The Right to Bear Arms

A well-regulated Militia, being necessary to the security of a free State, the right of the people to keep and bear Arms, shall not be infringed.

—Article II, The Bill of Rights (The Second Amendment to the Constitution)

THE RIGHT TO BEAR ARMS

by Carl Bakal

McGraw-Hill Book Company / New York Toronto London

Contents

To the manes of William Bakal, 1892–1961

America is the country where life is held
cheaper than anywhere else.

> —Andrew Steinmetz, an English
> visitor to the United States in 1868,
> writing of the frequency with which
> Americans shoot each other

1 Prologue: A Day of Death

A strange and peculiarly American plague has long swept our land—a plague of guns. Every year, firearms claim more and more lives in this country.

Since the turn of the century, this plague has brought death to the astonishing total of more than 750,000 Americans—men, women and children—a figure based on official, though incomplete, government records. Were complete records available for the years since 1900, and any records at all for the earlier years of our republic, the nation's cumulative toll of firearms fatalities would run into the millions. But even the figures we do have for the past sixty-odd years represent a civilian toll far greater than the 530,000 Americans killed in battle in all of our wars in our history—from the start of the Revolution through the current conflict in Vietnam. In no other country of the world do so many people kill and maim each other—and themselves—with firearms.

The fatal shootings in our streets, in our homes, and in other public and private places now continue at the rate of 17,000 a year—or nearly 50 a day.

On the eve of one such day not long ago ...

1

A smiling child named Belinda Gairhan sat down to celebrate her sixth birthday with her stepfather, Sammy Penter, and her mother, Juanita, in the family's modest five-room frame house near Trumann, Arkansas. Six hours later, only the half-eaten birthday cake, an empty whiskey bottle and an incomprehensible note scribbled in green crayon provided mute evidence to the horror that must have followed. By then, all three Penters and two other family members were dead.

Friends and neighbors later shed some light on the tragedy. They said that Sammy, who raised cotton and soybeans, and Juanita, a bookkeeper at the Trumann Implement Company, had been having domestic difficulties for some time. But this fact alone could hardly have explained what happened that evening. The house showed signs of a violent struggle. As police later reconstructed the sequence of events, Penter first shot his wife twice in the chest and head at close range with his .22-caliber pistol. It must have been bedtime, because Mrs. Penter was wearing nightclothes.

Hearing the commotion, Belinda, Mrs. Penter's daughter by a previous marriage, apparently rushed into her parents' bedroom, for her body was found there, near her mother's, with two bullets in the chest and one in the forehead, fired at close range from the gun used on her mother. At 11:30 P.M. Penter telephoned his wife's mother, Mrs. Vivian Byrd, and asked her to come to the house. Mrs. Byrd was shot in the right breast with a .30-30 rifle as she walked through the front door. The next to step through death's door was Mrs. Penter's sister, Patsy Moon, whom Penter had also telephoned. Her body was found on the living-room floor, with a .30-30 wound in the right breast.

At 11:50 P.M. Penter called his father-in-law, William J. Byrd, and said he would like to see him too. Byrd asked about his wife and daughters.

"They're all right; they're here in bed asleep," said Penter.

Alarmed because he could think of no reason why his wife would be sleeping in the Penter home, Byrd picked up two policemen and drove there. While the police waited in their squad car, he opened the front door and stood dumbfounded at the sight of the bodies. Then, suddenly hearing the click of the safety catch of a gun, Byrd leaped out of the doorway and ran back to the car. Penter was clearly visible standing inside the house with his rifle, but he did not fire.

The police officers radioed for reinforcements and waited, watching Penter first go out to the yard of the house and then walk around inside. Suddenly they heard a shot. On going inside they found Penter dead, among the four others, with a bullet in his throat. Ironically, the police officers knew Penter well, had frequently hunted with him, and considered him one of the best marksmen in the area.

It was shortly after midnight when they stood over his body. Penter's death probably marked America's first firearms fatality of the new day.

A robbery occurs in the United States every five minutes. Many involve the use of guns, and result in the injury and death of robbers, victims, policemen and others who happen to get in the way. On the day of the Penter tragedy, for example, in Brooklyn, New York, Walter Newling was fortunately just grazed by bullets and missed death by inches when he made a grab for one of four gunmen who were making off with his construction company's $12,000 payroll. On that day, too, in Wilmington, Delaware, Thomas H. Winsett was indicted for the shotgun slaying of State Trooper Robert A. Paris, who had had the misfortune of catching Winsett and two accomplices with a carload of stolen TV sets and other items at a motel.

Much more typical, however, are angry shootings by average citizens over money matters. There was the incident which the Los Angeles *Times* splashed over its front page early that same day under the screaming headline, MURDER OVER $20! The story said that Richard Claborn, an occasional photographer and paint factory worker, had been fretting over the $20 he thought he was owed for some odd jobs he had done for Louis Sanders, an advertising salesman. Sanders, however, apparently had mixed feelings about this; he had given Claborn a check for the sum in question, but then stopped payment on it.

"Lou's going to be awful sorry he didn't give me the twenty dollars," Claborn told Mrs. Sanders just before gunning down her husband in his office with a .30-30-caliber deer rifle.

Other equally tragic incidents occurred. In Atlanta, Georgia,

Everett Gross was shot to death during an argument with two men; one had taken offense at the slapping of his seven-year-old daughter. In Denver, Colorado, Shiro Matsuno died of a gunshot wound inflicted by another citizen who charged that Matsuno had hit him first—with a snowball. And the Albany *Times Union* made mention of the trial of Rufus Jackson for the fatal shooting of Melrose Spells in a dance hall in an argument over a woman.

In Santa Rosa, California, John K. Naumann, an eighty-year-old retired tool-and-die maker, exercising his so-called constitutional right to keep and bear arms, impulsively whipped out a pistol to kill his wife, Hedwig, age seventy-eight. Naumann harbored the belief —later described as "illusional"—that she was conducting an affair with an elderly next-door neighbor.

As happens every day, there were those who for a variety of reasons chose to turn a gun on themselves. In Falls Church, Virginia, Paul Nixon Gibson, the Washington *Evening Star* reported, drove to a cemetery, propped himself against a tree and used a 20-gauge shotgun to blast himself to eternity. And in San Francisco on the same day, Loudin H. Renshaw put a bullet from a .38-caliber revolver through his temple. He was finally successful in suicide after a previous attempt, three years before, had astonishingly given him little more than a violent headache.

Many inevitably fatal accidents with guns were reported, too. On that day newspapers reported the death of Charles Kenneth Stafford of McLeansboro, Illinois. Stafford, a farmer, chemist and Sunday-school teacher, with no thought of robbery, assault or suicide, had apparently been crawling through a fence when his shotgun discharged, the blast striking him in the head. In Danbury, Connecticut, Eugene Conklin, just home from the hunt, placed his 12-gauge shotgun on the kitchen sink. His wife, a mother of two, asked him to remove the gun. When he did so, it accidently discharged and fatally wounded Mrs. Conklin.

Listed among the Louisville *Courier-Journal's* "Kentuckiana Deaths" were two cryptic items: "Carl Crumbliss, Hopkinsville, accidentally shot," and "Ralph L. Schearn, Hawesville, shot to death in his home." And, in Baltimore, Daniel W. Bierer, a liquor store proprietor, rushing from his premises with a pistol in pursuit of three robbers fleeing with his $400, fired off a round at the dim shadows in a dark alley. Killed was an innocent bystander, Haywood Roscoe, who lived above the liquor store.

There were of course the lucky ones who lost, not their lives, but only a leg or arm, or suffered some other bodily damage. Among them was James Sykes, a fourteen-year-old Seattle boy, who was accidentally shot in the arm and abdomen by Robert Kotoff, a thirteen-year-old friend proudly displaying a shotgun from big brother's weapons collection. Young Sykes's arm was amputated at the elbow in the hospital that evening.

In a Miami hospital that same day was two-year-old Dwayne Saunders, struck in the head by a bullet discharged by his four-year-old brother James from a .22-caliber revolver discovered in Daddy's dresser drawer. "Gun, gun. Shoot me," Dwayne demanded. His brother obliged him. Mother had stepped over to a neighbor's while the two boys and a six-month-old brother were supposedly asleep. Fortunately, the bullet, though it traveled 3 inches under Dwayne's scalp, did not penetrate his skull.

Somewhat less lucky was eight-year-old Thomas Libby who at the same time lay in a Long Island hospital with a fractured skull—a souvenir from Michael Collins, a sixteen-year-old gun enthusiast with poor eyesight. (He ordinarily wore very strong prescription glasses.) Thomas had been reclining on a grassy slope reading a comic book. Michael, mistaking him for a squirrel, fired at him from a second-story window. The myopic marksman was chastised in court, was punished with a suspended sentence, and is now at liberty. Thomas had to have part of his brain removed, and today wears a metal plate in his head.

And so it went. The names are real. The incidents described did happen. The day was fairly typical of any of the others on which guns now claim, on the average, nearly 50 lives, or about one every half hour.

However, one incident that took place on that day shook the world. On that day—November 22, 1963—a President of the United States was murdered.

With the assassination of John F. Kennedy, the country was shocked into an awareness of the American plague of guns. Bullets had been aimed at seven and killed four of our nineteen Presidents within the past one hundred years. Yet no less real, though less publicized, are the hundreds of thousands of other victims of firearms.

Why do so many shootings occur here, with fatalities as much as five to ten times as high as those in other countries?

Why does a civilized society allow deadly weapons to be so readily available to everyone? Why aren't there laws that might serve to prevent at least some of the fifty firearms murders, suicides and accidents that will occur today and tomorrow and the day after tomorrow?

Why the apathy of most people to this firearms epidemic—one that could possibly take even *your* life?

Why is the subject of firearms control one of such seething controversy? Who are those who oppose control?

Is the so-called constitutional right "to keep and bear arms" so absolute that it can infringe on an even more fundamental right of people—the right to live?

2 License to Kill

> . . . it took only one madman to bend the curve of history with a single cheap Italian carbine. And there wasn't a law in the land that could have stopped him from obtaining the gun.
> —Jack R. Griffin, Chicago *Sun-Times*, December 1, 1963

In what must now surely rank as one of the most ironic footnotes to history, Senator John F. Kennedy rose in the Senate on April 28, 1958, to introduce a bill that, if enacted, would have barred from this country the very gun that was to kill him five years later. The bill sought to "prohibit the importation or reimportation into the United States of arms or ammunition originally manufactured for military purposes." Its special target was the gun being imported in greatest number, the 6.5 mm. Mannlicher-Carcano carbine, an early World War II version of a venerable series of short, bolt-action Italian military rifles conceived in 1891.

The Kennedy bill was given the number S. 3714, was read twice, referred to the Committee on Foreign Relations, and seemed to have every chance of success. For shortly before, a companion House measure, sponsored by Representative Albert P. Morano of Connecticut, had been favorably reported from the House Foreign Affairs Committee by a vote of 26 to 0.

That both bills miraculously came to naught may occasionally stir the collective conscience of one of the nation's most powerful yet least-known lobbies, the National Rifle Association, which is headquartered—within gunshot of the White House—in a gleaming glass and marble $3.5-million structure with a rifle and pistol range in the basement. Purporting to speak for the nation's estimated 30 million gun owners, the 700,000-member organization has opposed and managed to scuttle virtually any legislation seeking to impose sensible controls on the availability, sale and use of firearms in the United States. In the NRA's view, almost all gun laws are bad laws. To promulgate this dogma, the NRA has for nearly four decades conducted one of the most intensive and imaginative lobbying operations witnessed in Washington. It has also been hard at work in state capitals and county and city legislatures. Encrusted with respectability and a self-applied patina of patriotism, the NRA has propagated the myth that any control of firearms by law would infringe on the so-called constitutional "right to bear arms."

What prompted Senator Kennedy's interest in 1958 in a law limiting the importation of foreign military firearms was neither mysterious prognostic powers nor any great humanitarian concerns.* The Senator rested his case solely on economic grounds. The influx of foreign guns, he said in his short speech to the Senate at the time he introduced his bill, had "helped spoil our domestic market," and particularly that of the firearms manufacturers located in his home state. Massachusetts is the base of operations of names known to every gun owner—Savage Arms, Smith & Wesson, Harrington & Richardson, Noble, and Iver Johnson.

Representative Morano of Connecticut no doubt had a similar motivation. His state houses the main offices and plants of such other big industry names as Winchester-Western (a division of the Olin Mathieson Chemical Corporation), Remington Arms (60 per cent owned by du Pont), Colt, High Standard, Marlin, Mossberg, and Sturm, Ruger.

Between 1955 and 1958, according to the *Wall Street Journal* of December 4, 1959, domestic gun sales had fallen off 50 per cent, and profits of the industry had dwindled to the vanishing point. During this period, U.S. firearms manufacturers had had to lay off one-third of their skilled production workers. There were a number of reasons

---

* Many of the imports were regarded as hazards to the shooter as well as to anyone within shooting range. The Carcano, in particular, had even been declared unsafe for military use by the Italian government because of the tendency of the barrel to explode and blow up in the face of the shooter.

for this. Most important was the competition of foreign military weapons, which had become outmoded in Europe in the mid-1950s when the armies of the North Atlantic Treaty Organization (NATO) decided to switch to a common-sized cartridge. American imports of the rifles thereby rendered surplus multiplied 14 times between 1955 and 1958. In 1955, only 14,000 old foreign rifles were imported into this country; in 1957 the total was 129,000 (of which, incidentally, about 100,000 were Carcanos); and by the end of 1958 the import figure had climbed to 198,000, or nearly one-third the number of the 677,000 manufactured in the United States that year.

Domestically produced rifles, though far superior in quality, could scarcely compete with the surplus weapons from all over the world. In addition to the Italian Carcanos, there were British Enfields, German Mausers, Norwegian Krags, and Swedish, Belgian and other foreign military cast-offs. In many cases, these rifles cost their importers less than $1 apiece. Add the average import duty of 52 per cent and their cost still came to as little as $2. The guns eventually sold in America for as little as $12 or $13, and this price still permitted a handsome profit for the importer, dealer or any other middlemen concerned. Although some of the foreign surplus items would go for as much as $30 or $40, this price was well below the $80 to $100 cost of most American-made high-powered sporting rifles.

Domestic gunmakers complained in vain about the low-priced imports. They claimed that diminishing domestic sales of their products had forced them to lay off skilled gunsmiths and to scrap modernization projects, and they contended that this would in turn imperil the national security. To plead their case, the importers, on the other hand, fired back that half of the outdated war rifles sold went over mantels or into gun collections, and so weren't competitors of new sport rifles. No matter where the truth lay, the guns—obsolete handguns as well as rifles—flooded into this country, and into the hands of almost anyone with $12 or so to spend for one.

Although exact figures are unavailable, it is estimated that some 5 million, perhaps as many as 7 million, foreign weapons, both old and new, poured into this country from 1959 through 1963. Today the United States is the dumping ground for about 75 per cent and, according to some estimates, for as much as 90 per cent, of the world's war-surplus weapons.

Why? Because few other nations would have them. Indeed, nowhere but in America is there such a fascination for firearms. And nowhere in the world are they so readily available, legally, to almost anyone.

With the exception of the United States, most civilized countries have laws which make it illegal for anyone to own a firearm without some sort of special permit. In Britain, for example, you need a certificate from the local police in order to buy or own a rifle, pistol or revolver.* Since few people with the exception of farmers, acknowledged hunters, and members of shooting clubs can give any valid reason for wanting these guns, such certificates are rarely issued. Even the police do not carry guns routinely. Nor do prison guards or private guards employed by armored car delivery services. In Britain the only bodyguards normally armed are those assigned to protect the members of the Royal Family and the Prime Minister, and, unlike the situation in gun-toting America, only one guard is considered sufficient protection per person.

Personal protection is hardly ever accepted as a valid reason for wanting a firearm. A London publisher who tried to justify his illegal possession of a gun on the ground that he needed it to defend himself against burglars was fined $45 and told by the judge: "Defend yourself with your fists."

Of all the 400,000 criminals arrested in England and Wales over a recent three-year period, only 159 were carrying guns. In 1962, only 29 persons were shot dead in all of England and Wales; the United States, with four times the population, had 4,954 firearms murders. That year, only 73 British robbery victims reported even seeing a gun. The country's $7-million Great Train Robbery of August 1964, the biggest cash haul in history, was carried off without a gun.

* For practical and also legal purposes, the most commonly used firearms are generally classified into the following groups: shotguns and rifles, which are long arms, those designed to be fired from the shoulder; and pistols and revolvers, which are handguns, that is, guns made to be held and fired with one hand. The shotgun, the most widely used hunting gun, is a smoothbore gun that fires a number of pellets (or "shot") at one time. The rifle, which gets its name from the spiral grooving cut into its bore or barrel, fires bullets, as do also handguns. There is some popular confusion as to the exact distinction between a pistol and revolver, and the two terms are often used interchangeably. In the strict sense, though, a pistol, also often called an automatic, is a magazine-loading gun, whereas a revolver, or six-shooter, is distinguished by its revolving chambered cylinder which holds the ammunition that feeds into the barrel. For a further description of all these types of guns, see the Notes to this chapter.

The British, however, are not entirely without firearms. Britain has 4,500 shooting clubs. Valid sportsmen, by obtaining an annual license, can avail themselves of shotguns and air guns, but they can be used only in specified places. However, no person under fourteen is allowed to buy or have a gun of any kind. Adolescents between fifteen and seventeen can use shotguns only under the chaperonage of a person over twenty-one. London gunsmiths say their sales are confined almost entirely to shotguns; pistol sales, in particular, are rare. One large London gunsmith reportedly made its last pistol in 1880, and virtually all of the pistol certificates issued authorize the pistol only for range use.

In the Netherlands there was not a single firearms homicide during the three years 1960, 1961, and 1962; no firearms can be lawfully bought or owned there without a permit. The same holds true in Italy, where, as in England and elsewhere in Europe, firearms cannot be sold by mail. In France, guns specifically made for hunting or target shooting can be bought freely, but handguns of every kind and military rifles are rigidly restricted to those with police permits. In addition, users of these guns can have a supply of only up to fifty rounds of ammunition, and need special permission to buy more.

Similar restrictions on firearms and ammunition apply in most other European countries, many of which also forbid firearms licenses to juveniles. When applying for a license in Sweden, you must also show that you need the gun and know how to handle it. The sale of military-type rifles is completely *verboten* in Germany, and permits to use hunting or sporting rifles are issued only to registered hunters and members of shooting clubs.

Japan goes so far as to prohibit entirely the private ownership of handguns. If you are over twenty you can buy a shotgun or rifle for hunting, but it must be registered and checked annually by the police. Japanese law also requires that you take three hours of instruction and pass a written examination before being issued a hunting license, and that you turn in all unused ammunition at the close of the season.

Closer to our borders, Canada requires that all pistols and revolvers be registered. As in other countries, dealers must also be licensed.

In America, however, as Lee Harvey Oswald demonstrated, the easy accessibility of firearms is a national scandal. Indeed, no other modern nation makes death-dealing weapons so freely and cheaply available. Until Oswald pulled the trigger of his Carcano in Dallas on November 22, 1963, he had not broken a single law, Federal, state or city, pertaining to firearms.

There are practically no such laws to break. The few existent "laws," though possibly well intentioned, are either ineffectual or unenforceable, being riddled with as many holes as a marksman's target. Virtually anyone with a few spare dollars and old enough to walk into a sporting goods store and peer across the counter can buy some sort of gun, with no questions asked. Anyone able to write—a child, ex-convict, drug addict or lunatic—can order some sort of gun by mail—and get it. Oswald did. An untold number of unidentified Oswalds can continue to do so today.*

However questionable his background, Oswald resorted to a really unnecessary subterfuge in cloaking his Carcano purchase with a false name and the added anonymity of a mail order. This is indicated by the following conversation, which was reported by *The New York Times* as having taken place in a midtown Manhattan store the day after the Kennedy funeral:

CUSTOMER: If I buy a gun, do you check my identification or forward my name to any police agency?

SALESMAN: No; all we do is mark down the weapon number and keep the sales slip for our records.

CUSTOMER: What if I ask for a rifle just like the one Lee Oswald bought by mail?

SALESMAN: Here's the exact model. It's all yours; all you need is to be eighteen and have $15.95.

A similar conversation could be repeated across the United States, for nowhere in this country are there any enforceable restrictions on the sale of rifles or shotguns to adults, and even children.

Buying a gun that can be hidden or concealed, that is, a pistol or revolver, may be a little more difficult, but not much. For here

---

* To commemorate the second anniversary of the assassination of President Kennedy, the Paterson, New Jersey, *Morning Call*, on November 22, 1965, announced that it had ordered a .38-caliber revolver by mail in the name of L. H. Oswald—and promptly received it, though the newspaper did not have the gun permits required by both its city and state.

again, firearms controls are left to the tolerance of the individual state.* In all but a few states, handguns, like shotguns and rifles, may be bought freely on the open market by practically anyone old enough to carry his purchase out of the store. No license or permit to purchase is needed; no registration requirements; no questions asked as to criminal record, dope addiction, drinking habits, commitment to a mental institution, nor any probing as to the purpose for which the weapon is being bought.

Only seven states require you to have a license or permit before you can buy a handgun: Hawaii, Massachusetts, Michigan, Missouri, New Jersey, New York and North Carolina. Some counties of Virginia also require such prior permission before purchase. One state, South Carolina, prohibits the sale of handguns. Only nine states and the District of Columbia specify a waiting or "cooling off" period, such as forty-eight or seventy-two hours, between the time you buy the gun and are actually allowed to have it. This ostensibly gives the local constabulary the chance to check the buyer's credentials, or allows the heat of passion prompting a purchase to subside.

Without specifying such waiting periods, other states delegate judgment of the customer's condition, character and other qualifications to the gun salesman, at least one state prohibiting the sale of guns to those "under the heat of passion" (Texas), one state to anarchists (Hawaii), and one to Indians (Colorado). Other proscribed categories of persons include prostitutes (District of Columbia), persons of unsound mind (Pennsylvania), idiots (New Jersey), tramps, and, in many states, the insane, drug addicts, drunks, aliens, felons of varying degrees of misbehavior, and fugitives from justice. Since confessions can hardly be expected from such would-be customers, screening them presumes certain psychic insights on the part of the sales clerk, to say nothing of a tenacity to resist the temptation of turning over a dollar through a quick sale to the armed anonymous.

In all fairness, it should be said that most states do prohibit the sale or delivery of firearms to those below a certain age, or at least to those who look below a certain age. (Nine states have no minimum age requirements at all.) In South Carolina you have to be at least twelve before you can be given one, in Utah and Oregon all of fourteen, and in Rhode Island the firearms milestone of manhood is

* For a detailed comparison of the various state firearms laws, see Appendix II.

fifteen—still somewhat below the usual minimum age requirement in most states for driving or drinking. Elsewhere, the gun-wielding ages usually vary from an actual or apparent sixteen to twenty-one, although few dealers are fussy enough to ask to see birth certificates.

Whatever other state laws controlling handguns there may be apply not so much to the purchase of the gun as to its possession and use. Only one state, New York, through its well-known Sullivan Law, requires you to have a license both to purchase and to possess a handgun. (In other states there is nothing to prevent one person from buying a gun and then giving it to someone else. Hawaii vainly tries to inhibit this by requiring that all firearms be registered.) The other forty-nine states permit you to have a pistol without a license as long as you keep your gun at home, or, as in the case of thirty-six states, as long as you carry it about openly. Some of these states impose certain "restraints" on this privilege. In Texas, you can carry a handgun only if you're "traveling." Hence every Texan is a traveler.*

There are a multitude of other quaint regional requirements, too. In Minnesota and Vermont you are perfectly free to carry your gun about either openly or concealed without a license just so long as you don't have the "intent" of assaulting someone. The same stricture also applies in Arkansas, which boasts one of the nation's highest homicide rates. In Arizona, anyone can carry a gun on the street, but not into a church. In Alabama, no hunting or any other type of shooting is allowed on the Sabbath. West Virginia, on its Biblical day of rest, allows shooting on "regularly used" ranges. One of the few restrictive statutes in Mississippi requires a pistol permit of "boys under sixteen or any student within two miles of his school or college grounds."

In the twenty-eight states in which you need a license to carry a handgun openly or concealed (some states flatly prohibit the carrying of concealed weapons), getting the license presents no insurmountable problem. In most places the procedure is no more complicated than that for getting a dog license—and no more expensive. In Georgia and South Dakota, the cost of a firearms permit is

---

* In tolerant, gun-toting Texas, even ex-convicts can freely buy guns, unless their conviction was for using a gun against another person. (Knives or other deadly weapons don't count). Not that gun dealers are inquisitive enough to check into their customers' criminal pasts.

50 cents. Supposedly prerequisite to the issuance of a permit or license is the absence of a criminal record. However, only a half a dozen states make mandatory the taking of fingerprints, the only reliable means of checking for a criminal record. Only twenty-three states and the District of Columbia even bother to license the handgun dealer. And in fewer than half our states are dealers required to report handgun sales to the police.

To compensate for the shortcomings of their state laws, some counties and cities have come up with laws of their own. Some of these local ordinances require the licensing of dealers, specify purchase permits or waiting periods, and permits for the possession or carrying of handguns. A few cities require the registration of all handguns.* Detroit, Flint and a number of other Michigan municipalities, in addition to requiring the registration of handguns, also call for them to be inspected annually. Most cities, of course, prohibit the indiscriminate discharge of firearms. Some cities have tougher laws on BB guns than those governing firearms. Indeed, in some towns a twelve-year-old boy may be picked up for walking down the street with a BB gun. But there is nothing to stop him from ordering by mail and legally having a rifle or shotgun or, for that matter, even a revolver, a grenade, a bazooka or cannon.

Aren't there any Federal laws against this sort of thing? Not really. The two main Federal laws dealing with firearms are antiquated and impotent legal travesties, both enacted in the gangster era of the 1930s and both virtually unchanged since then.

The senior statute, the so-called National Firearms Act, vintage 1934, may be aptly named in that it is "national," but the "firearms" in its title is merely a loosely used euphemism. The National Firearms Act does not even touch pistols, revolvers, shotguns and rifles. It is aimed at the special weapons used by our highly publicized gangsters of the 1920s and 1930s. The act prohibits the possession of all machine guns and other automatic weapons (those firing more than one shot with a single pull of the trigger), except those registered with the Treasury Department. To keep these to a minimum, a virtually confiscatory tax of $200 must also be paid every time each such gun is sold or changes hands. The law also places similar restrictions on the sale or transfer of sawed-off rifles and shotguns

* Among them: Detroit, Flint, Grand Rapids, Omaha, Peoria, Baton Rouge, New Orleans.

(those with barrels less than 16 and 18 inches long, respectively) and any mufflers and silencers.

The second Federal law, the 1938 Federal Firearms Act, prohibits the interstate shipment of all firearms to or by convicted felons, people under indictment, and fugitives from justice. It also requires that firearms manufacturers, dealers, importers and others doing business across state lines have a Federal license.

The act largely affects the seller, rather than the recipient of these arms, however, without specifying how old or young either must be. Needless to say, the law does not inhibit anyone from ordering a gun and getting it.*

Another joker in the act is that, with no minimum age specified, anyone can become a federally licensed dealer simply by declaring his intention of going into the firearms business. Applications are readily available from the Treasury Department's Internal Revenue Service. Even a criminal can get a gun dealer's license, for no fingerprints need accompany the application. Nor would the license fee required strain the budget of even a strapped juvenile delinquent —only $1.

Should any reader think all this incredible, he can try what I did. I decided to make a test by applying for a license myself. It was in my mailbox ten days later.

The holes in this loose network of Federal, city or county, and state laws should be apparent to a child, and often are. A few examples, among thousands:

In 1963 in New York, veteran police officials were shocked when Albert "Kid Blast" Gallo, Jr., of the notorious crime clan was discovered in broad daylight parked outside the Manhattan District Attorney's office with a 12-gauge shotgun conveniently located on the rear seat of his car. Also on the seat was a supply of shotgun shells. Yet there was nothing the police could do, not even confiscate the shotgun and ammunition. Why not? Because under the New York laws anyone can have a shotgun, provided he has not been convicted of a crime. And although Gallo had a record of twelve arrests, he had never been convicted. At the time there would have been nothing to prevent Gallo from loading his shotgun and carrying it down Fifth Avenue; on the other hand, he could have been arrested for carrying even an unloaded handgun down the street without a license. This

* For details of these and other Federal firearms laws, see Appendix I.

situation was somewhat corrected by a new city law, effective July 15, 1964, which now makes it illegal to carry a rifle or shotgun in public, unless it is unloaded and enclosed in a carrying case.

Although the Sullivan Law of New York, the nation's most severe gun law, restricts the purchase and possession of handguns, the ammunition for these weapons is freely and legally available to any New Yorker over age sixteen for about the price of a pack of cigarettes. In addition to being used in illicitly owned handguns, the cartridges also fit nicely into zip guns, those improvised favorites of teenage gangs, which any juvenile delinquent with the barest mechanical skill can fashion from a length of antenna tubing from a car, a piece of wood and some rubber bands.

The archaic distinction between concealed weapons and those more difficult to hide is found in many state laws, written with such ambiguity that it is almost impossible to enforce them. Said the Chicago *Sun-Times* on December 5, 1963:

> In Chicago, it is illegal to carry a concealed weapon. But any arrest on that charge probably would be thrown out of court. "Even if I saw the outline of a gun in a man's pocket," said Deputy Police Superintendent Joe Morris, "I couldn't make the charge stick. I'd have to prove I could see the concealed weapon before the arrest, and how could I see the gun if it's concealed?"

> Equally bizarre, Morris said, is that the top hoodlum in Chicago could walk unmolested down Michigan Avenue with a six-shooter strapped in plain sight on his thigh. Why? It's not a concealed weapon.

With the handgun, the biggest headache to police in crimes committed with guns, Chicago law, like that of New York, also requires a police permit for the purchase of a handgun. But the Chicago law does not cover handguns bought elsewhere or otherwise mysteriously acquired. So it is virtually meaningless, as Chicago police official Morris also points out:

> A guy can walk across 95th Street into the suburb of Evergreen Park and buy a pistol without any restrictions. And he usually does.

Most state and local gun laws do not touch the gun buyer who crosses the line to make his purchase in another jurisdiction. Often a person can easily go to another county, city or, if necessary, another state, buy the gun of his choice and return home with it—all perfectly legally.

A New Jerseyite, for example, who wants to have a handgun handy but does not care to go to the trouble of securing the necessary purchase permit from his local police, can go to neighboring Pennsylvania and buy his gun there. He breaks no law in having the gun in New Jersey as long as he keeps the gun at home or doesn't carry it around concealed.

Should he be too impatient for Pennsylvania's waiting period requirement (forty-eight hours) or wish to avoid any investigation of his record, he can go down to more tolerant Delaware and pick up his purchase immediately. Again no law may be broken, although the New Jersey and District of Columbia authorities can cite you endless cases of their citizens with criminal records buying guns over the counter in Delaware, Virginia and (until 1966) Maryland * stores, often with the expected grim consequences.

In Virginia, one of the many states where the laws vary from one county to the next, a seventeen-year-old boy walked into a Fairfax County gun shop several years ago, said he was twenty-three, gave a fictitious name and address, placed $65 on the counter, and walked out with a .38-caliber revolver. He used the weapon to kill another youth some months later. The gun transaction, if not the murder, was perfectly legal, as far as the seller was concerned. Under Fairfax County law no registration of weapons is required. The law only asks that the seller be "satisfied" that the buyer is at least eighteen years old.

If you don't care to show your face at your friendly neighborhood arms dealer, or perhaps would like some choice, cheap or condemned gun not available or allowed locally, you can always order a gun by mail. Delivery is usually made by Railway Express or another common carrier, because handguns cannot be sent through the mails—at least, theoretically. But the few Federal laws won't stand much in your way. And as former U.S. Bureau of Prisons Director James V. Bennett has noted: "Mail order sales, particularly, acknowledge no state laws. Handguns are still mailed into South Carolina, for example, although the state laws prohibit their sale and even manufacture."

To find out for himself how easy it is to buy a mail-order gun,

---

* On March 29, 1966, the Maryland Assembly enacted a law requiring a seven-day waiting period for handguns.

Mayor Frank X. Graves of Paterson, New Jersey, in a bet with two disbelieving newsmen in April 1965, ordered a .22-caliber revolver from a Chicago mail-order house. He sent along a money order for $13.95, giving no information except his name and address. The gun arrived a week later. The shipment circumvented New Jersey law which requires a permit for the purchase of a handgun.

"The company that sent me this gun," Graves told reporters, "had no way of knowing if I were a convicted murderer, what my intentions were, or whether I was five years old or one hundred five years old."

Coincidentally, at just about the same time, I conducted my own personal test by responding to an advertised offering of the Carcano—a duplicate of the gun that killed President Kennedy—in the May 1965 issue of *The American Rifleman,* official monthly of the National Rifle Association.* I sent the stipulated $12.95 for the gun to the advertiser, the Potomac Arms Corporation of Alexandria, Virginia. Ten days later, a long bulky carton containing the carbine was delivered to my door. I wasn't home at the time, so my wife received the package. But it could just as well have been my three-year-old daughter. Since no license is required for a rifle or shotgun in New York, no law was broken by this transaction, although the thought that a three-year-old could have been on the receiving end of this transaction is somewhat frightening. No less terrifying is the thought that the recipient—of this or other guns—could be a criminal or one of the two million persons who, the National Institute of Mental Health says, are walking the streets in dire need of psychiatric treatment.

As a display of good intentions, some mail-order dealers go through the motions of asking customers to furnish "affidavits" to the effect that they are over twenty-one, have no criminal record, and are not fugitives or under indictment. But this is a formality with which anyone who wants a gun badly enough will be glad to comply. The affidavit is just a scrap of paper. It requires no oath, and is in no sense a legal document. And at least some dealers don't seem to care whether you send in the form or not.

As Sergeant K. T. Carpenter of the Los Angeles Police Department told a wide-eyed congressional committee:

* Lee Harvey Oswald had ordered his Carcano on a coupon clipped from the February 1963 issue of the same magazine.

"Any nine-year-old can fill out the form as long as he has a piggy bank, can draw the numbers '21' and can scrawl his name."

If further proof were necessary, this was supplied some years ago by a New Jersey writer, who, in an article for *The Saturday Evening Post,* told how he ordered a .45-caliber Thompson submachine gun in the name of his two-year-old daughter. Wasn't the purchase in violation of either the Federal Firearms Act or the National Firearms Act? Not at all. In compliance with Federal law, the tommy gun had been advertised and sold as "deactivated"; upon arrival, its barrel was found welded in two places. "One weld closed off the chamber, making it impossible to insert a cartridge for firing," the author wrote. "The other weld secured the barrel to the frame so that the plugged barrel could not readily be replaced with a usable one." But it took little more than an hour of the author's amateurish efforts with hand tools and a freshly acquired new barrel to restore the gun to its original shooting condition.

Isn't a dealer violating the law by making such indiscriminate interstate shipments, if not to children, delinquents, drunks, dope addicts and psychopaths, at least to convicts and others proscribed from receiving guns by the Federal Firearms Act? Not necessarily. For a provision—Section 902 (d)—of the act specifies that the dealer is acting illegally only if he knew or had "reasonable cause to believe" that the customer was not lawfully eligible to receive the gun —something difficult for the government to prove. In fact, not a single conviction has ever been obtained under this provision of the statute.

"The reason some dealers ask you to fill out those forms, though they're not really required to, is only to protect themselves," a Treasury Department official told me. "They're much like those signs in restaurants and night clubs: NOT RESPONSIBLE FOR HATS UNLESS CHECKED."

Isn't the dealer violating postal regulations? Not at all. Actually, the term "mail order" is somewhat of a misnomer. Although guns may be ordered by mail, none (with the exception of unloaded rifles or shotguns) can ordinarily be shipped by mail, except to military officers, law enforcement officials, government watchmen, licensed firearms dealers and manufacturers, and other such specified persons. To get around this legal barrier, mail-order gun dealers have adopted the common practice of shipping pistols and revolvers by common carrier.

Isn't the common carrier, you then ask, supposed to notify the police or other authorities where the customer lives that a handgun is going to someone in their jurisdiction? There is no Federal law requiring common carriers to do this, or, for that matter, to look into the legitimacy of a purchaser.

Finally, as a close reading of the act's Section 902 (c) will suggest, the cagey mail-order buyer, even if he lives in a place requiring a pistol purchase permit, is offered another loophole in the form of that Federal dealer's license, available to anyone for $1. Treasury Department officials have estimated that of the some 60,000 such licenses issued or renewed every year a "substantial number," perhaps as many as 45,000, do not go to bona-fide dealers.

It is easy to understand why, because the license, apart from enabling a gun enthusiast to buy freely, if illegally, across state lines, offers a considerable number of fringe benefits to its lucky possessor. With the license, the holder can: (1) avoid police clearance on each gun purchased in cities and states that require such clearances; (2) avoid arrest for transporting guns in his car; (3) purchase guns at wholesale while also saving on sales tax; and (4) make bulk or multiple purchases without arousing any suspicions.

That's quite a lot for a dollar, as one wily individual obviously recognized when, for the benefit of those not in on this governmental gimmick, he inserted this advertisement in *Shotgun News:* "For Sale—guns, buy wholesale. Become a dealer, instructions, $1." Whoever responded was simply told to apply for a Federal license —for another dollar.

Some mail-order firms have also stepped up sales by urging their customers to become dealers and "go into business." One Los Angeles firm, according to testimony before a congressional committee, even had the audacity to mail a card advising its customers to lay out a dollar for a Federal firearms license "so that more guns can be sent."

The perils of doing an interstate business without a license is illustrated by the sad case of a Chicagoan named Willie E. Engram, who, inspired by accounts as to how Oswald had acquired his Carcano, decided to go into the mail-order gun business. Before long he had built up quite a lucrative business, purchasing by mail about 1,500 pistols in Texas and disposing of them to local teen-agers, drug addicts and criminals. When Willie was finally arrested in August 1964, it was not because he had been caught breaking any local laws. What led to his downfall was his failure to buy the $1 Federal dealer's license permitting him to do business across state lines.

The vast majority of the nation's 120,000-odd gun outlets, though in a sense merchants of menace, are no doubt legitimate enterprises —at least, to the extent the laxities of the law allow them to be. Few items are so easily available as firearms and in so great a variety of places. Catering to those who would exercise the right to bear arms are, in addition to gun shops, department stores and discount houses, sporting goods and hardware stores, dime stores and pawn shops, mail-order houses and army surplus stores, to name only a few. In the South one can even see a glittering array of guns in gaso-line stations. A Denver home furnishings store offers free rifles and shotguns with the purchase of furniture during the hunting season.

The selection available to shoppers—if not free, often on easy credit—ranges from BB guns and bazookas to the more conven-tional shotguns, rifles and revolvers. Some years ago, Hess Brothers, an Allentown, Pennsylvania, department store, offered .22-caliber revolvers in stylish blue, gold and pink tones for feminine protec-tion. In a similar bid for the feminine market, a shopper's column recently announced a product combining the aesthetic with the utili-tarian: pastel pistols in hues to match Milady's station wagon, tooth-brush or alarm clock, the choice of color presumably depending on where she expected to be when she wanted to shoot someone.

Eminently respectable and indisputably the Tiffany's of the gun trade is the venerable, seventy-three-year-old sporting goods firm of Abercrombie & Fitch, whose main store occupies a twelve-story building in midtown Manhattan. In the magnificent seventh-floor gun room, where sales are conducted with the dignity and decorum appropriate to a London banking firm, A & F. customers (which have included royalty and U.S. Presidents from Teddy Roosevelt to John F. Kennedy) can find just about every kind of firearm fabri-cated from cross-eyed guns (for people who shoot right-handed and sight left-eyed) to a line of Purdeys which, priced at $2,000 and up, are to sporting arms what the Rolls Royce is to automobiles. A. & F., however, disdains those cheap foreign war-surplus weapons and the kind of customers attracted to them.

On the other hand, far too many stores are not as scrupulous both with regard to the products they handle and their customers, although they may operate well within the framework of the law as now written. Consider the traffic in bazookas and mortars, for which no license is required in New York, and which are of dubious value for either sport or self-defense. True, there are some New York City dealers who refuse to sell such goods to anyone under eighteen, although the legal age minimum is sixteen. A short time after three anti-Castro Cubans fired a bazooka round at the United Nations Building in December 1964, there was a certain general wariness on the part of clerks in surplus army and navy stores. But a few months later an Associated Press reporter, Bernard Gavzer, was able to report business as usual in Manhattan.

"In one store, the clerk eyed me and we talked about World War II trophies and then he said: 'I got a British mortar from World War II, worth $50 right out of the case. I'll give you a good deal on it; it takes up too much room and I got to clear my space. Look at it.' "

Gavzer, upon looking, found himself staring at a British grenade launcher. A few minutes later, after laying out $15.60, he was walking out of the store with it.

"A grenade launcher cannot be tucked under a coat, and yet few New Yorkers seemed startled at the sight of a man lugging one along a business street," Gavzer reported.

About the same time in Michigan, where it can sometimes take months to obtain a permit from the police to purchase a handgun, Detroit *Free Press* staff writer Walter Rugaber reported a similar successful, if somewhat more costly, experiment in a story that began:

I bought a 25-mm. French antitank cannon last week from a suburban gun shop. It was easier than buying a package of fire crackers. The price was $150. The salesman told me: "You could blast a Brink's truck off the map with this thing." *

* In October 1965, a 20-mm. Finnish antitank gun was used to blast open a Brink's vault in Syracuse, New York. The imaginative safecrackers looted the vault of $423,421. Brink's entered a $1 million damage suit against the alleged source of the antitank gun, the Potomac Arms Corporation of Alexandria,

No one asked me what I wanted a cannon for. No one asked me much of anything. I supplied my name and home address for the sales slip, but since I was not required to produce identification it could have been a phony.

Concerned Detroit police and both state and Federal authorities, reported the Detroit *News,* conceded there was nothing they could do about the sale or use of the weapons. "There isn't a law on the books restricting the sale of such weapons," said John Sheppard, an assistant U.S. attorney. So far as statutes are concerned, Sheppard said that even a 25-mm. cannon, the largest of the commonly available surplus weapons, is considered "a large-caliber rifle."

Purchasing firearms by mail order has assumed the dimensions of a multi-million-dollar business, largely in relatively cheap, unsafe weapons. There are said to be at least 400 mail-order houses dealing in such weapons. One mail-order gun dealer, when asked to estimate the number of guns he sold every year, refused to commit himself. He guessed, however, that sales of one type of gun alone, the British Webley revolvers, were in "the millions." One Webley is so potent that it was almost barred by the Geneva convention. However, the Webleys are dangerous not because they are big, but because they are small, and therefore concealable.

To reach buyers, dealers use gun and cheap crime and sex-and-sensation pulp magazines, newspapers and catalogs. The moral caliber of many of these dealers, and the customers they seek, can be detected fairly easily by the lurid pose of the advertising message, which is aimed apparently at the thrill-bent, the sadist and the highly impressionable adolescent.

"Halt! You'll speak with authority!" exclaims an ad in a "men's" magazine offering at $19.95 a .45-caliber snub-nose revolver—"the ideal weapon for the plainclothes detective or personal protection." Novelty seekers flipping through another magazine can send away for a "New Amazing Ball-Point Pen Gun. $4.95. Looks like a ball-point pen and writes like a ball-point pen. *But* cleverly built into the other end is a .22-caliber pistol." Another ad made available to anyone "the pride of the Royal Mounted Police," a .45-caliber handgun which was also described as the "revolver that tamed the North-

---

Virginia (the source of my mail-order Carcano). Brink's charged that Potomac Arms had knowingly sold the antitank gun to a man giving a false name and address.

west—the revolver that made the most desperate desperado cringe with fear, yours at a token price, only $34.95." And, as a novel way of honoring Dad, an ad some years ago in the Los Angeles *Times* suggested a $49.95 "Submachine Gun for Father's Day."

Gun advertising is at its most uninhibited in the various mail-order catalogs. A Hy Hunter catalog and "training manual" devotes its sixty-four pages entirely to "that deceptively cute little gun known as the derringer." Hunter points out that this weapon was potent enough to polish off "two of our country's Presidents, Abraham Lincoln and William McKinley." The catalog features violence and physical combat, and throws in a dash of sex for good measure.

A sample of the catalog's advice: "Remember that no matter how tough or big your opponent is, if you learn how to use the Hy Hunter Frontier Derringer properly you will always be the victor." The "training manual" portion of the catalog illustrates certain situations in which the derringer can be called into use. The photographs bear such captions as: "With intruder making amourous [sic] kisses, housewife can use Frontier Derringer in forward thrust to the solar plexus ... it must be understood that a blow with the Frontier Derringer to the crotch, face, etc., may be used in any of the holds shown." Elsewhere in the catalog are shown illustrated instructions for concealing the derringer under a sports shirt, in a shoe, in a pack of cigarettes, in a handkerchief, under a book, and in a garter holster. The last-mentioned example is illustrated by a photograph of an unskirted and virtually bare-bosomed "movie starlet" comfortably perched on the knee of Hunter himself.

Leafing through the literature of the Service Armament Company of Ridgefield, New Jersey, is an exotic, if not erotic, experience. Cavalry sabers, "the choice of pirates everywhere," go for $10 to $15. Captain Kidd cutlasses, "guaranteed to cut hard and deep," are the same price. The bazooka is plugged in a Service Armament catalog with copy that reads as follows:

ACHTUNG! Here is the acme of all German ordnance. The original Bazooka used by German troops to smash American-British forces all-over [sic] Europe. We have these weapons in two varieties. One is the standard Wehrmacht model in regular olive drab color. The other is the camouflage color model used by fanatical SS Troops at the Battle of the Buldge [sic]. Both models are truly Germanic.

Others of the colorful inventory of items are also enticingly described in a prose which I am preserving intact, misspellings and all, this time without resorting to the use of what would be extremely repetitive "sics." For example:

JAPANESE NAMBU EIGHT MM. AUTOMATIC   Here's the gun that won the Far East and blazed it's way accross the wide Pacific during WW II. A veritable masterpiece of oriental craftsmanship . . .

BROWNING BELGIQUE AUTO CALIBER   .32 One of these guns was carried by Mousalini and also by Hindrich Himmler as well as other WW II notables.

M.K.V.D. SECRET POLICE PISTOL   The rare "Baby Nagant." FANATIC Russian Secret Police Agent used these rare revolvers to terrify and kill enemies of the State. These tools could tell of many a bloody tale when being used during the purges of the 1930s. Guns have original Bolshevick markings which identify them as to their ownership.

GERMAN G-43 SNIPER AUTOMATIC RIFLE   In caliber 7.92 mm. used by fanatic SS snipers during the Battle of the Buldge in 1944 and now available to collectors and ex-patriots.

20 MM. SEMI-AUTO ANTI-TANK RIFLE   This is the ultimate in autoloading Rifles. Fires a gigantic rimless belted cartridge with a two ounce steel armor piercing bullet. Ideal for long range shots at deer and bear or at cars and trucks and even a tank if you happen to see one.

And, finally:

U.S. 60 MM. MORTER   Complete with bipod and base plate, etc. An ideal item for your den or front lawn. Can be easily packed into trunk of any automobile. This is the perfect tool for "getting even" with those neighbors you don't like. Perfect for demolishing houses or for back yard plinking on Sunday afternoon. We offer these hard-shooting Morters at the popular price of $49.95 each.

Surely, you say to yourself, the Service Armament people must be kidding, for their copy seems akin to the sort that might be concocted by the editors of *Mad Magazine.** Asked about this and

* Shortly after writing this, I happened to pick up a new issue of *Mad* (June 1965) and in it found, much to my surprise, *Mad's* version of a mail-order gun ad:

AUTHENTIC DELUXE ELEPHANT GUN
ONLY $7.95 †

Here it is, sports lovers . . . the authentic deluxe elephant gun you've been waiting for! Fires .94-caliber shells and/or small Civil War–type cannon balls. Deadly accurate from 200–500 yards. After that, who knows what you'll hit!

many glorified references to the violence that was Nazi Germany, a spokesman for Service Armament explained: "Our ads are written with tongue in cheek. We think they're kind of cute."

Law enforcement officers, however, don't find anything at all cute about the availability of the weapons described. Several years ago, in Sussex County, New Jersey, a state game warden, noticing flashes in the sky that were obviously not due to lightning, investigated and found three youths staging what he described as a "private war." Attired in semi-military uniforms and Nazi helmets, the young fun-loving trio was firing live ammunition from a British jungle carbine, an Argentine Mauser rifle, an American M-1 carbine, two semi-automatic rifles (one of Russian manufacture), and two .38-caliber revolvers. The warden was astounded to find in the youths' arsenal a 20-mm. Finnish antitank gun, purchased for $90 from Service Armament. The gun had been used by one of the youths to shell a nearby farmer's shed, smashing a tractor housed within. Asked why he had done this, the youth replied, "I wanted to see just what the gun was capable of doing."

This is not a unique experience. Four California youths using a German-made 20-mm. gun purchased for $150 from the Culver City firm of Martin B. Retting, Inc., shot off a blast that set fire to an acre of the Angeles National Forest. Another youngster, the proud possessor of a mail-order bazooka, took it out into the countryside one day and began shooting transformers off utility posts. The repair bill came to several thousand dollars.

Adults are no less enthusiastic in their response to the advertisements. In September 1964 the FBI seized four Russian Army Tokarev semi-automatic rifles that had been shipped to members of the Ku Klux Klan in Mississippi. During the racial unrest in Birmingham, Alabama, the summer before, Federal investigators discovered that 180 shipments of mail-order guns had been delivered to

---

Wonderful for flattening big game or overweight people you don't happen to like very much.

† NO MONEY DOWN. TAKE 18 YEARS (OR LONGER) TO PAY. CREDIT REFERENCES DISCOURAGED.

NOTE: We are required by law to have all mail-order purchasers send us a signed statement to the effect that you are 21 years of age or over, not an alien, have never been convicted of a crime, are not now under indictment, are not a fugitive, and are not a drug addict. Naturally, we have no way of checking the authenticity of your statement. So we'll sell merchandise to anybody. Just remember what happens when you lie. You can get a pimple on your tongue!

the Birmingham Railway Express office. In the summer of 1965 a
Fern Park, Florida, gun shop offered a "Nigger Getter"—a 12-gauge
shotgun with a "nigger back guarantee." A clerk, explaining the
guarantee on the gun, said: "Shoot a nigger with it, bring it back
and we'll give you your money back—and we'll let you keep the
gun, too."

What do the gun dealers themselves say about all this? Seated at
his desk with an engraved Thompson submachine gun resting in a
rack at his side, Val Forgett, Jr., the head of Service Armament, said:
"Americans should have the right to possess firearms."

He was asked why. "Because of all the kooks, rapists and mug-
gers," he replied.

The Federal Alcohol and Tobacco Tax unit of the Treasury Department, under whose authority falls the enforcement of the National Firearms Act, has quite a file on Forgett, who was once associated with a now defunct group known as the American Automatic
Weapons Association.

This group advocated the organization of "hunter" teams, small
bands of highly trained guerrillas armed with automatic weapons
and capable of "holding a bombed-out section against enemy
groups."

Dealers often feel no responsibility for the consequences of a sale.
A Los Angeles dealer, who was also a convicted pornographer, when
told by Senate investigators that a sixteen-year-old boy in Fairfax,
Virginia, had accidentally killed a fourteen-year-old companion with a
gun purchased from his California firm, shrugged the matter off:
"I didn't break the law, did I? If they've got the money, I sell the
gun. I'm not responsible for what they do with it."

Another mail-order gun dealer was asked: "Don't you have any
moral scruples about the possibility of the gun which you send by
mail order going to ex-convicts, juveniles or mentally unbalanced
persons?" His answer was typical of the attitude of thousands engaging in the gun traffic: "If I don't get it, the next guy will."

With the ease of obtaining guns either by mail or over the counter, it can readily be seen why the United States is virtually an
armed camp. Nearly a million guns are imported, and 2 million
more are made and sold annually in this country. It is estimated, although no one really knows, that there are more than 50 million privately owned guns in the United States today. Some estimates place

the figure at 200 million, and one as high as a billion! Every other American household, according to a Gallup poll survey, has at least one gun. In the South, firearms were found to be in two out of three homes. In California, more than 2½ million handguns alone are now registered with the state Department of Justice. One study, unbelievable as it may sound, found 42 per cent of all our male senior-high students to own a shotgun or rifle, compared to the 27 per cent owning a typewriter.

There can be no question that the world's greatest arsenal of privately owned guns is in the American home.

3 Lethal Tools and the Lawless

The easy accessibility of firearms is a significant factor in murders committed in the United States today. It is a problem which the American public needs to examine closely.... The questionable traffic in deadly weapons in many sections of our country is a disgrace. To my mind, the public has a right to expect that the distributor and the purchaser of weapons so deadly and easily concealed as handguns must meet certain regulations and qualifications. The spotlight of public attention should be focused on the easy accessibility of firearms and its influence on willful killings.
—J. Edgar Hoover in the FBI *Law Enforcement Bulletin,* June 1963.

In addition to boasting the world's greatest private arsenal of small arms, the United States can also claim the dubious distinction of being perhaps the most lawless nation on earth. Our incidence of crime is probably unmatched anywhere, except in such traditional centers of violence as Ceylon and the hot-blooded Italian provinces of Sardinia, Sicily and Calabria.

During 1964 we set an all-time record of 2,604,400 serious crimes, or five every minute. The Federal Bureau of Investigation crime clock ticked off one murder, forcible rape or assault to kill every 2½ minutes, one robbery every 5 minutes, one burglary every 28 seconds, one larceny ($50 and over) every 45 seconds, and one auto theft every minute. A murder took place every hour. No less than 57 policemen were murdered in the line of duty, and 1 of every 10 were assaulted. Since 1958 the nation's crime rate has increased 44 per cent and has been growing six times faster than our population. FBI Director J. Edgar Hoover has estimated the annual cost of crime in the United States at $27 billion.

A money value can scarcely be placed on that most heinous of crimes—murder. In a cold, statistical sense, known murders in the

United States now number more than 9,000 a year—about one every hour of every day. There is a murder a day in New York alone. In Atlanta and Dallas your chance of being murdered is twice as high as in New York. You are also probably much safer practically anywhere out of this country than in it. France and Japan have murder rates less than a third of ours, Italy less than a fifth, England only a seventh, and the Netherlands only about a sixteenth.

It would be neither fair nor entirely accurate to say that "guns cause crime." But there is ample evidence indicating a causal relationship between the ready availability of firearms and the importance they assume in crime statistics. Of the 9,250 U.S. murder victims reported in 1964, more than half (55 per cent), or 5,090, were killed by guns.

By contrast, of the 1,469 homicides in Japan in 1962 (the last year for which figures are available), only 37 were by firearms. Of the 309 persons murdered in all of Britain that year, only 29—about the number murdered by guns in the U.S. in two days—were done in by firearms. Canada had 92 firearms homicides (out of a total of 266), and in Belgium there were only 9 (out of 53), in Denmark, only 6 (out of 23), in Sweden, only 5 (out of 86), and in the Netherlands, there were no firearms deaths at all for three recent years of record.*

Interestingly, we find that in those areas of the United States where guns can be more easily purchased they play a greater part in murder. Against their 55 per cent use in murder on a nationwide basis, firearms accounted for 35 per cent of such killings in the Northeast, where there are some gun restrictions, against 64 per cent in the Southern states, where controls are at a minimum and where handguns are displayed in showcases, like shoes, for anybody's buying.

While pointing out that controlling the sale of guns would not, of course, eliminate all willful killings, J. Edgar Hoover has commented: "A review of the motives for murder suggests that a readily accessible gun enables the perpetrator to kill on impulse."

This apparently holds true particularly when policemen are the victims. Of the 168 police officers killed from 1960 through 1963, 78 per cent were dispatched by handguns, and an astounding 96 per

---

* For an exact comparison of the firearms homicide rates and the total number of firearms homicides in these and in other principal countries of the world, see Appendix IV.

cent by firearms of all kinds. These figures also suggest the superb suitability of the handgun for murder. As the Washington *Post* editorialized on April 4, 1965:

> It can be fired from a distance, thus sparing the killer any dangerous or disagreeable contact with his victim. A child can handle it, and indeed many a child does. It is not an expensive weapon. It is easily obtainable, portable, concealable, and disposable. If you take the trouble to wipe off the fingerprints, no one will be able to tell where you got it or who fired it. Even the smaller caliber pistols are marvelously effective at reasonable ranges, and one wonders why anyone wanting to slay somebody else should ever resort to any other device for doing so. . . . One also wonders why the rational members of society interested in staying alive should permit any Tom, Dick or Harry—anyone at all, from the village idiot to the upper echelons of Cosa Nostra—to obtain one of these lethal gadgets at will.

The crime situation seems to be getting worse rather than better. Although the over-all homicide rate has declined considerably since the murderous 1930s and has leveled off in the last decade or so, the firearms homicide rate has been inching up in recent years.* Adding to the seriousness of the situation and not boding well for the future is the grim fact that crime, once the virtually exclusive province of hardened adult felons, usually members of highly organized gangs, has increasingly become the domain of youth. In 1964, for example, half of the more than 1 million persons arrested for burglary, our most common crime, were youngsters under eighteen. Of those arrested for larceny, 54 per cent were under eighteen; for auto theft, 64 per cent were under eighteen. The high arrest age group for aggravated assault was twenty to twenty-four years. And about one-third of those arrested for murder were under twenty-five years of age.

While the juvenile population increased by 25 per cent during the five-year period between 1955 and 1960, the number of youngsters arrested for carrying guns shot up 46 per cent. No doubt contributing to this statistic were three boys who in 1958 were arrested in Martinsburg, West Virginia, for carrying loaded revolvers and were booked for seven burglaries. The boys' ages were eleven, ten and five.

* See Appendix III.

National concern over the mounting rate of juvenile delinquency reached a focus during the first Session of the 83rd Congress (in 1953), when a resolution "to conduct a full and complete study of juvenile delinquency in the United States" was introduced by Senator Robert Hendrickson of New Jersey. The resolution, referred to the Committee on the Judiciary, resulted in the establishment of the Subcommittee to Investigate Juvenile Delinquency.... In 1954, the U.S Senate Subcommittee reported that youngsters ten to 17 years of age were being picked up by the police at the rate of 2,700 daily. In this same year, the U.S. Children's Bureau reported that delinquency had been increasing for five consecutive years.... —William C. Kvaraceus, *The Community and the Delinquent* (1954).

It was not until 1959, when the upward trend in juvenile delinquency had continued for the tenth consecutive year, that the Senate Subcommittee on Juvenile Delinquency, under the chairmanship of Senator Thomas C. Hennings, Jr., of Missouri, finally got around to taking a serious look into the possible relationship between the availability of firearms and youthful criminal behavior. When, in the late summer of that year, U.S. teenage terror mounted to a fury that shocked the world, and New York found itself the scene of five teenage killings in an eight-day period, the subcommittee decided to hold hearings in that city in order to determine what could be done to help remedy what Mayor Robert F. Wagner called "an epidemic of crime committed by teenagers."

The hearings opened on September 23 against a background of still another incident of teenage violence in New York. Just two days before, a sixteen-year-old street gang member had been ambushed in broad daylight and fatally shot as he fled up the steps of a Bronx high school where he sought haven. The young killer later told the police: "It was all a mistake. I never wanted to shoot anybody. I had a gun in my pocket. When I pulled it out, it went off."

During the hearings, a parade of witnesses ranging from the then Mayor Wagner to New York Governor Nelson Rockefeller described the huge dimensions of the juvenile delinquency problem. They discussed the difficulties arising from the easy accessibility of dangerous weapons, homemade, store-bought or stolen, which were falling into juvenile hands in increasing number.

New York Supreme Court Justice John E. Cone told the subcommittee that, although the city's sixteen-to-twenty-year-old population had declined 28 per cent since 1940, arrests of youths in this age group had increased in number from 89 in 1940 to 692 in 1958 —a rise of 678 per cent! In the same period, the number of youths arrested for felonious assault increased 506 per cent, and those for robbery, 140 per cent.

Cone showed the senators a graphic display of confiscated teenage armament: zip guns, starter pistols converted to use .22-caliber ammunition, sawed-off shotguns and revolvers. The display also included an outsize bowie knife, an industrial conveyor belt studded with staples, and a stick wrapped with a chain and a rubber hose. Justice Cone asserted that more than two-thirds of the firearms deaths and injuries in the United States could be prevented by improved legislation. He called for a law making it a federal crime to ship weapons into states banning their use. In addition, he asked for a law requiring the federal registration of all firearms.

Senator Hennings, the subcommittee chairman, noted that he himself had already repeatedly and vainly sponsored bills calling for stricter firearms control, and despairingly said: "Nothing counts except the votes."

"All the speeches and pious pronouncements are fine," he continued, just before he poised his gavel to recess the hearing. "Many members of the House and Senate will vote for construction of dams costing millions of dollars. But they won't vote a nickel to stop the tide of waste and tragedy and loss of good citizens. These things are a little more abstract, a little more difficult."

Over the next two years, similar hearings were held in Chicago, Los Angeles, San Diego, San Francisco, Miami and Washington, D.C.—all as part of the subcommittee's concurrent nationwide study of the gang problem. What contribution was the free and easy availability of firearms making to outbreaks of juvenile violence? To find out definitely, the Senate subcommittee launched an intensive investigation of this subject in March 1961. By this time, the subcommittee was headed by Senator Thomas J. Dodd of Connecticut, who became its chairman after the death of Senator Hennings in September 1960.

"As our investigation progressed," a subcommittee report later said, "it became apparent that a major source of firearms to juveniles and young adults was the mail-order common carrier route.... It was further determined during the investigation that not only juveniles were availing themselves of this source of firearms, but also young and adult felons, narcotic addicts, mental defectives, and others of generally undesirable character."

In the nation's capital, a check by police of some 200 mail-order gun recipients found 25 per cent to have criminal records for offenses ranging all the way from misdemeanors to felonies, including homicide. A Webley revolver was taken from one felon with a record of arrests five pages long. One weapon ordered could not be delivered by Railway Express only because the customer, a dope addict, was then an inmate of the District of Columbia's mental institution, St. Elizabeth's Hospital.

There were similar findings from other large metropolitan areas. Chicago's Superintendent of Police O. W. Wilson reported that in a three-month-period "13 Chicagoans, once arrested on murder charges, bought guns by mail." Other mail-order gun purchasers reported by him included 58 persons who had been arrested for robbery, 42 for burglary, 83 for carrying concealed weapons, and 111 for assault—or a grand total of 307 for the three-month period. This meant that an average of better than 100 firearms a month, or 3 a day, were being shipped to Chicago criminals. Apparently, they still are.

Pittsburgh, too, though in a state which requires a forty-eight-hour waiting period for local handgun purchases, had long been plagued by mail-order handguns. However, the increasing seriousness of their contribution to the city's annals of crime was not uncovered until 1958, and this in a rather curious and almost accidental way.

"While serving as an inspector of police in charge of a district station house," Assistant Superintendent William J. Gilmore told the subcommittee, "I was traveling down a main thoroughfare in my city when I perceived a man with a gun in his hands. A few seconds later I heard shots being fired. I alighted from the automobile and placed him under arrest. He stated that he was only firing at rodents behind a display advertising billboard.

"After questioning him as to where he obtained this gun, he stated that he had seen an advertisement in a printed periodical; that he had forwarded a money order to the American Weapons Company, Burbank, California.* A short time later he received the gun without

* A Hy Hunter enterprise. See pages 25, 206.

answering any questions or furnishing further information. This man, prior to this incident, was under investigation for armed robbery but was released because of lack of evidence. Since that incident, he was arrested on various other charges.

"It was not until 1960, when I was promoted to assistant superintendent of police, that I received information as to how these guns were arriving in the city of Pittsburgh, and the names of the individuals to whom they were being forwarded."

The information developed did indeed indicate that not only was there, as Gilmore put it, a "virtually uncontrolled traffic in mail order firearms into the city of Pittsburgh," but that their use in the commission of crimes was increasing significantly.

In city after city, the similar situations uncovered represented what Senator Dodd called "a national scandal of growing proportions," not only in terms of illicitly used mail-order guns but also with regard to those obtainable without much more difficulty and certainly much more quickly over-the-counter. In his testimony before the juvenile delinquency subcommittee, then U.S. Bureau of Prisons Director James V. Bennett described a number of robberies where the stick-up men actually bought their guns on the way to the scene of the crime.

"Securing a gun was the least troublesome element of their plot, presenting a problem no more difficult than purchasing a pack of cigarettes," commented Bennett. Even the lack of money, apparently, did not necessarily present an unsurmountable problem. In one case described by Bennett, a twenty-eight-year-old man, three days after his release from the Nebraska State Penitentiary where he had just served a one-year term for car theft, swapped his Bulova wristwatch in a pawn shop for a 9-mm. automatic Luger and a clip of shells. Then, proceeding to an Oldsmobile agency, he asked for a demonstration ride, during which he pulled his gun on the car salesman and told him to keep driving.

Together they embarked on a wild ride carrying them through three Western states, sometimes with the kidnap victim driving and at other times with the ex-prisoner at the wheel and the victim in the trunk of the car. Two days later, the distraught salesman was bound and robbed of his case, credit cards and, of course, the car. The criminal, soon apprehended, was confined in a Federal prison hospital as a certified psychotic patient with an extensive prison record.

His offenses included a previous kidnapping of a salesman, transporting a stolen car across state lines, armed robbery and hit-and-run driving. On each occasion, he was either confined or was paroled after serving a short sentence.

Another classic case Bennett described was that of a man with a record of crime and juvenile delinquency dating back eleven years. During his prison terms, he was twice diagnosed as a paranoid on the borderline of schizophrenia and was given psychiatric treatment. Three months after serving his last sentence, and again a fugitive from justice for a freshly committed crime, he went to a sporting goods store in a Milwaukee suburb and bought a .38-caliber automatic over-the-counter, with no questions asked. Then he kidnapped an Iowa dentist and shot him to death.

Bennett went on to recite still more cases. "Now serving a life term at our Springfield Medical Center, which is the place where we keep mentally ill prisoners," Bennett told the subcommittee, "is a young man who in 1959 escaped from a mental hospital in the state of Washington, drew some savings from a bank, bought a .38-caliber automatic pistol from a Portland pawn shop, and shot and killed a traveling business man."

Bennett, a lawyer, an internationally recognized crime authority and a keen student of the firearms problem for more than three decades,* told the Senate subcommittee: "All of the data I have points to the fact that many serious crimes could be avoided if it were made much more difficult for guns to come into the possession of the unstable, the embittered and the hostile."

Do guns play a crucial role in the commission of crimes? From opposite poles of the law, the consensus is that guns do indeed play a crucial role, particularly in the case of the more serious crimes.

"It's almost a necessity that you control the situation, no matter whether it is a grocery store, bank, or what it is," a knowledgeable and perhaps penitent inmate of Joliet's Statesville Prison in Illinois told a CBS reporter. "With a gun in your hand, it's a little bit easier. I mean, you can't go in with a broomstick and secure any authority for an armed robbery."

Certainly, there can be no question that to the bank robber a gun is a virtually indispensable tool of the trade. There can be no ques-

* He retired at age seventy in 1964, and is now a consultant to the Justice Department.

tion that the steadily growing number of guns in circulation is reflected in the fact that more people are now robbing more banks than ever before in history. During the past five years, reports an article in the October 19, 1965, *Look,* bank robberies have shown an astounding 250 per cent increase, far greater than that for most other crimes. During the past year, 1,030 federally insured banking-type institutions were robbed of more than $7 million, and robberies are now at the rate of close to 100 a month.

On a single day in early 1965, New York newspapers alone reported three attempted or successful local bank robberies, one for $23,200. One of the victims, apparently beloved by the bank-robbing fraternity, had been the subject of a previous loss (for $36,000) only six days before. Scarcely two weeks before that two messengers of a New Jersey bank, while making the rounds picking up Sunday church collections, were ambushed in a Roman Catholic rectory and robbed of $511,000 in bills and coins. This was the largest bank-robbery loot in New Jersey history. Four priests were also relieved of $449 in collection money, just as a funeral procession was pulling up in front of the church door.

About 1 out of 4 bank robberies are now committed by amateur felons. In a celebrated recent case, twenty-two-year-old Duane Earle Pope, just graduated from college, killed three people in a Nebraska bank robbery.

Although firearms are the favored weapons in most robberies, they are used to a lesser degree in assaults, figuring in only 15 per cent of the estimated 184,900 serious cases of this sort tallied by the FBI during 1964. The 15 per cent firearms figure represented 27,700 gun attacks that year. These refer only to incidents in which the victim survived; otherwise, the cases would have been classified as homicide.

Furthermore, when guns are used—whether in assaults or robberies—someone is most likely to get seriously hurt and, all too often, fatally. J. Edgar Hoover has declared: "A firearm is *seven* times more deadly than all other weapons combined." His statement is based on an FBI analysis of the types of weapons used in assaults and murders: 21 per cent of the assaults in which guns figured resulted in death to the victim, as compared to the only 3 per cent who died when all the other weapons were used.

It is interesting to speculate whether those fascinated by guns

would commit the crimes they do if their fascination were not forti-
fied by the physical presence of a firearm. After listening to the cases
cited by James V. Bennett before the Senate juvenile delinquency
subcommittee, Senator Kenneth B. Keating of New York asked:
"Would these men in your judgment . . . commit crimes without
guns? Or is there some aspect of their personality which induces
them to commit a crime once a gun is available to them?"

"I think the latter, Senator," Bennett replied. "I have cited cases
mostly of the mentally disturbed people, of juveniles, who have a
fascination for guns. I do not think that unless they were bolstered
up by a gun they would have committed those crimes. They are not
the type of person that commits that kind of crime."

With crime having changed from the exclusive province of hardened adult criminals to the special domain of youth, such questions
are particularly pertinent. Whatever the psychological, sociological
and other roots of the crime problem and, especially, the juvenile
crime problem, one cannot but agree with those police officials who
have said, in effect:

"Take away the young hoodlum's weapons and he ceases to be a
potential criminal or murderer. Without a gun, he is reduced to the
comparatively tame status of a bad kid."

With the sharpest upswing in crime occurring in the Southern
states, where the criminal homicide rate has long been the nation's
highest, cause for particular alarm is the continued boom in the
traffic in firearms to areas of special racial tension. In May 1965, civil
rights leaders expressed concern about a shipment of 492 surplus
military rifles en route from California to a Selma, Alabama, gun
dealer, Walter H. Craig. "I don't know why this shipment is causing
such a stir," said Craig. "I am a licensed gun dealer and I often receive large shipments of guns. I sell them for hunting weapons." The
shipment included M-1 and .30/06 rifles. The latter was the type
used to kill Jackson, Mississippi, Negro leader Medgar Evers two
years before. The one found at the scene of the crime was identified
as belonging to Byron De La Beckwith, a dapper fertilizer salesman,
gun enthusiast and Klansman.

Beckwith whiled away his time in jail awaiting trial for the murder of Evers by writing a letter to the National Rifle Association:
"For the next fifteen years we here in Mississippi are going to have
to do a lot of shooting to protect our wives and children from bad

niggers." The letter also inquired about setting up ranges for "white people" to practice shooting. Beckwith was set free after the second of his two juries could not reach a verdict.

In the fall of 1964, a Georgia white jury acquitted two other Klansmen, both avid gun collectors, accused in the shotgun slaying of a Negro educator, Lemuel Penn, who, ironically, was returning from his annual two-week tour of Army reserve duty. The nation was shocked by scores of similar unpunished fatal shootings by the unsavory who could seemingly arm themselves at will with shotguns, rifles and handguns.

In early 1965, a Detroit sports store owner reported that "pistols are scarcer than hens' teeth" and said that a gun dealer from Huntsville, Alabama, just 20 miles from racial-torn Selma, had dropped into his store several days before, trying to buy used revolvers.

"We simply can't keep up with the demand or get enough stock through regular channels to supply customers," the Alabama dealer explained.

On March 25, just thirteen days later, Mrs. Viola Gregg Liuzzo, a white Detroit civil rights worker, was shot and killed near Selma. The murder weapon turned out to be a used .38-caliber revolver. It could have followed her to Selma from that Detroit gun shop near her home.

4   Are You Ever Safe
from a Gun?

"I want to wait for Mommy. She'll be home soon." Dazed and near tears, pretty, frail Susan Didchenko, twelve, waited today in the Brooklyn home of attorney Harry Gulgulin for the return of her mother, Gertrude, forty-three. The little brown-haired girl was unaware that her vigil was in vain.

Mrs. Didchenko was fatally shot in the main hall of the American Museum of Natural History yesterday by her ex-husband, noted violin maker Dmytro Didchenko, seventy-two, in an explosive climax to years of bitter wrangling over visitation rights to the child.

"He just had the gun and shot at Mommy," Susan recalled, oblivious to the fact that three shots had hit their lethal mark.

"The thing I want to know is, how did this man get the gun?" asked Mr. Gulgulin, referring to the 7.65-mm. foreign-make automatic Didchenko allegedly whipped from the pocket of his tweed overcoat to blaze six shots at his divorced wife.

"In America anybody can get a gun," Didchenko was quoted as telling detectives after his arrest.—*New York Journal American*, February 8, 1965

In Parsons, West Virginia, during the course of the last weekend, police arrested a forty-eight-year-old man and charged him with the fatal shooting of a neighboring couple. They got into an argument, you see—nobody seems to know or even to care very much what it was about—and the man had this gun handy. So, naturally, being rather angry and wishing to settle the matter, he killed a thirty-five-year-old man and also killed the man's wife; and for good measure he wounded their two-year-old daughter and a babysitter, who just happened to be there at the time.

These shootings did not occur in the course of another crime. One surmises that they were not planned or viciously motivated and that the killer now greatly regrets what he did. But what is done with a gun is generally not remediable.—Editorial, *Washington Post*, April 13, 1965

As such incidents indicate, not all shootings involve professional killers, kooks or Klansmen, or their junior criminal counterparts. In fact, contrary to a fairly widespread popular belief, most murders are committed by persons who are generally law-abiding. In his well-known study of fifty-one murderers, sociologist Stuart Palmer of the University of New Hampshire found none whom he considered professional killers, and only 4 with records of prior conviction for murder or first-degree manslaughter. * "The majority of the 51 men had either minor or no conviction records," writes Palmer in his book, *A Study of Murder.*

FBI figures bear out the conclusion that if murder were left to only the hardened hoodlum, our murder rate would immediately drop to a mere fraction of what it is now. Of the 9,250 willful killings in 1964, only 1,350—or about 1 out of 7—were "felony murders," that is, those committed during the course of robberies, sex offenses, gangland slayings and other such crimes by persons of known homicidal background. The offenders were generally strangers to the victims.

The vast majority of homicides—at least 80 per cent—were by so-called "average," normally law-abiding persons actually known to the victim—friends, neighbors, even members of the same family. Indeed, from the FBI figures we learn that blood, though thicker than water, flows rather freely among kinfolk: nearly one-third (31 per cent) of all 1964's murders occurred within the family unit.

---

* Manslaughter, according to *Webster's New International Dictionary,* second edition, is "the unlawful killing of a human being without malice expressed or implied." Voluntary manslaughter is that resulting from a sudden heat of passion or quarrel; involuntary manslaughter is the by-product of "an unlawful act not a felony or the doing of a lawful act in an unlawful manner, as in culpable negligence" (an auto death resulting from speeding, for example).

The FBI's fact-filled 1964 *Uniform Crime Reports,* one of our most interesting social documents, also tells us that slightly more than one-half of these "involved spouse killing spouse and 20 per cent parents killing children." In most cases the murder weapon was a gun. Considering that guns are more readily available within the home than elsewhere, it is not surprising that firearms figure in 60 per cent of willful killings within the family unit, compared to 57 per cent in all willful killings and in only 44 per cent of felony murders.*

Murders not involving felons, family members or relatives usually resulted from altercations between so-called friends and acquaintances, these making up 49 per cent of the willful killings. In this category of killings, the biggest single sources of trouble were love (22 per cent) and liquor (17 per cent). The majority of the friendly killings, however, were difficult to categorize so neatly, being the result, the FBI says, of "impulsive rage involving a wide range of altercations, such as arguments over a cigarette, ice cream, noise, etc."

Indeed, outside or inside the family, some of the things people quarrel and try to kill each other over are almost beyond belief. In Michigan, some years ago, a fifteen-year-old girl was arrested for pulling a gun on another teenager in an argument over which one was entitled to permanent possession of a fan magazine article about Elvis Presley. In Jersey City, New Jersey, early in 1965, an apartment house superintendent and two of her sons were shot by a tenant, through the superintendent's closed door, after a spat over the building's hallway lighting. In an Arlington, Virginia, restaurant later that year, a dishwasher was shot by a pistol-packing patron who said he was distressed over his victim's "foul language toward the waitresses."

Even sheer noise can trigger death. In 1965, a seventy-one-year-old Chicago blind woman shot her husband to death, aiming in the direction of his voice, after he complained about the tapping of her cane and threatened to send her to a home for the blind. Four days later, a Brooklyn resident, annoyed at the chattering of a group of seven teenagers just returned from a party, hauled out a rifle and fired a shot, killing a fifteen-year-old boy. Not long before, another

* These firearms figures are from the FBI's 1963 *Reports;* there is no such breakdown in the 1964 edition.

fifteen-year-old boy was killed by a .22-caliber bullet fired through a bedroom window of his El Sereno, California, home. The shot had been fired by a hypersensitive neighbor who had become irate over the noise made by the youngster's skateboarding.

There is literally no end to the trivia that can trigger a shooting. One man, refused admission to a Pittsburgh tavern, shot three and killed two of the persons who just happened to be standing by its door. Another fatal shooting resulted during the course of an argument over a $1.50 pot in a crap game. A murder resulted one recent summer when two elderly baseball fans disagreed as to the relative merits of their favorite players. In another incident, one man shot and killed another whose beagle, the murderer claimed, had been bothering his cat. In the Bronx, New York, a place not notable for the best of manners, a woman who accidentally bumped into another while passing her on the street was shot to death when she refused to apologize. A Miami Beach motorist, angered by his arrest on a pair of traffic charges, shot a policeman in the pants and then pumped four more bullets into the station-house wall. In Wilmington, Ohio, a family breadwinner, fed up with his in-laws' habit of dropping in and pilfering his groceries, sprayed revolver shots at their car as it drew up to his house.

Adding to the already awesome list of auto fatalities are such incidents as these. A Detroit doctor, in late 1965, was shot to death at a red light by an irate armed citizen who claimed that the doctor had been trying to run him off the road. And in San Francisco some years ago, a gun-traffic fatality was a driver who wouldn't back up enough to allow another car to park. In October 1964, a Long Island highway duel which began with cars being used as the weapons (each repeatedly sideswiped the other) ended when one of the drivers pulled out a .22 derringer and sent three bullets into the body of the other.

Not all killings, of course, are the consequences of such wildly impulsive shots fired in anger; many are the result of pent-up passions, issuing from various injustices, fancied or otherwise. In March 1965, Lewis Delgado, an unemployed Bronx, New York, grocery clerk, was arrested in the fatal shooting of Benjamin Penofsky, the owner of a Manhattan Army-Navy store. The boy had been brooding over a shoving incident with Penofsky that had taken place two years before. Possibly with liquor as his unseen accomplice, a New York bar patron shot and killed two other men in a Harlem bar. Police said the killer was trying to avenge the stabbing of a friend in the same bar several days before. With such avengers presumably having more time to secure arms, it is not surprising that guns are used most in this type of killing, figuring in 76 per cent of all killings for revenge. FBI figures indicate that at least 150 revenge killings take place every year.

People kill each other over money and property—everything from the paltry proceeds of a crap game to various obligations of other kinds.* Some years ago, in Hollywood, Carl Switzer, a thirty-one-year-old actor, whom old-timers and television late-nighters may recall as Alfalfa, one of the child rascals of the "Our Gang" movies, was shot to death by a friend in a battle over a $50 debt. The money, Switzer had claimed, was due him as a reward for finding his friend's dog. One of the most publicized money killing cases in recent years resulted in the conviction in 1964 of Mark Fein, a Park Avenue executive who was sentenced to a thirty-year term for shooting to death a Brooklyn bookmaker. Fein and two friends owed the bookmaker $23,898 for being on the wrong end of a World Series bet. The debt and death were uncovered when the bullet-ridden bookmaker, with ankles bound, was found floating in the Harlem River.

On the battleground of love, which "can make us fiends as well as angels," † quarrels, often complicated by triangles, end even more frequently in killing, account for about 1 out of every 5 occurring outside the family. Here the motives become somewhat more murky than those which cause murders over money. Indeed, the motivations are often only superficially conveyed by the frequent tabloid headlines screaming PASSION MURDER. A nineteenth-century art critic, asked why he had killed a woman friend, offered as his original and aesthetic rationale that it was "because she had thick legs."

In a case that attracted considerable attention in New York in 1959, complicating the lives of Lillian Freiberg, a petite secretary, and her fiancé, John Conwell, a handsome former Air Force pilot, were differences about religion, money and a miscellany of other matters. Conwell criticized Miss Freiberg's use of makeup. She liked skiing. He didn't. She liked the theater. He liked movies.

All this was brought out when Miss Freiberg was brought to trial

---

* They comprised 5 per cent of all nonfamily killings in 1963, according to the FBI's *Uniform Crime Reports.*
† Charles Kingsley, nineteenth-century English novelist (*Westward Ho!*).

for the fatal shooting of her fiancé, supposedly after he had tried to rape her. She was found guilty of voluntary manslaughter.* A damning bit of evidence against her was the disclosure that she had made a trip to Georgia to purchase the death weapon (a .22 Beretta pistol) under an assumed name.

Such tragedies are duplicated almost daily throughout the land, though more typically with the man as the killer. (Moreover, when women are homicidally inclined, they are more apt to use knives, rather than guns, as the instrument of murder.) Often, too, a competing male figure may be found lurking in the background as an unwitting, or sometimes even actual, accomplice.

About the time of the Freiberg trial, Ira Schwartz, a Brooklyn law student, shot to death Sandra Chick, his pretty ex-fiancée who had jilted him for a lawyer. Then Schwartz killed himself with another two shots from his .22 rifle.

A typical "passion murder" also took place in Gutenberg, New Jersey, that year. Robert Sharp, a tavern manager, could not bear the fact that the object of his ardent affections, Mrs. Marianne Shabilon, a beautiful blonde divorcee, was about to marry another man. Two hours before the scheduled nuptials, he seized his M-1 service rifle and burst in upon the pre-wedding party. "If I can't have her, neither can you," Sharp shouted to Jacob Bronler, the successful suitor. With that, Sharp fired a fusillade of shots into Broner's body, killing the bridegroom-to-be.

Interestingly, as Dr. Walter Bromberg points out in his psychiatric study of homicide, *The Mold of Murder:*

In a triangle situation in which the cuckolded man is young, his impulse is to kill the erring woman. On the other hand, when the cuckolded individual is older, the erring man is more frequently the victim.

There is an interesting psychological reason for this differentiation of victims [Bromberg explains]. To the younger offender, the woman is the more serious psychological threat since her misbehavior reawakens his feelings of sexual incompetence. The young offender has given his "secret" of sexual desire to the *woman* and has achieved emotional ease through her. When the woman of his choice betrays his secret through entering a triangle (usually to an older man), his sexual guilt with its accompanying anger mounts to fury. Wife, sweetheart or "his" woman

---

* She was not charged with a higher degree of murder, because there were no eye witnesses to the shooting.

have shared the secret of his sexual desire and his unconscious hatred of the other man. His underlying fear and guilt trigger the explosive reaction. The "older" offender's problem, on the other hand ... is more apt to be related to competitive strivings towards other men.

Sometimes, the betrayed or rejected kills both the man and woman. An unusual case described by Bromberg, a former director of the psychiatric clinic of New York's Court of General Sessions and one of the nation's leading psychiatric criminologists, is that of a man he calls Aaron Waldman. A young eastern European refugee from Hitlerism, Waldman, the son of an Orthodox rabbi, converted to Christianity and became a Protestant "prairie teacher." At a church meeting in Arizona he met and married an attractive girl, Kathleen, who was Catholic. The couple decided to honeymoon in New York. Before their departure, Aaron, at his bride's suggestion, purchased a pistol to safeguard their money during their stay in New York. As Bromberg continues the story:

Their stay in New York was pleasant. Among the people they met at the hotel, one, a priest, invited them for cocktails and dinner. Several evenings later, they met again for a social evening, this time in the Waldmans' room. The drinking tempo increased and during the course of the evening the priest, who had been considered "mentally unsound" by his superiors and was undergoing psychiatric treatment, suggested he hear Kathleen's confession. In laughing agreement, the pair withdrew to the clergyman's room to obtain privacy, while Aaron dropped into the lobby. After some time Aaron returned upstairs. Opening the door to the priest's room he saw the priest and his wife of sixteen days, her skirt removed, standing in a compromising position. Stung into action, the defendant walked to the bureau and picked up his gun. With dramatic calm Aaron said, "You kissed each other and you are going to heaven." He fired the revolver, killing both.

Domesticity can often bring out the worst as well as the best in people. Killings among family members, as already noted, account for some 31 per cent of the nation's murders, or nearly 2,900 a year—8 a day! This is easily understandable. Familiarity, evidently, breeds more than just children. Conflict and friction are inevitably bound to develop among those who live on close terms and, quite often, in close quarters. Moreover, they are also bound to be more frequent and more intense, because of the vicissitudes of marriage and family life and the complex interrelationships and adjustments these necessarily involve.

It is therefore not quite so simple to categorize the causes of killings within the clan as it is homicides outside the family. In some cases, the motivations for murder seem to be the same, at least on the surface, the reported reasons running the gamut from love and money to other major and minor irritations.

Yet while immediate causes may vary considerably, intrafamily killings have a deadly superficial sameness. A wife is overwrought. A husband is jealous, or under emotional stress. A child is disturbed, although perhaps not to any obvious degree. Sometimes alcohol may play a role in liberating the inhibitions and unleashing the lethal impulses.

Take the Ridener couple of Joliet, Illinois. On June 1, 1965, just after returning home from a night of drinking, they had another of an apparently endless succession of arguments.

A year earlier, husband Harold, a retired Army sergeant, had been laid up in the hospital for a month after wife Opal had shot him in the foot. Now the Rideners were at it again. Harold struck his wife several times, she later said; whereupon she pointed a 12-gauge shotgun at him. "I'm going to make you eat that gun," he said, starting after her. She fired, the spray of buckshot this time leaving her a widow.*

It is outside the province of this book to probe the real causes of these and other killings. Commenting on the motivations for murder, a University of Pennsylvania criminologist Marvin E. Wolfgang points out, "Most underlying 'causes' and unconscious motivations usually lie beyond the realm of necessary police investigation."

---

* Married men may take some comfort in the statistical evidence that women, though no strangers to homicide, are generally unlikely to go after their husbands with guns, or for that matter, weapons of any kind. (Poison is a traditional feminine favorite.) When women kill, they are more likely to kill their children. (One of the many complex explanations is the relationship of infanticide to abortion.) However, the occasional deviations from this pattern in line with the legend holding the female to be the more deadly of the species should give every husband pause. There is, for example, the story of Mrs. Katherine Harrig of Laurens, New York, a twenty-five-year-old mother of four. She became understandably upset when she saw Alice Pierce, a twenty-one-year-old unmarried girl, walk into the family apartment, plop down on a sofa and clasp her twenty-eight-year-old husband, Howard, to her embrace. Mrs. Harrig stalked out of the room, got her husband's .45-caliber Army automatic, and shot the ardent couple to death.

But pertinent is the question: Would many killings within the family take place if a gun were not so readily available? It seems reasonable to assume that if a gun were not at hand (in many homes, as commonly as household utensils), the arguments and bursts of anger might, in many cases, have blown over with less harmful consequences.

So incidents of spouse killing spouse account for the greater part of family killings, as lovers' quarrels continue into marriage and often for much the same reasons—such as jealousy, infidelity or estrangement. A killing may result, not only because one has threatened to leave the other or has actually done so, but also because one is *unable* to leave the other. The murder is a means, so to speak, of securing a divorce Italian-style. Or the killing may stem from one of the many woes peculiar to marriage, manifesting themselves in arguments, trivial or otherwise, which, like those typically advanced as grounds for divorce, often conceal the real basis for dissension.

We therefore have that seemingly endless stream of newspaper stories of husband-wife shootings. Though possibly differing to some degree in detail, they are united in similarity in most cases by the common availability and use of guns. In the Bronx, New York, Herman Martin Rosenthal, a waiter, ends a seven-hour argument with his estranged wife by shooting her to death with his .22-caliber rifle. He then critically wounds himself, as their six-month-old baby screams in its crib, and horrified neighbors try to force their way into the apartment.

In West Islip, Long Island, Helen Latessa, a mother of four, is shot to death with a hunting rifle by her husband, Thomas, a bartender, less than a day after they had ended a three-month estrangement. The husband, hunted by police, is reported as owning "a number of guns," including, in addition to the hunting rifle, a 12-gauge shotgun and a .25-caliber pistol.

In Los Angeles, Milton Taylor kills his wife, Alice, with a slug from a .45-caliber automatic pistol during a "family quarrel." Five of the victim's children by a previous marriage, ranging in age from nine to fourteen years, are asleep at the time.

Whatever the basis for the connubial conflict, innocent children are often unwitting victims in the ensuing marital massacre. In one particularly gory episode in Troy, Michigan, William Gravelin, a former mental patient previously arrested, though never prosecuted, on a charge of feloniously assaulting his cousin's wife, killed his own wife and six children with a double-bladed ax, a knife and a shotgun. Troy's police chief said the "stench of death" was so strong when his men finally entered the house that they had to wear gas masks. Inside, they found pinned to each of the bodies a note reading,"I love you. I'm sorry, it couldn't be helped," and on a dresser a Bible opened to a page in the Gospel of Mark, the page containing the verse: "And if a house be divided against itself, that house cannot stand." Gravelin, a former fireman, confessed to the slayings. He said that he and his wife were having marital difficulties and had reached the point where they were talking about divorce.

In Roselle, New Jersey, about ten months before the Gravelin tragedy, another loving husband and devoted father, Donald Stafford, also went on a rampage of death. He wiped out his family of four, suffocating his wife with a pillow, shooting his two children, aged eleven and seven, and then firing a bullet into his right temple with a .22-caliber rifle. In the pockets of the dead man, who was without a previous history of mental illness, were found forty-seven rounds of ammunition. In the house was found a note which read: "I loved my little family. Now we will always be together."

Also common are shootings by women who, though mentally ill or under emotional stress, had no difficulty whatever in buying or otherwise having easy access to guns. The great tragedy is that most of these shootings could have been prevented. Early in February 1964, Mrs. Elizabeth Stevens Takagi, the wife of a Japanese-born physician and researcher at the National Institutes of Health, shot to death her thirteen-year-old twins, Diana and Daniel, after keeping them home from school in order to carry out the killing. Then Mrs. Takagi walked from her Wheaton Woods home in Montgomery County, Maryland, to the nearby home of her seventeen-year-old married daughter, Gloria, and killed her, too. Finally, she fired the last of eight bullets into her own head. One neighbor said that the late Mrs. Takagi had been "highly nervous and emotionally upset" for months. Another said that she had been "threatening to kill her children for some time." Yet Mrs. Takagi, using only her maiden name, had been able to buy the .38-caliber Smith & Wesson revolver used in the killings at a Silver Spring gun shop less than forty-eight hours before. At that time a bill introduced by a Silver Spring delegate, Leonard S. Blondes, was pending in the state legislature which would have required a three-day waiting period for gun purchasers, during which time investigators would interview neighbors, personal friends and members of the families of such would-be purchasers to make certain that weapons were not getting into the wrong hands. The bill did not become law.*

Less than two weeks later, on Valentine's Day, just across the Potomac in Fairfax County, Virginia, Mrs. Judith Eileen Cox, the wife of a Falls Church school principal, also used a Smith & Wesson revolver to shoot and kill all of her four children, ranging in age from four months to fourteen years, and then herself. At the time he was shot in the back of his head, Danny, the fourteen-year-old, was opening his Valentine's Day mail on the drainboard of the kitchen sink. Laurie Beth, eleven years old, killed by a single shot, was in her bedroom stamping Valentine cards. Timmy, the four-month-old infant, shot once in the back and again in the head, was in his red plaid plastic carriage in the nursery. Also in the nursery and at first expected to survive, though with a bullet in his head, was two-year-old Joel. Mrs. Cox was found with a bullet hole in the right temple, partially slumped over in a rocking chair in the basement utility room, her right hand still clutching the gun. She had bought it that very morning in the local Montgomery Ward store. Since Fairfax County places no inhibitions on gun purchasers, requiring them only to look or say that they are eighteen years old, the store clerk had no way of knowing that Mrs. Cox had been twice committed to a mental institution.

On a nationwide CBS-TV show, *Murder and the Right to Bear Arms,* the sole surviving member of the family, principal Thomas J. Cox, was asked if he knew that his wife wanted to buy a gun.

"If I had known, I could have helped by taking her back to the institution," Cox answered. "We should have laws providing at least a seventy-two-hour waiting period before a person would be permitted to buy a gun. In other words, you go over and apply for it and give the police, or the stores, time to check with the husband, parents, or some local people who would understand this person or know about him."

Cox was asked if he would tell why he had permitted the TV network to come into his house, set up its cameras and interview him.

---

* Another, specifying a seven-day waiting period, was enacted on March 29, 1966, during the last thirty seconds of the Maryland Assembly's session.

"The main reason," he answered, "is that I want, in any way I can, to help prevent some other person from having to suffer even one death, or one tragedy. I know there'll never be another one like mine—there couldn't be as many deaths at one time.* But anything that I can do to help prevent even one I'm willing to do. . . . And the main thing I think that we have to do here is to get tighter gun control laws."

Although 20 per cent of the willful killings within the family involve parents killing children, according to the latest available FBI figures, the reverse situation, that is, children killing parents, accounts for far fewer deaths. The reasons seem fairly plausible: children, particularly those below grade-school age, apart from being naturally intimidated by the superior strength and size of their seniors, may not have quite as easy access to guns and other lethal weapons, or perhaps the few dollars necessary to buy them. However, these difficulties are not insurmountable, as is evident by many tragic newspaper stories, of which the following, from the New York *Post* of March 30, 1959, is fairly typical:

So there they were on the bright March day, two cops and the kid, and what they had to do was go to a funeral. The kid, they say, killed the man for whom the funeral was being held. The man was his father.

They went to the services, the three of them, from the Sheriff's office in Wampsville, New York, with as little display as possible. One of the deputies is Rus Pinckney and he is fifty-two, a solid double-chinned man who has four grandchildren to play with on most weekends. The boy is

---

* On the very day Cox's words were telecast, a Midland, Pennsylvania housewife, Mrs. Mary Zlatovich, shot and killed four of her five children, ages two to five, as they slept, after a bitter quarrel with her husband. The fifth child, an infant of eight months, was spared only because Mrs. Zlatovich ran out of ammunition for her .32-caliber pistol. Such multiple murders by mothers are not as uncommon as Cox and others may think. During a three-month period in 1965 I spotted newspaper announcements of three.

In August, Mrs. Mary Sartin, a Sandusky, Ohio, housewife, killed her five sleeping children, ages seven months to six years, her husband and herself—also with a .32-caliber pistol. In Walla Walla, Washington, a month later, Mrs. Margaret Hastings, a woman just forty days out of a mental hospital, used a .22-caliber rifle to kill four of her seven sons (two others were also shot), her husband and herself. A month after this, in Laurel, Maryland, Mrs. Charlene Hargis, the estranged wife of a former Kansas congressman, murdered their four children, ages two to twelve, with a .25-caliber pistol—her husband's. Here again, the children were asleep, and never knew their own mother had killed them.

Stephen Girard, sixteen. The reports say that Stephen argued with his father last Tuesday about the farm chores and that the boy ended the argument with his .22-caliber rifle.

When they got to the little country funeral home where the services were being held for Ferdinand Girard, the officers were worried about how the boy would act. . . . but there were no tears even then from Stephen.

"It would probably take a psychiatrist to explain his actual feelings," Pinckney said. "Actually, he's a nice boy. But there was something . . ."

But even psychiatrists do not find it easy to explain killings of this kind. "The boy who kills wantonly, out of a background void of previous criminal offense, is difficult to understand in terms of psychiatric principles," says psychiatric criminologist Dr. Walter Bromberg.* "Contrary to the delinquent youth involved in a gang killing, or an attack in unison with his gang brothers on a single defenseless boy, the solitary killer is not found to be sociopathic [psychopathic]. More often, he is a mildly introverted or even a passive individual who passes for an 'adjusted' youth. He should be distinguished also from the sociopath whose rebelliousness is deep-seated, whose unadjustability has been evident from an early age. Parenthetically, most authorities feel that the 'true psychopath' shows his difficulty in adjustment as early as the sixth year."

In fact, many kids who kill are, like Stephen Girard, often described as "nice" or "normal." Back in 1959, in Auburn, New York, Johnny Jayne, later described as "perfectly normal" by his high-school mentors, impulsively killed his father, mother, sister and brother with a 12-gauge shotgun after eating ice cream and watching television with them. "I had been mad at them for some time because of the whippings my parents gave me, and because of the fights I had with my brother," the boy explained calmly and without remorse.

Often there is no seeming provocation at all. In Rye, New York, on May 14, 1957, fourteen-year-old Andrew Casey, known as a good, average boy and a member of what was regarded as a close-knit, happy family, suddenly got up from his homework, took his brother's .22-caliber rifle and killed his mother and sister. "I just got depressed-like," he told police.

* *The Mold of Murder*, p. 72.

What turns a quiet teenager from a good home into a killer? The same question arose in Great Neck, Long Island, a year after the Casey killings when, under strange, inexplicable and shockingly similar circumstances, another fourteen-year-old boy, James Wiener, suddenly got up from his stamp collection, went to his bedroom closet, took out his .22-caliber rifle and killed his mother as she stood in the kitchen preparing dinner. Then he killed his sister and himself. Again the police took down the same familiar phrases from friends and neighbors: "... such a quiet, lovely boy ... so devoted to his sister ... he seemed very average in all respects ... I can't believe he'd do it ... you never think it could happen. ..."

One could cite an endless number of similar cases involving the killing of parents, brothers, sisters and other relatives for—if any known reason at all—a miscellany of curious, improbable ones.

In a Cain and Abel case in Altadena, California, an eighteen-year-old boy bought and used a mail-order pistol to shoot and kill his fourteen-year-old brother. When asked why, he replied: "My brother was an inferior person."

"He wouldn't let me join the Peace Corps. ..." This, according to detectives, was eighteen-year-old Garry Klinger's explanation of why he killed his father, Bernard, a Brooklyn druggist, on April 1, 1965.

"I wanted to see the world," the soft-spoken youth, who alternately grinned and looked bored at his arraignment, said simply. But his father had insisted that the young intellectual, who had a near-genius I.Q. of 150, finish his premedical college studies first. "I went to Times Square and bought a rifle for $16 in a sporting goods store," Klinger told police. It was similar to the one that killed President Kennedy.

Other means, such as bludgeoning and stabbing, are of course also used in such family killings, but for obvious reasons the preferred, and often only possible, juvenile "equalizer" is a gun, particularly because of the ease with which it lends itself to murder—multiple murder.

The incidents are endless. On January 4, 1965, Harrison Crouse, a University of Illinois art and drama major, shot to death his father, mother and sister in their suburban Chicago home. To the eternal question "Why?," he, like hundreds of others who kill, could only reply, "I don't know."

In a study of 175 murderers, Dr. Manfred S. Guttmacher of the University of Maryland and director for over three decades of the psychiatric clinic of the Baltimore criminal courts, found 105—well over half—to have been "clearly nonpsychotic at the time of the murder." "Society's greatest concern," says Guttmacher, "must be with the nonpsychotic murderer, with the individual who exhibits no marked psychopathology, since by far the greatest numbers of homicides are committed by this kind of person." *

Whether some fatal shootings are homicides or the result of accidents often depends on who is telling the story and to what extent the court believes it. In the winter of 1965, Mrs. Hubert Marlin of Nashville, Tennessee, shot and killed a twenty-year-old college football star, Charles Ray Neal, when she happened to find him asleep in bed with her twenty-two-year-old daughter, Cynthia. To Cynthia, all was innocence, and medical testimony supported her statement: Neal was spending the night with her simply because the ice-covered highways would have made a return to the Tennessee State University campus hazardous.

Mrs. Marlin told the court that the shooting was accidental. "I guess I just wanted to scare him," she said as she described how she first attempted to awaken Neal by prodding him with the gun before it somehow went off. Naturally, she did not know it was loaded.

Every year more than 2,200 persons are accidentally killed by guns in the United States.† (As in crime shootings and in murder-by-gun, we lead the world in fatal firearms accidents.) Our death rate from this cause has been almost constant during the past decade, about 1.3 per 100,000 population, or as much as 8 times that recorded in England and Wales (.16) and the German Federal Republic (.17), 14 times the rate of Japan (.09), and over 40 times that of the Netherlands (.03)! It is also appreciably higher than the rate in Denmark (.32), France (.56), Italy (.36) and even neighboring Canada (.8)).‡

Although 2,200 firearms accident victims a year may not seem like very much in a country of nearly 200,000,000 people, the num-

---

* *The Mind of the Murderer*, p. 4.

† In 1963, a total of 2,263, according to the U.S. Office of Vital Statistics; in 1964, about 2,400, according to an estimate by the National Safety Council. See Appendix III.

‡ For a comparison with other leading countries, see Appendix IV.

ber works out to an average of six every day around the clock. Nine out of every ten victims are males. About a quarter of the dead—nearly 600 a year—are youngsters less than 14 years old. Many are five- and six-year-olds, often with the shooter the same age or even younger! * And, as with homicide, most are shot by friends and members of their own family. The three-month period October–December, during which hunting activities are at a maximum and firearms are handled most frequently, accounts for nearly two-fifths of the annual toll of fatalities, according to an estimate by the Metropolitan Life Insurance Company. However, an astonishing number—at least half—happen not in the woods but rather right in the home. (Others take place on farms, on the street, and in such other places as garages, taverns and stores.)

A particularly tragic case concerned the Manitz brothers of Secaucus, New Jersey. Carl, sixteen, and Charles, seventeen, were just about as close as brothers can be. They went everywhere together, shared their possessions, their secrets, their dreams. And because Carl thought his older brother was "the greatest," he patterned himself on Charles, watching him, learning from him, looking up to him.

While Charles was cleaning a .22-caliber rifle one day in preparation for target practice, Carl was with him in their room. Suddenly a shot cracked out. The discharge of the rifle struck young Carl over the right eye and he died an hour later, the shot separating the boys forever.

How often have you seen similar newspaper reports of people being killed while cleaning loaded guns, even though every gun owner supposedly knows that it is impossible to clean such a gun properly?

Family Safety (winter, 1964), a National Safety Council publication, tells of a woman in Louisiana who, worried about a couple of shotguns in the house, repeatedly asked her husband if they were loaded. "Of course not," he replied, for what was to be the last time. "I haven't used them for twenty years, but it's time I cleaned them anyway." After cleaning his 12-gauge, he picked up the .410, accidentally triggering it. A lone undiscovered shell exploded, blasting a fatal hole in his chest.

It's amazing how many people are killed by "unloaded" guns

---

* In February 1966, an eighteen-month-old Brooklyn boy shot and seriously wounded his two brothers, ages three and four.

playfully pointed at them. In Missouri, a mock "Wild West" card game played by two teen-age boys ended in tragedy when one of the boys said, "Let's pretend you cheated and we both pull our guns." As they did, a shotgun held by one discharged into the neck of the other, killing him instantly. The shooter told police he did not realize the gun was loaded.

Equally dangerous are guns—always "unloaded," of course—left lying around or in places where they can be easily discovered or knocked over. In Bellport, Long Island, a two-and-a-half-year-old boy shot and wounded his father with a newly purchased rifle which had been placed on a couch. A three-year-old Milwaukee girl on a camping vacation with her parents was shot and killed when she bumped against a .30-30 rifle leaning against a wall in the family trailer.

In Brooklyn, a thirteen-year-old girl shot and killed her sixteen-year-old sister with a hunting rifle taken from their brother's unlocked gun rack. She was trying to copy the manual of arms they were watching on television during President Kennedy's funeral ceremonies.

Many accidents are the result of self-inflicted wounds. In Washington, D.C., a three-year-old boy playing in his mother's bedroom came upon a .22-caliber pistol and shot himself in the stomach. In Miami, Eugibio Vargas went to sleep holding a pistol, dreamed he was being attacked, and awoke to find that he had shot himself in the left hand and leg.

Some of the things people do with guns are almost incredible. Not a few deaths—as many as 80 a year, according to a Metropolitan Life Insurance Company study—are due to that peculiar pastime known as Russian roulette. In this morbid game, a single cartridge is put into a chamber of the cylinder of a six-shooter. Then each participant takes turns twirling the cylinder, pointing the revolver at his head and pulling the trigger on the chance—the odds are 5 to 1—that the hammer of the gun will hit on an empty chamber. In one recent game played by four New Jersey teenagers, the first participant to try lost the game—and his life.

In a solo version of this old game, Robert Sunshine, a New York lawyer, after lunching with a woman companion, said he would like to show her a trick. As they were seated in the restaurant, he suddenly drew a .38-caliber revolver, removed four shells from the cylinder of the gun, and then pointed it at his chest. "I thought the gun was empty," the woman said, "but all of a sudden it went off and he fell on his back." Police listed his death as "an apparent suicide, possibly accidental."

Guns account for about half of the more than 20,000 suicides now recorded in this country every year.* Some authorities place the figure even higher. Louis I. Dublin, the eminent long-time statistician of the Metropolitan Life Insurance Company, estimates the number to be "about 25,000." Norman L. Farberow and Edwin S. Shneidman of the Suicide Prevention Center in Los Angeles feel that complete figures would show as many as 50,000 suicides a year. For reasons of delicacy, many of these embarrassing family skeletons are hushed up and passed off as accidents, or otherwise not reported as suicides at all.

Still they occur with sufficient frequency to make one wonder why firearms should be so freely available to people who may wish to put an end to their lives. On August 27, 1965, *The New York Times* reported in adjoining columns two gun suicides in Pennsylvania: one was that of seventy-one-year-old *Grit* publisher George Lamade; the other that of Edward F. Mack, the fifty-five-year-old president of one of the largest trucking companies in the East. Ten days later, newspapers reported the death in Chicago of Clifford Stanton Heinz 3d, scion of the food-packing company, also of self-inflicted bullet wounds.†

Commenting on suicides and guns, Dr. Renatus Hartogs, chief psychiatrist of the New York City Youth House (who examined Lee Harvey Oswald in 1953), has this to say:

Unfortunately, it is possible for an individual to go into a store and buy a gun without indicating and revealing the intentions for which he buys the gun, and also without giving any indication as to the emotional state in which this person is. The individual who wishes to terminate his life finds it very easy to pull the trigger and put an end to his sufferings, and the mere presence of a gun makes it so much easier for him to actually accomplish and go through in this wish.

* In 1963, 9,595 of the 20,588 suicides, according to the U.S. Office of Vital Statistics.

† Most firearms suicides are likely to be "affluent people rather than those of lower income," according to Edward Ellis, co-author of *Traitor Within: Our Suicide Problem.*

On April 7, 1965, in Bethesda, Maryland, Mrs. Doris Crowley, a mother of two, shot herself to death with a .38 revolver she had purchased only three hours before. Immediately below the account of the suicide in the *Washington Post*, a Maryland state senator, Frederick C. Malkus, Jr., was reported as defending the recent rejection of a bill in the 1965 General Assembly to regulate pistols. "I didn't think the bill would do any good," said Malkus. "All gun bills do is to keep good people from being able to buy a gun."

In Washington, D.C., later that year, Dr. Nan P. Van Wagenen, a mother of three, separated from her husband, died as a result of a bullet wound in the mouth. When found, the woman physician was moaning, "Help me! Help me!" On the ground beside her was a .22-caliber rifle she had bought in a local store two days before.

Immediately above the Washington *Evening Star's* account of the Van Wagenen suicide was another story, involving a Marine captain and father of four. He was found dead, apparently of a self-inflicted gunshot wound, in a Pentagon parking lot. Just eleven days earlier the New York *Herald Tribune* (October 18, 1964) reported the gun suicide of an Army major, also the father of four children. The dead officer was found at Miller Field, Staten Island, with a .38-caliber pistol in his hand.

The two military suicides seem to bear out Dublin's statement: "The suicide rate of Army personnel has been higher than that of civilian males of comparable ages, except under age twenty-five." Firearms were also employed in 62 per cent of the soldier suicides studied for the years 1910–1958. This is not surprising, in view of the greater availability of guns to soldiers than to the civilian populace. Guns are even more freely available to commissioned officers (who, in fact, are issued handguns as standard equipment). It is therefore also not surprising to learn that U.S. Army officers not only kill themselves with greater frequency than enlisted men, but also use firearms in a greater percentage (72 per cent) of the self-inflicted deaths.

Why do people kill themselves? Some do so for reasons that would seem superficial and trivial to a normal person. One boy in Spokane, Washington, wrote a note saying, "Goodbye, Cindy, you are my love," and shot himself in the head by pushing the trigger of his father's hunting rifle with his toe. Cindy was the boy's horse that had been recently sold.

However, though many who kill themselves are extreme neurotics, schizophrenics, psychotics and others suffering from some degree of mental illness, it is a myth that all suicidal persons are necessarily mentally ill. Dr. Herbert Hendin of Columbia University's psychoanalytic clinic says that the main causes of suicide are disappointments in performance, especially among students and creative people, plus today's fierce competition in all walks of life—and above all a terrible sense of loneliness.

Thus a man may kill himself because of the fear of facing a sudden, frightening advancement in job responsibility, or a student because of his inability to cope with his courses. This is not necessarily because these persons are not bright. In fact, quite the contrary. "I take it that no man is educated who has never dallied with the thought of suicide," wrote the philosopher and founder of modern psychology, William James.* In questioning 50 normal high-school children, Dr. Reginald S. Lourie, clinical professor of psychiatry and pediatrics at the George Washington University School of Medicine, found that 54 per cent confessed that they had thought of committing suicide.

A surprisingly large number ultimately carry out their impulses for various reasons. "The suicide of adolescents," says Dr. Lourie, "takes more lives than TB, appendicitis, rheumatic fever, streptococcal infections, diabetes, and all the contagious fevers." In many instances, the suicide weapon is a gun.

In Queens, New York, a boy, apparently upset over poor marks in school, shot himself to death in a bedroom of his home. A high-school student in Springfield, New Jersey, shot himself because he had not been able to make the friendships that he had made in Texas, where he used to live. Another New Jersey pupil killed himself because he was reprimanded for drawing pictures in his class instead of reading. Among creative people, a celebrated gun suicide of recent years was Ernest Hemingway, so obsessed in his writings with guns, danger and death.

Clinical evidence indicates that many otherwise unexplainable suicides are often the result of an overwhelming rush of hostility against someone else, and are acts of punishment or revenge. "By killing himself," an article in *Today's Health* points out, "the individual may seek to arouse sympathy, remorse and bitter feelings of

* Quoted in *The Unseen Killer*, by Donald McCormick, p. 9.

guilt in the other person. Hostility against the parents, or against one of the parents, often plays an especially important role in the suicides of young people. The poor mark at school or the embarrassment at a party may be merely a trigger that sets off this hostility."

How important is the availability of a method or a weapon, particularly a firearm, a factor in suicide?

Though many countries have higher *over-all* suicide rates than the United States, our firearms suicide death rate is the highest in the world. In total number, more Americans end their lives with guns than all the people in all the other countries of the world combined! *

Certainly, there can be no question that a person absolutely bent on self-destruction will somehow manage some means of carrying it out. On the other hand, there are also people who are finicky about the method used (this often having a specific symbolic meaning), and an individual, if unable to use this method, will rarely resort to another. Shooting, for example, is the preferred method of men; guns are generally also more accessible to them. Even allowing for the possibly special nature of the military mystique, the higher suicide rate among soldiers than among civilians can probably be attributed to the fact that guns are more readily available to the military.

In the case of suicide, there is some encouragement in the belief of many authorities that it is preventable to a large extent. Although no precise figures are available, most authorities estimate there are at least five attempts at suicide for every one successfully carried out; this would make for a minimum of 100,000 attempted suicides in this country every year. According to other estimates, there are now nearly 2 million people in the United States who have attempted suicide at least once.

Reporting on a New Jersey study of juvenile suicide, Dr. Stanley F. Yolles, director of the National Institute of Mental Health, says: "The critical difference between the attemptor who failed and the one who 'succeeded' was the presence—in the case of the child who lived—of someone to whom he felt close."

Two recent studies reported at about the same time seem to bear this out. Eight out of ten persons who try to kill themselves and fail are glad to be alive and probably will not try it again, a Philadelphia

* See Appendix IV.

neuro-psychiatrist, Dr. Morton Herskowitz, told a meeting of the American College of Neuro-Psychiatrists, according to the Philadelphia *Inquirer* of September 28, 1965. Coincidentally, the *New York Post* of September 28, 1965, reported Chicago's Mental Health Director, Dr. Thaddeus L. Kostrubala, a psychiatrist, as telling an interviewer that an unrecognized tragedy of suicides stems from the hope of eight victims in ten that someone will prevent them from killing themselves. "Eighty per cent of the persons who kill themselves don't want to die at all," said Kostrubala, as the result of a study of the circumstances surrounding 3,064 Chicago suicides. "They want somebody to stop them."

Recalling the woman physician's words, "Help me! Help me!," it is meanwhile somewhat chilling to read what Shneidman and Farberow say: "Once every minute, or even more often, someone in the United States either kills himself or tries to kill himself with conscious intent. Sixty or seventy times every day these attempts succeed."

In a recent year, 1963, there were 5,126 recorded homicides, 2,263 accidents and 9,595 suicides—or a total of 16,984 deaths, in which guns played a part. Roughly 1 out of every 100 deaths in the United States from all causes, natural or otherwise, was the result of either a firearms homicide, accident or suicide. If past figures hold to form and the toll continues its steady climb, this year another 17,000 lives will be blighted by bullets, striking 1 out of every 3,200 homes across the land.

These cold statistics do not even begin to tell the whole story. For an estimated 100,000 or so Americans are also now wounded or maimed by guns every year, by accident, or assault or through an attempted homicide or suicide.

The point can be made even more strongly if one knows what it means to be hit by a bullet. The odds are 5 or 6 to 1 that you'll live. If you're hit in the arm or leg, you would probably suffer some broken bones or, at worst, lose a limb, something that may happen if you're not treated quickly enough and gangrene sets in.

Even if you're shot in the spine, there's a good chance that you may live, too, although you may become paralyzed and never be able to walk again. If you're going to die anyway, probably the best place to get a bullet is in the brain; that way death is virtually inevitable and almost instantaneous. This is not to say that gun wounds elsewhere in the head are not almost as serious, too. But they give you a better chance of remaining alive, with perhaps only the loss of an eye or with such resultant complications as motor-aphasia, epilepsy or paralysis.

With a direct heart wound, however, you rarely if ever have a chance. About the worst and most painful place to get hit is in the chest or stomach. If a bullet punctures your chest, and the wound is not plugged up right away, air will probably suck in and out of the hole and gradually squeeze the life out of you as your lungs collapse. But if the bullet has also punctured one of your big arteries so that the blood spreads out, chances are that you'll bleed to death first. Getting shot in the stomach is particularly unpleasant: the intestines often work their way through the wound.

How badly you're hurt depends, of course, on from how far away you've been hit, and with what. The .22-caliber bullet is a favorite in the United States. A study of 83 cases of gunshot wounds treated at the Marion County General Hospital in Indianapolis showed a .22-caliber weapon to have been used in 19 cases, a .32-caliber in 13 cases, a .38-caliber in 21, a shotgun in 12, and an unspecified type in 18. Although a .22-caliber is sometimes thought of as a fairly inno-cent and innocuous weapon, at close range it can be as deadly as a .38-caliber weapon.

Shotgun wounds may be relatively minor at long range, for one thing, because the velocity of this type of gun falls off much more rapidly than does that of a pistol or rifle. At close range, however, the numerous pellets discharged by a shotgun blast can be even more deadly than bullets. In *Northwest Medicine* (September 1954), Dr. Millington O. Young of Bend, Oregon, reported a higher percentage—up to 80 per cent—of close-range abdominal shotgun wounds to be fatal (often almost instantly, "because of the terrible damage produced") than abdominal bullet wounds.

"Persons sustaining close-range shotgun wounds of the abdomen usually die within a few moments," wrote Dr. Young. "If they sur-vive long enough to receive medical attention, they do so by vir-tue of the fact that the larger vessels sustained little or no injury." Another study by Doctors James C. Drye and George Schuster of the University of Louisville School of Medicine in the *American Journal of Surgery* (March 1953) also reported shotgun wounds of the head to be "almost always serious," and short-range direct hits there "always fatal."

These are only some of the physical aspects of what it means to get shot. Few words can describe the wounds you cannot see, the grief, the suffering, the shame and sadness, the aching memories of those remaining in homes blighted by bullets.

Think for a moment of Tom Cox, the Virginia school principal who has made the fight for firearms controls his own lonely crusade. He travels widely urging legislators to pass laws making it impossible for those known to be emotionally disturbed to be able to buy or keep guns. Recalling the day his mentally ill wife killed herself and their four children, the grief-stricken Cox says to all who will listen:

I wonder how many of you have gone home and walked in the front door to find your child shot to death. You go in the kitchen and find another child dead. You go in a bedroom and find another child dead. You go in another bedroom and find another child dead. You go down to the recreation room and find your wife shot to death. I wonder how many of you have prayed to God all night for your last child to die, after the doctor tells you that if he lives, he will be crippled for life.

What are the chances of you yourself or a member of your family being murdered and, if so, by a gun?

Apparently in your favor is the downward trend in this country's over-all homicide rate over the decades (from 11.3 per 100,000 in 1925 to 4.5 in 1963), but don't be misled by these statistics. "The obvious decrease of the homicide rate in the United States should serve to put us on guard against ready generalization based on statistics which we do not fully comprehend," say sociologists Herbert A. Bloch and Gilbert Geis.* There are many factors, they point out, that have to be considered in interpreting these statistics. "Taking everything together, it appears quite likely that the drop in homicide represents nothing more than a tribute to modern medical and surgical advances. Many persons who formerly might have died from crimes of violence are now saved on operating tables, and their assailants are charged with assault with intent to kill rather than with murder or manslaughter."

Your vulnerability to violence also depends on where you live.

* *Man, Crime and Society: The Forms of Criminal Behavior*, p. 260.

Known murder rates are traditionally higher in the South than in any other region of the United States. The Southern states (including Texas), though constituting only 31 per cent of the U.S. population, are the scene of 45 per cent of all this country's murders—and 52 per cent of those involving the use of a gun. By contrast, the Northeast region (including New York City), with 25 per cent of the U.S. population, contributes only 17 per cent of the nation's murders—and only 11 per cent of those by gun.

You are safest, of course, if there is no gun in your home. But consider the case of a young Queens Village, New York, couple, Michael and Patricia Burke. In February 1964, married only ten days and just returned from their honeymoon, they were lingering over their very first meal in the new apartment. Suddenly, they heard the roar of a shotgun and saw a stream of pellets streaming through their living-room floor. Burke, a handsome graduate student, ran downstairs to see what was going on in the apartment below. As he reached the second-floor landing, stepping out of the apartment was neighbor Arthur Arendes, armed with a 12-gauge shotgun. Firing it once more, Arendes killed Burke instantly. "I shot a Martian," Arendes, a former mental patient, first told police. As for the earlier blast into the apartment above, he said: "I heard heads rolling around on the floor." Later, as he was booked for homicide, he added: "God told me to do it."

Death can also come through the door or window. Fourteen rifle shots fired into the home of Sylvester and Angelina Cerpe in Brooklyn, also in 1964, killed their two-and-a-half-year-old daughter, Rose Marie, who died in her mother's arms. The accused killer, John Chiarello, a former friend of the Cerpes, had a psychiatric record, a grudge—and a gun. Later that year, Charles W. Fitzmaurice, a Marine colonel and father of four, answered a knock on the door of his home in the quiet residential area of Springfield in Fairfax County, Virginia. As he opened the door he was shot in the abdomen with a shotgun and died almost instantaneously. No one knows who killed him—or why—to this very day.

If you're not safe in your own home, where can you be really safe from a gun? People have been shot at and killed everywhere—in schools, parks and playgrounds, in offices, hospitals and restaurants. Recently, two women were shot in the ladies' room of a New York nightclub. In Los Angeles, a divorcee shot a priest to death in a conference room of the Catholic archdiocese; in Detroit, a youth critically wounded a rabbi during services at a synagogue.

People can go berserk anywhere and at any time, and it matters little to them whom they kill. Who can ever forget the story of that mad, methodical walk a soft-spoken Bible-reading war veteran named Howard Unruh took through Camden, New Jersey, back in 1949—with a gun? During his legendary twenty-minute shooting rampage, Unruh calmly took a pot shot into an apartment window and a two-year-old boy fell back with a bullet in his head. Unruh then killed a six-year-old sitting in a painted carousel-type horse chair at the local barber's. Of his thirteen victims, three—two women and a nine-year-old boy—had the misfortune to stop for a traffic light while driving through town during those fatal twenty minutes. They were total strangers to Unruh. Yet he walked up to their car and fired through the windshield, killing them all.

Not even on our skyways are you ever safe. In September 1965, Tommy Robinson, a sixteen-year-old Texan who said that he wanted to free Cuban political refugees, tried to hijack a jetliner with 91 persons aboard. Armed with two guns, he fired a barrage of shots inside the plane before he was overcome. The year before, the shooting of the pilot and copilot of an airliner by a suicide-bent passenger meant death for all 44 persons aboard.

We also have snipers who fire away just for kicks, if for any reason at all. Not long ago, in Montgomery County, Maryland, three joy-riding seventeen-year olds crossed the county, shooting out the windows of 93 cars with BB guns. In Chicago, one New Year's Eve, 148 incidents were reported of people firing guns out of windows. Perched on a hilltop near Honolulu on July 4, 1965, Michael Patrick Moeller, armed with a .30-30 rifle, shot at a bus full of tourists, wounding three and killing a policeman. Five months earlier he had been committed to a mental hospital after being indicted in a similar sniping incident. In Long Island, two teenagers, bored with shooting at birds, also turned to vehicles on an expressway, bagging a bus, among five other vehicles. One boy, a fifteen-year-old was using a rifle a doting mother had gotten for him with trading stamps.*

---

* Overheard discussing the incident the next day were two Long Island Railroad commuters. "Well, now," said one, "these anti-gun nuts will be after us again." "Yeah," said the other, "and the kids weren't really doing anything. After all, they were only shooting at the backs of the cars."

Other citizens at arms prefer to practice their marksmanship on human targets simply because of the "urge to kill." In Redwood City, California, Rosemarie Diane Bjorkland, a blonde typist, was jailed for the murder of August Norry, a golf course gardener. "I had a terrible urge to kill someone ever since I started target shooting as a hobby," the sheriff quoted her as saying. "I wanted a human target. I used to go up there [to the golf course] and point my pistol at a target pretending it was a human being. Mr. Norry on that day was my target.

"Suddenly I had the overpowering urge to shoot him. I kept shooting, emptying my gun and reloading."

And then there is the recent story of the two San Pedro, California, boys who put a bullet in the groin and another in the spine of a man whom they had never seen before.

"One of the boys was fifteen, the other fourteen," began the account of the incident in the Los Angeles *Times*. "They crouched on a grassy slope in Peck Park, a peaceful expanse of shrubs and greenery. Below them and perhaps 50 yards away, a heavy figure shuffled toward a water fountain. It was 6:30 P.M. and dark but the lights beyond silhouetted the man against the early night sky.

"Neither boy had ever fired a gun. But one lay between them now—a .22-caliber pump-action Winchester repeating rifle. And it was loaded. Minutes earlier, just before they had walked down a slope into the park, the older boy had challenged the younger:

"'I wonder what it would be like to shoot a human being...'"

5 The Firearms Mystique

Murderous in their mien, the two men in high-heeled boots sidled and slunk toward one another, moving like bent-kneed partners in a slow-motion version of the Twist. Beneath their broad-brimmed hats, their eyes burned piercedly. They walked with shoulders hunched back, hips thrust forward, right hands itching and twitching near the cold bone grips of holstered .45 revolvers. Suddenly, with the men a scant thirty paces apart, the two pistols blammety-blammed orange-red flames, and from one of them a perfect circle of gun smoke floated upward . . .

A description from a Western novel of a gun duel taking place in the old Dodge City days? A scene from a cinema or TV Western? No, the words are from a *Sports Illustrated* report of a new and nervous sport—fast-draw shooting. The two grown men playing cowboy and snapping their six-shooters are participants in a fast-draw championship competition.

Fast draw represents only one of the many ways in which Americans use firearms *pour le sport*. Indeed, even though the American frontier has been a thing of the past for three-quarters of a century, and today's Americans no longer have to forage for their own meat on the hoof, or be prepared to defend their own homes against hostile Indians, the use of guns is booming as never before. The *Wall Street Journal* reported in 1964, "This year, in the golden age of golf, three times as many Americans will go shooting as will tramp the fairways. In all, some 20 million Americans, including an estimated 1 million women, will try their hand at shooting this year . . ."

Actually, the *Wall Street Journal* estimate is probably on the conservative side, although the following claim by an industry spokesman in the book *The World of Guns* is probably too exuberant:

Did you think that baseball, football, basketball, golf, bowling were our national pastimes? Then you, like most Americans, will be surprised to learn that guns provide recreation for more Americans than any of these sports—almost as many, in fact, as all of them put together. Guns are merely and incontrovertibly the biggest thing in the United States' recreational picture.

Boating, fishing and photography may have more followers than shooting, but shooting ranks only behind boating and photography in recreational dollar volume. Sales of firearms, ammunition and shooting accessories in 1964 were estimated at nearly $283 million by National Sporting Goods Association economist Richard E. Snyder. And few recreational activities have made such an impact on the American way of life—emotionally, economically and otherwise. "The "side" expenses of the sport alone now produce more than $1,000,000,000 of business annually for the makers of everything from automobiles to wearing apparel.

What purpose do guns ostensibly serve? Who, besides the comparatively few at opposite poles of the law, police and criminals, own and use these undeniably dangerous pieces of apparatus? And why?

The great majority of guns are owned by what the National Rifle Association likes to characterize as "honest, law-abiding citizens." A distressing number of them, however, manage to pop up on the wrong side of the law. But until they used guns to propel themselves to national prominence, people like Lee Harvey Oswald, Howard Unruh, or Medgar Evers' killer presumably broke no laws. Some misguided citizens justify the need for a gun for possible protection against their fellow man. Nine of every ten American farmers keep guns supposedly to protect poultry, cattle and crops against crows, woodchucks, rabbits, squirrels and other so-called troublesome species. But most guns are fired not so much for protection against man or beast, but rather in fun.

Most guns are in the hands of hunters, a formidable array of nimrods estimated at roughly 25 million. Certainly the number is at least 19,058,809, this representing the persons who bought hunting licenses, tags, permits and stamps in 1964.* In addition there are legions of the unlicensed, now estimated at anywhere from 2 to 6

* At a cost of $72,071,094.

million, although no exact count is possible. These include those who shoot sub rosa without bothering to buy a license, and the many who do not need a license because of who they are and where or what they hunt.

Exemptions are given in many states to landowners who hunt on their own property, youngsters and (in some states) oldsters, veterans and other special groups. Farmers can also shoot freely at certain animals and birds for which no licenses are required, such as woodchucks, chipmunks, rabbits, rats, coyotes, crows, prairie dogs, squirrels and other so-called vermin, or pests.

There are hundreds of thousands who find hunting more convenient and less chancey in pay-and-shoot preserves, which now number more than 2,000, although they were virtually nonexistent in this country two decades ago. Most are stocked with pheasants and other game birds which you are virtually guaranteed to get off some good shots at, if not bag.

No exact figures are available as to how many people are hit and killed while hunting, because not all hunting accidents are reported. The National Safety Council estimates the number of such fatalities at from 600 to 800 per year. Some years ago, the National Rifle Association came up with an estimate of 300, based on reports from about half our states. In recent years, however, the NRA has found it distasteful to make public its tally of the death toll, although its annual Uniform Hunter Casualty Report gives some proportionate, if not total, figures. From it we learn that around 65 per cent of hunting accidents are the result of one hunter's hitting another—the remaining injuries are self-inflicted; that between 15 per cent and 20 per cent of the accidents are fatal; that the greater part of the casualties are accounted for by shotguns; and that virtually all of the careless and inept shooters are male, with close to half in their teens.

Hunting, in terms of mortality, is by far the most macabre of all shooting sports and, when one includes the mishaps with hunting weapons at home and elsewhere, more hazardous than any other individual sport except swimming. In the case of drowning, however, you usually only have yourself to blame; when hunting you can be killed by anyone.

In one six-week hunting season in Maine, for example, the dead numbered 41,730 deer and 15 humans plus 53 more wounded. In other localities, a teenage daughter fatally shot her mother in the

back, and a teenage boy killed his brother. One man cutting under-
brush was wounded *three* times and finally expired after being hit by
two hunters. One lad answering a call of nature behind a bush was
dispatched by his father; he mistook his offspring for a rabbit.

In another case, a hunter left himself stranded in the woods when
the "deer" he downed turned out to be his saddle horse; and in still
another case, a hunter, though not depriving himself of his transportation, did some damage to it: Seeing what he thought to be a deer
looming above the laurel, he tore the top off his tan convertible.
More than one hunter has mistaken mules for moose. One Utah
hunter with a doe permit went so far as to "dress" (disembowel and
clean) his "deer" and head home with it, even though the beast—a
mule—literally died with its boots on, sporting a set of iron shoes.

Target shooters, as a group, luckily suffer few, if any, mishaps
when they fire on supervised ranges. But when they stage impromptu
shootings elsewhere, they, too, bag a stranger now and then. Three
Long Island men, firing away in a backyard, wounded a man and
hit two homes two-thirds of a mile away.

Unlike hunting, which is probably the oldest of outdoor sports,
target shooting with firearms is relatively new.* And with the growing urbanization putting a continual crimp in the wide open spaces,
target shooting has also grown into a great national sport. It has
brought a boom in business for the gun and ammunition makers,
who have gone all out in recent years to promote "inanimate shooting." It is not hard to understand why. Although many a hunter can
go a whole season without getting off more than a dozen shots, if
any at all, a target shooter can blow five dollars' worth of ammunition in an afternoon. Accordingly, the Winchester-Western Division
of Olin Mathieson in early 1964 launched the country's first nationwide shooting range franchise program, and within a year had forty-
five such franchised outdoor shooting clubs from coast to coast.

---

* Target shooting as a community sport in this country has its origin in the turkey
and beef shoots of our early settlement days. In the turkey shoot, a live turkey
was tied to a stake or put in a crate with only its head showing, and fired at
from a distance of, say, 300 feet. The first man to draw blood or succeed in
knocking off the turkey's head took the turkey. In giving our forefathers the
opportunity to combine fun and food-gathering in a single activity, the sport,
a colonial historian points out, was held "innocent in the eyes of the strictest
moralist."

Winchester outdoor ranges are lit up after dark for the night shooter. Remington, in recognition of the increase in night trap and skeet shooting, has just developed new types of tattletale shotgun pellets which, like the wartime tracer bullets, are coated to make their trajectory visible by day or night. By 1970, Winchester expects to have some 400 franchised ranges in operation and to take in from $30,000,000 to $50,000,000 annually in ammunition and target sales and rental fees.

A new attraction for marksmen who want more realistic targets is available through a budding franchise system featuring a life-size plastic "running" deer. (Actually it moves, rocking back and forth and swaying from side to side on a circular stretch of track.) According to the entrepreneurs of this unique franchise, other targets are on the way, such as a facsimile tiger, bear, lion, antelope, lynx, rabbit, woodchuck and, presumably for the training and titillation of law enforcement officers, a two-legged thug.

For those who want to be home on the range, articles in the gun magazines and manufacturers' informational material give instructions on setting up shooting facilities in the garage, backyard, basement, even the living room. One of the safety precautions urged in a pamphlet of the Detroit Bullet Trap Company of Arlington Heights, Illinois, is: "Keep any door along the side or in the target area *locked* while firing." For handy shooting, one Maryland millionaire has a 300-yard combat firing range set up on his estate.

Following in the footsteps of Annie Oakley, more and more women are becoming at home on the range. An Associated Press dispatch some years ago revealed the startling fact that nuns attending a summer session at Villanova (Pennsylvania) University had organized a rifle team, and a survey of the sporting goods field indicates that the percentage of women shooters has doubled in a period of three or four years.

One can only guess at the number of Americans who practice some form of target shooting, but the figure could easily be as much as 4 or 5 million. The more than 1 million individuals and club members of the National Rifle Association alone are for the most part target shooters of varying degrees of enthusiasm. More than 100,000 compete annually in NRA-sponsored rifle and pistol competitions. As one would expect, these comprise only the better shooters, and so provide but a fraction of the total picture.

Lowest in status, though probably the most numerous, are the so-called "plinkers"—kids from six to sixty who enjoy shooting informally at tin cans, balloons, bottles and other such improvised targets.* Virtually any gun can be used for plinking, although some are especially made for the sport. A new Daisy "fun gun," a semi-automatic handgun shooting BBs at 400 feet per second, is advertised as a "penny-pinching plinker with a punch!"

The largest organized target-shooting group in the United States is made up of the rifle and pistol targeteers who train their sights on the bull's-eye of a paper target. Most are individual NRA members, or are affiliated with one of the more than 12,000 NRA clubs. About 7,000 men and women vie for trophies each summer at Camp Perry, Ohio, in the sport's biggest competitive shoot, the National Rifle and Pistol Matches. These competitions are regarded as the World Series of the shooting world.

Growing fast in popularity is the number of gunners, running well into the hundreds of thousands, who prefer the pleasure of downing a clay pigeon in the related shotgun sports of trap and skeet. Says one participant in explaining the joy of trap: "There's a tremendous satisfaction out of taking a flying object out of the air with a gun and seeing it break. There's a tremendous amount of coordination involved between eye and body and mind to catch a flying object in an instant of a second and take it down from the sky."

Both trap and skeet evolved from the once-flourishing sport of shooting live pigeons, a sport now outlawed in most states. Both use a "trap," the device used to propel the clay targets or "birds." The term trap derives from the device originally used to liberate the birds as targets for the shooter. Many of today's traps, however, are fairly elaborate devices, often automatic and operated by push buttons. The modern clay "pigeon" is a disk-shaped target, about 4 inches in diameter and 1 inch deep. It is not actually made of clay, but rather of mineral pitch and sand.

Trap shooting, though dating back to eighteenth-century Eng-

* An article in the November 1964 issue of *Guns & Ammo* suggested Necco candy wafers as dandy targets ("If you have a yen to see things go up in smoke when hit . . . and best of all, the pieces vanish with the rain") for this probably most carefree of shooting sports. "A box of common soda straws," also suggested the article, "offers many hours of challenging plinking. They can be set up in rows and cut one by one."

land, now enjoys its greatest popularity in the United States, where the sport has a national group, the Amateur Trapshooting Association, headquartered in Vandalia, Ohio. There are more than 500 local clubs, and in excess of 25,000 members, double that in 1955. The average trapshooter, the ATA also reports, shoots at about 1,000 targets per year, and more than 2,000 ATA members compete each year on the world's largest trap-shooting layout at Vandalia. In competitive trap shooting, shooters fire five shots from each of five positions (twenty-five shots in all) in a crescent-shaped formation, 16 or more yards behind the trap, which throws out the targets at various angles unknown to the shooter. The targets usually sail about 50 yards and the average hit is usually on the rise about 35 yards from the shooter. A perfect score, or twenty-five consecutive hits, is called a "straight."

Skeet is a relatively recent American invention, though its name —selected from among 10,000 entries in a $100 prize contest—comes from an ancient Scandinavian word for "shoot." Devised in 1920 by a group of Andover, Massachusetts, upland game hunters interested in getting in some between-seasons wing shooting practice, the sport was also aimed at giving competing clay-bird buffs a varied but equal series of shots. Originally, the shooters were stationed and moved to different positions around a circle, but when a nearby chicken farmer complained about the shots coming at him from all directions, the circle was sliced in half. As the sport finally has evolved, the shooter fires in succession from eight different stations or positions located around the half-circle. From each station he fires at targets thrown from either a "high" trap house or a "low" house at opposite ends of the half-circle, or, in certain positions, thrown from both houses at once. Since the targets are always thrown in the same pattern of flight, the only thing that varies is the different angle of the shot from each position.

Although opinions differ as to whether skeet is harder than trap and which sport is the better preparation for field shooting, the younger sport has also been attracting increasing numbers of participants. The National Skeet Shooting Association, headquartered in Dallas, puts out a monthly magazine, the *Skeet Shooting Review,* and sanctioned over 1,400 registered shoots during 1964. The NSSA claims membership has doubled to 12,000 in the past six years and says it now has 450 affiliated clubs. Like the Amateur Trapshooting

Association, the NSSA says that many more clubs exist which do not hold registered competitive shoots. The NSSA estimates there are 1,500 to 2,000 small skeet clubs in the United States, with anywhere from 100,000 to 200,000 members who shoot on an informal basis. Trap shooting, no doubt, also probably attracts hundreds of thousands of participants.

There is now also a big boom in old firearms. An estimated 750,000, and perhaps as many as a million Americans, collect guns just as others compulsively collect old salt and pepper shakers, beer coasters, shaving mugs, autographs, stamps and coins. However, only some 15,000 gun collectors are said to be really serious. Their organizations range in size from the Ohio Gun Collector's Association, with nearly 3,100 members, down to the 12-man Maple Tree Club in Norwich, Vermont.

The avid collector will spend a fortune on his hobby * and, unless he knows what he's doing, can easily get stuck with a bogus bargain. "If all the guns supposed to have been owned by Jesse James were genuine, he had an arsenal bigger than the entire U.S. Cavalry," John P. Amber of Chicago, editor of *Gun Digest,* has said. Although some Civil War Army revolvers can be had for as little as $75, a really top pair of Colts in premium condition may run as high as $7,500. A price of $15,000 is not uncommon for a pair of fine seventeenth or eighteenth-century Brescian pistols, which makes some firearms literally worth their weight in gold. Prices have skyrocketed in recent years. A good so-called "Kentucky" flintlock rifle (actually made in Pennsylvania) which sold for around $75 in the 1930s would fetch upward of $375 today.

Most collectors, though they may hunt or do target shooting, wouldn't for the world think of firing any of their choice specimens; they just like to have them around to look at. Collections of several hundred firearms are not uncommon, and I have heard of some running into the thousands. To the dedicated armophile, there is nothing that quite compares with the thrill of looking at one's own collec-

---

* A Denver gun collector paid Oswald's widow $10,000 for the Carcano that killed President Kennedy. However, the Federal government beat him to the gun: Congress passed legislation authorizing the government to take possession of it. In February 1966, a Federal judge also ruled that the government could confiscate the weapon because Oswald, in purchasing it under a fictitious name, had violated the Federal Firearms Act.

tion, or holding and fondling a fine piece of weaponry, and running one's fingers over its curved butt.

The enthusiasm for guns reaches its highest extremes in California, where cannon shooting is a booming new sport. A recent issue of *Guns & Ammo* carried a picture of a man crouched behind a piece of field artillery to illustrate an article entitled, "If Your Shooting's Gone Stale—Try a Cannon!" The article described the activities of an organization known as BALLS, an acronym which, the author hastened to add, stands for Benevolent Artillery Loaders and Loafers Society, headquartered at the Gun Room in El Cerrito. BALLS-men tow their king-sized "sporting rifles," as the article termed them, behind the family car or haul them on a truck. They like to make it clear that they are not a paramilitary organization bent on defending the California coast against the Sino and Soviet hordes. However, when a BALLS truck carrying two cannons and towing another passed through Pacifica, a peaceful hamlet south of San Francisco, not long ago, the residents, mistaking the BALLSmen for Minutemen on maneuvers, ordered them to detour. The BALLSmen moved on and soon found a good range on a dairy farm, although just what they shot at is not clear.

The *Guns & Ammo* article concluded that cannon shooting might not be everyone's idea of fun. The author commented: "I'm afraid cannon shooting won't catch on like wildfire. It is fun, though, and if you haven't tried it, don't knock it, huh?" One Arizona dentist says he uses his cannon (a 20-mm. antitank gun) to shoot rabbits. "I don't hit many," he concedes, "but when I do—oh, man!"

Ranking with the cannoneers among the odd-balls of the shooting fraternity are the so-called muzzle-loader fans. These are the firearms counterparts of antique car fanciers, and are dedicated to collecting or making and shooting what one magazine has called "as rag-tag a collection of firearms as could be found this side of the Smithsonian Institution."

Muzzle-loading guns include old-style rifles, muskets, shotguns, and pistols (or replicas thereof) of Civil War vintage and earlier. They are of either the flintlock or percussion type. Some shooters who are loath to fire a particularly valuable antique buy a new replica just for shooting. The cost of a new Kentucky-style flintlock or percussion rifle runs to about $100. Those made by Elmer Herman, a renowned rifle maker of Pasadena, California, are about double or triple in price. Some buffs even make their own muzzle-loaders.

The guns are called muzzle-loaders because, like cannon, they load from the front, or muzzle, this entailing a troublesome and time-consuming procedure, and no little dedication and devotion on the part of the users. After a series of shots, a muzzle-loader is black with powder and half deaf. Yet in spite of all the trouble, muzzle-loading, though still practiced by only an esoteric few, has been attracting more and more devotees in recent years. The National Muzzle Loading Rifle Association, started in 1933 to perpetuate the use and memories of "the old muzzle-loading rifles of our nation's forebears," now maintains headquarters at Shelbyville, Indiana. Its monthly magazine, *Muzzle Blasts*, goes to the organization's 7,800 members in about 150 affiliated clubs.

Three major shoots are conducted by the NMLRA each year, the principal one at its range near Friendship, Indiana. Affiliated clubs in all fifty states also have their own annual shoots. An important one is held each fall at Fort Ticonderoga, New York, which attracts one hundred or so true believers who spend a smoky weekend happily blazing away while wearing such masculine millinery as skunk pelts, sombreros and bands of feathers. "They're all crazy," a Ticonderogan told *Time*, "but they have a lot of fun." Things are much more formal at Friendship, where one can see shooters in fringed frontier buckskins and in Civil War regalia.

The recently-ended Civil War centennial no doubt contributed to the rebirth of interest in muzzle-loaders, originals as well as replicas. The North-South Skirmish Association, another national muzzle-loading, rifle-shooting group, started in 1950 with eight "Confederates" and five "Yankees," now numbers over 2,000 members. Every spring and fall, some of these Civil War buffs crisscross the continent to appear at hallowed battle sites. There, attired in tailor-made, snappy but authentic blues or grays and firing their equally authentic muzzle-loaders, they refight the old battles, simulating the skirmishes of a century before.

"We're not just a bunch of clowns who lark around," said one Skirmisher shortly before he rode off with his group on the same retreat route Lee's worn troops took to Appomattox.

Also reliving the days of yore is a relatively new type of gun nut —the already mentioned gunslinger, or fast-draw fanatic. In what has already assumed the proportions of a craze, if not a national menace, the devotees of the fast-growing, fast-draw fad try to see how quickly they can draw or pull a handgun from a holster and fire it. They shoot at their reflections in mirrors, at dummy "bad-men," at balloons, at each other, or other appropriate targets. In competition they go through their pre-draw rituals and then pull their weapons against clocks calibrated in hundredths of a second.

During the past decade, the fast-draw fad has attracted a formidable following—one big enough to support two magazines, *Gunsmoke Gazette* and the *Gunslinger's News*. On a TV show an instructor at a California fast-draw school was shown giving some chilling advice to a young pupil: "Try to hit the man about in the chest. . . . Are you ready? When I say draw . . . draw."

Various estimates show that anywhere from 200,000 to 1 million of our citizens are now devotees of the fast draw. The vast majority, according to a group studied at one competition, are high-school educated and, when not with a gun at the ready, work as butchers, milkmen, truck drivers, locksmiths and other such blue-collar jobs or trades. The fad has also attracted a sprinkling of corporation presidents, professional men and celebrities. Robert Six, president of Continental Airlines, once had himself and five of his executives privately tutored (the group called itself the Six-Shooters). Sammy Davis, Jr., whose passion for hobbies is limitless, once demonstrated his skill with a six-shooter on the Jack Paar TV show. However, modern gunslingers, despite their numbers, have sought in vain to win social status, even among other gun enthusiasts. Said *Popular Science* (a brother publication of *Outdoor Life*): "Many hunters and target shooters look down on the leather-slapping slicks in much the same way as sports-car enthusiasts did the early hot-rodders."

Apart from the occasional mavericks and lone rangers, most devotees are banded into fast-draw clubs. More than 2,000 were estimated back in 1961. The clubs bear such robust names as Thumb Busters, Side Winders, Widow Makers, Hang Town Gunslingers, and Gunfighters of Horse Thief Hollow. Many gunslingers customarily carry business cards indicating their club affiliations. Many clubs hold weekly "shoot-downs" or "shoot-outs," and the more skilled practitioners of the art convene in state and regional competitions which offer as much as $5,000 in prize money. The gala event of the year, held in Las Vegas, sees some 200 of America's fastest guns shoot it out for national honors to the click of cameras and roulette wheels and the cheers and groans of a gallery of as many as 12,000 spectators. A contest may take one of the following forms, according to *Sports Illustrated:* *

A walk and a draw, in which the gunmen, weapons loaded with blanks, approach each other à la *High Noon*, then draw when a signal light flashes (to determine who fired first, microphones on the floor record the sound of the guns); standing reflex, also started by signal light, but commonly using loads against balloons or cut-out targets; and self-start, or off-the-button, in which the shooter holds one finger of his gun hand on a timer until he is ready to draw.

No self-respecting gunslinger would think of reaching for a draw without being appropriately attired in a fancy Western outfit complete from sombrero to boots and breeches and, often, tin badge. Many also give close attention to facial expressions and grooming— one fast-drawing California dentist sported sideburns to the bemusement of his pained patients. With a fancy Western outfit costing as much as $200, and a "rig" (gun, holster and cartridge belt) perhaps also as much, grievances can understandably arise in fast-draw households. One gunman's wife was reported as complaining, "He gets a new rig and outfit each winter, and I wear last year's dresses." However, some women also follow the fad. Between her domestic chores, Carole Hall, California's "fastest female" (36 hundredths of a second for walk and draw) practices fast draw an hour a day and helps her husband put out the *Gunslinger's News*.

With anywhere from 20,000 to 100,000 rounds of ammunition burned up in a single contest, the ammunition makers are doing well from the fast-draw craze. Admittedly, a big beneficiary and prime instigator of the fast-draw boom is Colt's Patent Fire Arms Manufacturing Company of Hartford, Connecticut, originator of the famous "Peacemaker." Even in the old frontier days, Colt never sold more than 8,000 of its guns a year. By 1940, demand had diminished to the point where Peacemaker production had been stopped completely. In 1957, however, Colt, awakening to the possibilities of fast draw, sent salesmen scurrying all over the country to help organize fast-draw clubs.

* December 11, 1961 issue.

"We got going like hell," former Colt president Fred A. Roff, Jr., told *Sports Illustrated*. By 1961, Colt claimed responsibility for forming 500 to 600 clubs. "We provided rules for contests and how-to-do-it instruction booklets. Of course, we also provided (for $125, blued; $137. 50, nickeled) the famous old Colt Peacemaker." Within five years Colt production had quadrupled. Western-style six-guns were selling at the rate of 150,000 a year, much more than in the days of the Old West.

Oddly enough, though, in spite of the penchant for authenticity in accoutrements—everything from clothing to Colts—the fast-draw fad is as phony as a nine-gallon hat. "With few exceptions, most experts agree, the average Old West cowpoke couldn't hit the broad side of a barn in a quick draw," says *Popular Science*. "The best guns took time to get off one well-aimed shot while their opponents pumped two or three misses at them."

This generation of gunslingers may be somewhat less handy than those of yesteryear. Fast draw, though daffy, causes no noticeable damage as long as the Colts are confined to competition, and only blank cartridges or wax bullets are used. But some shooters use live ammunition, with the expected results. One Phoenix fanatic, while getting in some fast-draw practice during his lunch hour, shot himself in the leg. In California, a nineteen-year-old shot himself in the right thigh when his gun fired as he drew it from the holster. Under similar circumstances a thirty-one-year-old Californian shattered his leg bone. Such self-inflicted injuries are usually the result of the gunslinger being quicker on the trigger than he is on the draw. They are apparently now frequent enough to be recognized as a syndrome (according to Webster, "group of concurrent symptoms characterizing a disease") and to be the subject of learned papers in medical journals. This peculiarly American disease triggered by fast draws is variously known to doctors as the "Fast Draw Syndrome" or the "Dodge City Syndrome." It was first described in 1960 by a Dr. J. V. Brown in the *Western Journal of Surgery* in an article called "Gunshot Wounds of Lower Extremity; Fast Draw Syndrome."

The real tragedies, however, come when persons other than the shooter are involved. In Korea, a soldier killed another during a fast-draw contest. *The American Rifleman*, in an editorial decrying the use of live ammunition by gunslingers, cited the following cases involving civilians: In Colorado, a twenty-three-year-old who "forgot the gun was loaded" shot and killed his best friend in a playful fast-draw contest. In Alabama, a sixteen-year-old was shot and killed instantly by a brother "demonstrating his fast draw." In Pennsylvania, another sixteen-year-old shot and killed his twelve-year-old brother in a "cowboy quick-draw contest."

At least one case has been noted of a husband killing his spouse in a fast-draw contest, and there have been many of parents, engrossed in practice, killing their own children. On a Christmas Eve, in one of the most tragic incidents involving one who fancied himself as a fast man with a gun, a Chicagoan, Jack Bender, father of five children, accidentally shot and killed his fourteen-month-old son. Ironically, the son had been christened Wyatt Earp after the TV Western hero. That none of the other children was even hurt is miraculous, for as a preliminary to his practice of fast draws, Daddy had tanked up on three or four quarts of beer and then pumped about seventy-five bullets into the Bender home.

"That's what they do on television," Bender later told the police.

For the sake of sport or otherwise, people do the most incredible things with guns. When a mouse invaded the apartment of one John Reinhardt of Baltimore, he cut loose with both barrels of a shotgun, blowing out an apartment wall. (The mouse got away, and Reinhardt was fined $125 and advised by the judge to try a mousetrap next time). In Birmingham, Mrs. Louise Bishop was fined $25 for tacking a picture of her husband on the wall and firing some seventy times at it with a .22-caliber rifle.

Unfortunately, we also have our William Tells. In December 1965, Eugene Van Denburgh of Santa Monica, using a .22 rifle he had just purchased, shot and killed his five-year-old daughter while trying to shoot a tangerine off her head. Only a week before he had suffered two self-inflicted bullet wounds from another gun.

What accounts for the fatal fascination that firearms exert over so many Americans? Just as facsimiles of the phallus were favored features in the processions of ancient Greek Bacchic orgies, and are to-day objects of veneration in some Oriental houses of worship, the firearm is a comparable American object of unreasoning devotion. Indeed, it is a fetish in this part of the Western world.

The image of the gun, Samuel Grafton has written in *McCall's*, "seems almost as much a part of American décor today as the maidenhair fern was a generation ago. It is impossible to play with a TV dial for long without coming on the tableau of a man, or a woman, for that matter, holding a handgun straight out and forcing another man or woman to do his or her bidding. In our entertainment culture the gun does the job that not so long ago was performed by a judicious remark. Now you merely pull out your gun, and that settles the argument."

Apart from the ubiquitous use of guns here in entertainment and sports, crime and homicide, the firearms fetish takes many forms. A midtown Manhattan bank in New York (Meadow Brook National) offers for the titillation of passersby periodic window displays of ancient muskets. Across the street, a luggage shop features a derringer gun-shaped cigarette lighter at $6.95.* For the drinker there's a decanter in the guise of an old blunderbuss dueling pistol ("a delightful way to serve a 'shot'") which with a squeeze of the trigger also plays a lively tune; and for the adventurous automobilist a "turnpike toll gun" which fires quarters into the receptacles of those "Exact Change" booths. For the motorist who has everything, there is also the Swifty defroster gun, furnished with a fast-draw holster and designed to melt ice and snow on windshields.

For the children, stores offer all sorts of gun goodies, real and facsimile. A relatively new one is "Bop-A-Bear," described in *Insider's Newsletter* as "a 12-inch-high teddy bear which rolls along until struck by a pellet from a toy gun . . . then the bear screams in pain and runs frantically around." There are also facsimile human targets like "Hands Up Harry" ("shoot off his hat and his hands fly up; hit his belt buckle and down go his pants"), and such make-believe military hardware as the Johnny Seven One Man Army gun that can function as a machine gun, grenade launcher, pistol and so on. American children are virtually weaned on weapons. There are even gun-shaped teething things, and diaper pins with miniature gun replicas attached.

"Guns, or replicas of them," says the Washington *Post's* Alan Barth, "are given as playthings to American boys in the same way

---

* A cartoon in the December 1965 *Playboy* showed a body sprawled on the floor as a man was lighting a cigarette with what appeared to be a derringer lighter. The caption had the surprised survivor saying: "Could have sworn this was the lighter."

that dolls are given as playthings to American girls. It is as though young American males were being prepared for careers in manslaughter just as young American females are prepared for careers in motherhood."

"Marksmanship," comments the Canadian magazine *MacLean's*, "in the minds of millions of Americans, is mysteriously linked with good citizenship." * *MacLean's* also notes, "It's always been a compliment to call an American a 'square shooter,' and the crack shot has been considered a valuable citizen since the days of wagon trains and Indians." One could cite countless other colorful colloquialisms, sprung from firearms phrases or remnants of the old frontier, which now persist in the patois of present-day American speech: going off half-cocked; cocksure; flash-in-the-pan; keep your powder dry; lock, stock and barrel; on target; I could shoot you; you ought to be shot —and many more.

Big business uses gun motifs to sell everything from beer to banking services. "I pack a Fistful of Flavor and I'll take on any beer in the house!" reads a Ruppert beer ad featuring a hand gripping a bottle of the brew like a six-shooter. To show the "Big Change in Tempo!," R. J. Reynolds Tobacco Company compares its king-size cigarettes with a cannon. Men's shirts are sold in "musket maize."

Thirty-four per cent of the industrial firms reporting to the National Industrial Recreation Association now include shooting in their employee recreation programs, a Savage Arms executive has written in *The World of Guns*, which reveals that "industrial shooting has grown 31 per cent in the last few years." The president of Daisy Manufacturing Company, also writing in *The World of Guns*, tells us that recognition of the fact that "boys and BB guns go together as naturally as bacon and eggs" has prompted the use of the BB gun by hundreds of thousands of boys in programs sponsored by the "Jaycees" (United States Junior Chamber of Commerce), YMCAs, Boy Scouts, private camps and schools.

"No matter how much you may want to turn your back on it," says Cass S. Hough of Daisy, "the yen for a gun on the part of a boy is as natural as his very growth. The ownership and use of a BB gun satisfies that yen, and with proper training helps produce a bet-

---

* In East Meadow, Long Island, a fifteen-year-old junior-high-school boy brought a loaded Luger for show-and-tell display before his class in citizenship; police later discovered that the pistol had been stolen.

ter citizen." Meanwhile, a poll of 400 Illinois doctors turns up 139 cases of children treated for eye injuries caused by BB guns during a recent year; at least one doctor reported removing an eye, and many commented that BB guns were an even greater danger to sight than fireworks.

In New York's Westchester County, a judge dismissed an injunction suit brought by a group of citizens complaining about the noises emanating from a nearby "sportsmen's center"; the judge ruled the bark of target practice to be part of American civilization.

Why are Americans, more than other people, so addicted to guns —perhaps the most romantic and certainly the most ubiquitous of American symbols? Why is our whole culture seemingly centered around the gun, to the point where perhaps as many as 40 million Americans have a fixation on firearms to an often passionate degree?

Guns, for one thing, are deeply rooted in American tradition. From the earliest frontier days, guns, because of their vital role in self-defense and the gathering of food, were to be found in the hands of nearly everyone, including women and children. "Shooting small game with a bow or a gun and throwing a tomahawk became lifesaving skills when Indians attacked," writes Daniel J. Boorstin in *The Americans: The Colonial Experience*. "A well-grown boy at the age of twelve or thirteen years," noted the Reverend Joseph Doddridge of Virginia in the 1760s, "was furnished with a small rifle and shotpouch. He then became a fort soldier, and had his porthole assigned him. Hunting squirrels, turkeys and raccoons soon made him expert in the use of his gun."

With the need for meat and protection, gun makers were challenged to bring about improvements in the American rifle. With the colonials accustomed to defending themselves on home ground, whereas in Europe professionals were usually employed on distant battlefields, every citizen was also an instant soldier, and with this came the beginning of the notion of "a nation of riflemen." With the Revolution, the gun was virtually enshrined as our historic symbol of freedom. In the name of freedom, and laying the basis for the long-standing American myth of a constantly prepared citizenry, with every man a "Minuteman," the Founding Fathers wrote guns into the Constitution. The relevant words of the much-misinterpreted Second Amendment state: "A well-regulated Militia, being necessary to the security of a free State, the right of the people to keep and bear Arms, shall not be infringed."

The interest in guns is also part of our heritage stemming from the days of the wild and woolly West, when holstered hardware came into its own as a visible insignia of virility. A gun was the great equalizer, "the final judge in disputes of land, water, title, gambling debts and 'wimmin,'" as long as each disputant carried one of Sam Colt's arbiters on his hip.

In one of his Texas tales, J. Frank Dobie writes: "A local citizen strode up to Judge 'Three-Legged Willie' Wilkinson's table, pulled out a bowie knife and said: 'Your Honor, this is the law in this country.' Said the judge, pulling out his six-shooter: 'This is the constitution that overrides the law.'"

It makes little difference that most of the legendary lawmen and gunmen of that era, actually at its height for only two brief decades ending about 1886 or 1887, bore little resemblance to their sweet-smelling cinema or TV reincarnations. They were indeed inept with their equally legendary though clumsy and ineffectual equalizers. Beyond a distance of 20 feet, anybody hit would be hit by accident. The long, wary walk down a dusty main street was usually nothing more than a bluff-calling charade of a duel with no one getting hurt, and the crude custom certainly had nothing whatever to do with the winning of the West. Yet, as such legends live on, gun enthusiasts speak of "reliving our American heritage," and think of the gun as a somewhat romantic tool of violence and virility.

Feeding the fantasies of adolescents and contributing to the arrested development of adults are the imaginative versions of history furnished by the Western—in print, in video, and on the screen.* In the Western, the human drama of Western man may be seen in stark, simplistic opposites, like good and evil. There is, of course, also vicarious violence, or in psychological terms, aggression. One can think of his worst enemy in the villain's role. And if a man is hagridden, he has all outdoors in which to get away from women.

"I just naturally love history," a fast-drawing truck driver from Hattiesburg, Mississippi, told *Sports Illustrated*. "I read a lot of it in *Man's Magazine* and *True West* and in *Fast Draw*. I feel I become a part of it in a sense."

* The fantasies frequently become realities. A TV Western about a stagecoach robbery admittedly inspired two New Jersey youths to hold up a 59-passenger bus.

Surprisingly, although occasional more or less scientific studies have measured and mused on the motivations of stamp collectors and skiers, boaters and chess players and the pursuers of other such pleasures, physical or intellectual, none of a significant nature has ever delved into the psyche of the shooter. With but a few scattered references to him in the psychological and psychiatric literature, little therefore is known about the mores and motivations of the hunter, or for that matter other types of shooters. For some reason, shooters are generally a suspicious lot, shy about submitting to testing. One psychologist who recently tried without success to test various groups was turned down either for no reason or because, in the case of one group, of the fear of being "misquoted and misinterpreted." The leaders of some groups berated him as a busybody, and even as a Communist.

This defensive attitude is apparent in a *Guns & Ammo* article entitled "Are Shooters Psychotic?" The answer to be given by the author, Jeff Cooper, is apparent from the article's opening:

One of the more repelling characters in modern society is the amateur sociologist. Perhaps the professionals are equally offensive, but I don't know any so I can't say. The principle these people seem to have fastened upon is that nobody ever does anything just because he wants to: there must always be a deeper reason—some sick frustration or Freudian urge. Presumably a man's real *desire* is to sit and vegetate.

"Weaponcraft does not need any labored psychological analysis," Cooper goes on to say. "It is probably the most natural and normal attribute of man. Almost the best definition of man is 'the weapon-bearing animal.'"

Cooper, after confiding that among the standards the prospective husbands of his three daughters would have to meet would be skill at arms ("a young man who is unfamiliar with firearms, or timid about their use, is a poor prospect as a husband and father"), concedes that some gun lovers might be pretty kooky ("if you do much shooting you run into them all the time"). As for himself, Cooper concludes, he shoots for a number of reasons:

Partly for the feeling of reach and power it provides, partly for the satisfaction of controlling my own nerves and muscles with precision, partly for the sense of human mastery over immense mechanical forces, partly for the joy of competition against skilled human opposition, partly as a means of maintaining what I believe to be an essential attribute of any responsible, adult male.

But mainly I shoot because I enjoy it. And I hunt because I enjoy it. Really, Doctor, I am not trying to prove anything at all to anybody. I think that a good part of this half-baked psychological analysis stems from the increasing tendency to watch rather than to do . . .

Still, even some of Cooper's colleagues are not quite so cocksure. Lucian Cary, long-time gun editor of *True* magazine, writes:

All shooting is related psychologically to killing. When you shoot at game you are trying to kill it. When you shoot at clay targets with a shotgun or at a paper target with a rifle or a pistol, you are doing something symbolically similar. You are, whether you are conscious of it or not, indulging the fantasy to kill.

And says *New York Times* outdoor columnist Oscar Godbout, in an article for *Esquire:*

There is a strong emotional bond between most serious sportsmen and the firearms they use. They may not recognize it; if they do, they may be reluctant to admit it. But it is there. Without getting deeply immersed in the psychology of the hunter-gun relationship, it involves personal image, ego, and sense of power. A man with a gun imposes his will far beyond himself and his sense of power is increased manyfold. With these factors at work, his image of himself changes to a degree, depending on what his personality is to begin with. He is likely to see himself as more of a take-charge man, more of a masculine force to be reckoned with. Something sexual mixed in there? It goes without saying.

Atavism is at work, too. Within memory of living man, Americans have had to live, literally, by their firearms, not only in terms of defense and offense but equally for sustenance. When today's sportsman knocks over a running white-tailed deer or elk, doubles on quail or mallards, or stops a ton of annoyed Cape buffalo, he feels an emotional kinship with ancestors who had to do for survival what he's doing by choice for recreation. The gun is the connecting link between him and his great-grandfather.

Though the notion is plausible that there should be at least some difference between hunters and target shooters, to say nothing of collectors, cannoneers and other types of gun enthusiasts, generalizations of any kind can often lead to very shaky ground. But some conclusions can be drawn from the common denominator of all shooting sports—the gun.

Much, for example, is made of the gun as a sex symbol. Ian Fleming, speaking through one of the characters in his final Bond book, *The Man with the Golden Gun,* says:

It is a Freudian thesis, with which I am inclined to agree, that the pistol, whether in the hands of an amateur or of a professional gunman, has significance for the owner as a symbol of virility, an extension of the male organ, and that excessive interest in guns (e.g., gun collections and gun clubs) is a form of fetishism. The partiality of Scaramanga [in the book, the villainous wielder of the title weapon] for a particularly showy variation of weapon, and his use of silver and gold bullets, clearly point, I think, to his being a slave to this fetish and, if I am right, I have doubts about his alleged sexual prowess, for the lack of which his gun fetish would be either a substitute or a compensation.... So I would not be surprised to learn that Scaramanga is not the Casanova of popular fancy.

I asked a psychiatrist friend, Dr. Alfred J. Siegman, to expand on the thesis which sees guns as sex symbols.

"Is such symbolism attached to the gun because of its size and shape?" I asked.

"Well, not only for that reason," he said. "It pierces, it penetrates, it discharges, much like the penis."

"Can you explain why more men than women use guns?"

"You can say that men are more preoccupied with the idea of power in shooting than women. The idea of being masculine is perceived as involving the use of penetrating, aggressive, hurting things. And there may be people who, because of the need for particular reassurance about their masculinity, resolve their problems by means of guns."

"Man, when you've got a piece on your hip, you're nine feet tall," says a New York *Journal American* feature article * quoting a citizen stating his views on his reasons for carrying a gun. Summing up the views of psychiatrists and criminologists who hold a gun to be a great equalizer because "it makes a little man feel big, a stupid man

* New York *Journal American,* February 18, 1965, "Are You Gun Shy? . . . Read This and Be Happy."

feel clever, a frightened man brave and an insecure man feel sure," the article classifies the following types of persons as finding comfort or fulfillment from the feel of the "piece on their hip":

1. The basically insecure individual who is in touch with reality but gripped by anxiety. Like a teenager with an automobile, he feels the weapon gives him power.
2. The criminal sociopath who is in touch with reality but has emotional problems. Typically, he has no regard for others and is unable to "feel" for them.
3. The psychotic out of touch with reality and irrationally fearful of power symbols such as the FBI and the CIA, the Communists or his boss. He presents a threat because he may misidentify a complete stranger as an agent of persecution and shoot him dead. [Hence, as the feature also points out, in the mind of a seriously disturbed man with complicated delusions of persecution, a gun may offer "protection" against imaginary persecutors.]

"A gun carrier is often a very insecure individual," comments Dr. David J. Owens, clinical director of St. Elizabeth's Hospital, the national hospital for the mentally ill in the District of Columbia. "They tell us they're going to get their equalizers," says Owens in speaking of his mental charges, some of whom had ordered mail-order weapons from within the hospital's confines. Whether as a result of unrealistic fears, a desire to appear more manly, or for other reasons, Dr. Owens says, a gun may be one way for a person in a deprived area to "compensate" for insecurity.

"Athletics are, in our society, the almost perfect outlet for aggressive feeling," says sociologist Stuart Palmer of the University of New Hampshire in his *A Study of Murder*. "Athletics and the competition they involve are highly approved by the society. The physical energy expended directly or indirectly against opponents can serve quite clearly as an escape valve for aggression." However, Palmer found that the fifty-one New England murderers he studied made "relatively little use of that escape valve," and preferred hunting as a way of venting aggression. In the cases where he was able to determine definitely which murderers hunted and which didn't, Palmer found 36 per cent to have hunted at least occasionally. Indeed, reported Palmer, a number of the murderers to whom he talked expressed an "almost fanatical" liking for hunting. One man, a quiet middle-aged farmer who had shot and killed his wife, told Palmer, "Oh, I love hunting. I'd rather do that than anything I can think of." The farmer's eyes lit up as he explained, "Out there by yourself in the woods, nothing to worry about."

"How do you feel about animals in general, apart from hunting?" Palmer asked him.

"I like them. Always have. Why, when I was a kid I always had pets around. Always."

"But, in a way, doesn't hunting go against that?"

"No! Why should it? It's different. They're not pets. You don't know them."

Although it would be erroneous to conclude from this that only hunters, or for that matter, even predominantly hunters, are capable of murder, it is also interesting to note that more than half of all hunters—according to one well-known survey—agreed that they couldn't be satisfied with a hunt if they didn't kill any game. Palmer also ventures that his murderers' preference for hunting as an escape valve might be partially explained by the fact that "most athletics require a degree of social participation ability which the murderers lacked.... They tended, by and large, to choose solitary channels of release. Hunting is an example of a type of aggression release which from the individual's point of view is, by and large, a solitary one." A study of Minnesota hunters also showed them to have a "mild tendency to social introversion," as compared to the average normal personality.*

* Perhaps the most penetrating, though informal, analysis ever made of the hunter is in the composite portrait put together by Pittsburgh psychiatrist Dr. Stonewall Stickney, himself a hunter, for a book *Motivation in Sports*, edited by Dr. James A. Knight of the Department of Psychiatry of the Tulane University School of Medicine. The book is to be published by Charles C. Thomas, Springfield, Ill. In a letter to me, Dr. Stickney said he has noted a "shy, inarticulate aestheticism" in many hunters. He has also been impressed by the sadistic love many hunters have for the animal victim as well as the totemic and "latently homosexual quality" of, say, big Southern deer hunts. In his manuscript for the book, Dr. Stickney also wonders if there is something homosexual about a hunt. At the same time, he finds it difficult to imagine "that such virile characters as hunters (and athletes) could harbor such tendencies. Their manly recreation proclaims their virility and aggressiveness." Yet he recalls, "Playful invitations and nicknames referring to homosexual acts would be offered from time to time (especially on drunken deer hunts), and nobody's masculinity seemed to be impugned by all this loose talk. To my knowledge these suggestions were never acted upon, at least during the hunt, but the openness and innocence of them were astonishing. Perhaps they only

To some people like author-naturalist Joseph Wood Krutch, it is "inconceivable that anyone should think an animal more interesting dead than alive." Literally thousands of people give up hunting every year without suffering any trauma or damage to any of their instincts. One of the disenchanted, Dr. Karl Menninger, one of America's leading figures in psychiatry, wrote me:

As a former member of the joyous gang which sallied forth each fall to see what they could knock the guts out of at 100 yards, I can tell you why I turned against it. In the first place, there are just too many of us on this earth and too few of the poor animals that we are so eager to kill. Normal, natural and universal as the urge to murder something may be, it no longer serves social usefulness to turn it on defenseless wildlife, and it ought to succumb to the restraining effects of our civilization before all of the interesting fauna in the world are wiped out.

Most hunters, as well as other gun enthusiasts usually venture a simple explanation, or possibly rationalization, for their obsession. Hunting and shooting, they say, are wholesome forms of recreation, physically stimulating and full of thrills and excitement, as well as fun. In loftier terms they may even proclaim the sport as "healthful" and "character-building." To proselyte the sport among youngsters, gun organizations and firearms manufacturers and dealers also cite the value of guns in contributing to good physical and mental growth, self-discipline, initiative, team spirit and an abundance of other admirable traits. They urge that every youngster be given a gun, a real one, perhaps at first preceded by a toy replica. Such devices are suggested as useful, if not essential, to enable Junior to develop masculinity and give vent to his aggressive impulses.

Naturally, most medical people take issue with such dogmatic lay opinions. Guns appear nowhere on the list of recommended toys in Dr. Arnold Gesell and Dr. Frances Ilg's authoritative *Infant and Child in the Culture of Today,* a work based on the two eminent child specialists' years of research at the renowned child clinic of the Yale School of Medicine.

Dr. Lois Barclay Murphy, a child psychologist at the world-famous Menninger Foundation in Topeka, Kansas, was quoted by

---

seem so now after a few recent years of reading and observing, just as it now seems hilarious that many people down here will call a man a sissy or an 'Aunt Puss,' and never imagine that he may be a practicing homosexual!"

Look as saying that "there are better ways, such as sports and games, for a boy to develop masculinity, without encouraging warlike attitudes at a time when the world faces destruction." Dr. Michael B. Rothenburg, clinical professor of child psychiatry and pediatrics at the Albert Einstein College of Medicine in the Bronx, New York, and director of children's psychiatric services at Beth-El Hospital in Brooklyn, told the *New Republic:* "If children must release aggressive emotions, they should do it against bowling pins or dart boards, not against human effigies or the symbols of civilization. ... If children are conditioned to work out their aggressions with such things as atomic cannons, or if they are encouraged to think of all who oppose them as subhuman, and that the proper way to deal with these opponents is with Polaris submarines, then we are developing an adult population which, some years hence, will find it relatively easy, if not even natural, to put such horrifying weapons to actual use."

Dr. Benjamin Spock, America's most famous pediatrician, has long been of the opinion that playing with guns will not by itself turn a well-brought-up boy into a belligerent militarist or aggressive delinquent. However, in recent years, Spock too has taken a stand where he would also be inclined to discourage the use of toy guns and other war toys. What brought Spock to this position, he told *Redbook,* were examples he had seen of how "mock violence can lower a child's standards of behavior," and, more important, "the assassination of President Kennedy, along with the reported cheering of some school children, and the immediate murder of Lee Harvey Oswald."

It is also not easy to forget the picture of a young Bronx boy once drawn by a neighbor for a *New York Times* reporter. "We all thought that he was kind of queer," she said. "He liked Western comics. All you could hear was 'bang, bang, bang.' He would play by himself with his toy guns."

The boy's name was Lee Harvey Oswald.

6   Inside the World of Guns

> By a faction, I understand a number of citizens, whether amounting to a majority or minority of the whole, who are actuated by some common impulse of passion, or of interest, adverse to the right of other citizens, or to the permanent and aggregate interest of the community.
>
> —*The Federalist,* Number 10 (James Madison)

There could be no more shocking example of what can result from the absence of controls on the sale and use of firearms than the murder of President Kennedy in 1963. By a strange irony, only fourteen months before the assassination, a Dallas judge had declared unconstitutional a city ordinance making it "unlawful to have in one's possession within the city or upon any property owned by the city, any firearms, rifle, revolver, pistol or any other weapon." * And in Washington, less than four months before the mail-order Carcano was put to use in the crime of the century, a bill had been introduced in Congress regulating the sale of mail-order guns. This bill was still pending in Congress on November 22, 1963. Within a matter of weeks, some seventeen other firearms control bills were introduced in Congress.

"By the ordinary rules of the game," said *The Reporter,* "the event in Dallas should have ensured prompt enactment, just as the news

---

* The ruling, in *Texas v. Kelvin O. Jenkins* in September 1962, reversed the conviction of a man found with a revolver in a Tom Thumb Food Store. However, the ordinance had hardly been enforced anyway, being applied only in instances of misbehavior with firearms.

of Thalidomide-deformed babies had provided the long-needed impetus for passage of stricter drug regulations in 1962." Popular support for gun control legislation was widespread. A nationwide Gallup Poll taken in January 1964 showed 78 per cent of the American people in favor of a law requiring a police permit for the purchase of a gun. In Congress, Senate Majority Leader Mike Mansfield joined the Republican leader, Senator Everett McKinley Dirksen, in eloquently voicing the need for at least some firearms regulation.

But by the time the session had ended, nine months later, Congress had not acted. The proposed legislation had been the target for the deadly aim of one of the most extraordinary and powerful lobbies in the United States.

The lobby includes hunters and other gun owners, vendors of sporting arms and allied goods, manufacturers, wildlife preservation and conservation organizations, gun clubs and associations, outdoor and gun magazines, and assorted superpatriotic organizations, including militant right-wing extremist groups. Collectively, this loose alliance exerts an influence far greater than its true proportion of the country's population.

The lobby is highly vocal and often downright vitriolic. Over the years, it has managed to thwart all efforts made to introduce new and stricter firearms regulations. It matters little what type of legislation is proposed. To all such proposals, as far as the gun lobby is concerned, there is seldom any compromise. Any additional firearms legislation, no matter how mild, is bad legislation. Accordingly, proponents of gun-control laws are characterized as "anti-gun." To the lobby one is either "anti-gun" or "pro-gun," and there is no reasonable middle ground in its view.

"Probably no proposed legislation in city, state or Federal circles, can arouse the controversy, the arguments, or the bitterness that additional restrictive firearms laws or regulations can," said the Toledo *Blade,* shortly after the Kennedy assassination. "So bitter has this become that many legislators refer to any proposed gun laws as 'kiss of death' legislation, and veteran lawmakers shy away from it as they would from legislation that would advocate sin or belittle motherhood."

"Few issues kindle such an emotional response as the debate over firearms legislation, which invariably flares up in the wake of a publicized crime," editorialized the Washington *Post*. The *Post* stated that "the manner of President Kennedy's assassination has prompted many questions about how and why the killer was able to obtain the murder weapon together with demands for stricter laws regulating the sale of firearms to the public."

That at least some new and stricter firearms regulations would come into being seemed a virtual certainty after that fateful day in Dallas. The 18 bills in both houses of Congress represented a surge of firearms legislation unparalleled in congressional annals. More than 170 laws were proposed in state capitals. In Massachusetts alone, 35 new bills were introduced; in New York, there were about 80.

The proposed legislation, both Federal and state, was comparable to that already long in effect in most other countries. It ran the gamut, from laws prohibiting ex-felons, narcotic addicts, minors, and the mentally ill from possessing rifles and shotguns, to those requiring police permits for the purchase of any kind of a gun, as well as registration of all gun owners. One proposed bill sought to limit the sale of ammunition to persons displaying a hunting license or gun permit.

A substantial majority of the country has long favored stricter firearms control. Although opponents of gun laws charged that post-assassination hysteria had influenced the Gallup Poll of January 1964, a previous poll taken little more than four years before had shown similar results. At that time, 75 per cent of the people sampled had expressed themselves as being in favor of a permit's being required for the purchase of any kind of a gun. Even as far back as 1938, what was perhaps the first Gallup Poll on this subject showed more than 80 per cent of the American people as favoring registration.

Although opposition to bills restricting the purchase of shotguns or rifles has usually centered on the argument that they would be unfair to persons using these guns, the 1959 Gallup survey showed that even gun owners would be willing, by a ratio of 2 to 1, to get a police permit before buying a gun. Even in the South, where gun toting is inhibited by few laws, 2 out of 3 persons said they would be willing to accept the suggested curb. More than half (54 per cent) of the persons surveyed also favored restricting the sale of ammunition to those with a police permit.

Leading citizens' groups and professional organizations, ranging from the General Federation of Women's Clubs to the American Bar Association, have also gone on record as favoring stricter firearms control. In New York City, the National Committee for the Control of Weapons, composed of several hundred religious, civic, legislative and judicial leaders, has been pressing for stricter laws since its origin in 1947.* This group was instrumental in having Federal legislation enacted which outlawed the manufacture, sale and distribution of switch-blade knives. In December 1963, the committee, through its chairman, New York State Supreme Court Justice John E. Cone, recommended state laws calling for the registration of rifles and shotguns as well as handguns, a forty-eight-hour "cooling-off period" between the time of purchase and delivery of guns, and limiting the sale of ammunition to persons holding gun permits or hunting licenses.

On the Federal level, Judge Cone also called for legislation which, among other things, would prohibit the shipment in interstate or foreign commerce of rifles and shotguns to persons not registered by states to possess them, and to ban the importation of foreign surplus and obsolete military rifles. With the aim of taking "guns out of the hands of thugs, psychopaths, drug addicts and teenagers," the committee also urged more stringent regulations on the issuance of hunting licenses, including fingerprinting of applicants to determine if they had criminal records.

With but few exceptions, every recognized law enforcement official and agency from the Justice Department down has taken a stand in favor of stricter controls. In a report to the House Subcommittee on Appropriations in January 1964, FBI Director J. Edgar Hoover stated: "I have felt for many years there should be some statute enacted by Congress, with some steps taken to have the enactment of state laws to supplement it and buttress it, that would restrict the obtaining of guns without some type of ownership registration." A 1957 survey by the Senate juvenile delinquency subcommittee showed 63 of 69 city police chiefs to be in favor of more Federal control over firearms entering their jurisdictions. That year, the International Association of Chiefs of Police, a professional

* The National Committee is an outgrowth of the Committee to Ban Teen-age Weapons.

association of some 5,500 top echelon police executives and administrators, issued the following policy statement concerning firearms:

The primary concern of the IACP, and the Police Agencies of the United States is to make sure that there is no weakening of the present controls on the use of these weapons, particularly revolvers and pistols, which are the guns most commonly used by criminals. The Association has traditionally supported legislation which, in the opinion of its governing body, would strengthen existing controls of the sales of firearms and ammunition in the public interest.

Two years later, the IACP sent its membership a questionnaire regarding the proposed firearms legislation then before Congress. Summing up the comments of the police administrators was the statement by Chief Anthony C. Bosch of the Toledo, Ohio, Police Department: "Removing any control on firearms could have a tendency to increase crime." Other advocates of gun registration or other firearms controls include America's leading crime prevention experts, prosecuting attorneys, state attorneys general and federal government officials, up to and including the Attorney General and the President of the United States.

Reflecting and encouraging the strong public and governmental support for control over the traffic in guns is an overwhelming majority of the magazines, newspapers and radio and television broadcasters. Magazines which have at one time or another editorialized or run articles underlining the need for firearms legislation range from mass circulation publications such as *Life, Look, The Saturday Evening Post, McCall's* and the *Ladies Home Journal* to intellectual journals of opinion such as *Harper's, Saturday Review, The Reporter, The New Republic,* and *The Nation.* Radio and television stations across the country have also editorialized or featured programs emphasizing the need for firearms controls. So have virtually all the newspapers of consequence in the nation. Some, like *The New York Times, Christian Science Monitor* and Washington *Post,* have even made stricter controls the matter of a crusade; in 1965, the Washington *Post* ran editorials on the subject for seventy-seven consecutive days. According to an analysis of editorial opinion made by the Senate juvenile delinquency subcommittee, newspaper proponents of such legislation were found in 1965 to have a combined circulation of more than 42 million, as compared to the less than 3 million circulation of newspapers editorializing against controls.

The proponents of stricter firearms controls concede that controls will not provide a panacea for the gun problem. But controls on the purchase and possession of guns, they argue, would prevent or at least make it more difficult for some people to have guns, and certainly cut down on many of the impulse killings in which a readily accessible gun so often figures. Restricting weapons to mature people of unblemished background and character with a proven ability to handle guns safely, it is also pointed out, would prevent many of the firearms accidents that take place both inside and outside the home.

While it is conceded that laws would not necessarily keep guns out of the hands of all criminals or other unauthorized persons, the laws would at least provide some basis (at times perhaps the only one) for the arrest and conviction of such persons. A registration requirement, for example, apart from preventing criminals, minors and mental incompetents from legally obtaining firearms, would also make it easier for the authorities to determine who was armed with what in the case of a shooting. The registration of firearms would admittedly cause some inconvenience, as do most exercises of police power. But, as *The New York Times* has pointed out, "nobody objects today to the universally required registration of that other dangerous 'weapon'—the automobile—or to the licensing of the operator of a motor vehicle." And as J. Edgar Hoover has also observed: "Automobiles and dogs are licensed—why not guns?"

The wide array of interests forming the gun lobby takes issue with all this. However, they number many who cannot oppose firearms controls for the real reasons underlying their opposition. To claim that controls would diminish their dollar intake would smack too much of self-interest. To assert that guns are fun or a boon to health might be regarded as frivolous, or hardly sufficient compensation for their evils. Therefore, a somewhat loftier motive must be advanced as justification for opposition to gun control laws. What better than an appeal to patriotism?

Let us sustain abiding faith in the Second Amendment of the Constitution. Let us also not forget what took the Minutemen from Lexington and Concord to Yorktown and the Marines from Guadalcanal to the top of Mount Surabachi on a place called Iwo Jima. Our traditional American heritage includes the inalienable right to keep and bear arms and should the day arrive when any government fears the lawful use of arms by its citizenry, on that day such a government will have abrogated its good faith in governing free men.

So reads an advertisement by the International Armament Corp., also known as the Interarmco Group, the nation's—if not the world's—largest weapons dealer. The patriotic business of catering to those who would exercise the right to keep and bear arms has grown into what the *Wall Street Journal* estimated in 1964 as a $1.5-billion industry. Comprising the hard core of the industry are the some forty companies making U.S. firearms and about ten commercial ammunition producers. (The latter group, however, also numbers some who produce guns as well as ammunition.) To supplement the basic weaponry of shooters, there is also a multitude of makers of accessory equipment ranging from eardrum protectors and camouflage clothing to telescopes, game lures and scents. To market all this paraphernalia as well as guns and ammunition by mail and over the counter, there are, as already noted, some 120,000 retail outlets. Rounding out this distribution system are also several hundred wholesalers, importers, and any combination of the foregoing.

Apart from what is spent on guns, ammunition and accessories, there are the "side" ramifications of shooting. According to the National Shooting Sports Foundation, these in 1963 produced more than $1 billion annually for the makers of automobiles, car accessories and fuel ($261 million); boats, boating equipment and services ($225 million); wearing apparel ($268 million); lodging ($30 million); food ($100 million); transportation ($10 million) and for such things as camping equipment, cameras and accessories, licenses and highway tolls. Needless to say, all these diverse groups are in general agreement that what is good for the gun industry is good for America.

When Samuel Cummings, the thirty-seven-year-old boss of Interarmco, was informed at a Senate juvenile delinquency subcommittee hearing in 1965 that eighteen of his rifles and 10,000 rounds of ammunition were sold to a Mississippi dealer who was a known member of the Ku Klux Klan, Cummings simply responded, "He was a licensed dealer." *

Cummings, an ex-CIA operative, does his biggest business in supplying the armies of foreign nations with everything from machine guns and rifles to antitank guns and mortars, as well as other surplus military appurtenances, including heavy tanks and jet planes. To fill the various needs of his clientele, Cummings' nine bonded Interarmco warehouses clustered along the Potomac River in Alexandria, Virginia, a few miles from Washington, are said to have a larger arsenal of weapons—their number is reputed to range to as many as 500,000 or 600,000—than the British and U.S. Armed Forces combined. Though an American, Cummings resides in tax-lenient Monaco; he also maintains a chalet in the Alps, and owns his own bank in Geneva, the Banque Genèvoise de Commerce et de Crédit. Cummings apparently sees no embarrassment in the ethic of servicing the needs of such politically diverse clients, past and present, as Cuba's Batista and Castro, the Dominican Republic's Trujillo, Yugoslavia's Tito, Guatemala's pro-Communist Guzmán, and Indonesia's Communist-leaning Sukarno.

"It's not my job to be a moral judge of humanity," he once said, brushing off responsibility for what happened to the guns and equipment he sells.

Speaking for the industry as a whole, E. B. Mann, writing in *The World of Guns*, says:

Cliché artists have painted us as fat monsters feeding on the profits of war—ignoring the fact that no other industry has given as generously of its patents, its methods, its men, and its tools to other makers in order to meet national needs for more guns than we could manufacture alone; ignoring the fact that no industry sets higher standards of product ex-

---

* Under our present laws, the transaction was perfectly legal, although four of the rifles were later found in the possession of Paul Dewey Wilson when he was arrested on October 2, 1964, in connection with the racial bombings in McComb, Mississippi. Also found on Wilson's person and in his home were gun dealer price lists, a tin star "sheriff's" badge of the type found in Crackerjack boxes, and cards signifying membership in the United Klans of America, The Americans for the Preservation of the White Race, and the National Rifle Association. Wilson and his fellow conspirators received suspended sentences and were placed on probation after pleading either guilty or *nolo contendere* (no contest).

cellence or more demanding margins of product safety, at low margins of profit on massive investments.

On April 20, 1965, however, came the revelation by Drew Pearson that Olin Mathieson had charged over $1 million in excess profits for blank cartridge powder. The giant corporation had charged $1.72 a pound for powder similar to that which the Army had previously procured for 90 cents a pound. "When the excessive prices were eventually disclosed by an Army Audit Agency review," reported Pearson, "Olin Mathieson and the Army negotiated a significantly lower price for future delivery."

Until recently, the gun industry did not do as well as it would have liked in civilian sales. As mentioned earlier, the year 1958 was a particularly bad one for rifle and revolver manufacturers, with sales off from 25 to 40 per cent as U.S. surplus military arms and those from Italy, Germany and England cascaded on to the market here at cut-rate prices. To aim for a bigger share of sporting goods sales, the gunmakers sought to capture new converts to shooting by, said the *Wall Street Journal,* "drawing a bead on every member of the family, including Mom" through a variety of promotional tactics. The Daisy Manufacturing Co. which holds that a boy's "yen for a gun is as natural as his yen for a dog" and, even more important, that "the BB gun bridges the gap between father and son," began to step up its stress of educational programs for children with the cooperation of the United States Junior Chamber of Commerce. Olin Mathieson's Winchester-Western division distributed propaganda aimed at the young shooter, although it may be wondered whether the message suggesting shooting as a wholesome alternative to juvenile delinquency was motivated more by the desire to sell guns than to save America's youth. "To help convert Mother herself to shooting," as the *Journal* put it,* Winchester also distributed to women's organizations pamphlets offering advice on how to conduct programs on gun safety, and gave TV stations free film clips showing proper gun handling and shooting by smartly dressed women. The company also brought to the fore the "Winchester Man" as the theme of a new advertising campaign.

To boost business during slack shooting periods, an issue of Winchester's monthly news magazine for dealers suggested opportuni-

* *Wall Street Journal,* August 5, 1964.

ties for seasonal promotions. During late spring and summer, it was suggested, "you can still sell .22 rifles and ammo by setting up a display combining picnic equipment and .22's and suggesting how much fun could be had by doing a little plinking on the family picnic."

Dealers were also urged to make use of holidays, too, although Winchester conceded that associating some holidays with shooting might seem a bit far-fetched at first—at least, until one gave some thought to the matter. "The Fourth of July is a natural for an Independence Day window display featuring flintlock and Kentucky rifles. Thanksgiving leads to thoughts of turkeys and Pilgrim muskets (and a live turkey as a prize in a Turkey Shoot or other types of contests). Veterans' Day is a good time to put up your World War I machine gun, and a sign saluting your town's ex-servicemen. Father's Day is the perfect day to suggest that youngsters give their dad supplies of ammo for their favorite rifles or shotguns."

At a Senate Commerce Committee hearing in December 1963—less than a month after the Kennedy assassination—Thomas L. Kimball, executive director of the National Wildlife Federation, rhetorically asked:

Will the enactment of laws controlling the sale and possession of firearms, short of complete and effective disarmament of the citizenry, prevent the brutality and senseless murder committed by the assassin, the felon, the criminally insane, the juvenile delinquent? Would such laws if in force at the time have prevented the assassination of one of the greatest men of our time? Insofar as the National Wildlife Federation is concerned, the answer is a forceful and resounding "No" to both questions.

Any contemplated firearms laws, Kimball went on to say, "should be directed toward the criminal element and unlawful use rather than mere possession or registration of firearms. Gun registration lists, no matter how subtly obtained, or how intensely desired by law enforcement agencies, can and will provide the most effective and convenient way of disarming the private citizens should a subversive power infiltrate our police system or our enemies occupy our country."

In commenting on a firearms bill in Congress in 1965, an editorial in *Virginia Wildlife,* a publication of the Virginia Commission of Game and Inland Fisheries, stated: "Truly there exists a foul conspiracy to disarm the law-abiding American public." This interesting flight of fancy, said the Washington *Post,* referred to a bill carrying into effect a recommendation for firearms controls made by President Lyndon Johnson.

Conservationists, at first thought, might seem oddly out of place within the firearms lobby. Many gun users are, after all, dedicated to decimating the wildlife of forest and field. But this seeming anomaly is explained by the simple fact that hunters are the financial backbone of state game departments, which in 1964 collected $72 million from hunters for licenses, tags and permits. The money goes to pay the game wardens' salaries, plus the bill for buying and preserving breeding grounds, feeding and generally caring for wildlife.

Under the Pittman-Robertson Act of 1937, an 11 per cent federal excise tax on sporting arms and ammunition, currently totaling $20 million a year, is apportioned to the state projects. Other revenue from the sale of Duck Stamps ($80 million worth sold through post offices since 1934) and private contributions to organizations like the National Wildlife Federation make up the remainder of the $150 million that hunters now spend each year to protect and increase wildlife. Without this money, wildlife programs as they are now conducted would perish, as would many of the organizations and persons depending on their support.

The National Wildlife Federation, a private nonprofit group dedicated "to the attainment of conservation goals through educational means," is the world's largest organization of its kind. Through its affiliated conservation organizations in every state it has an estimated membership of 2 million persons. Another influential group is the 15,000-member Wildlife Management Institute, also headquartered in Washington, which is concerned with the technical and research aspects of wildlife restoration. Among the better known of the hundreds of other national organizations having their own particular conservation axes to grind are Ducks Unlimited (for the perpetuation of wildfowl), the Izaak Walton League of America (now concerned with both hunting and fishing), and the Boone &

Crockett Club (best known for its scoring and keeping of records of game trophies).

Not surprisingly, the National Wildlife Federation and the Wildlife Management Institute are creations of the arms industry. They were born at a three-hour dinner meeting held on April 24, 1935, at the Waldorf-Astoria Hotel in New York—a meeting attended by representatives of Hercules Powder, Remington Arms, and du Pont (which two years earlier had acquired control of Remington). At the meeting, the three companies agreed to subscribe the funds which led to the birth of the American Wildlife Institute (predecessor of the Wildlife Management Institute), and the National Wildlife Federation, and for the support of a number of other conservation groups. (The National Audubon Society was later invited to share in this industry largesse, but refused.)

In 1937, Remington (which today contributes significantly to the support of the Wildlife Management Institute), du Pont and Winchester-Western were instrumental in effecting passage of the Pittman-Robertson Act (officially known as the Federal Aid in Wildlife Restoration Act). All three companies plus Hercules are members of the Sporting Arms and Ammunition Manufacturers' Institute. The letterhead of the Wildlife Management Institute makes interesting reading. Listed as treasurer is Harry L. Hampton, Jr., who serves simultaneously as secretary of the Sporting Arms and Ammunition Manufacturers' Institute. Vice President C. R. ("Pinky") Gutermuth of the Wildlife Management Institute also holds life membership in the National Rifle Association. Nor should it seem strange that the National Wildlife Federation is joined with du Pont, Remington, Winchester and other manufacturers, gun dealers, and gun magazines in the industry group known as the National Shooting Sports Foundation.

Small wonder that conservationists often sound like die-hard gun lovers. For example, the Michigan United Conservation Clubs, one of the fifty such state groups affiliated with the National Wildlife Federation, published the following editorial in its monthly journal in December 1963:

In the wake of the tragic assassination of President Kennedy, the anti-gun cranks can be expected to make another strong push in their campaign to restrict the constitutional right of law-abiding Americans to bear arms.

We will grant that these highly vocal people mean well and have "good intentions"—but we are all aware of where that road leads. The fact is that these anti-gun people are grossly misinformed and misdirected.

The sort of police control programs these people advocate would discriminate against the honest sportsmen, but would mean nothing to the hardened criminals and psychopaths who would continue to have easy access to whatever weapons they desire.

We will not at this time enter a long argument as to why these people are wrong in their premises and proposed methods. The time for that will come later.

We simply want to alert the sportsmen of Michigan, so that they can be ready when the attack comes.

Having similar views about gun laws to bona-fide sportsmen are many who merely masquerade as sportsmen—the para-military superpatriots of such wild-eyed militant extremist groups as the Minutemen, Rangers, Paul Revere Associated Yeomen, and the American Nazi Party. The sentiments of these superpatriots were once well synthesized by Goldwater's ghostwriter, Karl Hess,* in an article for the April 1957 *American Mercury*. "The question of freedom, when stripped to its steel center, is just this: Who has the guns?" he wrote. "[Ours] is the sort of freedom which, based upon an ideal and an image, was born in gunfire, preserved in gunfire, and which is, even today, maintained by a ready strength of arms."

On another occasion, Hess, a life member of the NRA, wrote: "It would not be America really if it did not produce men who suddenly tire of palaver and reach for the rifle on the wall, to use themselves or to hand to the underdog who needs it."

In fact, guns are valued accessories of the ultras, antis, fanatics and assorted crackpots who hold that crack shots are our last defense against Communist enslavement and, accordingly, profess that firearms legislation is part of a vast Communist conspiracy to disarm red-blooded American citizens.

When William H. Garland, a member of a far-out California-

* Author of that now-historic phrase: "Extremism in the defense of liberty is no vice." Hess, it should be said, is not a member of the groups mentioned.

based "white Christian" sect known as the Christian Defense
League, affiliated with the Rangers, was arrested for the illegal
possession of eight machine guns (he also had nearly 100 other
weapons), his explanation was that he had amassed the arsenal as a
"patriot" for the purpose of repelling "invaders." The Southern-
oriented National States Rights Party, which has ties with the Ku
Klux Klan, urges all "our people" to be armed with at least one rifle
or pistol to withstand the siege by "an army of Kikes, Kommunists
and Koons." Indeed, as Samuel Johnson once said, "patriotism is
the last refuge of a scoundrel."

The Paul Revere Associated Yeomen (PRAY) warns that unless
all Americans stock up on firearms and "lots" of ammunition, "your
wives and daughters will be chattels in Mongolian and African
brothels." Probably the largest and most fanatical of these groups is
the Minutemen, with a claimed following of 25,000. They have been
called "idiots and screwballs" even by leaders of the far-out John
Birch Society (although the two organizations probably have some
overlapping membership). Preparing for the day when the Communists strike, an event expected by 1973, the Minutemen practice
guerrilla maneuvers against an imaginary enemy. Members are also
required to fire at least 500 rounds of ammunition a year to keep in
sharpshooter trim. "When murdering Communist bands come roam-
ing through your community," says the Minutemen recruiting booklet, "they must find a vigorous and well-armed civilian population."
An issue of *On Target*, the group's official publication, published the
names of twenty members of Congress accused of following the
Communist line: they were listed under a heading "In Memoriam,"
with the warning: "Traitors beware. Even now the crosshairs are on
the back of your neck." *On Target*, speaking of the time when
bullets may have to replace ballots, also ominously warns: "We are
not going to have a free election in 1968."

Such are the incitements that some take as invitations to assassination. The national leader of the Minutemen, a group conceived on a
duck hunt in 1960, is Robert Bolivar de Pugh, proprietor of a Norborne, Missouri, veterinary pharmaceutical supply house. He does
not indicate concern about Minutemen activities' possibly being in
violation of Federal statutes against private armies. "We're only exercising our constitutional right to bear arms," he says.

In the summer of 1965, de Pugh was arrested on a charge of

kidnapping at gunpoint two girls whom he planned to use, the girls said, to seduce and blackmail high U.S. government officials. Although the kidnapping charge was dropped, de Pugh was indicted on charges of contributing to the delinquency of a minor (one of the girls was seventeen) and possessing bombs and bombshells.

With an overwhelming majority of the nation's newspapers and general magazines in favor of more severe firearms control, the press campaign against controls is led by the so-called men's magazines, the outdoor and gun magazines, and the outdoor columnists and writers of various magazines and newspapers.

The newspaper columns devoted to the great outdoors are not backed by substantial gun advertising. It would therefore hardly be expected that the men who write these columns should have any particular commercial axes to grind. Probably, however, an occasional invitation to the Remington Arms experimental farm in Maryland for a few days of shooting does help some columnists see things the industry way. In any event, there is almost universal agreement between the writings of the outdoor columnists on firearms legislation and the industry point of view.

For Tucson *Citizen* outdoor writer Bill Davidson to suggest, as he once did in a column on "Firearms Legislation Sportsmen Could Live With," that "a Federal approach is the only real solution" would be regarded as heresy by most members of the firearms faction. But this is about as far as any rod-and-gun writer would dare to go if he wants to remain in good standing in the shooting fraternity.

When the nation's outdoor columnists are hard put for a subject, particularly during the lull between the close of the hunting season and the beginning of the spring fishing season (December to March), they can always contrive a lively column by taking a few whacks at New York's Sullivan Law or some threatened local law. In one typical outburst, the New York *Journal American*'s Ed Moore wrote:

The Sullivan Law, which was supposed to solve forever New York's problems with firearms, has only taken firearms away from good citizens, leaving them helpless in a crime wave of armed hoodlums, and built up a lucrative racket in the sale of firearms to the underworld. Few states have laws as restrictive and stringent as the Sullivan Law. Few states have as much violence with firearms as New York. And in no state are there the problems that New York police and politicians imagine would result from firearms in the hands of honest citizens.

And here is the late Dick Cornish of the New York *Daily News:*

Every year, sportsmen have to fight gun legislation that gets crazier and crazier, the only result of which can benefit criminals who don't give a hang for the law in the first place. The Sullivan Law, I am sure, has never deterred a single stick-up man.

Manifesting concern for the coffers of conservationists is Arthur Sullivan of the Boston *Record-American.* In a column of January 12, 1965 beginning, "It is law-making time in the state and in the nation," and noting the great increase in proposed gun laws in the nearby hunting state of Maine, Sullivan asked: "Can Maine, for instance, that sees thousands of dollars poured into its coffers by the hunter each year afford to start a restrictive gun law era? If it does, can its tourist trade in the outdoors survive? Remember most shooters are fishermen, too. They can lose patience, go elsewhere."

There is also a concern for the kiddies. "Boys and guns are compatible, and no amount of legislation will make them incompatible," wrote the New York *Journal American's* Ed Moore, quoting a past president of the Southern New York Fish and Game Association.

"Go ahead and take away our Daisies, make our kids really gun-dumb. Reds should love the idea," said Dick Cornish of the New York *Daily News.* And tugging at the heart strings was the New Haven *Register's* outdoor man, Bob Bolton, in a column beginning, " 'They're not going to ban BB guns before Christmas, are they?' my son asked in a whimpering voice tonight."

The last-mentioned complaint was voiced shortly after the assassination of President Kennedy. The wave of firearms legislation at the time brought other columnists to the aid of the outdoor writers. Said Scripps-Howard syndicated columnist Richard Starnes in a brief headed "A Kind Word for Guns": "All that can be accomplished by the wave of anti-gun hysteria that is now being fanned by poorly informed organs of opinion is to hand some chinless bureaucrat another means of depriving 20 million American hunters and/or target shooters of a portion of their liberty."

Also heard from was the late Robert Ruark: "Before we go entirely hysterical about guns, because Mr. Kennedy was shot by one, let us calm down and consider that some of the most effective weapons ever made were produced by the scientifically ignorant people of Kenya, called Mau Mau, who constructed them from door bolts and strips of rubber tire to provide the action." Ruark's column went on to say, "The knowledge of guns and the handling of guns is basically a good thing for a kid to grow up with."

At least one outdoor column is devoted entirely to the subject of legislation. Sam Maxwell of Edmonds, Washington, turns out a weekly feature called "Pro Gun Corner" for Seattle's *Fishing & Hunting News* and for newspapers in seven Northwestern states. Maxwell, whose affiliations include life membership in the National Rifle Association, the National Shooting Sports Foundation and the Wildlife Committee of Washington, once sent me a sheaf of his columns and a note which explained, "The prime purpose of the column is to keep gun owners up to date and informed on activity of the anti-gun types. . . ." Maxwell added that reader response indicated "very favorable acceptance of the column." *

Of the general sporting or outdoor magazines, the largest and most influential are *Field & Stream, Outdoor Life* and *Sports Afield*, each with circulations of about 1,300,000. All are slickly edited, eminently respectable magazines of long standing that serve up their readers about equal doses of hunting and fishing fare. They also manage to get in their anti-gun legislative licks now and then. This is not surprising, since each nets about $500,000 a year from arms and ammunition advertising, such advertising accounting for about one-sixth of their total advertising income.

Perhaps the most prestigious of the three and having a sizeable advertising and slight circulation edge over its rivals is *Field & Stream*.† The magazine was taken over by the publishing firm of Holt, Rinehart and Winston, Inc., in 1950 and celebrated its seventieth anniversary in 1965. Its pages have featured an array of

---

* A typical response: "Our impression has been that these anti-gun people have a big preponderance of left-wing, liberal, or socialistic advocates."
† July 30, 1965 ABC circulation 1,333,116, compared to *Outdoor Life's* 1,330,063 and *Sports Afield's* 1,242,057.

writers ranging from Zane Grey to that contemporary old master, Ted Trueblood, whom *F & S* hails as "probably the most beloved of present-day outdoor writers." The magazine also relishes the phrase, "He is the *Field & Stream* type," used now and then to describe the prototype of the supposedly superior sort of outdoors man.

Back in 1940, the humorist Corey Ford, touched off by the death of his dog at the hands of a trigger-happy hunter, castigated the hunter in an uncharacteristically poignant piece which has become a classic of its kind. Among its concluding phrases were: "I hope that you will remember how she looked. I hope that the next time you raise a rifle to your shoulder you will see her over the sight, dragging herself toward you across the field, with blood running from her mouth and down her white chest. I hope you will see her eyes . . . whenever there is a flick in the bushes and you bring your rifle to your shoulder before you know what is there."

Without minimizing the tragedy of the author's loss, one cannot help wondering why comparable pieces about human beings killed by hunters never appear on the pages of the sporting and gun magazines. Ford, a long-time *Field & Stream* contributor, is also responsible for one of the magazine's most popular fictional features, a never-ending stream of stories about the Lower Forty, a mythical band of sportsmen who conduct their well-lubricated club meetings at the village store of one Uncle Perk. The running recital of club activities frequently involves the Lower Forty's feud with Deacon Godfrey, a hypocritical rascal who would ban hunting but who is not above killing trout with dynamite.

The magazine's never-ending war on those it considers anti-gun fanatics dates at least as far back as 1941, when an *F & S* cartoon depicted a heroic-looking Minuteman, rifle at the ready, bedeviled by a horde of sinister little monsters variously labeled "fifth columnists," "bureaucrats," "spies," "nuts," "anti-firearms propagandists," "ignorants" and so on. Lest any readers be in doubt as to the *F & S* credo, the following statement appeared in the April 1964 issue as a two-page spread, available upon request in parchment for framing. Under the usually abridged quotation from the Bill of Rights, it stated, among other things:

WE BELIEVE that no law which lacks either enforceability or public respect, or which is devised merely as a further extension of police authority or which would turn law-abiding citizens into either deliberate or unknowing violators, can be legally or morally justified. . . .

"Strict restrictive laws," once explained Clare Conley, *F & S* managing editor, "would encroach on gun collectors, sportsmen and just plain Americans who want their wives to be safe when they are home alone."

Outdoor Life, only three years younger than the venerable *Field & Stream,* is a product of the Popular Science Publishing Company and, according to Editor Bill Rae, also has a gun-law policy that "pretty well parallels that of the NRA." The magazine has published articles with such titles as "Gun Owners Should Switch to the Offensive," and, in one recent issue, a quiz feature, "What Do You Know about Gun Laws?" In the latter, one typical question reads, "Can a gun commit a crime by itself?," and you are supposed to answer "No," *Outdoor Life* explaining, "Guns can't commit crimes, only people can."

The seventy-eight-year-old *Sports Afield,* a Hearst publication, ventures into the realm of world affairs in pursuit of its anti-gun villains. In a polemic in the August 1963 issue entitled "Blueprint for Peace—A Threat to Gun Ownership?" Pete Brown, the magazine's arms editor, charged that the American government was "about to sell the Second Amendment for a doubtful peace." This threat, Brown said in presenting "the grim, hidden facts," loomed in the form of the proposed three-phase disarmament treaty, referred to as an "instrument for national suicide," that President Kennedy had presented to the General Assembly of the United Nations on September 25, 1961, just two days after Congress had approved the Disarmament Act establishing that sinister bureaucracy, the United States Arms Control and Disarmament Agency.

In addition to the outdoor magazines there are the strictly gun magazines. Altogether, there are about fifteen gun magazines with a *total* circulation of somewhat less than 1,500,000 copies a month. What the gun magazines may lack in numbers they make up in noise. Perhaps because of the fervor of their readers, collectively they are probably the most influential of any of the magazines in influencing the fate of firearms legislation.

The most potent voice and by far the leader in its field, accounting for about half of the combined circulation of all gun magazines, is the venerable *American Rifleman,* official monthly of the 700,000-member Nation Rifle Association. Most of the 749,000 print order (as of June 1965), nearly five times as large as that of *Guns & Ammo,* its nearest competitor, goes gratis to each NRA member; the rest are distributed through a selected number of sporting goods stores and gun shops. A veritable graybeard among gun magazines, the *Rifleman* dates its origin to 1885, having metamorphosed since then under a variety of auspices and names. When taken over by the NRA in 1916 it was known as *Arms and the Man,* becoming *The American Rifleman* in 1923.

Among its loud and lurid competitors, the relatively low-key and somber *American Rifleman* occupies a position similar to that of the august *New York Times* among its newspaper competitors. "You'll notice an absence of hoopla—no cover banners, no screeching or screaming, no howling, no scaring people," editor Walter Howe told a visitor. "We are rather straightforward. We have a broad variety of subject matter to cover, and I'm an absolute nut on accuracy. Some articles are checked by as many as eight different people. There is a lot of material put out in this field that doesn't meet that." Although Howe won't single out any of his competitors for criticism, the impression given is that he looks down on the blood-and-gore gun magazines and considers his an Olympus in a class by itself—which, in a sense, it is. "Our aim is to produce an accurate, definitive magazine," he says. "I have been accused of turning out a cold magazine," he says, "but that's exactly what I aim for. There are enough hot ones around. I try for a total lack of passion."

In addition to its frequent editorials and articles on legislation, the magazine has a regular feature called "What the Lawmakers Are Doing," a concise bill-by-bill summary of firearms proposals and legislative action at both the Federal and state levels. Otherwise, *The American Rifleman,* in spite of its name, now ranges far beyond the confines of just rifles or things American. Nonlegislative articles in a typical issue covered types of German pistol holsters, coaching a small-bore rifle team, woodchuck hunting, building a private shooting range and shotshell loading data. In this issue there were also the regular monthly features on court cases of consequence, famous firearms and a column, "The Armed Citizen," an account of episodes in which heroic citizens used firearms to kill or wound robbers, burglars and other criminals.

Just as mention of death is taboo in the *Christian Science Monitor,* there is a general avoidance of the term and subject, at least insofar as they apply to human beings, in *The American Rifleman* and other magazines catering to shooters. When I edited a men's magazine, I once had the idea of running an article on firearms accident prevention; the article was to mention the appalling number of deaths due to guns, and give some examples of the foolish ways in which they occur. My gun editor, however, disabused me of the notion of including the case histories and number of deaths.

"The gun and ammunitions manufacturers wouldn't like it," he said. "It might give some people the idea that shooting and guns are dangerous."

Even when referring to animals, the magazines often prefer to use such euphemisms as "harvest" and "take" for words like "kill" or "slaughter," just as many people prefer the term "pass away" to refer to the death of a person.

Most of the remaining major magazines in the gun field have come into being during only the last ten years and strongly resemble one another, even to name. They bear such titles as *Guns & Ammo, Guns and Hunting, Guns and Game, Gun World, Gunsport* and simply, *Guns.* There are also a *Shooting Times, Shooting Industry* and *Precision Shooting.* Most of these are not the sort of magazine you would want to display on your coffee table. With the exception of *The American Rifleman,* which does manage to maintain a certain dignity, the others tend to the sensational. The covers are often cluttered with colors, huge type, question marks (ARE HUNTERS AND SHOOTERS REALLY "PSYCHOTIC"?) and exclamation points (MEET THE PEOPLE WHO WANT TO TAKE AWAY YOUR GUN!; and WE MUST KILL MORE DEER!!!).

The cover illustrations are usually carcasses or heads of snarling beasts or closeups of various types of armament. One favorite version of the latter depicts the gun shown against a background of the Bill of Rights. *Shooting Times,* published in Peoria, used this cover theme (featuring a Colt revolver) for its November 1963 issue. By a remarkable stroke of timing, the big cover blurb of the issue, which was on sale at the time of the Kennedy assassination was: BIG GUN IN THE WHITE HOUSE. This wording, however, referred to Teddy Roosevelt, described by the magazine as "a real 'gun bug,' a man whose love of firearms was a true joy!" On the March 1964 cover of *Guns*, the Bill of Rights provided the background for a Sharps sporting rifle, a box of cartridges and, in large important-looking type, the blurb: A *PRO* GUN LAW NOW!

Inside, the magazines serve up much the same gamy fare, the bulk of their editorial content being devoted to hunting. The modern deerslayer can learn all he cares to know about how to stalk one, shoot one and skin and convert his trophy into an enduring, enjoyable article of interior decoration. "Hang Your MEMORIES on the Wall" read the title of a *Shooting Times* article blurbed, "Through the skills of taxidermy, the hunter can relive exciting experiences many times over." There are also occasional recipes and related hints, the now defunct *Guns Illustrated* advising: "A good dinner depends on the first fifteen minutes after the deer drops dead. There is absolutely nothing more detrimental to the flavor of the meat than delayed or improper gutting right on the spot of the kill."

Off the beaten track are articles on such subjects as "Crazy Coon Calls" (about a new way of luring raccoons out of the treetops) and "I weaned my boys on . . . ARMADILLO SHOOTING!" In the realm of child upbringing, there are also such articles as *Guns & Ammo's* "Teach 'Em Young—Teach 'Em Right," an accompanying illustration showing a three-year-old girl being introduced to a revolver.

However, no type of article is as likely to set up such sympathetic shock waves and roil the readership more than one lambasting laws aimed at curtailing the uninhibited traffic in guns, or invoking the Bill of Rights. Featured on the cover of the January 1964 *Guns* was the bold-faced blurb: THE SECOND AMENDMENT IS NOT ENOUGH! The September 1964 *Guns* cover called attention to an article, THE SULLIVAN LAW MUST GO! And *Guns & Ammo* magazine reminds readers monthly to SUPPORT *YOUR* RIGHT TO "KEEP AND BEAR ARMS."

Whether such hortatory advice is offered by selfless crusaders out to save our society or by commercial exploiters attuned to the times and out for a fast buck may perhaps best be gathered by taking a close look at some of the principal promoters of these patriotic philippics.

Guns & Ammo, which, with a circulation of about 170,000, ranks second only to *The American Rifleman*, is a publishing house stablemate of some eleven other magazines. The two largest, each with circulations of about 750,000, are *Hot Rod*, angled at youthful car enthusiasts, and *Teen*, which serves up a combination of entertainment gossip, fashion tips and advice to adolescent girls. The rest of the magazines are devoted either to automobiles or to such activities as surfing and skin diving.

All of these, along with *Guns & Ammo,* are brought out under the imprimatur of the Los Angeles–based Petersen Publications, a firm of 400 employees headquartered in a former automobile showroom on Hollywood Boulevard. The firm also publishes a flock of paperbacks and "one-shot" magazines on subjects ranging from cars and football to photography and jazz (one big success was a 35-cent number called *Bandstand Buddies*) and recently ventured into the hard-cover publication field with two gun books (one a $12.50 biography of Colonel Townsend Whelen, generally considered the dean of American riflemen). From all of these publishing activities, it derives an annual revenue of about $12 million. In addition, the company has extensive real estate holdings, a large investment stake in a California sports-car raceway, and has also placed a foot in the door of TV production.

The sole owner and builder of this empire is Robert E. Petersen, a thirty-nine-year-old former movie press agent whose life story reads like the fulfillment of the American dream. At age twenty, he was laboring at M-G-M as a junior publicist. Laid off with scores of others when TV began to hurt the movie business, Petersen next did publicity for a variety of enterprises ranging from Prince Sua and his Royal Samoan Dancers to midget-car racing and hot-rod shows. Possessed of sound commercial instincts, he sensed the need for a magazine catering to hot-rodders. With four hundred borrowed dollars, he and a former M-G-M colleague brought out the first edition of *Hot Rod* in January 1948. The magazine was an almost instant success, and was soon followed by a succession of other mechanistic monthlies: *Motor Trend, Car Craft, Rod & Custom* and so on. *Guns & Ammo* came along in 1958, born of Petersen's lifelong love for guns.

The magazine has been self-described as "written, edited and published by men who believe deeply and unshakably that personal weapons are essential to personal and political liberty," and is presumably aimed at people of similar mind. In any event, *Guns & Ammo* readers are apparently well armed, one survey showing a sampling to possess an average of 11.8 guns each.

As part of its campaign to help what it calls "the cause," *G & A* offers its readers lapel buttons ($1), embroidered emblems (also $1), and bumper stickers (10 cents), all emblazoned with the magazine's motto: SUPPORT YOUR RIGHT TO "KEEP AND BEAR ARMS." The items are also available together in a "promotion kit." T shirts at $2, with the motto imprinted, are also available from the magazine in both children's and adult sizes. The magazine proclaims the shirts as "real conversation starters on the vital issue confronting all gun-owning citizens and shooters!" At one time, the slogan was even available on stationery and envelope stickers.

One wonders what sort of people buy this sort of thing. Editor-publisher Thomas J. Siatos, a forty-one-year-old ex-Marine, acknowledged to a visitor that there probably are some extreme right-wingers among his readers. Not long after making this acknowledgment, he admitted to past membership in the John Birch Society, and said he still continued to support the society's precepts. Siatos also said that his political views, which he blandly describes as "on the conservative side," do not find their way into *Guns & Ammo.* "The kind of information we publish," he says, "is not directed at the extreme right wing." The magazine's firearms legislative policy, he says, "completely concurs" with that of the National Rifle Association.

What kind of information, then, does *G&A* publish? *G&A*'s editorial comment and articles on firearms legislation are usually confined to the magazine's "Keep and Bear Arms" Department. In addition to this, however, special features are also devoted to the subject, and the magazine's sentiments often spill over into other department columns. In the June 1964 issue, for example, the magazine's big-game hunting columnist, Elgin T. Gates, expounded on "anti-gun" legislation in the full page allotted to him. "Who would want to totally disarm all American citizens, including us honest hunters?" asked Gates. "The answer is very simple. The Communist criminal conspiracy. Nothing would suit them better than to see America disarm herself. We would then, as Lenin predicted, fall like a ripe fruit into their hands.

"Who is helping them towards achieving this end? Every politician who introduces an anti-gun bill is an unwitting dupe of the conspiracy. Eventually the only guns left in America may be in the hands of those who knock on your door at midnight."

Guns is the third biggest-selling gun magazine in the United States, with a claimed monthly circulation of about 150,000. It is published by a small but diversified firm in Skokie, Illinois, called Publishers' Development Corporation. The firm is the brainchild of George E. von Rosen, a late-fortyish entrepreneur who, after serving an apprenticeship as circulation manager of *Down Beat*, a Chicago-based jazz magazine, formed his own magazine distributing company and then decided to start publishing magazines as well. His current string of magazines includes *Modern Man* (185,000, newsstand), a monthly "adult" picture magazine interspersing run-of-the-mill nude spreads with features on such sports as auto racing and wrestling, *Modern Sunbathing,* a nudist picture monthly blurbed as presenting "The UNCENSORED *truth* about Nudism," *Figure Quarterly* and *Sunbathing Annual.*

An avid hunter and gun collector, von Rosen started *Guns* in 1955 and, several years later, *Shooting Industry* and *Guns Annual.** To edit these publications, he brought in E. B. "Bev" Mann, a Western novelist and long-time veteran of the firearms field (he was a former managing editor of *The American Rifleman*). One of *Guns'* current contributors, and once listed as its technical editor, is William B. Edwards, who makes no secret of the fact that he is a recruiter for the Minutemen. Edwards, widely known in the gun industry for his fund of technical and historical knowledge, is the proprietor of a San Francisco gun shop where a sign on display says, REGISTER COMMUNISTS—NOT FIREARMS. In his shop Edwards hands out leaflets which urge, JOIN THE MINUTEMEN. Printed at Minutemen headquarters at Norborne, Missouri, the leaflet states that one of the goals of the Minutemen is "to form in advance of actual need a secret underground organization equipped to spy upon, harass and destroy troops of any foreign power that might occupy United States territory." Another stated goal is "to investigate, by means of our own secret membership, the possible infiltration of Communist sympathizers into American organizations of government, business, labor, religion and education."

Apparently there is much to investigate, according to a declaration on the back of the leaflet: "It has been authoritatively estimated that the Communists now have an army of 500,000 combatants al-

* Another recent company publication is the book *The World of Guns,* heralded as "A complete arsenal of Pro-gun information."

ready landed on American shores and already working by the most insidious means to destroy our American way of life."

Guns Editor E. B. Mann, like his other gun magazine counterparts, professes concern over the possibility that irresponsible people sometimes get guns through the mail in response to the ads in his magazine. "We're perhaps more sensitive to and more infuriated by the possession of guns in the wrong hands than anybody else, because we're hurt by it more than anybody else," says Mann. Yet, while saying that he is for "anything that would keep guns out of criminal hands and unsupervised juvenile hands," he has consistently opposed all legislation aimed at accomplishing this. He suggests instead that the solution lies in intimidating potential armed wrongdoers with the threat of more severe penalties, rather than in preventing their getting a gun in the first place. Mann, who says that he takes "pretty much the same position as the NRA," of which he is a life member, has long felt that even the laws now on the books are too strict.

As a gimmick to boost circulation, *Guns,* in 1962, organized the Shooters Club of America; with every new subscription to the magazine went a free membership in the club. Today, club membership is no longer tied to subscription, although the magazine continues to sponsor the club and promote it in its pages. Coupons in each issue solicit memberships from those who want to support their "constitutional right to own and *enjoy* firearms" (emphasis added). For $3 a year, members—there are now about 13,000—receive, among other things, a decal for their cars, a brassard for their hunting or shooting jackets, a quarterly newsletter (in an envelope marked IMPORTANT!) warning of objectionable proposed legislation, and, suitable for framing, a color illustration of the gun that killed Lincoln.

Speaking for the industry, in addition to the magazines mentioned, is the *Sporting Goods Dealer.* This monthly, published in St. Louis, is often caught on the horns of a delicate dilemma because of the diversity of interest among dealers. Those doing an over-the-counter business naturally favor tighter restrictions, if not the prohibition, of mail-order gun sales, particularly those involving cheap, imported arms. Understandably, those dealing only in guns would also not be unhappy if sales were taken away from discount houses and department stores. The *Dealer,* in trying to steer a middle course, editorializes weakly as it did in December 1963:

Most suggested laws are based on the erroneous theory that legislation restricting the rights of law-abiding citizens to own guns will stop crime. This ignores the basic fact that criminals seldom get guns through legitimate channels and that they could hardly be expected to register them in any case.

About ninety leading manufacturers, dealers, distributors, magazines, organizations, and individuals having some financial stake in the health of shooting sports are joined in the National Shooting Sports Foundation. Organized in 1961, the NSSF is a collective public relations and promotion arm for the industry. Member manufacturers, whose dues are scaled to their gross annual volumes, include such prestigious names as Remington, du Pont, Winchester, Colt, Browning, Smith & Wesson, and Hercules Powder. Other NSSF members range from Abercrombie & Fitch, *Field & Stream,* and the National Wildlife Federation to *Guns* magazine, *Sporting Goods Dealer,* and Klein's Sporting Goods, Inc., the Chicago mail-order firm which numbered Lee Harvey Oswald among its customers.

Another industry group is the Sporting Arms and Ammunition Manufacturers' Institute, known as SAAMI, a trade association of leading U.S. makers of sporting firearms and ammunition. Founded in 1920, the Institute now has nine members: du Pont, Federal Cartridge, Hercules Powder, High Standard, Ithaca Gun, O. F. Mossberg, Remington Arms, Savage Arms, and the Winchester-Western Division of Olin Mathieson. A promotional program of the institute conducted by its Sportsmen's Service Bureau was incorporated together with the bureau itself into the National Shooting Sports Foundation in January 1963.

The foundation was created to promote shooting sports in this country. The NSSF constitution defines its purpose: " . . . to foster in the American public a better understanding and a more active appreciation of all shooting sports . . ." One of the vexing and persistent problems the foundation faces in working toward this goal is how to eliminate the impression so many people have that guns are rather dangerous. To help overcome this obstacle to firearms sales, the foundation spent more than $200,000 on public relations and advertising in 1963. Part of the money paid for a one-minute "public service" spot announcement distributed to 572 TV stations.

Accordingly, that fall, television viewers could see Dan Cartwright, the white-haired patriarch of *Bonanza*, draw his six-shooter and say: "On our show we act with guns every week—real guns.* But we always handle them with respect." Then two other *Bonanza* cast members were seen giving a brief demonstration of proper gun handling. To impress upon the public the importance of the industry, the foundation grinds out press releases such as one beginning: "The United States sportsman-hunter feeds more than $1 billion into the nation's economy annually, aside from what he pays for sporting firearms and ammunition."

The foundation also does considerable lobbying. In fact, this was the reason actually behind its creation. It was conceived on June 8, 1960, at a New York seminar on "antifirearms legislation" moderated by Frank Daniel, secretary of the National Rifle Association. An informal proposal was made to start a national organization to oppose legislation restricting or regulating the use of sporting firearms. The seminar was part of an all-day national conference on shooting sports at New York's Waldorf-Astoria Hotel under the sponsorship of *Field & Stream* magazine, and was attended by firearms trade people, outdoor writers, conservationists and educators. The idea for the new organization was advanced by Warren Page, *Field & Stream*'s shooting editor, and head of a committee formed a year before to investigate methods to promote shooting and defeat gun control legislation.

At the seminar, *The New York Times* reported, the conferees agreed that some central agency was needed "to coordinate these efforts of many public and industrial groups that already monitor vigilantly a yearly torrent of bills in Congress, legislatures and city councils aimed at the regulation of firearms."

The committee was asked to report back to members of the conference at a later date. The following year the nearly 100 participants in *Field & Stream*'s Second National Conference on the Shooting Sports, held in New York City on May 25, 1961, pledged over $10,000 in start-up funds for the establishment of a National Shooting Sports Foundation. It was incorporated in October of that year.

Elected as president of the NSSF and to a seat on its Board of

---

* A related, amusing story: Some years ago, in California, a dope addict was caught with seventeen guns—real guns. They had been stolen from the set of the television program, *The Untouchables*.

Governors was Fred A. Roff, Jr., then president of Colt's Patent Fire Arms Manufacturing Co. The NSSF got off to a shaky start when some major manufacturers, such as Remington, du Pont, Smith & Wesson and Hercules Powder, unable to resolve certain differences, decided to stay out. Soon afterward, however, they all joined the fold.

The fledgling foundation was soon hailed throughout the industry. *Shooting Times,* after an interview with then Executive Director A. Robert Matt, reported to its readers in February 1962 that they would benefit through the NSSF program "to educate the American public—to get across the *facts* about guns and shooting, and counter the Red-inspired propaganda 'scare' articles such as appeared recently in two women's magazines."

Today, the NSSF, after several shifts of operational base and directors, is headquartered in Riverside, Connecticut. Charley Dickey, a veteran firearms man, heads the staff of seven. Before becoming NSSF director, Dickey, a moon-faced, cigar-smoking Tennessean in his forties, was for eight years the Southeastern field man of the Sportsmen's Service Bureau, and before that was with Winchester.

"I certainly believe in the Constitution," Dickey assured me in his office. "I believe it's the greatest document of human freedom ever written. Nothing can touch it. If we don't like it, we can change it, amend it. But those fellers in Washington . . ."

To win friends and influence people in Washington, one NSSF ad, which ran in most outdoor and gun magazines, used a big illustration of a pair of hunting boots. Under it was the heading, "Put a Senator in Your Shoes." The copy continued:

Or State Legislator or Local Councilman.

If he has never been hunting, or shot skeet or trap, or tested his skill on a target range, you can hardly count on his support when firearms control bills come up.

So why don't you invite him out shooting?
Show him a good time, get him interested.

Talk to him—as only you can—about fine guns, and about shooting as a family sport.

Try it. Lawmakers who know the feel of the field can become great marksmen. Good enough to shoot holes in the anti-firearms argument.

Other NSSF ads have such themes as, "The hand that rocks the cradle" (an inducement to get Mom to take up shooting), and "A *Man* in the making" (indoctrinating Junior). The ads at the bottom bear the legend: "Carry your firearm proudly. It is part of your great American heritage—a symbol of freedom."

Perhaps because of such lofty, advertised sentiments about freedom, the NSSF is often free with facts in the publicity it circulates. In December 1964, *Harper's* magazine published an article of mine which described in detail how all the bills introduced in Congress shortly after the Kennedy assassination had been shot down by the NRA and other elements of the gun lobby. My work on the article had been subsidized, in part, by a grant from the Society of Magazine Writers, the leading professional organization of free-lance nonfiction writers. The society, in order to encourage articles it feels to be of public interest, has a program by which writers can qualify for grants to prepare articles of this sort. The reason for the grants is that the preparation of such articles quite often requires a degree of research, time and monetary expenses far beyond the budgetary capabilities of the magazine most likely to publish them —limited circulation, though influential, magazines like *Harper's,* for example. Contingent on the grant, which is to supplement the magazine's normal fee, is an expression of interest or an assignment from some magazine, which in my case came from *Harper's.*

With the publication of the article, the NSSF rushed out a memo, presumably to its entire press list, for the foundation's comment on the *Harper's* article soon began popping up all over the country. The NSSF did not challenge the accuracy of my article. Neither did the NRA or others named in the article. Instead, the NSSF, on the basis of an "investigation," questioned my eligibility for the grant, and claimed that it was supposed to go only to writers *without* assignments. Moreover, the NSSF said that the society was "upset" by the article's contents. Of course, neither statement was true.

Could the NSSF simply have been careless with the facts and made an honest error? The society and I wrote to the NSSF, to *Guns* magazine, and to others to point out their errors and ask them to correct the misstatements. None of our letters was ever answered.

On another occasion in April 1965, the foundation circulated a memo irresponsibly describing the modest budget of Senator Thomas J. Dodd's Juvenile Delinquency Subcommittee as a kind of slush fund for an anti-gun propaganda campaign run by Carl Perian, described disparagingly as "a sociologist." Perian, a member of the subcommittee staff for eleven years, is a recognized criminologist.

The NSSF, with its big budget, is certainly qualified to speak about propaganda campaigns. Charley Dickey in a subsequent appearance before the Dodd Committee confessed that the NSSF had footed the bills for TV actors to come to Washington to work against pending firearms control legislation. He also conceded that the NSSF had circulated misleading statements about firearms proposals then pending in Congress.

Although the gun groups have a lurking fear of the police, feeling that law enforcement officers generally view the possession of private firearms with a jaundiced eye, the lobby strains to invoke *some* seemingly competent authority to state that guns don't cause crime. Anointed some years ago for this purpose was an organization called the National Police Officers Association of America. It is easy to understand why. Back in 1959 or 1960, the organization, through its then president and current executive director Frank J. Schira, issued a statement of its position on firearms control. After giving the matter "considerable thought," Schira said, "We feel that an American citizen of voting age and of good character should have the right to purchase without restriction a handgun, pistol, revolver, rifle, shotgun or a like item without interference by a government body." In what would seem to be an unflattering reference to his police colleagues, Schira also said that "to place the purchase of firearms in one official would give cause in some cases to abuse."

In 1962, the year-old National Shooting Sports Foundation, casting about for an "objective" yet authoritative-sounding police partner, sat down in Chicago with the National Police Officers Association of America. The two groups, with the behind-the-scenes help of the National Rifle Association, drafted a joint resolution. The resolution, since then reprinted in gun and outdoor magazines, presented solemnly before congressional committees and cited endlessly in speeches and statements, reiterated the earlier NPOAA statement that any citizen of voting age (even the earlier proviso specifying "good character" was now missing) should be allowed free access to handguns, unhampered by any red tape whatsoever. The resolution, among other things, also stated that "restrictive anti-gun laws have never been, and never will be, a successful deterrent to crime, organized or otherwise, and . . . do not succeed in disarming the criminal, but do disarm the law-abiding citizen. . . ."

It matters little to the lobby that the NPOAA has little, if any, standing among criminologists or members of the law enforcement community. No police officer of any repute belongs to the group, but few people know this. In fact, few of the police officers I once queried in various parts of the country had ever heard of it.

Actually, the NPOAA is a small, fraternal-type, insurance benefit organization set up in 1955 by Schira, who is a sixteen-year veteran of the Chicago Police Department, and at present a detective in its Homicide and Sex Unit. Now listed as president of the organization, which claims a membership of 11,000 police officers (out of the 360,000 in the United States), is Donald Snyder, a patrolman from Braintree, Massachusetts. Among the national vice presidents are chiefs and assistant chiefs from such places as Sleepy Hollow, Illinois; Sheboygan, Wisconsin; and Clinton, North Carolina. By contrast, the International Association of Chiefs of Police, with a membership of 5,500 police commissioners and high-ranking staff officers, has as its current president Atlanta Police Chief Herbert T. Jenkins and, among its vice presidents, the police commissioners of New York, San Francisco and St. Louis.

The NPOAA has since 1962 been headquartered in Venice, Florida, where with a staff of five (compared with the IACP's staff of sixty) it is housed in and operates the "National Police Museum and Hall of Fame," a tourist attraction "dedicated to officers killed in the line of duty" and having on display such things as the artifacts of John Dillinger, specimens of counterfeit money, lie detectors and leg irons, machine guns and billy clubs, police uniforms from the world over and an electric chair in which you can sit and have your picture taken. The site of this house of horrors was donated by a public-spirited land development corporation interested in inducing police officers to eventually settle in retirement homes in the community.

Also housed in the National Police Museum Hall of Fame building and said to be the creation of the NPOAA is an organization called the International Association of Auxiliary Police. The IAAP runs coupon ads headed: "You Can Help Stop Crime!" in magazines

like *True Detective Story* and *Guns & Ammo*, soliciting memberships
(at $5 a year) from civilians who want to "join other interested citi-
zens to aid professional police to stop crime." Benefits include an
"official" membership card, a car emblem which "assures you of
quick recognition by law enforcement officers," and a subscription to
Valor, the NPOAA's bi-monthly.

Because of the vague credentials offered by advertising solicitors
for *Valor* and other NPOAA publications, the two organizations
have attracted the attention of, among others, the Attorney General
of Ohio, who issued a warning about the organizations in a "Con-
sumer Fraud and Crime" Bulletin dated May 1964. The Better Business Bureau of Greater Miami also carried the following item in its
March 1965 News Bulletin:

NATIONAL POLICE OFFICERS ASSOCIATION, Venice, Florida:

A telephone promotion is now being carried on for the sale of advertising in the "Annual Program." The professional telephone promoters
who are calling business people for ads are notably vague about what
police organization they are representing. Some business people who
have called the Bureau thought it was the Miami Police Department, and
some thought it was the Sheriff's Office. The Bureau has contacted the
Dade County Sheriff's Department and several City Police Departments
in Dade County and have not found any local police who are members
of this organization and have found that local police have very little
knowledge of the activities of this organization. Information furnished
to the Bureau by the National Police Officers Association has been somewhat vague as to the value of the organization to police officers and the
value of advertising to local businesses.

Attending the 1965 annual convention of the NPOAA at a New
York midtown motel, I also found the officers of the group vague
and evasive.

"Can you give me the names of some of the best-known police
officers in your group?" I asked Executive Director Schira.

"We are all equal," he replied. "If I gave you some names, it
would be unfair to the others—like Joe there" (he pointed to a shirt-
sleeved cop across the room).

"Well, what about yourself? Can you tell me something more
about your background in law enforcement?"

"You can read about me in our directory."

"Where can I see a copy?" (The public library didn't have any).

"We'll sell you one."

"What do you think about the Sullivan Law?"

"What Sullivan Law?" asked Schira, looking at me blankly and then up at the ceiling.

"The handgun law here in New York. Do you think other states should have such a law?"

"As a national organization, we don't comment on local laws."

"Do the police officers in your organization really feel that *every* citizen should be allowed to buy and have a handgun for self-defense?" (Virtually every recognized police authority to whom I have spoken discourages this practice.)

"Read our resolution."

"How did you happen to write it?"

"The National Shooting Sports Foundation people contacted us and we prepared it together with the help of the NRA," Schira said.

It is evident that the elements of the gun lobby are closely inter-related. Frank Schira is listed as a member of the "editorial advisory board" of *Guns*. E. B. Mann, editor of *Guns,* to give some further examples, sits on the Board of Governors of the National Shooting Sports Foundation. Corporate members of the Foundation like Winchester, mail out reprints of an editorial entitled "Assassination—by Hatred," asserting that President Kennedy's death "was not basically caused by a bullet." Every important manufacturer and large dealer has at least one key executive in the NRA. Also within its ranks as a life member is Robert de Pugh, national leader of the Minutemen. It may seem an anomaly only to those outside the firearms fold that Harry L. Hampton, Jr., serves as secretary of the Sporting Arms and Ammunition Manufacturers' Institute, while serving in another executive capacity at the Wildlife Management Institute, a creation of the arms industry.

The gun lobby leaders cannot understand why they are so cruelly misunderstood, why their public relations and propaganda, though effective in legislatures, fail to win them friends from among the public at large. They wonder why this should be, and why the communications media do not so readily accept the facts they so freely offer to support their views. Even an attempt at a balanced presentation of the pros and cons of firearms controls is evidence that they are being persecuted. In their view, there is only one side to the story.

On the phone with the NSSF's Charley Dickey, I was discussing the one-hour CBS-TV program *Murder and the Right to Bear Arms*, just after it was shown on June 10, 1964. I thought that both sides of the story had been represented with about equal time and fairness, and I told Dickey so.

"You thought that was fifty-fifty?" he said from his base in Riverside, Connecticut. "I thought it was more near eighty-twenty. Why, they hit the damn roof in Washington! You could hear them screaming all the way up here!"

He was referring to the officials of the National Rifle Association, the spearhead of the gun lobby.

7 The NRA:
Vigilante on the Potomac

I think strong laws should be passed restricting the sale of guns, but when you try, you run head-on into collision with the National Rifle Association.
—J. Edgar Hoover, quoted at a press conference by
The New York Times, November 19, 1964

Hardly known to the public at large, and seldom found on any list of those who labor on behalf of a special interest in Washington, is the leader of the firearms faction—the National Rifle Association. The NRA is a nonprofit, private organization of more than 700,000 gun owners. Its income for 1964 was nearly $4,500,000. Its command post, an imposing modern structure on Scott Circle, has office space for a staff numbering about 250, and houses a museum of over 700 firearms and a 10-point range. Though not even registered as an organization that carries on lobbying activities, the NRA ranks high among the big lobbies of the Capitol, functioning with an efficiency and speed that few others can match. A standard boast of NRA officials is that they can flood Congress with more than 500,000 pieces of mail virtually overnight in opposition to any proposed gun legislation. To do this the NRA can not only invoke the support of its 700,000 registered members, but can also mobilize another 400,000 followers in some 12,000 NRA-affiliated gun clubs and other groups whose many interests "touch common ground in an affection for guns and shooting and in love of country," as the NRA official monthly, *The American Rifleman*, once put it. More than any other
128

organization, the NRA, encrusted with respectability and shining with true-blue patriotism, has been the unwavering Galahad of the gun crusade.

Its zeal in the cause spans nearly half of its ninety-five-year history. The NRA's unparalleled success is indicated by the fact that no Federal firearms laws whatever have been enacted in nearly three decades. And there have been only two major ones in our entire history, both measures rendered almost worthless by emasculation at the hands of the NRA. With few exceptions, hardly any of the 1,000 Federal, state or local gun laws that are proposed annually ever emerge from committees. In short, our firearm laws in most areas of the country are scarcely more stringent than they were in the frontier days. No other lobby can claim such a record in its particular sphere of interest.

Although the million or so NRA members and followers represent but a fraction of the nation's estimated 30 million or more gun owners, they make up in fervor what they lack in number. Applicants for membership must be citizens of "good repute," must be endorsed by a member in good standing, a public official or a member of the U.S. Armed Forces, and must sign a loyalty oath which, among other things, calls for the fulfillment of the "obligations of good sportsmanship and good citizenship." The NRA's 700,000 registered individual members pay dues of at least $5 a year ("life" members pay one-time dues of $100).

For their dues members receive such benefits and services as a subscription to *The American Rifleman,* a gold-filled lapel emblem and auto decal, free answers by mail to their personal gun and shooting inquiries, advice and reports on guns and shooting equipment, the privilege of buying surplus U.S. Army guns at cut-rate prices, a chance to win marksmanship qualification and hunting awards, information on where to hunt and what to hunt with, discounts on books of interest to the gun enthusiast, low-cost gun and personal accident insurance, and the camaraderie of their fellow members. The NRA, in its own words, "represents and promotes the best interest of gun owners and shooter-sportsmen, and supports their belief in the ideals of the United States of America and its way of life." Accordingly, a brochure soliciting prospective members promises "prompt notification of any attempt to limit your right to buy, own, use or sell guns."

Actually, lobbying was far removed from the NRA's original purpose and program of activity. The organization was formed in 1871 by a small group of New York National Guard officers "to promote and encourage rifle shooting on a scientific basis." The officers, the Civil War still fresh in their memories, were worried about the low state of American marksmanship. "In that conflict the shooting on both sides was terrible," says a history of Remington Arms. "Northern statisticians figured that the Grand Army of the Republic had 999 misses for every hit, and the Confederates were only a shade better." The *Army-Navy Journal*, in an 1871 issue, urged the formation of an association, editorializing: "The National Guard is today too slow in getting about this reform. Private enterprise must take up the matter and push it into life. We would suggest that a meeting of those favorable to such a project be called."

Chartered that year as a nonprofit organization, the group lost no time in displaying its considerable political potential. "Before the New York State legislature had adjourned its 1871 session," recounts an NRA history, "it had passed a bill authorizing the infant association to purchase a range site, construct and operate a range. The state would appropriate $25,000 if the National Rifle Association contributed not less than $5,000. The cities of New York and Brooklyn also were authorized to contribute $5,000 each."

Three decades later, the marksmanship of our citizenry was apparently still wanting. Rankled by the lack of shooting ability displayed by our citizen-soldiers during the Spanish-American War, and recognizing the possible value of civilian marksmanship training, the Army in 1903 established a National Board for the Promotion of Rifle Practice. Together with the NRA, the National Board organized a civilian training program and conducted shooting competitions.

As the years went by, the NRA moved its headquarters to the nation's capital (in 1908), and developed into a sportsmen's organization. Preoccupied at first with the promotion of military-type rifle practice, the NRA did not pay much attention to pistol men until the 1920s. Since handguns are of scant military significance, the NRA, in 1925, established a Police Division to assume the leadership in this field of marksmanship, and to conduct missionary work among law enforcement officers. Soon police pistol teams sprouted everywhere, and their activities led civilians to follow suit. Reporting at one point on the phenomenon of civilians and policemen shooting side by side on municipal ranges, the NRA said: "The cleanliness of pistol and revolver shooting appeals to business and professional men and to women. The speed with which it moves appeals generally to the American character."

In the 1920s the NRA set its sights on the junior shooter. The NRA junior program was started in 1925 when the NRA took over the Winchester Junior Rifle Corps, a company promotion program which had bogged down because of its commercial affiliation. Although suspicion as to the motives behind the program continued to persist for years, by 1931 there were 800 NRA junior rifle clubs with 38,788 qualified junior shooters.

By the 1930s, NRA membership had risen to a total of about 50,000, and it remained at that figure through most of World War II. With demobilization, membership zoomed rapidly, climbing to about a quarter of a million by 1947. It fluctuated around that figure until 1957, then crossed the 300,000 mark. Since 1957, the NRA membership has more than doubled to its present 700,000, thanks largely to an intensive membership drive initiated as part of a "Build NRA" campaign in 1960. The initial goal of 500,000 members was reached in 1962, and the NRA, in its own words, is now "shooting for a million" by 1971, its 100th anniversary year. Today the membership consists of all types of gun enthusiasts: hunters and plinkers, target shooters and tinkerers, gunsmiths and ballisticians, collectors and armchair gun enthusiasts and others fascinated by firearms for some reason. In addition to children, women of all ages are enrolled, even though they would seem to be unlikely candidates for eventual military service and therefore hardly in serious need of marksmanship training.

Obviously, a membership so broad in character has brought with it a need to restate the organization's original objects and purposes, which, in the official words of the NRA, have been expanded to embrace the following aims:

To promote social welfare and public safety, law and order, and the national defense; to educate and train citizens of good repute in the safe and efficient handling of small arms and in the technique of design, production, and group instruction; to increase the knowledge of small arms and promote efficiency in the use of such arms on the part of members of law enforcement agencies, of the Armed Forces, and of citizens who would be subject to service in the event of war; and generally to encourage the lawful ownership and use of small arms by citizens of good repute.

In the pursuit of these purposes, the NRA is involved in a welter of activities, ranging from programs in marksmanship and firearms safety to the sponsorship and sanctioning of thousands of shooting tournaments every year. As the governing body of U.S. competitive rifle and pistol shooting, the NRA, in cooperation with the National Board for the Promotion of Rifle Practice, sponsors the big annual event, the National Matches, held over a three-week period in late summer at Camp Perry, near Toledo, Ohio. There, in about 100 different events, some 7,000 of the nation's finest shooters, both soldiers and civilians, converge to compete for national honors. To the winners of the matches go handsome trophies, gold, silver and bronze medals, guns and shooting equipment, colorful brassards, and, to the winner of the most important service rifle match, a congratulatory message from the President of the United States.

The NRA selects the rifle and pistol teams to represent the United States in the Olympic Games, the Pan American Games and the other international competitions sanctioned by the International Shooting Union, the governing body for the world sport. Appropriately, the NRA's executive vice-president is a member of the executive committee of both the International Shooting Union and the U.S. Olympic Committee. Among other things, the NRA establishes the rules for organized shooting, maintains tournament records, classifies competing shooters, designates national champions and is the certifying agency for the nation's tournament referees and firearms safety and marksmanship instructors.

At the heart of the NRA training program are now more than 86,000 volunteer certified instructors. "It is through the unselfish devotion of these dedicated members that much of the work of spreading the influence of the NRA is accomplished," says the organization in its annual reports. Since 1950 about 2½ million novice hunters, mostly teenagers, have successfully completed the NRA hunter safety course. Marksmanship training, the NRA's primary reason for being, has continued unabated over the years with a high priority on the program. Since 1925, the organization has issued nearly 6,500,-

000 awards for shooting skills demonstrated in its marksmanship qualification courses.

Although the NRA does not list lobbying among its official purposes, the organization says it "stands squarely on the premise that the ownership of firearms must not be denied American citizens of good repute so long as they use them for lawful purposes." It also states that "the strength of the NRA, and therefore the ability to accomplish its objects and purposes, depends entirely upon the support of loyal Americans who believe in the right to keep and bear arms." Accordingly, as the self-appointed, if unofficial, "guardian and bulwark against the forces of anti-gun sentiment in the United States," the NRA has long devoted a good part of its time and effort to lobbying against virtually all legislation that would in any way restrict in the slightest the sale and use of firearms.

What sort of laws would be so restrictive? The NRA's current views are set forth in a "statement of policy," a manifesto issued in—of all places!—Dallas, back in 1958, and reaffirmed without a word of change immediately after the Kennedy assassination. As a reading of the statement of policy indicates,* it is plain that the NRA abhors and suspects any enforceable preventive laws; the only ones it countenances are those providing postfactum penalties for the "misuse" of firearms—in other words, laws taking effect after the damage is already done. "There is no 'pro-gun' law," NRA Secretary Frank Daniel told an NRA annual convention, "which by some legerdemain or sleight of hand can remove you, full time, from the necessity as private citizens of protecting rights guaranteed to you under the Constitution."

Yet the NRA is clearly aware that these vaunted "rights" are limited. As one of its information folders concedes: "There can be no doubt that the states, under their broad 'police power,' can enact legislation controlling the possession and use of firearms by private citizens. Such controls are not necessarily unconstitutional, and many existing firearms laws have been repeatedly upheld by the courts."

As the NRA sounds the call "to keep and bear arms," it invokes the memory of the self-armed Minutemen of Lexington and Concord. It maintains that a similar armed citizenry is still necessary, even in this nuclear age—and in spite of our modern armed forces,

---

* Its full text is in Appendix V.

National Guard and local police—to protect the country from peril. Indeed, living as it does in the past, the NRA likes to characterize itself as a "Paul Revere organizaton," eternally vigilant against constitutional and other encroachments from enemies without and within.

To this end, a widely distributed NRA folder urges readers to "watch for firearms control proposals that may appear in Congress or your state legislature, in your community, city or town," and to oppose them "by letter, telegram or telephone call to your elected representatives or by your appearance at open hearings."

From NRA headquarters emanate similar warnings regularly in the *Rifleman* and, in the case of proposed legislation demanding special attention, through special legislative bulletins mailed directly to members and clubs. A flow of folders with such titles as "The Gun Law Problem" and "The Pro and Con of Firearms Registration" offers an arsenal of arguments with which to convince the unknowing.

The rationale behind the propaganda strategy was graphically described in a December 1948 *Rifleman* report, which pictured members not merely standing as sentries, but also working as "doctors" in fulfillment of their membership obligations. Referring to the gun ignorance of the public as a "disease," the *Rifleman* said:

The real job before us is education of the public to cure their ignorance regarding firearms and the men who use them. This educational job is not one which can properly be done by NRA headquarters people working alone. Special articles, features, radio broadcasts, letters to newspaper editors originating in Washington at NRA headquarters are viewed mostly as propaganda. Exactly the same arguments, when advanced by local citizens, are listened to with respect. The NRA headquarters can, and does, supply "medicine" in the form of a continuing array of arguments, facts and figures through *Rifleman* editorials and special bulletins to members of the Association. Each member must consider himself as a local "doctor" who is responsible for curing the disease of gun ignorance by administering this "medicine" in convenient doses to his neighbors, local politicians and newspaper editors.

The National Rifle Association is tightly controlled from the top. The governing body is a board of seventy-five directors, elected by the life members for three-year terms. In fact, the board is virtually self-perpetuating: Selection by a nominating committee is tantamount to election, and the committee's choices are for the most part present or past directors. The board meets once a year to determine policies, review NRA programs, fill board vacancies and, every two years, to elect a president and vice-president.

The power base, however, narrows down to a 20-member executive committee (selected by and from the directors) and to the president, whose duties include the appointment of the nominating committee members. There is also a fourteen-member executive council made up of NRA elders, but its function is only advisory.

The current president (until 1967) is Harlon B. Carter, fifty-two, Texas born and reared and now a resident of Garden Grove, California. Carter is a former physical education instructor, U.S. Border Patrolman and Chief, and the holder of three national marksmanship records and of several state championship titles, with both rifle and pistol. When not shooting or occupied with his NRA duties, Carter is southwest regional commissioner of the Immigration and Naturalization Service, whose parent body, the U.S. Department of Justice, is as much in favor of firearms control as Carter and the NRA are opposed to it.

The other key officials of the association are the NRA's three top salaried staff officers, who direct the staff of 250 at Washington headquarters:

Franklin L. Orth, a fifty-eight-year-old attorney, wartime colonel with Merrill's Marauders in Burma and a former Deputy Assistant Secretary of the Army, has been executive vice-president of the NRA since 1959. Together with the NRA president, Orth represents the organization in public, and the two usually speak for the NRA at congressional hearings.

Louis F. Lucas, fifty-four, a certified public accountant who joined the NRA staff in 1948, doubles as executive director and treasurer.

NRA Secretary Frank C. Daniel, Jr., fifty-two, holder of a degree in business administration and on the NRA staff since 1940, now also heads the organization's legislative and public affairs division.

All three are ex-officio members of the board, with voice but without voting privileges.

"If we are a lobby, everyone's a lobby," Lucas told me. "Actually, we don't put any more about firearms legislation into our magazines and bulletins than the newspapers do. We just bring all the information together as a service to our members."

To show me how this is done, Daniel led me on a tour of his legislative and public affairs division, which, according to the NRA's annual report, spent $157,388 in 1964 to support a staff of thirteen (double the spending figure and personnel of two years before) and, among other things, to produce the legislative bulletins to inform members about proposed anti-gun laws. (By comparison the American Medical Association budgeted $160,000 in 1964 to maintain its Washington lobby office with a staff of twenty-two.)

One of the NRA's top legislative experts and key propagandists is Jack Basil, a slim, swarthy man in his thirties, who holds a master's degree in political science from Georgetown University. Lining the walls of his office are books on law, criminology and weaponry, and adorning the walls and the tops of bookcases are memorabilia of his military service, which included a tour of duty as a major with the military government in Germany. On his desk the day I was there were two right-wing paperbacks: *Suicide of the West* by James Burnham, and *None Dare Call It Treason* by John A. Stormer. The Stormer work, which was bought by the millions by Goldwater backers during the 1964 campaign, is an extremist Birchite warning of an imminent Communist take-over, and, in a concluding chapter, makes a membership pitch on behalf of the John Birch Society.

I asked Basil if there were any subversives or extremists in the NRA. Not any more than in the government, he said, speaking with his characteristic, hearty self-assurance. One of the functions of the legislative and public affairs division, he said, was to serve Congress, formally and informally, as counselor, guide and information specialist on matters pertaining to firearms legislation.

To do this and keep their fingers on the pulse of propaganda offensive to NRA policy, Basil and his legal and public affairs colleagues receive an endless stream of news items, articles and comment about firearms legislation from a press clipping service, members and allied interests. Typical of the items routed to Basil is an October 20, 1964, column by Andrew Tully headed "Aim: Sensible Firearms Limit." In it the syndicated Washington writer, irked by the letters of the "Dear Sir, You Cur" type he had been receiving, had taken the occasion to reply: "I should like to say that I have never suggested that sporting guns be taken from the hands of the American public. I do not desire to repeal the Bill of Rights. I am not a Russian spy, either."

Attached to the Tully column was the following memo:

To Members SAAMI Accident and Crime Prevention Committee
    cc: Dickey, Orth, Daniel, Scott
For your info. This and earlier columns by Tully makes it rather clear that this columnist considers this topic as "crusade material."

                                                   hlh/10-22-64 *

Reports on state and local bills also come in regularly from NRA members and local "watchdog" committees. A teletype just outside Basil's office clacks out instant around-the-clock warnings of state bills the moment they are dropped into state legislative hoppers. Copies of the bills themselves come a few days later, together with the name of the committee to which each bill has been referred.

Bills reported to NRA headquarters are, after analysis, categorized as "good," "severe," "restrictive" or "undesirable"—presumably in order of increasing obnoxiousness (or, from the other point of view, desirability). Details and analyses of the more important bills are the subject of the legislative bulletins which are dispatched to individual members and club officers in the areas concerned.

During 1964 the NRA mailed twenty-six legislative bulletins to 141,000 members and clubs in eleven states. And when necessary, Basil said, the association doesn't hesitate to get on the phone or send wires. Somewhat impressed by the efficiency and thoroughness of this operation, I asked Basil, "Doesn't all this put you to a lot of trouble?"

Basil's answer was short and emphatic: "We don't run any nickel-and-dime operation here, you know."

Indeed it doesn't. The NRA's income and net assets (more than $8 million in 1964) have been enough to pay for a massive publicity campaign budgeted at about $100,000 annually, and utilizing every medium of communications. As part of this campaign, the NRA's two

---

* The initials "hlh" are those of Harry L. Hampton, secretary of SAAMI (the Sporting Arms and Ammunition Manufacturers' Institute); Dickey is Charles Dickey, executive director of the National Shooting Sports Foundation; Woodson Scott is an NRA director and head of its legislative committee.

outside consultants, James B. Deerin and John E. Horton * produced a motion picture entitled *To Keep and Bear Arms*, which features a Kentucky rifle that talks with the voice of television's Peter Gunn. "Men with their guns fought for freedom, won our struggle for independence, made it possible for our representatives to write some good rules for all of us in the Constitution," says the rifle. "Yep, they mentioned fellers like me, too, in the Bill of Rights." The campaign also includes NRA floats in the annual Tournament of Roses parades saying "The Bill of Rights—Freedom to Keep and Bear Arms." A recent float featured a printing press that actually produced copies of the Bill of Rights for distribution to spectators.

In 1963 a special weekly column on NRA activities and programs, under the heading "Target, Woods and Gun Room," was offered free to the nation's newspapers, and by the end of the following year was reportedly carried by nearly 500. That none of the newspapers in the nation's capital have ever carried it is a source of considerable frustration to the NRA. The columns range over such subjects as selecting a shotgun, how to hunt safely and kill game cleanly, and shooting in summer camps. (The latter begins: "A summer camp without a rifle range is like a Beatle without bangs.") In some columns, the NRA manages to work in an occasional blast at the evil of firearms legislation. In a typical year, 1964, the NRA also sent out a total of 48,600 copies of press releases and 4,582 photographs.

NRA propaganda is by no means confined to such publicity efforts. The NRA's editorial division in 1964 spent a total of $1,617,303, a major portion of this in connection with the publication and distribution of *The American Rifleman*. During the year, the *Rifleman* devoted a total of fifty-three pages to articles, features, and editorials on firearms legislation. Any reckoning of NRA lobbying expenditures must also take into account at least some portion of the executive staff budget ($392,672 in 1964), which, in addition to the salaries of the NRA's top officials, covers four field representatives, who, to promote the NRA's varied interests, are constantly on the go.

Among the many organizations with which the NRA maintains close ties are: the Boy Scouts of America, the National Education Association, the National Safety Council, the U.S. Olympic Commit-

* Horton is a son-in-law of former Secretary of the Treasury John W. Snyder (under Truman).

tee, the International Shooting Union, the American Legion, the Bureau of Outdoor Recreation, the Forest Service, the Izaak Walton League, the National Industrial Recreation Association, the International Association of Game, Fish and Conservation Commissioners; the National Guard Association; the National Park Service; the National Recreation Association; the National Wildlife Federation; the Public Health Service and the Reserve Officers Association.

Although considerable political leverage can be exerted from its Washington headquarters and those of its friends, the foundation of the NRA's lobbying strength, like that of the American Medical Association, also lies in its component parts—its 12,000 clubs and, particularly, its state associations, which are essentially miniature versions of their Washington parent organization. With the financial resources of the fifty state associations, plus one in the District of Columbia, the funds put to use by the NRA could well run into the tens of millions of dollars.

Why, indeed, is the NRA, with all the appurtenances and outward signs of a lobby, not registered as a lobbying group? The Federal Regulation of Lobbying Act of 1946 requires all groups attempting to influence the course of Federal legislation to register with the Secretary of the Senate and the Clerk of the House, and to file quarterly reports of its lobbying expenditures. The Lobbying Act, however, is filled with inadequacies. Senator William Proxmire has dismissed the law as "a farce." John F. Kennedy, when a Senator, once termed it "practically worthless."

Thanks to the escape hatches in the Act, the NRA claims it is not required to register as a lobby, because—allegedly—its function is not to influence legislation, but merely to "inform" or "educate" its members and the public.

One may also wonder how the NRA can take so active a part, directly or indirectly, in legislative and political battles and still maintain its status as a nonprofit, tax-exempt organization.

The common statutory tax exemption for religious, charitable or educational organizations under Subsection 501(c)(3) of the Internal Revenue Code explicitly bars "carrying on propaganda or otherwise attempting to influence legislation." The NRA's tax exemption, however, is not under that subsection but under 501(c)(4), which exempts "civic leagues or organizations not organized for profit but operated exclusively for the promotion of social welfare . . . and the net earnings of which are devoted exclusively to charitable, educational or recreational purposes."

A pertinent question one could ask is: To what extent has the NRA overstepped its stated mandate "to educate and train citizens of good repute in the safe and efficient handling of firearms," to the point where the promotion of the public welfare is secondary to the promotion of the private interests of the American gun industry? This question is particularly pertinent, because the NRA is the beneficiary of certain rather special governmental privileges. Though it is not generally known, the NRA is probably the only private pressure group to receive public bounty—one amounting to millions of dollars a year—to say nothing of considerable aid from industry.

The NRA publicly denies that it is an industry "front," and asserts that it represents the interests of the sportsmen of America—the "users" of the products of the arms industry. It claims it has no other axes to grind, and is beholden to no one else. It also denies that it receives any government aid. A notice in the *Rifleman* reiterates monthly that the association "is supported by membership dues and contributions" and "does not receive any grants or subsidies from the manufacturers of arms and ammunition or from the Federal government."

Yet this is to ignore completely that advertising space bought in *The American Rifleman* by makers and vendors of arms, ammunition and related products provided the NRA with $1,121,574 in 1964, a quarter of its entire income. Nor, as already indicated, does the NRA pay any taxes on this income, some of which comes from advertisers registering their opposition to gun legislation.

Rifleman advertising revenue alone is virtually enough to pay for the entire cost of putting out the magazine and distributing it to members. As a free give-away and a superior publishing product, the *Rifleman* is quite an incentive to membership. And more members lead directly to higher advertising income. As Secretary Frank Daniel explained this to me: "Even with increasing membership, we haven't had to raise our dues in many, many years. When our membership goes up, the circulation of *The American Rifleman* also goes up. This means we can raise our advertising rates."

Thanks to an indulgent Congress, NRA members in about 5,500 of the association's 12,000 affiliated clubs receive free ammunition and free or bargain-priced guns. This partnership between the government and the NRA stems from a Defense Department program run by the Army's National Board for the Promotion of Rifle Practice, which the NRA was instrumental in setting up back in 1903, admittedly to secure government aid. The idea for the board was the NRA's very own. A report of the NRA for 1902 said that early that year, a committee headed by the then NRA president, General Bird W. Spencer, "waited on the Secretary of War and submitted to him a plan of reorganization which would make the Association more national in its scope, and other suggestions looking to the advancement of rifle shooting among the citizens of the country. The Secretary of War requested that the suggestions be presented to him in writing." This was done in a letter dated January 25, 1902, from General Spencer to the Secretary of War, then Elihu Root.

If results of any importance were to be obtained, the letter said, "exceptional facilities should be provided for the National Rifle Association, and its affiliated organizations, and to that end, if legistion does not already exist, it should be had, in order that the National Rifle Association may purchase arms and ammunition at cost. Later if circumstances seem to warrant it, legislation can be sought to permit of the issue of arms or ammunition on a more liberal basis."

The National Board came into being on March 31, 1903. In the early years, the annual appropriation for the board (or, in effect, the NRA) amounted to only $10,000, but it has grown tremendously in the years since.

For the five-year period ending in 1964, the National Board program cost taxpayers at least $12,000,000. Of this, $7,200,000 were spent for 247 million rounds of free ammunition for NRA affiliated clubs, and $2,300,000 for guns and other equipment on loan to the clubs. As of early 1964, 35,000 guns were on loan. The remaining $2,500,000 were used for the other incidentals involved in the National Board's civilian marksmanship program. In effect, the NRA is also the sole beneficiary of the National Board's annual appropriation,* most of which goes to pay for NRA facilities (for example, to lease Camp Perry, Ohio, site of the National Matches), for transporting shooting teams to matches here and abroad, and for targets, trophies, badges and medals.

Apart from all this regular bounty, NRA members, and *only* NRA

* $506,000 in 1964; $471,000 estimated for 1965.

members, can from time to time buy surplus U.S. military rifles, carbines and pistols, as they become available, at "cost-to-government" prices, about one-third to one-quarter of their usual retail value, through the Army's Office of the Director of Civilian Marksmanship. During the recent five-year period, NRA members were able to buy such surplus military U.S. arms as Springfield Model '03 rifles for $14.50, .45-caliber automatic pistols for $17.50 and M-1 carbines for $20. The NRA attributed its 20 per cent growth in membership in 1963 to, among other things, "the carbine sale influence."

To what extent the NRA depends on government aid may be deduced by the following sequence of events in 1948. On June 19 of that year Congress adjourned without providing the NRA with its requested funds. On the same day, the NRA executive committee met and decided to raise the association dues for the first time in twenty-one years, individual annual membership rates going from $3 to $4. The national matches at Camp Perry were also canceled for that year. And with free ammunition cut off during the next few years, too, NRA membership dropped from its then all-time high of nearly 300,000 in 1948 to about 230,000 in 1950.

In recent years the question has been raised whether the government's civilian marksmanship program is being abused by extremist individuals or groups who join or form NRA clubs in order to receive free government guns and ammunition.

One who feels strongly that this is so is Representative Henry Gonzalez, a Texas Democrat, who read into the May 26, 1964, *Congressional Record* a newsletter from the rightist Paul Revere Associated Yeomen, Inc., also known as PRAY. This document predicted there would soon be a "revolution-insurrection" inspired by "the diehard liberals and Reds who have controlled our government for thirty-one years." Against this ominous possibility, readers were urged to "stock up on rifles, shotguns, pistols . . . arm every member of your family," and join the Minutemen and the National Rifle Association. Representative Gonzalez also charged that the Minutemen, the grass-roots guerrilla group, was "in part supported, subsidized and encouraged by the Federal government" through the Civilian Marksmanship Program.

Several months later, Robert B. de Pugh, national leader of the Minutemen and a life member of the National Rifle Association, told a *New York Times* interviewer that it was a "common tactic" for

Minutemen, without disclosing their affiliation, to organize or join gun clubs in order to gain access to rifle ranges for target practice. Accordingly, thousands of Minutemen, said de Pugh, had joined the National Rifle Association in order to get free ammunition through the Army program and, by their dues, to support the NRA's fight against gun control legislation.

The NRA, without denying de Pugh's claim to life membership in its organization, has vehemently disclaimed connection with the Minutemen, Paul Revere Associated Yeomen, or "any group which advocates or condones activities of violence," and has said there is no hard evidence that extremist groups have infiltrated its gun clubs. Indeed, NRA officials resent the attempt to link the organization, even in the role of an unknowing host, to "private armies and guerrilla forces." At the same time, NRA Secretary Frank Daniel admits: "We could never be sure that someone who is a member of the NRA wasn't a member of the Minutemen or the Black Muslims or some group like that."

No doubt most NRA members are citizens of impeccable reputation. The NRA claims that its roster has borne the names of five Presidents of the United States plus those of two Chief Justices. On the other hand, present and past members have included such people as Minutemen leader Robert de Pugh, Klansmen Byron de la Beckwith and Paul Dewey Wilson and bank robber-murderer Albert Lee Nussbaum.

How closely are the credentials of would-be members or affiliates really examined? The evidence indicates that joining the NRA is not much more difficult than joining the Book-of-the-Month Club. The NRA by-laws specify that individual applicants must be endorsed either by a member in good standing, a public official, or an officer of the U.S. Armed Forces. To test this rule, I once sent for an NRA membership blank and had it endorsed by a relative who is not an NRA member, or a public official, or an officer of the U.S. Armed Forces. In fact, he had never even handled a gun. Nonetheless, eight days later I received my NRA membership card along with literature which informed me that I was now eligible to buy bargain-priced guns from the Army. Lest you think my acceptance was a fluke, Tom Nolan of the Washington *Daily News* applied for membership as recently as December 1965 by filling out an application clipped from a barber shop magazine. "For the 'endorsement,'" says

Nolan, "I just printed the first name that came to mind—out of the air." Nolan's membership card arrived in the mail a week later.

And so far as affiliated groups are concerned (a minimum of ten members is required), there is nothing really to prevent, say, ten Minutemen or Mafia mobsters from forming a gun club and then applying for affiliation.

Approval of would-be affiliates is usually routine after the Adjutant General and NRA office in the club's home state "review" the club application, supposedly to determine whether the officers listed have criminal records. (Oddly enough, however, fingerprints—the only reliable way of checking criminal records—are not required with the application). Once it has its NRA charter, the club can then apply to the Army for its free quota of guns (eight for a ten-member club).

The chief of the New York State National Guard, Major A. C. O'Hara, has frankly admitted that he can't perform the check prescribed by the NRA. Consequently, he told *The New York Times*, every time he receives a list of club members from the NRA he simply sends it back without approval or disapproval. Yet there has been no slowdown in the chartering of NRA clubs in New York State: the number there grew from 1,430 in 1962 to 1,713 in 1964.

Back in 1960 an enterprising resident of Los Angeles was able to form a "one-man" authorized NRA gun club, presumably padding out the membership application to show the required ten members. He ordered, and actually received, a full club quota of free rifles and ammunition. His deception was discovered when he was later arrested on a charge of theft and failed to appear at a local Army Supply Depot to pick up a subsequent order of targets mailed to him by the Army.

With the NRA affiliates multiplying in California, authorities there are especially worried about the formation of local private armies of fanatics. In 1963 State Attorney General Stanley Mosk had established that the Minutemen had formed units within the California National Guard, and that they were recruiting members from cells of the John Birch Society and from other extremist groups. The NRA's western field representative and local lobbyist, Colonel E. F. (Tod) Sloan, promptly branded Mosk's action a "witch hunt."

Mosk asked the Army's National Board a simple, straightforward question. He wanted to know the names of the members and officers of all the NRA gun clubs in the state, and the amount of free ammunition and firearms each had received. His letter, addressed to the NBPRP's administrator, Lieutenant Colonel C. J. Shaffer, went unanswered. Frustrated, Mosk then wrote directly to Defense Secretary Robert McNamara and asked him to "unfreeze" the information. He charged that Army secrecy had stymied his efforts to prevent the formation of private armies by "fanatics and extremists." "It is disturbing to consider that the U.S. Army may aid such violence through its distribution of free ammunition," Mosk wrote.

Eventually, after this prodding, the Army revealed that California had 420 NRA clubs, armed with 2,500 .22-caliber rifles and 2,500 .30-caliber M-1 military rifles on loan from the Army. An Army spokesman also said that *any* NRA club qualified for the loan of weapons. The only requirements were that they have access to a rifle range, have a certified NRA instructor, conduct continuous marksmanship training and submit annual inventory reports on weapons and ammunition.

But Mosk's successor as California Attorney General, Thomas C. Lynch, was still trying to determine the membership makeup of the clubs themselves a year later. "The Adjutant General here says he gets the lists, but doesn't keep them. He sends them to the NRA," Lynch's administrative aide, Tom McDonald, told me. "The NRA told us to write to the Army. The National Board said all they could give us was a list of the clubs and the secretaries of each." The list, when finally received, proved of little value; many of the clubs had as their addresses only a city and a post office box.*

The characterization often made of the National Board as the NRA's little empire within the Army is apparent from the makeup of the 23-member National Board: all of its eleven civilian members

* Representative Henry Gonzalez of Texas had similar difficulties. In January 1966 the Texas Congressman, after two years of firing questions at the Army about its weapons distribution, characterized the Department's answers as "sometimes evasive, often slightly less than candid and invariably slow in coming." Gonzalez repeated his charge that the Army may inadvertently be handing out free guns and ammunition to Klansmen, right wing extremists and "other nuts" because of "negligent and slipshod" controls. According to the Washington *Post* of January 30, 1966, Gonzalez had also concluded that the Army has no idea whether the ammunition "is being used for target practice, stored in secret ammunition dumps, sold to racists or rioters or shipped to foreign governments."

are NRA directors. Colonel Merle E. Preble, executive officer of the National Board, is also an NRA director. The other of the military members of the board, appointed by the Secretary of the Army from the upper echelons of the services, are friendly to the NRA.

At the annual NRA members' banquet, the guest speaker almost always is from the top brass. Guest speakers since 1955 have been Secretaries of the Army Stephen Ailes, Elvis J. Stahr, Jr., and Wilbur Brucker, Secretary of the Navy Fred Korth, Chief of Naval Operations Admiral David L. McDonald, Deputy Secretary of Defense Robert B. Anderson, Marine Corps Commandant General David M. Shoup, Army Chief of Staff General Lyman L. Lemnitzer, Air Force Vice Chief of Staff General Curtis Le May, Selective Service Director General Lewis B. Hershey, and Representative John J. Flynt, Jr., of Georgia. The latter, a dues-paying NRA member, was honored no doubt because of his position on the House Committee on Appropriations.

The NRA is well represented in Congress. No one knows just how many NRA members it has. But as *Guns* editor E. B. Mann, an NRA life member, once reported to his readers, "We have friends in Washington, more of them than you may think." Arizona's Carl Hayden, President pro tempore of the Senate, is an NRA member, as is also Senator Bourke Hickenlooper of Iowa. Former Senator Barry Goldwater is a member, and many friends and members, like Carl Hayden and John Flynt, sit on key committee posts (Senate and House Appropriations, respectively). Senator Warren Magnuson of Washington is Chairman of the Senate Commerce Committee, which must rule on most firearms bills. The NRA's influential friends also include Representative Wilbur D. Mills of Arkansas, chairman of the House Ways and Means Committee, to which most of the proposed House firearms measures are usually referred; the committee's number two man is Representative Cecil R. King of California, an NRA director.

King, along with Representatives John D. Dingell of Michigan and Robert L. F. Sikes of Florida, are among the staunchest advocates of the NRA in Washington. Sikes, also an NRA director, is a frequent sponsor of NRA-written or approved legislation, and is a ranking member of the House Appropriations Subcommittee of Defense which passes on the annual budget request of the National

Board. The recipient of an instant commission, Sikes rose rapidly in the Army Reserves, and is now a major general—in the words of Drew Pearson, "as stern and distinguished a major general as ever fought for more appropriations for the Army."

In January 1964, because of the still-fresh impact of the Kennedy assassination, the House Appropriations Subcommittee on Defense, when considering the National Board's appeal for legislative largesse —the ultimate recipients to be the NRA—sought special assurance that members of the NRA were carefully screened, law-abiding citizens. Such a justification was deemed superfluous, declared Representative Daniel J. Flood of Pennsylvania, "as long as General Bob Sikes is on this committee."

Less than three months later, Sikes, twenty-three years a Congressman, recipient of the Florida governor's conservation award for 1960, and a presumed signatory of the NRA membership pledge of "good sportsmanship and good citizenship," was fined $50 after pleading guilty to violating hunting laws.* Sikes and a number of hunting companions, including General Nathan F. Twining, former chairman of the Joint Chiefs of Staff, had been caught hunting turkey over a baited field. The practice (which involves scattering corn or other grain to attract the turkeys) apart from being illegal, is regarded as heinous by hunters. Those abiding by the NRA Hunter's Code of Ethics agree, among other things, to "obey all game laws and regulations" and "insist" that their companions do likewise, and to use "hunting skills which assure clean, sportsmanlike kills."

Sadly enough, another member of the Sikes family has had difficulty with guns. A UPI dispatch of November 2, 1958 revealed that Sikes' daughter, Bobby Serrene Wicke, confessed shooting and wounding her sleeping husband, Florida State Attorney Edward F. Wicke, after an early-morning argument.

Interestingly, it was a Sikes measure that, earlier in 1958, was finally adopted by Congress in place of the NRA-repudiated bills introduced by Representative Albert P. Morano of Connecticut and then Senator John F. Kennedy to keep all surplus foreign military weapons out of this country. The watered-down Sikes substitute, approved by the NRA, simply prohibited the return to these shores of only those military arms the United States had sent abroad under

* AP dispatch of April 21, 1964, datelined Chatom, Alabama.

our foreign assistance program. The bill, passed on June 23, 1958, left the loophole that made it possible for the Carcano that killed Kennedy to enter this country.*

Sikes also had a hand in what was perhaps the NRA's biggest *positive* legislative triumph of recent years. In 1963 the association wrote the language for one of the provisions in a bill to amend the Arms Control and Disarmament Act. The provision, introduced in identical versions by Sikes and by Senator Bourke Hickenlooper of Iowa, read:

Nothing contained in this act shall be construed to authorize any policy or action by any Government agency which would interfere with, restrict, or prohibit the acquisition, possession, or use of firearms by an individual for the lawful purpose of personal defense, sport, recreation, education, or training.

The words were accepted by the House and Senate the day before President Kennedy died. The provision was enacted the day after his funeral.

---

* Through a weird freak of journalistic juxtaposition, the Carcano was featured in an ad of the Chicago firm of Klein's Sporting Goods, the source of Oswald's Carcano, in the June 1958 *American Rifleman*. The reverse side of the page contained some of the NRA's critical barbs at the Kennedy bill. In fact, the names Kennedy and Carcano were virtually superimposed.

8 The Futility of State Laws

Control of firearms presents a twofold problem: how to make guns safer in the hands of people legitimately entitled to them, and how to keep them away from the emotionally unstable, the immature and the criminal.

With wild illogic, opponents of firearms control claim that any restrictions on guns should also apply to everything else, from knives to nylons, which may be used as instruments of homicide. They conveniently ignore the vital difference. The other items have a primary purpose that is nonlethal; but guns are made only to put a bullet through a living body, in order to kill. As Lucian Cary, gun editor of *True* and a prominent member of the firearms fraternity, once wrote: "Shooting is the only sport that requires a weapon designed to kill violently."

Prohibitions on owning and carrying dangerous weapons date back to at least the Middle Ages. In England, as early as 1328, the Statute of Northampton, which remains in force today, forbade any man to "go nor ride armed, by night or by day in fairs, markets, nor in the presence of the justices or other ministers, nor in no part elsewhere ...." Going armed in places of public assembly was apparently regarded as tending to terrify the peaceful populace and to provoke breaches of the peace by the impetuous and unscrupulous. The offense was indictable under the common law, a fact indicating that, contrary to what some people now assert, weapon-bearing was not really an unassailable common-law right, like that of trial by jury.

The Statute of Northampton became the basis of our early colonial laws. In 1692 the Province of Massachusetts enacted a similar prohibition on carrying "offensive" weapons in public, and this law was re-enacted in 1795 after Massachusetts became a state. Unlike the Massachusetts law, virtually all the state laws later enacted were curbs on the carrying of concealed weapons. Curiously enough, the first such statute was enacted in 1813 by the frontier state of Kentucky, then a backwoods region, where the common practice of gun-toting made it particularly hazardous for the average citizen to venture about unarmed. The Kentucky law prohibited the carrying or "wearing" of concealed pistols, except when traveling. A commentary on the Kentucky law states:

Traveling in those days was a much more precarious and dangerous undertaking than it is now, when one can go from any part of this country to almost any other part in about the same degree of safety, personally, as one finds in his home town. Travelers were exempted; they were expected to look after themselves.

Indiana followed Kentucky's lead in 1820, and Arkansas and Georgia followed in 1837 with similar concealed weapons legislation. In court tests they were found to be constitutional. Like other of our early firearms laws, they sought to regulate not the purchase or possession of weapons but rather the carrying of them. And they applied, as do most of our laws even today, almost entirely to small guns that could be carried concealed—handguns. As the frontier receded, concealed weapons laws became more and more common and, in some states, were made more stringent. Today the right to carry a concealed pistol is either absolutely prohibited, or permitted only with a license, in every state but six.*

* Minnesota and Vermont, for example, forbid concealed carrying only when there is an "intent" to use the weapon against another person. Of course, after the intent is realized, it is too late. For the other permissive states, see Appendix II.

The rationale for the emphasis on concealment in our weapons laws had its roots in the good old American belief in the "fair fight," and the traditional abhorrence of sneak attacks. In theory, a man who was planning to shoot at another should have his weapon out in the open, so that his enemy would be fairly forewarned. An opinion delivered in a case tried under New York State's concealed weapons law (enacted in 1881) held that:

> The purpose of all concealment statutes is clear. At the time that they were enacted the open carrying of weapons upon the person was not prohibited. The purpose of the concealed weapons statute was to prevent men in sudden quarrel or in the commission of crime from drawing concealed weapons and using them without prior notice to their victims that they were armed. The person assailed or attacked would behave one way if he knew his assailant was armed, and perhaps another way if he could safely presume that he was unarmed.*

Although originally intended to apply only to concealed small arms such as pistols, many of the statutes were broadened to cover either deadly weapons in general or additional specified weapons. New York's concealed weapons law featured a long list of banned articles, including sandbag, blackjack, bludgeon and stiletto. The Texas law catalogues a list which includes:

. . . pistol, dirk, dagger, slingshot, blackjack, handchain, nightstick, pipe stick, sword cane, spear, knuckles made of any metal or any hard substance, bowie knife, switchblade knife, springblade knife, throwblade knife, a knife with a blade of over five and a half inches in length, or any other knife manufactured or sold for the purposes of offense or defense.

Nothing in these early laws required anyone to get permission to purchase such weapons. This new concept, controlling the owning of weapons, did not appear in law until 1911. In that year New York State enacted its much-discussed, still controversial Sullivan Law, which is known in police circles as "Old 1897" after its section number in the state's penal code. The Sullivan Law of New York requires a license to purchase as well as possess a handgun or other concealable weapon. It is generally acknowledged as the most re-

---

* *People* v. *Raso*, 170 N.Y.S. 2d 245 (1958).

strictive state firearms law in America. Understandably, the New York State law enrages the gun lobby.

"No other state has gone so far in the field of firearms legislation. It is fervently hoped no state ever will," the National Rifle Association declared recently. NRA spokesmen have maligned the law as "ill-conceived," "a legal monstrosity," "the continuing sorrow of collectors, shooters, and hunters," and "a tool of the criminal." The gun lobby fancies that in a hypothetical "revolution," the "Communists" would seize the list of licensees in order to confiscate every gun, as the first order of take-over business pending a Soviet invasion.

"Communists love this kind of law. There have been some who championed it," a newspaper interviewer was once told by Karl T. Frederick, a former president of the National Rifle Association and champion pistol shot on the 1920 Olympic Team. Frederick even went so far as to declare that the law filled him with a "sense of shame" at being a citizen of the State of New York.

Timothy D. Sullivan, the New York legislator whose name the law bears, was a prominent Tammany Democratic leader, State Senator, and former Congressman. A genial Irishman who rose from the tenement to the top of Tammany and, in the process, accumulated untold wealth, much of which he lavished on the poor, he typified the big-city politician in a place and era when ballot-box stuffing was a common practice. Two bills he sponsored, however, were to give Tim Sullivan a certain claim to fame. As a history of Tammany Hall tells it:

One was a bill making Columbus day a legal holiday, and the other was the bill which still bears his name making the carrying of firearms without a license a penal offense. The first pleased Tammany's Italian constituency, and the other enabled the Senator and his associates to keep these same friends and their Jewish and their Irish compatriots under control. Whenever a gangster who led repeaters, those who voted two or more times at elections, or an influential brothel keeper grew obstreperous enough to prove inconvenient to the plans that were made in Tammany Hall, he could usually be found with a gun, or a gun could be planted upon his person, and he could be sent to the State Prison under the Sullivan Law for a long enough time to keep him from being annoying. One of these men, "Big Jack" Zelig, found that the better part of discretion after the Sullivan Law was passed was to sew up all his pockets. . . . The Sullivan Law was, however, useful to Sullivan and to

Tammany Hall because it enabled them to control their gunmen friends when they should become their enemies.*

Although there would seem to be nothing wrong with placing gunmen behind bars, this historical excerpt does not tell the whole story. For a little-known fact is that the law bearing his name did not originate with Sullivan. Moreover, however questionable Sullivan's own personal motives may have been, there can be no challenging the motives of others who favored enactment of the law.

Actually, its father is George Petit LeBrun, then the secretary to New York's Medical Examiner's (or Coroner's) office.† In 1910, when a prominent New Yorker, David Graham Phillips, was shot to death on the steps of the Princeton Club by a madman with a pistol, LeBrun first conceived what was to become known as the Sullivan Law. Armed with statistics on other such crimes, LeBrun drafted an outline of the bill and induced Tim Sullivan to sponsor it. LeBrun then began a campaign for its enactment by writing to twenty influential civic leaders, among them John D. Rockefeller, Jr., Nathan Straus, Dr. Simon Baruch (Bernard's father), and Arthur Brisbane. This part of the story is ignored in the NRA's account of the history of the Sullivan Law. Nor is the NRA correct in stating that State Senator Sullivan "personally steamrollered" the bill through the Legislature. In his own house of the Legislature, the bill passed by 37 to five, the most vigorous opposition coming from an up-state Senator who had two arms factories in his district. Said Tim on the Senate floor:

Now I ain't alone in wantin' this little measure . . . There's the Merchants Association and the City Club and District Attorney Whitman and Police Commissioner Cropsey and the American Museum of Safety and Schiff, Jacob H. Schiff, and Henry Clews and Isaac N. Seligman and Rockefeller, John D., Jr., a social acquaintance of mine . . .

There was a need for the law at the time, as even the NRA has conceded in *The American Rifleman* (April 1962):

. . . There was a good deal of truth in the claims of the proponents of the Sullivan Law which led to its passage. Without question, this

* M. R. Werner, *Tammany Hall*, pp. 506–7.
† Astonishingly, LeBrun is still alive at this writing, having reached the age of 103 in Florida on July 27, 1965.

law was immediately useful to the police. Professional criminals were frequently known, but their crimes almost impossible to prove. Since most of them possessed pistols, and all had "dangerous weapons" in their homes, they could be sent to jail, if caught, to the general benefit of the police.

Belying the NRA's concern with Sullivan's motives, Karl T. Frederick has also ascribed the passage of the law to the changing tenor of the times during the early 1900s: the great increase in population, particularly in the cities; the corresponding decrease in the familiarity on the part of the public with firearms; the rise of organized or "professional" crime; and the introduction and growing use of the automobile which favored the mobility of the public in general and of the criminal in particular.

Among the objections raised to the law is the claim that it must be inherently defective and unworkable because of the need to amend it (or "patch it here and there," as the NRA puts it) over the years. Actually, most of the 50-odd provisions added to the original statute have merely been procedural in nature and were needed to cope with the changing times. The main thrust of the law has not been touched by the amendments. Efforts are also made to cloud the constitutionality of the law, usually by quoting minority opinions from the many court cases in which the majority of the judges has repeatedly held the law to be a valid exercise of the state's inherent police powers. Moreover, the courts have held that the law does not interfere with the citizens' vaunted arms-bearing right.*

The most frequent argument against the Sullivan Law, however, is that it burdens the "decent and law abiding citizen" without keeping guns away from the criminal, who will not obey the law but who will steal, bootleg, or make any needed handgun. Defenders of the law have never denied this. As a prominent attorney and authority on crime pointed out back in 1934:

One benefit to be derived from this type of firearms legislation is that it provides a basis for easily convicting gun-carrying gangsters when witnesses have been intimidated or when there is not sufficient evidence to prove guilt beyond a reasonable doubt for a major offense. Proving

---

* Among the many New York court cases sustaining the law: *People* v. *Ryan* (1911), *People* v. *Persce* (1912), *People* v. *Warden of City Prison* (1913), *People* v. *Murphy* (1939), *People* v. *Terra* (1951), and *Moore* v. *Gallup* (1943).

that a gunman possessed a gun without a license is a simple matter compared with proving that he participated in a bank robbery. It is a type of "public enemy" statute, simple in operation. For example, in 1933, 1,003 persons were arrested and temporarily detained for carrying concealed weapons in violations of the New York Sullivan Law. One hundred fifty-four of these persons are now serving prison sentences, many of them notorious gangsters, such as Morris Grossman, alias Irving Bitz, Harry Kagel, and Stanley Tomasetta.*

As for the burden the law imposes on good citizens applying for handgun permits, this is often greatly exaggerated. The procedure involved, critics of the law would have you believe, is the equivalent of the labors of Hercules and requires the patience of Job. According to one critical article, the applicant has to fill out an application requiring him to answer "forty searching questions." Another article has given the number of questions as "nearly 100". In addition he must pay a "substantial" fee, submit to fingerprinting "as though he were a felon," and then wait for perhaps a year or so before his application is granted, if at all.

Actually, the procedure is not quite so formidable, although it is rigorous enough to discourage the frivolous and screen out the unscrupulous. Under the law as it now stands, pistol licenses are issued by police commissioners in New York City and Nassau County, and elsewhere in the state by a judge of a court of record in the applicant's county of residence.

You go first to your local precinct station or court and get the necessary applications. To fill this out and answer its 24 (not 40 or 100) questions takes about five or ten minutes. The questions are mostly of the yes-no type. On the application you have to show "proper cause" for wanting the license. There are really only three standard reasons accepted for possessing a "handgun": for target shooting, in which case the applicant has to present proof of membership in a gun club; for protection of premises and property; and for transporting valuables. Most permits are issued to private detectives, bank clerks, payroll messengers, art buyers, rent collectors, jewelry salesmen, liquor store owners and to other merchants.

You can't get a gun permit just because you feel nervous walking the streets at night, or because some hot-tempered neighbor is mad

* John Brabner-Smith, *Law and Contemporary Problems*, I (1934).

at you, although some permits may be granted for very special reasons. But the law makes it clear that a permit should not be issued to an applicant having a police record with a conviction for a felony or certain specified misdemeanors, or to one who is insane, or whose "temperament is unreliable."

You must with the application submit sworn statements from three references, attesting that both they and you have led virtually blameless lives, and provide six photographs of yourself. Then you have your fingerprints taken, pay a fee of $20, and wait for your application to be checked, something that takes about three or four months in New York City and less elsewhere. If your application is approved, you are given a "purchase document" in the form of a coupon on your license. You give this coupon to the man in the gun store where you buy your weapon. New York City permits must be renewed each year; elsewhere in the state they are valid for longer periods of time, in many places indefinitely. Your permit can be revoked for various reasons: if you are arrested, threaten someone, or expose the gun without cause, or if you are found out to be hot-tempered, or hang around drinking places, or are in the habit of leaving your weapon lying around where it is accessible to others. Some years ago, New York authorities refused to renew the license of a rifle instructor with a spotless record simply because his son, with whom he lived, had been in trouble with the police. And if you don't have your license with you whenever you carry your gun, this leaves you open to having it revoked. Licenses are of two general types: one for the gun's on-premises use, the other allowing you to carry it around within certain reasonable bounds. Licenses for target shooters, for example, are validated to cover carrying the gun only to and from the range. And in New York one may not legally carry or own a pistol unless he *first* gets the license to buy it.

The law also makes it illegal to own a machine gun, sawed-off shotgun, or the like. Nobody may have these except the police, the military, bank guards and others in special groups, or those registered under the provisions of the National Firearms Act. *

Banned, too, as a carryover from the state's old concealed weapons laws is an array of other "dangerous" and "deadly" items. Mentioned specifically in the law are the blackjack, bludgeon (loaded stick), billy, slingshot, sandbag, sandclub, and metal knuckles. Also

* Appendix I.

taboo are daggers, dirks, stilettos, razors, gravity knives, and switch-blade knives (with blades springing open by the pressure of a button). This part of the Sullivan Law received national prominence in July 1964 when Arlene Del Fava, a pretty, young New York secretary, was charged with a misdemeanor for using a switchblade knife in repulsing a rapist. By merely carrying the switchblade knife, she had broken the law. As one detective advised her, however, she would have been legally clear had she responded to the attack with a ten-inch butcher knife. A kindly grand jury refused to indict her, permitting her arrest record to be erased.

In the case of some weapons, mere possession is enough to send one to jail. Otherwise, possession must generally be linked with the intent to use the weapon *unlawfully* against somebody. The first offense is usually considered a misdemeanor, and later ones as felonies.

Of all weapons, the hardest to explain away are unlicensed hand-guns. If you have a pistol stashed away in your dresser drawer or in your desk or on your hip, you can get up to a year in jail and be fined $500 to boot, provided the weapon is unloaded and it is the first offense. If it is a second offense, or the weapon is loaded, the penalty is up to seven years and $1,000. If the unlicensed gun is used in a crime, the criminal can get up to ten years extra just for having the gun.

It is often charged that the procedure specified by the law for owning a pistol is not worth the nuisance. It is also charged that the clause requiring applicants to show "proper cause" is used by the authorities to deny handguns to deserving applicants. Yet neither charge is borne out by the record. According to a 1964 tally by the State Investigation Commission, 444,043 New York State residents were found to have licenses to own an estimated 750,000 handguns —or one for every *sixteen* men, women and children in the state. And the Commission's total did not include licenses held by dealers and gunsmiths. Nor did it include an estimate of handguns owned illegally. Nor did it touch shotguns and rifles, which do not have to be licensed.

Many permits,* the Commission found, had been issued in rural

---

* The terms, permit and license, are generally used interchangeably. Getting a license or permit may or may not involve the registration of the gun, that is the recording of its serial number and the name of its owner. In New York,

areas to sixteen-year-olds, to former mental patients, to the aged and physically infirm, and to others of somewhat questionable character. In New York City, where applicants are more carefully screened, there were only 17,087 valid licenses outstanding, roughly one for every 470 persons. Because New York City is also among the few areas in the State requiring the periodic renewal of licenses, these are valid throughout the entire state; however, licenses issued in other counties of the state are not valid in New York City.

The Commission urged the strengthening of existing laws and the enactment of new ones to tighten controls even more. It said that in some counties licenses were given to persons too feeble to be entrusted with firearms. The Commission report told of one case in which a woman complained that her husband had threatened to kill her. Investigation disclosed that her husband had obtained a pistol permit eight years after he had been discharged from a mental institution.

Yet it is clear that the Sullivan Law has had some effect on public safety. As far back as 1932, the state had a homicide death rate of only 5.8 per 100,000 population, against 9.2 for the country at large. The highest death rate for homicide that year was for the state of Florida, where it reached 27.7, or about three times the national average. Similar relationships hold true today. In 1964, Florida's homicide rate of 8.6 was the nation's fourth highest (exceeded only in Georgia, Alaska and Alabama); New York's was 4.6. And New York's rate would be even lower than it is if the Sullivan Law were more rigidly administered and strengthened. For example, the law imposes no controls on the sale of ammunition that can be used in handguns. Nor does it cover rifles and shotguns, which can be conveniently cut down and so converted into concealable weapons. The carrying of a rifle or shot gun concealed on one's person under a coat is also not a violation of the Sullivan Law.

Although reputable firearms dealers will not sell a rifle, shotgun or ammunition to a person under eighteen years of age (even though the legal minimum is sixteen) because of a fear of legal complications which could arise if the weapon is misused, this self-imposed regulation does not deter the minor who wants to own a gun. He can simply order by mail.

---

it does. On the other hand, a registration law may not necessarily require a gun owner to have a permit for purchase or possession. In this sense, registration does not restrict possession as broadly as licensing.

New York State can, of course, do nothing about the absence of control in other states. This permits a hoodlum to take a ride out of New York to, say, Maryland or Delaware in the morning, buy a pistol there and be back home in time for dinner. Naturally, no amount of legislation on the part of New York State has been able to prevent such activities. Even America's toughest state gun law is therefore easy to get around.

Perhaps the most obvious shortcoming of the nation's state firearms laws has always been their diversity; even among the various pistol or concealed weapons laws, there had never been a semblance of uniformity from state to state. Back in the early 1920s, three states prohibited the carrying of all pistols, two the carrying of all but military pistols, two the carrying of pistols in certain places, and twelve the carrying, with certain exceptions, of concealed pistols. In addition to statutes regulating the carrying of pistols, some states prohibited their sale to certain persons, such as minors, drug addicts, and criminals. The states, however, left it to such persons to voluntarily reveal their identity to the sales clerk. Other states provided for an additional penalty for those committing crimes of violence when armed. The mere pointing of a gun at another, within shooting distance, was regarded as an assault at common law, whether the gun was loaded or not. New York's Sullivan Law was unique in requiring a permit for both the purchase and possession of a handgun.

Shortly after World War I, there was a growing current of public opinion against the easy access to firearms by everyone. There also grew the feeling that handgun laws should be substantially uniform throughout the states. An effort was begun in a number of states to adopt the provisions of the Sullivan Law.

"I am sorry to say that that was before the NRA exhibited any interest in the subject," Karl T. Frederick recalled before the 1951 NRA annual convention. "You, who are old members, will remember that for quite a number of years the NRA regarded itself as exclusively a rifle association and left the pistol men to themselves as being a rather small group of people that it was not so very much interested in."

To forestall the dire eventuality of the Sullivan Law spreading throughout the nation, Frederick and a small group of members of the United States Revolver Association got together in 1919 to draft legislation much less drastic than the New York Law. The strategy was to urge a weak "model law" as a standard for all the states. The group labored until 1923, when it finally offered its product to the legislatures of the various states. A grand total of only three (California, North Dakota, and New Hampshire) saw fit to adopt it.

Feeling the need for a somewhat broader base and more eminent auspices, Frederick and his associates then brought their model firearms statute to the attention of the National Conference of Commissioners on Uniform Laws. Their joint efforts resulted in 1926 in a proposed so-called "Uniform Firearms Act." The title was a misnomer, since the act dealt only with pistols and revolvers. Not surprisingly, it did not require a license of handgun purchasers, as did the New York law, or the statewide registration of firearms, as did then a subsequently repealed Arkansas law.

Its main provision banned the possession of handguns by persons previously convicted of a crime of violence, and also by drug addicts, habitual drunkards and minors under 18. It required a license only to carry a concealed pistol. It provided for the licensing of dealers, and a 48-hour "cooling off" period before delivery of the pistol to the buyer. It added penalties for any crime of violence committed by one armed with a pistol.

The proposed act, though adopted in 1926 by the Conference and also approved by the American Bar Association, immediately drew severe criticism as not being sufficiently drastic. On December 24, 1926, New York City's Police Commissioner, George V. McLaughlin, sent the President of the American Bar Association, Charles A. Whitman, a letter in which he stated:

A cursory examination of the proposed act leads me to the conclusion that instead of helping, it would be handicapping those who have to do with the apprehension of persons who, without authority, are carrying firearms.

McLaughlin then pointed out what he regarded as some of the defects in the Act.

Take the definition of a pistol. It states "any firearm with a barrel length under 12 inches in length." The law could be completely evaded by having a pistol 13 inches in length.

Section 3 would seem to provide that a person who commits a crime of violence, such as murder, manslaughter, robbery, burglary, and house breaking, would be completely absolved if he had a pistol permit.

Section 4 limits the denial of a pistol permit to those who have committed a crime of violence. In other words, counterfeiters, pickpockets and forgers could have a pistol permit.

Section 5 prohibits a person from carrying a weapon concealed in a vehicle. Now you know, the crooks nowadays carry them on the floor of the automobile, and it is doubtful if this could be construed as a concealed weapon.

"The whole bill seems to be a compromise affair gotten up for the benefit of the manufacturers of firearms," concluded McLaughlin. "I hope you will see that this bill receives further consideration before the American Bar Association again gives its approval."

In addition, the Act was also offensive to the newly organized National Crime Commission, which received so many protests from police organizations and law enforcement officers that it organized a committee to study and propose uniform firearms legislation of its own. The Commission's draft of a proposed uniform act, considerably more drastic than that proposed by the Conference, was submitted to the state legislatures in 1927. It got nowhere, principally because of the opposition of the National Rifle Association, which was then awakening to its destiny as special pleader for the gun interests.

Meanwhile, the Conference's Uniform Firearms Act was the subject of further study. For four years, the Act was considered and reconsidered. At length, in 1930, it was approved once more, with only minor modifications, by both the Conference and the American Bar Association. Hailed by historians of the NRA as a "modern, forward-looking" statute, it was enacted in whole or in part during the 1930's by five states (Alabama, Indiana, Pennsylvania, South Dakota, and Washington) and the District of Columbia. Whether the Act was not accepted by other states because it was too weak or too strong is an interesting subject for speculation.

As part of its persistent efforts to erase the Sullivan Law from the statute books, the NRA tried to have its "model" uniform law enacted in New York. It very nearly succeeded. In the fall of 1931, two New York State legislators with the improbable names of Hanley and Fake introduced a firearms bill. If enacted, it would have replaced all of the state's other firearms laws, including the Sullivan

Law. The Hanley-Fake Firearms Bill was essentially the NRA's model Uniform Firearms Act. Athough the Hanley-Fake Firearms Bill passed both state houses, it was vetoed by Governor Franklin Delano Roosevelt at the behest of New York City's police commissioner.

As the years went by, many serious authorities had become disenchanted with the Uniform Firearms Act. "Developments since it was drafted have thrown new light on several of the problems with which it deals," said Professor Sam B. Warner of the Harvard Law School in the *Journal of Criminal Law and Criminology.* "For example, experience has demonstrated the futility of further increases in the maximum sentence of persons convicted of crimes of violence. The various studies of the lives of criminals have shown that those already convicted of crimes of violence are not the only potential gunmen . . . More and more it has been recognized that the possession of a pistol that can easily be concealed in the pocket furnishes a temptation which many young hoodlums are impotent to resist. Thus, the relation of strict control over the purchase and carrying of pistols to the problem of reducing crimes of violence has become clear."

Such considerations led the Interstate Commission on Crime in 1937 to designate Professor Warner, one of the nation's most distinguished legal scholars, to head a committee to draft a *new* uniform act. The new act, adopted by the Interstate Commission the following year, was known as the Uniform Pistol Act in order to avoid confusing it with the older Uniform Firearms Act.

Among other things, the new act provided for *minimum* penalties for armed crimes, rather than for merely imposing heavier penalties or adding to the penalties for such crimes as provided in the Uniform Firearms Act. "The catch in this scheme," said Warner, "is that today in nearly all states the judges are already authorized to impose sentences of imprisonment for 20 years or more for all the more serious crimes of violence. Either the judges do not impose such sentences or they impose long maximum sentences with short or no minima.* These judicial practices together with early release on parole result in most convicted offenders serving only short

* That is, a sentence specifying both a maximum and minimum or indeterminate term allowing for the prisoner's early release.

stretches, even for serious crimes of violence committed while armed with a pistol." Warner cited a U.S. Census Bureau report, showing that 40 per cent of all persons convicted of robbery, for example, were not sentenced to any period of imprisonment, that 57 per cent served either no imprisonment or less than two years, and that only 9 per cent served six years or more.

Another important provision of the proposed Uniform Pistol Act placed an absolute ban upon the possession of a pistol by anyone previously convicted of a serious crime, not just a crime of violence. Echoing New York City Police Commissioner McLaughlin's earlier reservations about the Uniform Firearms Act, Warner's reasoning was:

Robbery and other crimes of violence are occasionally committed by young men without prior criminal records, but not usually. Ordinarily a young criminal cuts his teeth on larceny and other minor offenses, including such nonviolent ones as making or possessing burglar's tools, of buying or receiving stolen property, of aiding escape from prison, of extortion, of dealing in drugs, and so on. Only after he has had a few convictions and "done time," does he graduate into robbery. The transition may be intentional, but often it is due to chance and the presence of a pistol. He has the pistol and the opportunity for easy money seems Heaven-sent. Hence a strenuous effort should be made to keep pistols out of the hands of boys and young men whose prior conduct shows them to belong to the class from which gunmen spring.

Most controversial, however, and absent from the Uniform Firearms Act, was a provision in the new act requiring a license for the purchase of a pistol. "Experience seems to show that this requirement has worked well in New York, especially in New York City," Professor Warner commented, adding:

The efficacy of a statute that aims to prevent criminals from securing arms depends upon the kind of criminal to which one refers. A law, which like the Uniform Firearms Act, merely imposes a slight delay in the sale of pistols, may supply a cooling time for a disgruntled lover or a jealous husband. A law, which like the Uniform Pistol Act, requires a license to purchase a pistol would probably also prevent the insane and the feebleminded from securing pistols. If well administered, such a law might prevent otherwise law-abiding citizens who are addicted to alcohol or fits of temper from securing pistols to their detriment and that of others. It might even keep a young hoodlum without underworld connections from embarking accidentally upon a criminal career.

Primarily because of the provision for a license to purchase a pistol, it goes without saying that the Uniform Pistol Act was unpalatable to the NRA.* However, the new Act was approved in 1940 as a successor to the innocuous Uniform Firearms Act by both the National Conference and the American Bar Association. This fact is one that the NRA does not find worthy of mention in its various published accounts of the history of uniform firearms legislation. It does, however, boast that the act "never gained acceptance by any state," although it does not claim a much deserved credit for this.

Instead, says a NRA brochure, *The Gun Law Problem,* "In 1949, the National Conference of Commissioners recognized that the Act was unsatisfactory and, consequently, killed the Uniform Pistol Act by withdrawing approval." This statement takes some liberties with the facts. The National Conference has informed me that it declared the Uniform Pistol Act obsolete in 1949, not because it was unsatisfactory, but rather because it did not have much chance of adoption. "As you may know," the Conference also told me, "there are powerful organizations and lobbies that oppose any type of gun regulatory legislation, and we have found it impossible to get our Act on the subject enacted by any large number of states." †

One of the NRA's most profound regrets is that it was not sufficiently prophetic or powerful back in 1911 to prevent passage of the much-hated Sullivan Law. "There was no organized opposition in those days to ill-conceived firearms laws," said an article in a 1962 issue of *The American Rifleman.* "The Sullivan Law is really no worse than many introduced into other state legislatures each year. But now they are properly analyzed and usually killed before they get to the floor for discussion. Today, as for the last 30 years, the full

* Among the NRA's other principal objections to it: the provision for a "target shooter's" license, and the requirement that any target pistol have a barrel at least six inches long.

† As recently as 1964, the National Conference again considered and vetoed a suggestion to draft a uniform act. "In view of past history," the Conference wrote me on October 16, 1964, "it was the consensus of our Executive Committee that the Conference should not spend a lot of time and energy drafting legislation that would not have much chance of being adopted by the states."

strength of the membership of NRA would be marshaled against any such proposal. Unfortunately, in 1911, there was no such organized strength."

However, such strength during the past three decades has been sufficient to see to it that the only alternative to stringent and uniform state laws—a meaningful Federal law—has never been adopted.

9 Federal Controls—A History of Failure

While Congress had, from time to time, pondered the need for firearms controls, it was not until 1927—some 138 years after the birth of the Republic—that it got around to enacting its first such measure. This was a law prohibiting the sending of pistols and other concealable firearms through the mails.*

Since the National Rifle Association had only then just begun to welcome pistol shooters as brothers-in-arms and to assume the mantle of chief defender of the citizens' "right" to bear arms, no one appeared at congressional hearings to oppose the bill. After passage, however, it proved innocuous enough to gun lovers; it was easily circumvented by the simple device of shipping handguns by express, instead of by mail. Rather than resort to this ruse, a few conscientious mail-order merchants discontinued the sale of pistols and revolvers. The president of one large mail-order house, which had done an annual pistol business amounting to $250,000, said: "We found that most of these pistols were being bought for unlawful purposes." And impatient people, unwilling to wait for express shipments or with some nasty business to get over with at once,

* Exceptions were made for certain persons. See Appendix I.

could of course continue to procure handguns locally over the counter.

The issue of gun controls was thrust suddenly on the public early in 1933 by one such person, Giuseppe Zangara, a 32-year-old unemployed Miami bricklayer with an ulcerated stomach. Zangara was a demented man, filled with deep hostility toward the world in general and toward kings, capitalists and Presidents in particular. When he read in the newspaper that President-elect Franklin D. Roosevelt would be in Miami, he resolved to kill him. On the evening of February 15, Zangara, armed with a revolver purchased for $8 in a local pawn shop, proceeded to the city's Bay Front Park where Roosevelt was to address a rally from the rear seat of his open car.

"I sat there in the park waiting," Zangara later said, "and my stomach kept aching more than ever. . . . I do not hate Mr. Roosevelt personally, I hate all Presidents, no matter from what country they come, and I hate all officials and everybody who is rich."

After Roosevelt had delivered a short, informal talk, Zangara, from 35 feet away, fired five bullets at the Presidential car. Possibly because the assassin's arm may have been jogged by the shot, the bullets went awry and hit, instead of the President, five other bystanders. One of them, Mayor Anton Cermak of Chicago, died of his wound on March 6.

The shock of the Presidential assassination attempt, creating the momentary fuss that such matters invariably do in this country, was transformed into a demand for meaningful Federal firearms legislation. At the trial of Zangara,* Judge Thompson of the Eleventh Judicial Circuit Court of Florida declared his firm conviction that Congress should pass an act providing for "confiscation of all firearms that may be carried or concealed about the person."

Three Presidents of the United States have been assassinated. We have had just a few more than thirty Presidents, so that out of every ten, one has been killed, so far, by an assassin. One other ex-President was shot in a public appearance . . . These assassinations have either been perfected or undertaken by a man armed with a pistol, and yet the people of this country steadfastly permit the manufacture, sale and possession of such deadly and useless weapons. I say "useless" for this reason: A pistol in the hands of an assassin is sure death and murder,

* Zangara was electrocuted on March 20, 1933.

while a pistol in the hands of you good people, and the good people of this country is about the most useless weapon of defense with which you can arm yourself.

Also giving fresh impetus to the demand for federal controls over guns were a number of other jolting facts. Guns were continuing to flow in unrestricted quantity not only to criminal mobs, but to the population at large. The toll of deaths—homicides, suicides and accidents—attributed to firearms had been steadily increasing over the years, rising from 11.6 per 100,000 population just before World War I (1913) to a rate of 15.4 in 1932. The victims of bullets, self-inflicted or otherwise, numbered 18,461 in that year. In the twenty years from 1913 through 1932, there had been the astonishing total of 243,153 firearms deaths in the United States.*

It was brought out that three-quarters of our firearms murders were committed by concealable firearms. Equally significant was the fact that in those states, such as New York and Massachusetts, where a license was required for the purchase of pistols and revolvers, the homicide rate was far lower than that of other states. As we have already learned, in New York, for example, the homicide rate in 1932 was 5.8 per 100,000 population against 9.2 for the country at large. And as the attempt on Roosevelt's life clearly illustrated, most of the states had failed to come up with effective measures of their own. Said J. Weston Allen, then a special assistant to the U.S. Attorney General:

The provisions of the Sullivan Law restricting the purchase of pistols are of little avail in New York, if the gunmen can cross the Hudson River by ferry and purchase the latest model automatic pistol without restriction in Jersey City. A similar law in Massachusetts is rendered ineffectual if pistols can be purchased by the criminal over-the-counter by crossing the Rhode Island state line to Providence.†

By 1933, at long last, it seemed almost inevitable that Congress would act. At the request of Attorney General Homer Cummings, an unprecedented number of bills regulating the manufacture, disposal or transportation of small firearms was introduced in the Seventy-

* For year-by-year figures, see Appendix III.
† This is no longer true. However, New Yorkers can still go to other nearby places. See Digest of State Laws, Appendix II.

third Congress. Seven bills were introduced in the House, and five in the Senate—one under the impressive bipartisan sponsorship of such illustrious names as Senators Copeland of New York, Vandenberg of Michigan, and Murphy of Iowa.

Basically, there are three areas of constitutional power under which firearms controls may be legislated. One is the power of the Federal government to regulate interstate and foreign commerce. Another is the Federal taxing power. Finally, there is the residual police power of the states, which the states can use to maintain law and order. The last-mentioned power derives from the Tenth Amendment: "The powers not delegated to the United States by the Constitution, nor prohibited by it to the States, are reserved to the States respectively, or to the People."

Although some of the bills introduced in the Seventy-third Congress exercised the Federal power over interstate commerce, most of the bills were based on the Federal taxing power. As Attorney General Cummings later explained, "The traffic in firearms is not always interstate. For example, we want a record of the guns which were shipped from Philadelphia to Pittsburgh within the same state, and we want every owner of a firearm in both these cities to be subject to the terms of the statute. The taxing power, consequently, seemed the only basis upon which to frame a registration statute."

A typical bill of this sort, H.R. 9066, required all manufacturers, dealers, importers and pawnbrokers dealing in firearms to pay an annual occupational tax, and to keep records of all their transactions. Firearms were defined to mean pistols, revolvers and such "gangster weapons" as machine guns, silencers and sawed-off shotguns and rifles. Ordinary shotguns and rifles were bypassed, because Cummings and members of Congress wanted to avoid arousing the hostility of the organized shooting fraternity. Among other things, H.R. 9066 required that each weapon be registered, and a tax be levied on its transfer, the new owner to be identified by certain information, including fingerprints and a photograph. Another bill also provided for the regulation of the sale of ammunition for the firearms specified.

At a hearing before the House Ways and Means Committee in April 1934, the Attorney General pointed out the need for the proposed legislation: "All of these bills ... are predicated upon the proposition that there has developed in this country a situation which is far beyond the power of control of merely local authorities." He took occasion to reaffirm a statement which had previously astounded the country. He declared there were at least 500,000 lawless persons "who are carrying about with them, or have available at hand, weapons of the most deadly character."

In rebuttal, the National Rifle Association in the person of its then president, Karl T. Frederick, protested against the provision for fingerprints. Drawing upon the organization's well-worn analogy between auto deaths and firearms fatalities, Frederick said that automobile owners, though not fingerprinted, were "as a class, a much more criminal body, from the standpoint of percentage, than pistol licensees."

"Do you make that statement seriously?" asked Chairman Robert L. Doughton of North Carolina.

"Yes, sir," Frederick replied.

"That the ordinary man who owns and operates an automobile is more likely to be a criminal than the man who arms himself?" Doughton persisted. "On what do you base that statement? Have you statistics upon which to base that, or is it a guess?"

Frederick confessed that he had no statistics, and said that his information came from "numbers of high police officials," whom he did not name. Nor did he mention that in a survey made by the National Crime Commission of the chiefs of police in all the metropolitan areas of the country, the reply in every instance favored the licensing of gun purchasers.

"Would not the interesting analogy be more between the pistol and dope peddling?," asked committee member John W. McCormack of Massachusetts.* "Would not that be a closer link than the link of a pistol with an automobile?"

"I do not think so," said Frederick.

"The use of dope is recognized by mankind as inherently harmful to the human being."

"Except as prescribed by physicians," said Frederick.

"That is the exception," said McCormack, "but, as a general rule, it is recognized as inherently dangerous. The same applies to weapons; they are recognized as inherently dangerous."

At the time, the NRA was relatively unknown in Washington legislative circles, its initials commonly being taken to refer to that then-

---

* Since 1962, Speaker of the House.

familiar New Deal bureaucratic creation, the National Recovery Administration. Consequently, Representative McCormack manifested some curiosity as to the character of the organization and, more pointedly, its possible connection with a stream of letters and telegrams he and other committee members had recently been receiving from gun clubs and hunting associations all over the country.

Several minutes later, Major General Milton A. Reckord, the NRA's executive vice president, after some persistent questioning by McCormack, explained: "In each state, or practically every state, we have a State Rifle Association, and we advised a number of those people that the hearing would be held today."

"Did you ask them to wire in here?" McCormack asked.

"I do not recall the exact language of the telegram," General Reckord replied. "I would say yes, probably we did . . ."

Even then taking umbrage at its characterization as a "lobby," the NRA some weeks later sent a mass mailing to its "members and friends" urging them to "personally communicate with your congressman asking him to oppose H.R. 9066." With the letter was enclosed a circular and the additional advice: "You should show the circular to your local dealers and have them do the same [that is, express their opposition to the measure]. Contact your local sportsman's organization, American Legion post, etc., and have similar action taken. Do not delay."

The circular, in addition to giving a detailed description of H.R. 9066, made a rather startling admission: "All guns, shotguns and rifles, as well as pistols and revolvers, must be included in the Federal statute if it is to serve any useful purpose. If they are not included, H.R. 9066 is not worth the paper it is printed on as a crime preventive measure."

"This bill," the circular then commented, "is undoubtedly presented in its present form because there are fewer owners of pistols and revolvers than there are shotgun owners, and it is hoped in that way to get the law passed." Once the law was on the books, the circular warned darkly, the Attorney General could go to the next Congress and have the law amended to include all firearms. The circular continued: "Within a year after the passage of H.R. 9066, every rifle and shotgun owner in the country will find himself paying a special revenue tax and having himself fingerprinted and photographed for the Federal 'Rogues Gallery' every time he buys or sells a gun of any description."

The NRA followed this prediction of things to come with an amazing public statement:

"The issue is clean cut between the Attorney General and his undesirable law on the one side, and the sportsmen of America and other law-abiding citizens on the other side, with the armed criminals of the country on the side lines rooting for the Attorney General."

On May 28, Senator Royal F. Copeland of New York opened the Commerce Committee hearings on several of the bills, which had been introduced in the Senate, with the statement: "A great deal of misinformation has been sent out over the country about the purpose of these bills. One would think from reading the records printed that it is the desire of the Senate to disarm good men and to furnish arms only to men who are bad."

Copeland was a physician, a former medical school dean and president of the New York City Board of Health, who had fruitlessly introduced firearms control bills annually during his nearly dozen years in the Senate. He clashed almost from the start with General Reckord, who, Copeland brought out, was a high-salaried official of the National Rifle Association.* After questioning Reckord sharply about the NRA—its membership, activities, source of financial support, relations with the firearms industry and efforts to influence legislation—Copeland asked, "Is there anything in these bills that interferes with the possession of arms by reputable private citizens?"

"A great deal," Reckord replied. "For instance, it says sawed-off shotguns without specifying the length of the barrel."

"All right," said Copeland, "We'll strike that out; anybody can saw off a shotgun."

"Then it regulates the sale of ammunition for all the weapons mentioned," Reckord continued. "We object to that; ammunition is not firearms and is not in itself dangerous."

"Is it your view that anybody in the world should be permitted to buy ammunition?"

---

* Now in his middle eighties, Reckord today lives in a Baltimore suburb. He still serves as Adjutant General of Maryland, an official post he held while he was the NRA's executive vice president. Currently, he is also a member of the NRA executive council.

"Yes, with certain regulations, such as licensing dealers to make them amenable to discipline."

"Should Dillinger be allowed to buy it?"

"He shouldn't be allowed to buy anything."

"All right, call him Brown."

"If he's an honest citizen, he should be allowed to buy freely."

"How are we going to know?" Copeland protested. "And a gun would not be any good without ammunition, would it?"

"No, sir."

"Well, then, it is just as important to regulate the ammunition as it is the gun, isn't it?"

"We don't think so, Senator."

The two then turned to a provision prohibiting anyone but a licensed manufacturer from shipping arms in interstate commerce. "Do you see any objection to that provision?" Copeland asked.

"Yes," Reckord replied. "I don't see why you should not be allowed to ship a gun to me, if you want to ship a gun to me."

"If I can freely ship a gun to you, I can ship one to Dillinger," Copeland said.

"Well, if you license the dealers, we think you will regulate the traffic in firearms sufficiently," Reckord answered. "We don't think you should inconvenience the honest citizen by Federal law. But I don't think you should be permitted to ship a gun to Dillinger."

"Are you going to write in the law that you can ship to anybody except Dillinger?"

"No, you cannot do that, Senator, but you could write into a law that if Dillinger were found with a gun on his person that had been shipped in interstate commerce illegally then he, Dillinger, should be sentenced because he had disobeyed that law."

"Then all we would have to do is to catch Dillinger," said Copeland, a model of forbearance. "That's a beautiful idea, but show me how it can be made to work."

Senator Copeland patiently and persistently tried to pin the NRA spokesman down in regard to any practical gun control law that his organization would favor, but Reckord just as persistently squirmed away. It became obvious that he would not approve any control measure designed to cover lawless men that might inconvenience the firearms fraternity in the slightest. One proposed provision, Reckord said, would place a "terrible burden on the manufacturer."

"Of course, you're not interested in the manufacturer?" asked Copeland with elaborate casualness. "You speak for the National Rifle Association."

"Well," replied Reckord, "it would be a terrific injustice which the committee ought not to vote in justice to itself."

Reckord finally closed his testimony with the plea: "The only thing we are asking is we don't want you to include pistols and revolvers."

The plea was really unnecessary, for on that very same day, a report from the other side of Capitol Hill recommended the elimination of pistols and revolvers from the newly consolidated House bill, H.R. 9741, which was hurriedly enacted into law on June 26, 1934, just before Congress adjourned. The strong gun law that had been deemed "inevitable" in February 1933 had been hacked down to a basket case.

With pistols and revolvers eliminated, and with ordinary rifles and shotguns never even considered, the law, though entitled the National Firearms Act, was nothing more than a Federal machine-gun act. It provided principally for the registration and tax of $200 on the making, sale or transfer of machine guns and other similar fully automatic firearms (including machine pistols), sawed-off shotguns (that is, those with barrels less than 18 inches long), cut-down rifles (barrels less than 16 inches long), and mufflers and silencers. There was a lesser tax, plus registration, on the transfer of "gadget" guns —such deceptive esoterica as flashlight guns, pen guns, palm guns, cane guns and cigarette lighter guns—which are not quite what they might appear to the unwary eye. The annual occupational tax decreed for all doing business in this array of weapons was $500 for manufacturers and importers, $300 for pawnbrokers and $200 for dealers.

Although the National Rifle Association had charged that the legislation culminating in the National Firearms Act was the product of "an effort to disguise as a revenue bill a Federal police measure," doubts as to its constitutionality were put to rest by a Federal District Court in 1935, in the case of *United States* v. *Adams,* and by the U.S. Supreme Court in 1937, in *Sonzinsky* v. *United States.* In the Sonzinsky case, Justice Harlan Fiske Stone said that in exercising its constitutional power to tax, Congress may choose the subject of taxation, and that a tax does not lose any of its character because it has a regulatory effect.

In spite of its limitations, the act was not without some effect. It resulted after three years in the registration of 9,316 submachine guns, 11,520 machine guns and machine rifles, 16,456 miscellaneous weapons, and 769 silencers. For the most part, they were held by law enforcement officers whose official duties required the use of these weapons. The law virtually put an end to their private ownership and casual sale to the public. The smoking tommy gun ceased to be a symbol of organized crime. In spite of the occasional rumblings of underworld warfare, there were no more big barrages of machine-gun fire.

The traffic in firearms continued in the years that followed.

"The criminal's arsenal is today not only made up of pistols and revolvers, but of ordinary shotguns and rifles," said Attorney General Homer Cummings, speaking before the Annual Convention of the International Association of Chiefs of Police in Baltimore on October 5, 1937.

A typical arsenal described by Cummings consisted of 30 weapons, including 3 .45-caliber Colt revolvers, 3 .45-caliber Smith & Wesson revolvers, 12 .38-caliber Smith & Wesson special revolvers, 6 .38-caliber Del Colt special revolvers, and 6 .45-caliber Remington derringers. All were purchased in a sporting goods store by someone who represented himself as a hardware dealer and gave a fictitious name. Three of the weapons were later found in a car used in a murder, others at the scene of gang killings at Oak Park, Illinois; Newark, New Jersey; and Philadelphia.

Referring to long arms, Cummings said: "These weapons continue to take their terrific toll. The high-powered rifle which will kill big game at tremendous distances is, unfortunately, equally effective against human beings. During the past two years, improvements have been made, both in hand arms and the quality of ammunition, which have already rendered obsolete much of the protective equipment of law enforcement agencies. We cannot longer remain blind to these facts. Are we altogether realistic when we require the registration of a shotgun with a barrel of less than 18 inches in length and overlook the weapon which measures 19 inches? Why should we require the registration of the short rifle and exempt the automatic pistol or the newer type revolvers?"

Cummings, a tough attorney, though slow in speech and movement, went on to pledge a "fight to the finish" for a Federal law requiring the registration of *all* firearms. "No honest man can object to registration, a procedure much simpler than the registration and licensing procedure applicable to automobiles. Show me the man who doesn't want his gun registered, and I will show you a man who shouldn't have a gun."

At the time, a bill submitted by Cummings had been quiescent in Congress since May. He had been vainly calling for public hearings on the measure, which extended the provisions of the National Firearms Act to cover all types of firearms. Then Cummings, as a realistic concession to the power of the gun lobby, altered his original proposal. In the spring of 1938 he agreed that it should apply only to pistols and revolvers, but not to rifles and shotguns. Nonetheless, the bill languished in the House Ways and Means Committee. With it was another Justice Department proposal, one to end the indiscriminate mail-order sale of pistols and revolvers to minors, criminals, mental defectives and other such persons, by prohibiting the shipment of these weapons even by express.

The Cummings bills had the backing of the American Bar Association and the International Association of Chiefs of Police, two organizations intimately in touch and directly concerned with the crime problem. The bills were also endorsed by the General Federation of Women's Clubs, which then represented organizations with a membership of more than 2 million women throughout the country.

Although the gun lobby had fostered the impression in Congress that there was widespread opposition to the registration of firearms, a nationwide poll conducted by the newly formed American Institute of Public Opinion (founded by a fledgling pollster named George Gallup) indicated that more than five-sixths of the nation's population favored registration.

In a letter to the *New York Herald Tribune*,* J. Weston Allen, special assistant to the Attorney General, wrote:

When it is considered that deaths from homicide in this country are ten times more frequent than in Canada and twenty times more frequent

* May 10, 1938.

than in Great Britain, and that in this country 70 per cent of the homicides are committed with firearms, as compared with 30 per cent in Canada, it is clearly apparent that to attempt to legislate against the criminal use of firearms in this country without including pistols and revolvers is like playing Hamlet with Hamlet left out.

If an insistent public demand is made for favorable action on the pending bills [Allen's letter concluded], there is every prospect that there is yet time to secure their enactment into law during the present session of Congress.

However, just as four years before, the NRA sounded a call to action.

"The Attorney General's previous efforts to secure drastic Federal firearms laws have been killed by the active and audible objections of the sportsmen of America," the NRA trumpeted in *The American Rifleman*.

"Once again, the members of the National Rifle Association will need to be represented by their officers in pointing out to Congress the hidden dangers of such a plausible legislative scheme to end crime. Once again we ask every active member to use the coupon below to say: 'The right of the American citizen to bear arms shall not be infringed.'"

The message concluded with the suggestion that each NRA member "start the New Year" by persuading "another good American to join the NRA and thus take an active, intelligent part in this new campaign to save the sportsmen's guns from registration, confiscation or further taxation."

Subsequent 1938 issues of the *Rifleman* continued to castigate the Attorney General's bill while enthusiatically advocating the passage of the NRA's suggested solution to the crime problem, Senate Bill No. 3, which did not require the registration of firearms. Instead, it merely provided for the licensing of manufacturers, importers and dealers at modest fees. The bill contained a meaningless clause enjoining dealers from doing business *knowingly* with a list of proscribed people—criminals, fugitives from justice, and the like. The measure also placed a ban on interstate and foreign commerce in stolen firearms, or those from which the serial number had been removed, obliterated or altered.

The shortcomings of this bill were obvious. Nothing in it could effectively prevent a criminal from sending for a gun and getting it.

He would be breaking the law, of course, but if he used a false name in ordering his gun, it is unlikely that anyone would ever catch up with him. The bill did not require express or other common carriers to notify local authorities to determine the legitimacy of a gun customer, or that he verify his identity himself. And with no fingerprinting requirement in the bill, there was nothing to stop any criminal from lying about his identity and getting a Federal dealer's license.

Yet the strategy of the NRA was clear enough: "The passage of this measure," said the May 1938 *American Rifleman*, "would mean the death of the Attorney General's bills."

Equally significant and buried away among the numerous provisions of the original draft of S. 3 was a brief sentence calling for the repeal of the 1934 National Firearms Act. The sentence was promptly deleted with no dissent after it was spotted by a sharp-eyed Justice Department official.

Not surprisingly, playing a major role in the drafting of S. 3 was none other than General Milton Reckord of the NRA. More curious is the fact that the nominal sponsor of the bill was that veteran fighter for firearms control, Senator Royal F. Copeland of New York. What Copeland's motives were in lending his name to the legislation is not quite clear. Some historians of that era have attributed to him a flexible ethical sense. This sense, wrote Arthur M. Schlesinger, Jr., in *The Coming of the New Deal*, enabled Copeland to accept broadcasting fees from Fleischmann's Yeast, Eno Fruit Salts and Phillips Milk of Magnesia while a pure food and drug bill of which he was the nominal sponsor was under discussion. More radical proponents of food and drug control, said Schlesinger, dismissed Copeland as a tool of the drug interests. Or it may be that Copeland in his waning years was given to accommodation and compromise.

Just as Copeland's controversial food and drug bill suffered a series of dilutions under his management in 1933–34 because he said that his bill would be better than no bill at all, so also did he believe, in the case of his newest firearms bill, that it was better to get "half a loaf than none."

Actually, S. 3 had first been conceived back in 1935. When the Justice Department objected to it at its first hearing then, Copeland stated: "I have had a bill here for twelve years. That bill received no favorable consideration, but did receive drastic criticism. That is true of the bill which we presented last year." Speaking of S. 3, he then said, "I believe that this bill is as far as we can go with any hope of passing the legislation. If the Department of Justice can put over a more drastic law, God bless them. But I feel that it is my duty to say, with reference to this bill, that it is my judgment that no more stringent law than this can be enacted."

S. 3 was enacted as the Federal Firearms Act on June 30, 1938. Senator Copeland did not live to see it, because he had died just thirteen days before. But his prophecy has proved correct, in that no more "stringent" law, indeed, no further Federal firearms legislation of any consequence, has been enacted down to this very day.

Any possibility of S. 3's having any meaning had been lessened at the 1935 hearings. This is when the Senator, in response to a request by the NRA, had acquiesced to the words "knowing or having reasonable cause to believe" in the provision which now reads:

It shall be unlawful for any person to ship, transport, or cause to be shipped or transported in interstate or foreign commerce any firearm or ammunition to any person knowing or having reasonable cause to believe that such person is under indictment or has been convicted in any court of the United States, the several States, Territories, possessions, or the District of Columbia of a crime punishable by imprisonment for a term exceeding one year or is a fugitive from justice.*

As time was to show, the government could not easily prove that a dealer or a manufacturer was *knowingly* shipping guns to persons in the prohibited class. In fact, the government has never obtained a single conviction under this provision of the Act.

True to form, the NRA heralded the enactment of S. 3 as a sweeping victory for "the gun lovers of this nation," and stated that the Attorney General had been given "a workable law . . . all the law he needs." †

Just as the courts had upheld the 1934 National Firearms Act as a valid exercise of the taxing power, so also was the Federal Firearms Act subsequently declared constitutional ‡ in its use of the commerce clause.

---

* The provision in the original 1938 Act proscribed only persons convicted of a *crime of violence*. The somewhat broader present definition of prohibited persons was effected by an amendment adopted in 1961.
† *The American Rifleman*, August 1938.
‡ *Cases* v. *U.S.*, 131 F. 2d 916 (1st Cir. 1942).

Since the new 1938 Act also contained some provisions for the collecting of excise taxes, it was placed under the custodial wing of the Internal Revenue Service, which had earlier been given the unhappy task of administering the National Firearms Act.

In order to execute these duties effectively, it was assumed that the Commissioner of Internal Revenue could prescribe and promulgate any additional rules and regulations he deemed necessary, without first having to go to the trouble of securing the sanction of Congress. But the commissioner took no such action for the nineteen years from 1938 to 1957.

Meanwhile, there had been but one abortive attempt to pass a strong Federal gun law: In 1947 Senator Alexander Wiley of Wisconsin, at the request of Attorney General Tom Clark, introduced what the NRA was soon to term an attempt "to revive the idea of a Gestapo-type Federal firearms registration law."

Wiley gave compelling reasons for his proposal which would not have required a person possessing a firearm to procure a license, but merely to register the firearm and to record any transfer of it. On the floor of the Senate (January 24, 1947) Wiley said:

"At present, thousands of small arms, principally revolvers and automatic pistols, orginally issued to the members of the Armed Forces, are in the possession of persons who do not appear to have acquired them legitimately." Pointing out that the Armed Forces had been reporting a "tremendous number" of small arms lost or unaccounted for and that servicemen returning from abroad had been bringing back firearms by the thousands, Wiley stated that a considerable number of firearms had recently been found in the possession of members of the underworld. The seriousness of the situation is indicated by the fact that in 1946 more than a half million major crimes were committed in the United States by minors under eighteen, the majority of them with firearms.

But the NRA's propaganda wheels were once more set in motion, against the Wiley bill and against Attorney General Clark * for having proposed it. Soon after, Wiley recanted. He lamely explained to the NRA: "I introduced this measure merely at the Attorney General's request in my capacity as chairman of the Senate Judiciary Committee." Wiley then withdrew his bill.

* Since 1949, an Associate Justice of the U.S. Supreme Court.

Another ten years was to go by before the attempt came to do with regulation what appeared impossible to achieve through legislation. In 1957 the Internal Revenue Service, in order to strengthen the 1938 Federal Firearms Act, proposed for the first time in nearly two decades a number of changes in the IRS regulations used to implement the Act.

With the announcement of these proposed changes, the NRA once more was up in arms. Its protest culminated in a government hearing perhaps unparalleled in Washington annals—a noisy free-for-all that one startled government onlooker called "a disgrace." Packing the hearing room were hundreds of gun lovers who had descended on Washington from all corners of the country—lumberjack types from the Far West wearing checkered sport shirts, watery-eyed sons of the South, tanned stalwarts from Texas sporting Stetsons and bolo ties, and, somewhat more restrained in raiment if not in decorum, delegates from firearms manufacturer and dealer groups. Members of Congress friendly to the firearms interests were also present.

During the hearing, it was intimated that some powerful pressure group had exerted undue influence on members of Congress with a tremendous letter-writing campaign, and that the large crowd in attendance was due to "organized opposition," namely, that spear headed by the NRA.

To refute this charge, Representative Bruce Alger, ultra-conservative Dallas Republican friendly to the NRA, rose and remarked: "While opposition in our area to these regulations has been to some extent organized, I can assure you that the majority of letters appear to come from thoughtful and responsible citizens who are expressing their own feelings in this regard. The organization referred to would appear to have been only something of a Paul Revere effort to inform and alert individuals to the necessity of expressing their own thoughts."

The "Paul Revere effort," however, was a considerable one. The announcement of the proposed regulatory changes had first appeared in the May 3, 1957, *Federal Register,* an official government publication which the NRA staff reads as religiously as stock market devotees do the *Wall Street Journal.* According to the announcement, the new regulations were due to go into effect on July 1.

Under the established procedure, any objections to them would have to be registered within thirty days of the announcement, that is, by June 3. The NRA did not have too much time to lose.

"As soon as the National Rifle Association observed these proposed regulations," an *American Rifleman* editorial later recalled, "it was realized that 'the Redcoats were coming!' The signal light was hung and the alarm was spread." *

The proposed changes did not seem to warrant such alarm, as they gave no indication of inhibiting the activities of any shooter-sportsman. Indeed, the changes were only minor in character and, in most instances, represented no marked departure from the spirit, if not the letter, of the provisions in the 1938 Act.

One change, for example, would have required all manufacturers and importers of guns to stamp each with a serial number and other identifying information. This was a practice already followed by most major U.S. manufacturers, including those responsible for about half of the domestic output of all shotguns, and one-third of the production of rifles. Moreover, the Act had already recognized the importance of serial numbers by outlawing the traffic in any firearms "from which the manufacturer's serial number had been removed, obliterated or altered."

Another clause would have simply required a person to sign his name when buying a firearm or ammunition for a handgun. This did not seem to be in conflict with the requirement already on the books that a dealer make a record of the buyer's name. Still another proposal would have required manufacturers and dealers to retain their records *permanently*, something already specified in the original Act, although back in 1943 a period of six years was for some reason set down by the rule-makers as the life of records.

Valid as the IRS proposals were, they were obnoxious to the NRA and its friends in the arms business. By May 15, an NRA legislative bulletin sounding the alarm was quickly on its way to all firearms manufacturers, leading dealers, gunsmiths and outdoor writers. An extra 37,000 copies were prepared for and at the expense of the Winchester-Western Division of the Olin Mathieson Chemical Corporation; Winchester mailed these together with a covering letter to its

---

* The editorial, in the same Paul Revere vein, also stated, "Fortunately for the gun owners of America, we have our 'observation post' and our 'courier' to inform the public," and, fittingly, reprinted a portion of Longfellow's poem about America's most famous horseback ride.

largest dealer list. The Remington Arms Company followed suit with a newsletter of its own, as did also several other manufacturers and important firearms dealers groups. Although the June *American Rifleman* was about to go to press, rushed into it was a box announcement summarizing the principal proposed regulatory changes.

Having been so alerted, NRA members and the others reached made their feelings known, not only to the Internal Revenue Service but also to their senators and representatives. "The effect was almost immediate!" crowed the NRA, for before long the Internal Revenue Service announced a public hearing to take place in Washington on August 27. The August *Rifleman* brought news of the hearing to NRA members, together with further comments which concluded with the statement:

"The issue is whether under the guise of Executive Department regulation, our rights in the private ownership of arms can be strangled little by little without legislative action of any kind. Do not leave this for someone else to do. This is your battle!"

Members were urged to attend the August 27 hearing in person if at all possible, and to continue to make their feelings known through letters and written statements.

Letters poured into Washington, several thousand registering protests directly to the IRS. More than 350 people appeared on August 27, so many that it was necessary to shift the scene of the hearing from a small room in the Internal Revenue Building to the spacious Department of Commerce auditorium. The hearing, originally scheduled for one day, required two days, and the testimony was eventually to fill more than 350 typewritten pages.

Of the sixty-two witnesses who had the opportunity to testify, there were only four to speak in favor of the changes. Together with the six IRS officials present, they were lonely figures who took quite a pummeling from the opposition.

Speaking first was James L. Sullivan, Chief Counsel of the U.S. Senate Subcommittee on Juvenile Delinquency. Sullivan pointed out that 43.2 per cent of all the robberies in the United States in the year before were committed by persons under twenty-one years of age. Pistols and revolvers were the most frequently used weapons in the commission of these crimes, he said. The proposals, Sullivan stated, "would not be the complete answer to keeping firearms out of the hands of the criminal element, the mentally unbalanced and the juvenile. They will, however, provide the community with some safeguard, now lacking, and give law enforcement agencies clues in solving crimes they do not now have."

Stating that his subcommittee investigation had found police departments and other law enforcement agencies to be "overwhelmingly in favor of more stringent controls over the sale and distribution of firearms and other dangerous weapons," Sullivan cited a murder case where the police were able to trace a weapon by the serial number in a matter of hours.

"This particular gun," said Sullivan, "was traced from the manufacturer through many dealers and owners, and the fact that the police department had the serial number played a major part in the solution of this crime."

Sullivan said further that the requirement of a signature would possibly be a deterrent to persons buying guns or ammunition for illegal purposes. "Since it is already required that every dealer make a record of the name of the person to whom a firearm is sold, it is difficult to see how there could be objections," he said.

Sullivan, the government's key witness, suddenly found himself berated from all sides. As the surprised Sullivan listened, thirty-two-year-old Representative John D. Dingell of Michigan, one of the nine Congressmen to testify personally (another fifteen did through their administrative assistants), opened his remarks with the astonishing words:

"Now, I want to start out by stating that I heard a do-gooder come down here on behalf of some Senate committee, a member of the committee staff, and he proposed to speak on behalf of the Congress of the United States. [Sullivan, of course, had done nothing of the sort.] And I want to make it very clear that he does not speak on behalf of the Congress of the United States . . ."

Detective Sergeant Joe Chennault, representing the Metropolitan Police Department of Washington, D.C., deplored the "distortions" used by the "organized opposition." "The material that was presented to us," said Chennault, "would make an uninformed citizen conclude with certainty . . . that not only should we discard these proposed amendments, but we should hasten to repeal the regulations that now exist and the acts of Congress which authorized these regulations."

Obviously alluding to Dingell's charge that Sullivan did not speak for Congress, Chennault went on to say that during the course of an investigation* he had once talked to over 200 members of the House of Representatives. "A great majority of that number expressed to me appreciation for what firearms regulations we did have," said Chennault, "and many of them stated that they wished that they could be improved."

Of similar mind was Leroy E. Wike, executive secretary of the International Association of Chiefs of Police. Wike said that most of the proposals were "merely extensions of regulations already in force," and stated that it would be "difficult to overstress the importance of firearms identification in the prevention and detection of crime." Wike added that "the average citizen who likes to own and use a fine firearm should not object to an accepted means of positively identifying the piece when he registers no objection to the manufacturer's name, serial number and type of product on his television, camera, radio, air conditioner or outboard motor, his wife's food mixer, electric range, garbage disposal or any of the dozens of mechanisms necessary for modern living."

Apparently, however, not many at the hearing agreed with the law enforcement officers on the usefulness or desirability of the regulations. Some even read into them a sinister motive. James H. Holton, representing the Veterans of Foreign Wars, warned: "We must not shut our eyes to the fact that there are, in our country, subversive elements which desire a police state." His lengthy written statement concluded with the declaration, "We Believe That the Ultimate Defender of His Personal Liberty Is an Angry and Resolute Free Man, Armed with a Firearm."

Representative Leroy H. Anderson of Montana went so far as to threaten the Internal Revenue Service. Shaking his finger at the tax officials present, he said, "Need I remind the bureau that we have both direct and indirect ways," as the hearing room rocked with laughter. "We hold the purse strings," he slyly suggested, "and I think it is not an idle threat to say that the appropriations of the bureau will be very seriously scrutinized if such a thing as this is put into effect." And Representative John Dowdy of Texas blithely assured the assemblage that the Communists would desire the adoption of the proposed regulations.

The rest of the two days of testimony also roamed over such mat-

* This stemmed from an incident involving five men who had shot up the House of Representatives several years before.

ters as economics and aesthetics. The new rules for record keeping, some argued, would result in an increase in the cost of firearms. The "unsightly" stamping of serial numbers, others protested, would disfigure firearms. Many felt the proposed regulations impugned the honesty and character of members of the shooting fraternity. "There is nothing abnormal about us gun lovers," said Herb Glass, a Bullville, New York, dealer, in speaking of his relish for hunting. "I have killed bobcats and snakes with a pistol. I get a big bang out of that, and I think that is normal."

Another typical gun lover heard from was Charles Brees, representing the Daniel Boone Hunters' League of Milwaukee. Brees, explaining that he was "visually handicapped" (which presumably did not interfere with his shooting activities), asked a friend to read his statement, which called for the repeal of all existing laws. Then there was C. Alfred Bergsten of the Minnesota Rifle & Revolver Association, who said, "I have never found any group that I feel more at home with then with these good, honest, Christian, clean, upright citizens in the gun shooting fraternity." Ending on a personal note, Bergsten, admitting to an arsenal of some twenty-five guns, said, "I tell you now, no government body is going to get available to them the serial numbers on those guns that I have—and if that be treason, make the most of it."

And so it went. Needless to say, the new regulations, as finally adopted on January 18, 1958, contained virtually none of the features found objectionable by the NRA. The new regulations called only for the retention of dealers records for ten years, instead of the former six-year period. They required the serial numbering of only handguns and high-powered rifles, but not of shotguns or .22-caliber rifles. In heralding the victory, *The American Rifleman* said:

"Members of the NRA, and all others who raised their voices in opposition to the regulations as originally proposed, have every reason to take pride in a job well done."

As the years went by, there were no more serious attempts at Federal firearms controls—by regulation or legislation. In 1961, only one firearms bill of any consequence was introduced in Congress. Sponsored by Representative Victor Anfuso, a Brooklyn Democrat, it proposed that all privately owned handguns be registered with the FBI. The result again was a flood of letters to Congress. Anfuso alone was the recipient of some 850 letters and postcards. One, from Amarillo, Texas, began, "Have you lost your mind?" It went on to say, "Your bill H.R. 613 is the most ridiculous, insane, cowardly piece of legislation ever proposed to the Congress of the United States." A Florida correspondent wrote: "I am going to keep plenty of ammo on hand and the first son-of-a-sea-cook who tries to take my guns from me will have to shoot me first." Others accused Anfuso of trying to sell out the United States to its enemies, of undermining the Constitution, and of proposing a law that would enable the Communists to take over.

Some of the opposition mail came from Dallas, where Dan Smoot, a former booster of the late Senator Joe McCarthy, conducts a right-wing radio program and sends a newsletter to gullible readers. A March 14, 1962, Smoot newsletter appealed to readers to pressure Congress to reject the proposed Anfuso legislation. It eventually died, without once getting a hearing by any committee.

Unfortunately, there was no public clamor for the Anfuso bill. President John F. Kennedy had not yet been assassinated.

10 The NRA Versus Senator Dodd

Slumbering in the Senate of the Eighty-eighth Congress at the time of the Kennedy assassination was a bill designed to curb the uninhibited traffic in mail-order firearms. Sponsored by Senator Thomas J. Dodd of Connecticut and four other Senators,* the bill was the fruit of nearly two and a half years of toil by Dodd's Senate Juvenile Deliquency Subcommittee. The subcommittee, as we know, had long been looking into the role of weapons, especially firearms, in juvenile delinquency. In 1959 it had managed to secure passage of a bill outlawing switch-blade knives. In March 1961, as a result of the large increase in the mail-order gun business, it began its full-scale investigation into the availability of firearms to juveniles.

Several years before, the subcommittee had sent questionnaires to virtually every important police chief and commissioner in the United States. Of the 69 who responded, an overwhelming majority favored the need for stronger Federal firearms controls. There were 46 respondents, representing every major urban center plagued by juvenile and adult crime, who agreed that the National Firearms

* Birch Bayh, Indiana; Sam J. Ervin, Jr., North Carolina; Hiram L. Fong, Hawaii; and Estes Kefauver, Tennessee.

Act should be broadened to cover the registration of pistols and revolvers, as well as the other weapons already specified in the act. As already noted, of the 69 law enforcement authorities, 63 said that they favored amending the Federal Firearms Act to prevent the interstate shipment of any firearms into their jurisdictions without their being notified in advance by the manufacturer or dealer making the shipment.

The subcommittee also sent more than 200 questionnaires to psychiatrists, psychologists and criminologists, to obtain their observations on the rise of youth crimes. It made field visits to twenty-six cities with known gang problems, and took testimony on gangs during hearings held in New York, Chicago, Philadelphia, Los Angeles, San Diego, San Francisco, Miami, and Washington, D.C.

No other firearms proposal in our history was based on such extensive research as the measure that was to become known as the Dodd Bill.

Recalling the inquiry launched in March 1961, Eugene Gleason, a subcommittee staff member, told me, "We put two additional investigators on the problem, and subsequently had conferences with industry, law enforcement people, gun dealers, government officials and representatives of the sportsmen's groups, before even thinking of putting together a legislative proposal. We examined all the previous legislative attempts and all the changes in the law, none of which had ever really succeeded, and decided that the best way to do it now was in a way that would irritate the fewest people. We sent more questionnaires to the police, and tried to see how the data reflected the crime rate so that we could track down the general areas where the mail-order houses did most of their business.

"We concentrated on mail-order guns, because the gun laws of most states that permit this traffic generally run from poor to weak. Then we subpoenaed multitudinous records from mail-order dealers and examined them. It was a monumental job. You'd get four or five packing crates of records, in each of which there might be 30,000 or 40,000 sales slips."

"Two of the largest mail-order dealers didn't care what they sold and who they sold them to," Gleason commented. "George Rose and Martin Retting alone each sold 3,000 guns in a year, and most of them went into only a few precincts in Chicago—the high crime areas. I personally flew to Chicago and checked each name on the mail-order sales slips against the Chicago Police Department records. I came up with a figure that 25 per cent of the guns—and this is only a minimal figure—were going to people with police records for anything from repeated drunkenness and wife-beating up to murder, to say nothing of assault, robbery and burglary."

Armed with this and other data, the subcommittee held five days of public hearings in Washington during January, March and May of 1963. It received testimony from police, prison, Treasury and shipping officials, and, of course, from executives of gun clubs and industry groups. Among them was the ubiquitous, ever-watchful National Rifle Association. The testimony bore out the ample need and demand for more effective Federal firearms controls. It showed that mail order was a major source of firearms to juveniles and young adults, as well as to adult felons, narcotic addicts and mental defectives. James V. Bennett, then director of the U.S. Bureau of Prisons, testified:

"Today we do not have the organized bands of desperate criminals that we had in the Thirties, and some of us have therefore concluded that we no longer have the bank robberies and kidnappings that we once had. The truth, however, is that we have more bank robberies than ever, and the number of kidnappings has not declined. Only the nature of the criminals committing these offenses has changed. Instead of the 'professionals' like John Dillinger and Machine-gun Kelly, we have now the economically desperate amateur, the emotionally disturbed, the impulsive, the unstable, and the heedless individual and juvenile. All they need is a gun, and their warped ideas or mentality lead inevitably at least to violence and frequently death. Our files are full of such cases."

The bill that finally emerged from the subcommittee provided that a mail-order gun purchaser must submit a notarized statement attesting to his criminal record, if any, and stating that he was over eighteen and that his purchase would not be contrary to his state or local laws. It was also proposed in the bill that license fees be increased—manufacturers' from $25 to $50, and dealers' from $1 to $10—and that holders of the Federal dealer's licenses be at least twenty-one years old.

On August 2, 1963, Dodd introduced the bill in the Senate, as an amendment to the Federal Firearms Act. Because it involved the movement of goods in interstate or foreign commerce, the bill, designated S. 1975, was appropriately referred to the Senate Commerce Committee. Once there, it was promptly forgotten.

After several months Dodd grew restive about his seemingly moribund bill, and on November 1, 1963 sent a lengthy brief on its behalf to Senator Warren D. Magnuson, chairman of the committee:

I am writing to you in reference to S. 1975, which I and several of my colleagues on the Juvenile Delinquency Subcommittee introduced on August 2, 1963, relating to the mail-order traffic in lethal weapons across state lines. The bill was the result of over two years of investigation and hearings conducted by the subcommittee. Our investigations disclosed the fact that "mail-order" weapons were delivered to felons, minors, narcotic addicts and, even in some cases, to mental defectives. For example, in checking the police records of approximately 200 recipients of "mail-order' weapons in the District of Columbia, subcommittee investigators determined that 25 per cent of them had criminal records ranging in seriousness from misdemeanors to felonies. . . .

Our spiraling crime figures also underscore the role of the lethal weapons traffic in this country. Of 8,600 murders in 1961, 53 per cent were committed by guns in the hands of mentally ill or criminalistic individuals. Of nearly 500,000 robberies and burglaries in 1961, most were committed with the assistance of firearms. Half of the persons committing suicide in the United States used guns and, in addition, killed 700 defenseless people without warning.

One of the most startling discoveries made during our hearings was the fact that between 1955 and 1960, when the juvenile population increased 25 per cent, the number of youngsters arrested for carrying guns increased almost 50 per cent.

Since the bill has been introduced, we have further evidence of the continuance of this traffic in lethal weapons, and, until the loopholes in the Federal statutes are closed, as provided by S. 1975, I feel this traffic will continue to flourish. . . .

In view of the fact that this is a relatively noncontroversial bill which would definitely cure a serious flaw in our local and Federal law enforcement machinery, I would hope that this measure could be considered in the very near future.

From the outside world, there was also an occasional plea for the all-but-forgotten bill. To cap a series of nine articles it had just run on the mail-order gun problem, the *Christian Science Monitor*, one of the few newspapers to devote any extensive space to the subject, published an editorial on November 19, just three days before the

Kennedy assassination. Headed "Murder by Mail Order," the editorial read:

Congress has been handed an antiweapon weapon with which to crack down on crime, crime made easy through the wide open sale of mail-order handguns.

This weapon is in the form of a new bill introduced by Senator Thomas J. Dodd (D.) of Connecticut and now before the Senate Commerce Committee. The committee so far has taken no action on this legislation which would crack down on "murder by mail order," as it has been called, through an amendment to the Federal Firearms Act.

If passed and enforced, it would keep mail-order guns out of the hands of trigger-happy juveniles, criminals, mental defectives and others who use the anonymity of this type of purchase as a means of obtaining firearms. . . .

Then came the terrible tragedy in Dallas. In the space of a few seconds, Lee Harvey Oswald—with a cheap foreign surplus military rifle, purchased under a phony name from Klein's Sporting Goods, a Chicago mail-order house—had murdered the President. On the rifle was a telescopic gunsight which had originated from another mail-order house, Weapons, Inc., of Los Angeles. Less than an hour later, Oswald had killed police officer J. D. Tippit with a .38-caliber revolver purchased from still another mail-order house, Seaport Traders, also of Los Angeles. Two of the three mail-order houses had been under investigation by the Dodd subcommittee staff: Weapons, Inc., whose president was Martin Retting, and Seaport Traders, owned by George Rose.

An old political truth holds that the provisions and intentions of a given bill are not so important as the men who consider it and the atmosphere in which they function. The National Firearms Act, innocuous though it was, had become law on the strength of the crime wave of its era, and the near-assassination of another President back in 1933. For the following thirty years there was a virtually unbroken record of failure. From 1955 through 1962, some 35 firearms bills were introduced in Congress; none met with any success. During the same period nearly 2,000 bills were introduced in state legislatures, with only a scattered success here and there. Now, just thirty years after the attempt on the life of F.D.R., it seemed that the time had finally come once more. After months of being mired in the Commerce Committee, S. 1975 suddenly sprang to life.

For tactical reasons, the bill had been drafted to cover only pistols and revolvers; its sponsors had so hoped to neutralize the opposition of the hunting interests. Of course, in this form the bill would not have prevented Oswald from buying a rifle; it would not even have made the purchase more difficult. "The big argument of the opposition was that all rifles are used for hunting," recalled Gleason. "Well, here was a gun—a standard military carbine—made for just one purpose, and that was to kill people. And, incidentally, Oswald ordered it by clipping a coupon in *The American Rifleman.*"

So, shortly after the assassination—on November 27—Dodd amended his bill to cover *all* firearms, rather than just handguns, and also extended its provisions by requiring mail-order purchasers not only to fill out an affidavit but to have it "authenticated by the highest local law enforcement authority in his community."

As for the new provisions, Dodd said he felt confident that "responsible law-abiding sportsmen and gun owners will be willing to tolerate what I feel is only a slight inconvenience at the worst."

The NRA acquiesced, if somewhat reluctantly, to rifles and shotguns being brought under the coverage of the bill. But the requirement of police authentication stirred the NRA's lurking fear of local police. Thereupon, the NRA's executive vice president, Franklin Orth, sat down with staff members of Dodd's subcommittee to urge that this provision be deleted. When it dawned on Dodd that it might be impossible for the Federal government to force some local police to cooperate, he agreed to eliminate the requirement of police authentication. Substituted instead to appease the NRA was the weaker requirement that the gun purchaser simply include in his affidavit (made out in duplicate) the name and address of the local ranking law enforcement officer. The dealer, before shipping the gun, would forward a copy of the affidavit by registered mail, with a return receipt requested, to the police official named. This would place the official on notice that someone in his locality was going to receive a firearm of a certain description from a specified source.

Even in its newly amended form, as in its original version, S. 1975 was regarded by many people as a mild, middle-of-the-road proposal, no more than "a step in the right direction," according to then U.S. Bureau of Prisons Director James V. Bennett. It was among the

weakest of all the firearms bills offered in Congress immediately
after the assassination. Even its sponsors did not claim the bill, if
enacted earlier, would have prevented the assassination. The provisions of the bill would not necessarily prevent anyone from getting a
mail-order gun; theoretically, one could by filling out a false statement which the police would be unable to or not bother to check.*
Nor would the bill prevent over-the-counter purchases. The bill's
backers, however, argued that it would have a substantial impact on
mail-order sales to juveniles.

"Throughout two and a half years of investigation," said Dodd,
"we have found that the secrecy which shrouds the mail-order gun
business has allowed those with the capability of committing mon-
strous crimes against society to clandestinely avail themselves of
means to do so. My bill would insure that the purchaser of a mail-
order weapon could not use the privilege of the mails to disguise his
identity and eventually his evil deed. . . . Lee Harvey Oswald purchased his terrible weapon by concealing his true name and address.
What more do we need than the death of a beloved President to
arouse us to place some regulation on this traffic in guns for crime?"

The NRA gave lip service to the Dodd bill, perhaps in deference
to public opinion or perhaps because it had helped draft the measure. As far back as 1961, NRA officials, flanked by an array of gun
manufacturers, dealers and other industry influentials, had sat down
with Dodd and his aides in a series of behind-the-scenes meetings,
and carefully worked out the details of the bill. Its motive, of course,
was to see that the bill would hurt as little as possible. Consequently, the NRA officials present were generally concerned with
protecting the interests of the shooting fraternity. The measure that
finally emerged was largely their handiwork.

Inevitably, Dodd was to be accused of capitulating or selling out
to the gun interests, just as Senator Copeland had been some thirty
years before. A genial, pipe-smoking, white-maned man in his late
fifties, Dodd would certainly seem a most unlikely proponent of firearms control, representing as he does Connecticut, the nation's leading producer of firearms and ammunition. Known since colonial
days as "The Arsenal of the Nation," the state today houses the
home offices and plants of some of the most glittering names in

---

* According to a later amendment to the bill, the dealer could make shipment
if the police for some reason refused to accept the registered letter.

gundom, including Winchester-Western, Remington Arms and Colt.*

For their part, Dodd's subcommittee aides say that the product of their legislative labors, S. 1975, had to conform to certain realities. "Personally, the senator would have preferred a stronger bill," one staff member told me, "but ours was a reasonable bill, one that even the pro-gun people would support. Getting Orth [the NRA's executive vice president] to sit down with Dodd was the coup of the century. We didn't want to antagonize the NRA. This wasn't a sellout at all. We simply had to be practical. You must remember that the Federal Firearms Act hadn't been changed in nearly thirty years. We had to come up with something that would pass."

Accordingly, Dodd issued periodic statements making much of the "support" his bill was receiving, not only from government and private groups, but also from the firearms industry and the NRA. Unbeknownst to him, however, the NRA had other ideas.

The shock of the assassination thrust the association on the horns of a rather delicate dilemma: how to continue to pretend to support the bill, at least until the public passions had subsided, and at the same time see that it was never enacted.

The Dodd bill seemed to make sense to most citizens, and the public would actually have preferred a stronger one. So the NRA had no choice but to go along with S. 1975, even though it had been broadened to include rifles and shotguns and provided for notification of the police.

Meanwhile, support for the Dodd bill was gathering rapid momentum. Mail received by Dodd's office reportedly ran 8 to 1 in its favor, and newspapers and radio and television stations across the country, including many customarily at opposite ends of the political spectrum, editorialized on its behalf. In many cases, editorials called for even stronger legislation. One typical example, from the Bridgeport, Connecticut, *Telegram:*

---

* Pertinent may be the statement made by gun dealer William B. Edwards (see page 117) for the House Ways and Means Committee in the summer of 1965: "Senator Dodd, according to Mr. William V. (Bill) Hollander, arms product manager, Winchester-Western Division, of Olin Mathieson Chemical Corp., New Haven, Conn., was got into the anti-imported and mail-order gun business by Winchester in his reasonable role of representing a Connecticut industry in its commercial struggles in competition. Mr. Hollander, when asked by this petitioner in January 1963, what he thought 'of his fair-haired boy' (Dodd) fervently replied: 'We wish to Christ we had never got him started.' "

Count us in with Senator Thomas J. Dodd, Democrat, of Connecticut, for a Federal law to control the sale of firearms. He is doing a great public service in trying to get better Federal controls which are long overdue. We supported his first bill. This earned us the criticism of various organized rifle groups and gun lobbies. They failed to convince us we were wrong. Therefore, we support his new, strengthened bill which he has just introduced. As a matter of fact, we think that it doesn't go nearly far enough.

The bill also had the solid backing of the Administration. In rapid succession, it was approved by the Treasury, State and Commerce Departments and then by the Justice Department, although the latter indicated it would have preferred a stronger bill.*

In Congress, support for the bill cut across party lines. Senate Majority Leader Mike Mansfield of Montana told Dodd, "You keep after that gun bill. I'm with you." Republican leader Senator Everett McKinley Dirksen voiced the need for such legislation. Dodd also received assurances from more than a dozen other Senators, Democrats and Republicans, that every effort would be made to enact the bill as quickly as possible. On November 29, just one week after the assassination, Senator Magnuson, after polling his Commerce Committee, announced that since a majority of its members had spoken in favor of the legislation, he was ready to report S. 1975 to the floor of the Senate for a vote. No new hearings on the bill would be necessary, Magnuson said, in view of the Juvenile Deliquency Subcommittee's already exhaustive study and hearings on the subject of the bill. Time, it seemed, was running out on the NRA.

However, another week went by. Still Magnuson did not report the bill from the Commerce Committee. Somehow, Dodd must have had a premonition of disaster. On December 6 he wrote each member of the committee a detailed letter outlining his bill's lengthy legislative and investigative history, and describing the exhaustive combination of private meetings and public hearings that had preceded its introduction. The letter closed with the plea:

I submit that recent events have now offered us unquestionable proof of the inadvisability of indiscriminately selling firearms by the mail-order, common carrier route. Therefore, I ask that you as a member of the

* Such as the one introduced by Missouri Representative Frank Karsten, and limiting mail-order gun sales only to dealers.

Committee on Commerce do all that you can to see that the bill is considered and reported as quickly as possible so that we can prevent not only events such as those that occurred in Dallas, but tragedies which are occurring every day in the United States.

On December 10, apologetic replies to the Dodd letter started to trickle in. The same day, the Commerce Committee, after meeting in executive session, suddenly announced that it had decided to hold public hearings on the bill before taking any further action on it. The *Christian Science Monitor* sounded an ominous warning:

Don't expect Congress to rush through legislation curbing or stopping the wide-open sale of mail-order guns despite the Kennedy assassination. A powerful lobby is pressuring for time, urging against haste, apparently hopeful that, as in the past, such legislation will come to naught.

When the hearings opened to a packed house in Room 5110 of the new Senate Office Building on December 13, Chairman Magnuson did not choose to preside. In fact, Magnuson was virtually absent from the hearings, showing up only now and then to pose for news photographs. Other committee members also pleaded business of various sorts. By default, the acting chairmanship fell to the committee's lowest-ranking Democrat, the aptly-named Howard Cannon of Nevada. However, Magnuson's presence was felt throughout the hearings.

"You always have to remember that he's Big Daddy. The committee is controlled by Magnuson," said a Washington insider. "When it gets to a vote on a bill, the bill will not come out unless he calls for it." In fact, a statement by Senator Magnuson read into the record at the opening of the hearings set the tenor of what was to follow. Magnuson made his own opposition to the Dodd bill evident, by saying that "neither the present legislation nor any other Federal legislation will or can provide effective firearms control." Warning against action conceived in an atmosphere of "hysteria" and "born of ignorance," he said that the committee "would be derelict in its responsibility to report out legislation which would mislead the public into believing that a problem had been solved when in fact it had not."

Magnuson also said that he would oppose any bill that would shift the responsibility for preventing the circumvention of local law from the states, "where it belongs," to the federal government, "where it does not belong, and where meaningful control cannot be effected." Magnuson said that he had directed his staff "to consult with Federal, state and local authorities, the American Bar Association and other interested parties," presumably to come up with a uniform law. He said he had no doubt that this would result in a "reasonable" solution, one that would "depend largely, if not entirely, on the cooperation of the states."

Senator Bourke Hickenlooper of Iowa, an NRA member, also attacked the proposed legislation on states' rights grounds. Hickenlooper read the NRA statement of policy into the record, vented his feelings about the futility of Federal firearms controls and said, "I think the states are perfectly capable of handling these things."

Dodd, who led off the string of witnesses for the day, agreed with Magnuson that S.1975 was not a "cure-all," but said he thought the bill would help solve the country's gun problem. The purpose of the bill, he said, was to "place reasonable controls on the interstate commerce in deadly weapons." He also suggested that at some later date "a uniform law among the states be adopted" for the sale and delivery of weapons to remedy the "crazy-quilt" pattern which had made the Federal Firearms Act "for all purposes ineffective with respect to many jurisdictions."

Originally, according to a committee spokesman, the thought was to have one day of hearings during the congressional session, then finish up early the following year promptly after the start of the new session. But the hearings were ultimately to consume five separate days, stretching to the end of January 1964, and were resumed for still another day in March.

Testimony at the hearings was overwhelmingly against the Dodd bill or, for that matter, any gun legislation. It ranged from the argument that the bill would be ineffective in curbing the acquisition of firearms, to the seemingly contradictory argument that it would disarm the United States. Witness after witness counseled the committee not to act out of "hysteria." The record, noted *The Reporter*, was "replete with inferences that to be for the bill was to be against father and son enjoying the outdoors together or, worse, to be against man and his dog." Among other things, it was also argued that the Dodd bill amounted to firearms registration.

These sentiments were echoed in the barrage of mail that descended on Congress. "So much mail came in that it was stacked knee-deep in the office," said a Dodd aide. "We got thousands of letters and telegrams—maybe as much as 20,000—on this from all over the country," said Bill Beeks, a Magnuson staff man, who also indicated the changing character of the mail since the start of the hearings. "Up to December there were few protests against the bill. The mail ran 300 or 400 to one in favor of it. Yet by February it had completely shifted, and ran 10,000 to 1 opposed," Beeks said. In the Dodd office, the tide of mail, formerly 8 to 1 in favor of the bill, started to turn *against* it after the hearings got under way.

"We heard from everyone from hunting clubs to the same claque of nuts and Birchers who will write us about anything," said one senator's staff man. "This is almost as emotional and irrational an issue as whether children ought to pray in school," said another.

Senator Philip Hart of Michigan, the state which ranks second nationally in the sale of hunting licenses, reported an inundation of mail on the Dodd bill, mostly from what Hart called the "nut fringe." In a single day, Senator William Proxmire of Wisconsin, the sixth largest hunting state, received well over a hundred letters. Many used the usual distorted and irrelevant arguments, some set down in childish scrawls: "There are strick [sic] laws of the highway with automobiles and yet they take more lives, than the gun does," one citizen wrote Proxmire.

"The mail I got was about 75 per cent slanted by someone who had completely misrepresented the legislation I introduced," said Representative John M. Murphy of New York, who had proposed a bill in the House similar to S. 1975.

Hostile correspondents accused Dodd, who had labored on his bill for nearly three years, of hasty action. Many cited the cherished Second Amendment and warned that the bill was part of a Communist conspiracy to disarm America. This was an odd charge to level at former FBI Agent Dodd, who has been perhaps the most persevering anti-Communist in Congress.

A Tennessee correspondent linked as elements of the "international Communist conspiracy: the Dodd Bill, the Geneva Disarmament Conference, and civil rights legislation." Many letters were miraculously similar in erudition and argument and almost identical in wording, though emanating from widely separated places. There were the usual diatribes against the Sullivan Law and the arguments to the effect that guns did not kill people.

Such a homogeneous outpouring, no matter on what subject, can usually be traced to a single fountainhead, and in this case it was not hard to identify the likely source. The deluge of mail, apart from reflecting the NRA gospel, also bore frequent references to Dodd's deviation from the organization's stated legislative policy. However, the then NRA President Bartlett Rummel piously assured the Commerce Committee on January 23, 1964: "We have not drummed up people from all over the country to contact you. . . . We have made no concerted effort to bring pressure on Congress through [NRA] members. . . . These communications to you have more or less arisen spontaneously."

But many people felt otherwise, including Dodd, who had even received letters, telegrams and telephone calls threatening him with assassination. On March 4 he made a surprise appearance before the committee and spoke bitterly of "a concerted attempt to kill the bill" through "an irresponsible lobbying campaign." Inveighing against the "lunatic fringe," he charged that "row upon row" of witnesses, posing as supporters of the bill, had given false or misleading testimony to discredit it. He accused these persons of sowing confusion by attributing provisions to S. 1975 which were not in the bill at all.

To support this contention, the presiding chairman, Senator Cannon, said that many of his correspondents had been objecting to the "gun registration provisions" in the Dodd bill.

"That is an example of which I speak," said Dodd. "As you know, Mr. Chairman, there is no registration at all in the bill . . ."

For some reason difficult to fathom, Dodd did not identify his adversaries by name and even took special pains to absolve the NRA. "There has been a studied effort to have it appear that the National Rifle Association is opposed," he said, adding that even members of that organization "apparently got this impression some way or other."

This "impression" was not surprising, for the NRA hierarchy was exceptionally adroit in concealing from its members, and virtually everyone else except the wishful-thinking Dodd, its alleged enthusiasm for the Dodd bill. Thus, the day before the Commerce Committee hearings opened, December 12, NRA President Rummel, in a newspaper interview, urged Americans to make a "careful study of any anti-gun laws." The account of the interview referred to the Dodd proposal as a registration measure—"the 'hot' bill as far as sportsmen are concerned." Just before granting the interview, Rummel had attended a meeting of the policymaking NRA executive committee.

At the opening of the hearings on the following day, an exchange between NRA Executive Vice President Franklin Orth and the committee's Senator Philip Hart went like this:

HART: Lest a reader of this record or others present may have any doubt, does the association support the bill in the form introduced this morning by Senator Dodd?

ORTH: In the form introduced this morning, the association supports the bill of Senator Dodd. I would like to add, parenthetically, that normally we are opposed to legislation relative to guns of any kind because we don't think they reach the criminal. We think the criminal gets the gun anyway. You mentioned, Senator Hart—

HART: Don't leave me hanging there. It that a "Yes, but . . ." or—

ORTH: No, it is not a "Yes, but . . ." We support Senator Dodd's bill as presented here this morning.

This "support," however, was not indicated in a four-page legislative bulletin that the NRA mailed ten days later to each of its then 11,500 affiliates. After tersely summing up the provisions of the Dodd bill, the bulletin merely stated that Orth had "testified in opposition to any proposal which violated NRA legislative policy."

"Others testified in similar vein," the NRA message went on, "and it became apparent that the Senate was not going to take seriously restrictive action in haste or in a highly emotionalized climate." The bulletin also contained the astonishing revelation that none other than the NRA itself had prompted the decision to hold hearings: "So great was the public pressure to do something that there was fear at first that legislation would be forced to the floor of the U.S. Senate without hearings of any kind.* Fortunately, through NRA friends in the Senate and by direct contact with members of the Senate Committee on Commerce, this did not happen."

*This, of course, ignored the extensive hearings held by the Dodd subcommittee earlier that year.

Nor did the January 1964 *American Rifleman* refer to the Dodd bill in any terms calculated to rally NRA members to its support. "Within a matter of days after the shocking incidents in Dallas," said the *Rifleman*, the bill "which had been *lying quietly* in the Senate Committee on Commerce, was *dusted off* by its sponsor and *significantly* amended." (Author's italics.) After describing the Dodd bill in detail, the *Rifleman* then listed the various other firearms bills in Congress and informed its readers that their text was not being reported in full "because each is either identical to the amended Dodd bill or even more restrictive and severe." In its first four 1964 issues, the *Rifleman* devoted thirty-one columns and every editorial to firearms legislation and urged its readers to make known their views to their elected Representatives and to members of both the Senate Commerce Committee and House Ways and Means Committee.

Any mystery as to the fealties of the "row upon row" of witnesses whom Dodd had castigated as giving false or misleading testimony was cleared up by a follow-up NRA bulletin in February which listed and neatly catalogued all 34 witnesses who had testified at the hearings. Of these, only 6 were proponents of the Dodd bill or of stricter firearms controls. The remaining 28 were either NRA members or designated as "NRA-oriented"; the latter included high officials of such groups as the American Legion, National Muzzle Loading Rifle Association, and the National Wildlife Federation.

One of the "NRA-oriented" was also Representative John Dingell of Michigan, who testified that while the Dodd bill was "perhaps less onerous and less objectionable" than others, it was still "clearly not in the public interest." Thomas L. Kimball, executive director of the National Wildlife Federation, another of the NRA-oriented, called the Dodd bill "good," but suggested some further modifications, contending, for one thing, that if "police have the serial numbers of guns, they will use the information to set up firearms registration." (The bill at no point ever called for the recording of serial numbers.) "This," Kimball went on to say, "would provide the most effective and convenient way of disarming the private citizen should a subversive power infiltrate our police system or our enemies occupy our country."

Later, David J. Steinberg of Alexandria, Virginia, one of the few favorable witnesses, sardonically suggested even a better way: "An efficient army of occupation would probably not take the time and trouble to seize the files of all the police departments and game wardens of the country, but might prefer . . . a quick single trip to 1600 Rhode Island Avenue, Washington, D.C., the headquarters of the National Rifle Association."

George N. Craig, a former governor of Indiana and past national commander of the American Legion, which has long reflected the NRA's views,* said he supported the Dodd bill, but also expressed agreement with Kimball that it should not require the recording of serial numbers [*sic*].

None of the gun manufacturers who had worked with Dodd in forming the bill materialized before the Commerce Committee to testify on its behalf. A vice president of one company who wanted to testify in favor of the bill, said *The Reporter* magazine, was voted down by his board of directors. The feelings of the industry were also made plain by some of the advertising that appeared in the gun magazines while the hearings were in progress. Redfield, a Denver gunsight firm whose ads in the past usually showed a greatly enlarged scope framing a white-tailed deer or a woodchuck now ran ads placing in the middle of the scope the slogan "Let's Aim for Good Gun Legislation." The ads also urged readers to join the National Rifle Association immediately "to help insure the rightful passage of *sane, sensible* gun legislation and prevent *bad* gun legislation which not only infringes, but is dangerous!" The president of Redfield, E. H. Hilliard, Jr., is also president of the National Shooting Sports Foundation.

Indeed the only outside support for the bill came from people like citizen Steinberg, U.S. Bureau of Prisons Director Bennett, a Treasury Department official, a New York City deputy police commissioner, and then New York Representative John V. Lindsay,† author of a stronger firearms bill than the Dodd bill. Lindsay appeared before the Senate Committee brandishing a Carcano identical to the one used to assassinate President Kennedy. He said that the Italian carbine had just been purchased in Manhattan for $15.55, and urged

---

* The American Legion, at its 1963 National Convention in Miami Beach, called upon the state and Federal governments to: (1) defeat all state and Federal legislation which infringes the basic right to keep and bear arms, as guaranteed under the Constitution; (2) promote and encourage the accurate use of firearms.

† Elected Mayor of New York City in 1965.

that the Constitution be interpreted "in the light of the times." He added that the nation no longer depended upon the "citizen's weapon" for its national defense, as it did when the Second Amendment was written. "Our right to keep and bear arms does not mean that you or I have a right to walk down the street with a bundle of hand grenades tied to our waist or to obtain a high-power rifle with a telescopic sight by mail order." Protection today, Lindsay said, "means the reasonable regulation of firearms, not the absence of any regulation."

Somber though the hearings were, they were not without their lighter moments. In a brief but memorable appearance, Arizona's senior senator, eighty-six-year-old Carl Hayden, president pro tempore of the Senate and an NRA member, was introduced by Senator Magnuson as "the rootingest-tootingest sheriff that Arizona ever had." Hayden was then handed a .38 Colt revolver (from an arsenal seized by the District of Columbia police) which he jovially aimed at Senator Strom Thurmond of South Carolina, who ducked in mock fright; Hayden also waved the weapon at others in the room asking, "Who shall I shoot?"

With these preliminaries out of the way, Hayden proudly introduced constituent Ben Avery of Phoenix, head of a contingent of Arizonans who had driven the 2,500 miles to Washington in fifty-four hours in order to "help stem the tide of unreasoning emotionalism aimed, apparently, at disarming the American people."

After objecting to "bad" features of the Dodd bill, Avery, an NRA director, produced a sheaf of statements from Arizona rifle clubs. "The first," he began, "is a statement by the Mesa Gun Club in which they oppose the registration and licensing of all firearms—"

Senator Cannon interrupted, "That, of course, is not required in the bill; do they take a position on the bill that we are considering or not?"

"Sir, they didn't know what was in the bill," said Avery. "They were honestly trying to express their opinion."

Another Arizonan, Dr. William E. Gorder of the mining town of Bagdad, told the Commerce Committee: "The Dodd bill represents a further attempt by a subversive power to make us part of one world socialistic government, and this bill owes its birth to the favorable climate generated by too many years of our Federal government's socialistic trend."

The charge drew an astonished reaction from Senator Ralph Yarborough of Texas, who was presiding. Stating that he "emphatically disagreed," Yarborough asked, "Surely you don't believe that Senator Dodd's bill represents an effort by a subversive power to take over this government?"

"Yes, I do," Gorder replied.

The liberal Texas Democrat asked the question three times, and each time the witness quietly and calmly replied in the affirmative.

"The gun is the standard of freedom in the United States of America," declared Thurman Gibson, also of Bagdad. "When there are restrictions placed on the right of the American citizen to keep and bear arms, then it is only a matter of time before the Communist take-over. Furthermore, I want to say that if our country is invaded by the enemy, I hope that the National Rifle Association is right in its estimation that there are 50 million armed Americans." Still another Bagdad resident, Burr Marley, said, "Now, to me, freedom does not come without some effort. It is a price I must pay. Now, I think we realize that there is a problem when we own guns. Somebody is going to get shot. . . ."

Though reports from Capitol Hill indicated that his bill would not pass, Dodd was determined to fight the issue through, despite the strength of the opposition. He told the *Christian Science Monitor*, in an interview reported on February 14, "I don't propose to let this legislation fade away. The arguments against it are weak, and the minorities who oppose it are small in number, but they are loud and well organized." It is possible, he agreed, that there may be an effort to "drag consideration of the bill out as long as possible in the hope it can be killed with time; that people will forget it after a while. I am going to resist that very strongly."

In having his last word at the March 4 hearing, Dodd threatened to "expose" the opponents of his bill. "I intend to continue my fight for adequate firearms controls in this country, and I will not be intimidated by those who would defame my colleagues and myself." He concluded with a plea to the members of the Commerce Committee to "discharge S. 1975 as quickly as possible so that we can vote the bill out and get it signed into law. I can see no reason for further hesitation or delay."

As time went on with no further committee action, Dodd and his assistants on the Juvenile Delinquency Subcommittee staff continued to generate publicity by showing how easy it was for a teenager to buy a handgun by mail order and how often these guns became robbery and murder weapons, a situation reflected by the repetitive daily headlines in the press. They also decided to hold additional hearings of their own, these taking place on March 26, April 24 and April 25, 1964.

The new Juvenile Delinquency Subcommittee hearings focused on whether the importation of foreign firearms, which Dodd called "one of the prime causes of our current gun problem," should be restricted. Summoned to appear before the subcommittee were two of the largest Los Angeles importers and distributors of these firearms; they were Haywood "Hy" Hunter, president of the American Weapons Corporation, and George W. Rose, president of Seaport Traders.

Both Hunter and Rose, long under investigation by the subcommittee, had already been identified in earlier testimony by Los Angeles police officials as maintaining questionable business operations, as well as being former traffickers in pornographic materials. Hunter, for example, prior to his entry into the firearms business, had been a purveyor of nude photographs. In this connection he had on his record a conviction for contributing to the delinquency of a minor.

The flourishing firearms firm owned by Hunter, once the subject of a *Cavalier* magazine article entitled "He Can Sell You a War Wholesale," had been doing a business with an annual volume at $600,000. Rose's Seaport Traders, the country's largest importer of the German-made Rosco, had brought in and disposed of 77,000 of these snub-nosed .22-caliber revolvers, many to children, crooks, dope addicts, assorted imbeciles and other citizens who for some reason wanted a weapon unsuited for such conventional sporting purposes as target shooting and hunting.

Through cross-examination, Dodd and his staff sought to establish how these two firearms entrepreneurs were operating their mail-order businesses by circumvention of local, state and Federal firearms laws. The testimony showed, for example, that both dealers only casually complied with Federal record-keeping requirements; Hunter, when asked for his records, said they were in Germany. Both had also frequently imported their firearms as "scrap," in order to take advantage of the lower tariff rates for disassembled material.

More seriously, both had been in continuing conflict with law enforcement authorities by shipping handguns and other weapons into New York City, Baltimore and other proscribed jurisdictions.

The records of Rose showed that he had, during the years 1961, 1962 and 1963, shipped handguns to 2,577 residents of Chicago. Of these recipients, 554 were found to be criminals, murderers, narcotic addicts and juvenile delinquents.

Rose, when confronted with this information, said that this could not possibly be true, because, as he said, "On every sale I have made, I have been very careful in getting a statement of age and character as required by the Federal Firearms Act."

"Well, we have records here of sales to children fifteen and sixteen years old by you in Chicago," said Dodd. "There's no controversy about the records. If you want to look at them they're here, and you may do so."

"Senator, may I say, please, that if a child lies about his age, I cannot do anything about it," Rose replied.

Dodd then questioned Rose about a $49.95 submachine gun his company had shipped to a student at the University of Mississippi on April 7, 1962.* Rose claimed that the gun was a deactivated gun that could not be fired, and was sold as a souvenir item "that can be hung on the wall."

"Well, I want to tell you something," said Dodd. "Our staff very easily made this an operable gun. They did it in about two minutes, and they will be glad to show you how it's done, if this is news to you. Now, may I again direct your attention to the sale to the student at the University of Mississippi." This exchange then followed:

DODD: Did you know that there was some trouble brewing in Mississippi or there had been trouble about the time that this sale to this student was made?

ROSE: There was some trouble in Mississippi about what, sir?

DODD: You never heard of any trouble in Mississippi?

ROSE: I don't know what trouble you're talking about, Senator.

DODD: Did you hear of any civil disorder in Mississippi at any time in the last few years?

ROSE: Yes, there must have been civil disorders, yes, sir.

* The year before, Rose's Seaport Traders had won some notoriety with its newspaper ad suggesting a "Submachine Gun for Father's Day" as an unusual way of honoring Dad.

DODD: Anything having to do with the University of Mississippi?

ROSE: Senator, if you are trying to say that I sold this machine gun, which was deactivated, for the purpose of any—something that was going on in Mississippi, I certainly will say that I have no knowledge of anything going on, nor was I interested in selling any type of weapon for any disturbances. I am strictly in the business of selling target pistols and souvenir items.

Both Rose and Hunter, the testimony also revealed, were members of the NRA; Hunter, in fact, indicated that he had been an NRA life member for fifteen years.

The NRA's lobbying strategy was clearly revealed about the same time when Franklin Orth, on April 6, told the NRA annual convention in Los Angeles:

The Congress is well aware of our reluctance to support any* firearms legislation because of the general ineffectiveness of such laws in accomplishing the intended purpose. Consequently, in focusing national attention on the Dodd bill, concerned only with juveniles and those who misuse firearms, we have all but eliminated the serious threats contained in the registration and licensing bills.

NRA Secretary Frank Daniel told the same convention:

So far as I can see now, we are pretty well out of the woods. . . . It would appear that there is little likelihood of our being forced to accept, in 1964, any legislation at either the Federal or state level which does violence to the NRA's announced policy on firearms legislation. That we have been so largely successful is a tribute, not to your staff whose job it is to simply report, but to you, the members, who, in all cases, have listened, have understood, and have taken prompt and effective action in truly the finest tradition of our democratic life.

The NRA Board of Directors, meeting behind closed doors on April 8, secretly passed a resolution gratefully citing Senator Magnuson for "displaying leadership and calm judgment" in handling anti-firearms legislation "in the face of hysteria."

Understandably, Magnuson did not think it propitious to reveal himself as the recipient of so signal an honor until June 24, some ten

* Author's italics.

weeks later, at a time when his committee was still theoretically considering the Dodd bill. The bill, of course, was dead, though not yet
officially interred. For some reason, however, Dodd was evidently
not yet aware of this, although his aides were beginning to fear for
S. 1975.

Dodd still labored under the illusion that the NRA favored his
bill, and he spoke to this effect in public and in private. Several reasons have been advanced to explain this. For one thing, he had
plainly not read, and, in fact, was probably unaware of, the NRA's
legislative bulletins pertaining to his bill. Secondly, Dodd had a
genuine personal liking for Orth, and could not fathom the possibility of the NRA executive vice president's doing him dirt. Thirdly,
Dodd may have been aware of the shenanigans behind his back and
yet may have felt the need to use the name of the NRA as a sort of
endorsement to lend weight to the backing for his measure. Finally,
Dodd may simply have been a victim of wishful thinking.

And so, during the long, hot summer of 1964 Dodd continued to
press for action on his bill. Again and again he appealed in person,
by phone call and by letter both to the Commerce Committee as a
whole and to its individual members. On August 6, with Congress
close to adjournment, the desperate Dodd took to the floor of the
Senate.

"I know personally that a number of committee members favor
the bill," said Dodd. "Yet despite the fact that every procedural requirement has been met, that every preliminary legislative hurdle
has been overcome, we cannot get action on the key step, the voting
on this bill, either up or down, by the full committee. What seems to
be influencing some members of the committee to withhold action
on this bill are the protests of people who are either misinformed or
bamboozled."

Nonetheless, the protests could not easily be ignored. Nine of the
Commerce Committee's seventeen members (for the most part, senators from noncommercial old frontier and hunting states) were up
for re-election that year.

Knowing that the committee was expected to have its probably
final meeting of the session on August 11, Dodd addressed "one last
appeal" to each committee member the day before. "While I realize
how busy you are in these closing days of the Eighty-eighth Congress, I felt that the problem of mail-order firearms is such a press-

ing one that I must tell you once again of the concern I have over the passage of S. 1975," wrote Dodd.

Nevertheless, bearing out conjectures that Magnuson would try to prevent a vote that might send the measure to the floor, the Dodd bill was officially interred the following day. The committee, without taking a roll-call vote, decided to defer action on S. 1975, ostensibly until the absent Senator Cannon, who had presided over its hearings, could be present. No later meetings were ever scheduled.

"There was," said one of those who attended the August 11 meeting, "an overwhelming sentiment for doing nothing."

Dodd called the committee action—or rather, lack of it—"an avoidance of the issue" and an indication that "the gun runners, the hoodlums, the crackpots and the self-styled 'vigilantes' were more powerful than the American people, who I believe want this law."

"The American people," he said, "will not forget the assassination of President Kennedy with a weapon fraudulently obtained through the mails, nor can they forget the other needless tragedies that they read about every day."

11 "This Stain of Violence"

By the end of 1964, not a single Federal, state or local law of any consequence had been enacted to register or strictly control the sale of firearms. Although more than thirteen months had elapsed since the assassination of President Kennedy, it was still just as easy for a madman, criminal or child to buy guns as it had been in November 1963—or for that matter at the time of the near-assassination of President-elect Roosevelt in 1933.

But the prospects for 1965 looked unusually bright. Though only 25 of our 50 state legislatures had been engaged in lawmaking the preceding year, 47 would convene in 1965. Most would consider means of coping with the growing traffic in guns.

Many more Federal bills were also expected, under somewhat less emotional circumstances. The likely enactment of at least some firearms control legislation by the Eighty-ninth Congress was enhanced by the anticipated support of the Johnson Administration, the compliant attitude of the overwhelmingly Democratic Congress and, no less important, the overhanging threat of Senator Dodd, "to identify and expose the activities of the powerful lobbyists who have successfully stopped gun legislation from being passed in every Congress."

On January 6, 1965, Dodd, declaring what he called "war on the gun lobbies," again introduced his bill to curb the mail-order traffic in guns. Now designated S. 14, it was virtually identical to his S. 1975, which had failed to get out of the Senate Commerce Committee during the Eighty-eighth Congress. In introducing his bill, one of fourteen introduced shortly after the convening of Congress,* Dodd urged that "each day of added delay is costing human lives."

A graphic example was furnished little more than three weeks later about 60 miles from the nation's capital. On January 30, in a Baltimore suburb, Wayne Knautz, a 15-year-old high school freshman, killed his father, mother and sister with a .38 caliber revolver he had bought the week before by mail from the Los Angeles firm of Martin Retting. As the boy was being arrested, *another* gun was being delivered to him from the same firm—the company that had imported and sold the telescopic sight used by Lee Harvey Oswald to focus on President Kennedy.

S. 14, like its predecessor would not stop the sale of mail-order guns. It merely set up purchase requirements that would help prevent the sale of these guns to minors, known criminals and the mentally unstable. Any of these persons would still be able to buy guns over the counter without much difficulty. But, mindful of his experience in the preceding Congress, Dodd did not dare to go further than this moderate bill. The big question hanging over Capitol Hill was whether President Johnson would go further and ask for stronger legislation in his forthcoming message to Congress on crime.

On March 8, the President sent Congress his message outlining a broad campaign to check crime. The President said that it was vital that every citizen help to "arrest and reverse the trend toward lawlessness." "The people," he said, "will get observance of the law and enforcement of the law if they want it, insist on it and participate in it."

Citing as a significant crime factor "the ease with which any person can acquire firearms," the President asked for a complete ban on the mail-order sale of guns to individuals.

"Lee Harvey Oswald sent for and received a rifle through the United States mail," the President said. "I believe that the people of the United States have learned, through the recent tragic loss of President Kennedy, the need for strengthened control. There the

* Before the session ended, a total of 34 bills was introduced.

Federal government's jurisdiction is limited. State and local action will be necessary. But at minimum, we must make effective local regulation of firearms possible by increasing Federal control over interstate shipment of firearms. In addition, limits must be imposed on the importation into this country of surplus military weapons and other used firearms."

Reflecting the recommendations of the President were two new bills which Dodd introduced on March 22 with the comment: "It is with a sense of thanksgiving and hope that I introduce on behalf of the Administration legislation calling for controls more comprehensive and stringent than I dared hope for in the heedless and complacent years gone by, when 10 million weapons were placed in unknown hands."

What promised to be the most controversial bill was S. 1592, a detailed amendment to the Federal Firearms Act. Among its three cosponsors was Senator Robert F. Kennedy of New York. The bill would put an end to the mail-order sale of all guns to individuals, as opposed to dealers. Further, it would raise the Federal license fee for interstate gun dealers from $1 to $100; would restrict the over-the-counter sale of handguns to persons who lived in the state where the dealer conducted his business; would prohibit the sale of handguns to persons under twenty-one and of rifles and shotguns to those under eighteen; and would require sellers to "ascertain" (according to regulations later to be prescribed) the identity and address of the buyer; and not sell to anyone they knew or had reason to believe was a felon or fugitive from justice.

Knowing what the fate of the bill would be in the Senate Commerce Committee, Senator Dodd received permission to have S. 1592 referred to the Judiciary Committee, where he, as chairman of the Juvenile Delinquency Subcommittee, would be able to preside at the inevitable public hearings.

Meanwhile, the National Rifle Association was girding for a giant campaign to defeat the Administration's proposed gun control laws. The association had just unaccountably suffered what it termed its "perhaps biggest major setback in years" when the city of Philadelphia in March passed a law requiring a permit for the purchase, transfer or possession of any kind of firearm—handgun, rifle or shotgun. Even guns bought outside the city and brought into it, the law specified, had to be reported to the police, who could refuse to authorize permits to dope addicts, habitual drunks and persons convicted of crimes of violence.

The stringent law would no doubt save the lives of innumerable citizens of the City of Brotherly Love. However, it was mocked by an enterprise called Guns International, Ltd., located just outside of the city's jurisdiction, which advertised: "GUNS INTERNATIONAL guarantees all qualified Philadelphia area residents the handgun of their choice WITHIN 48 HOURS at the LOWEST PRICES IN DELAWARE VALLEY." The advertisement, displaying photos of two handguns, offered buyers a choice between a six-shooter and an automatic. The Philadelphia ordinance again pointed up the futility of local laws in the absence of statewide and Federal legislation.

The NRA annual convention in Washington in early April turned into a noisy, emotional rally protesting any gun curbs at all. The cry was sounded to stimulate gun lovers into sending "a million letters to President Johnson" protesting any new legislation. One member suggested spending $1 million to "hire a high-powered Fifth Avenue public relations firm" to improve the shooter's image. "As Philadelphia goes, so goes the nation," declared a New Jersey gun dealer, who proffered this advice: "We should also get in touch with every member of the National Rifle Association that is in stage, screen, radio or television. There is Buddy Hackett and there is Mel Torme and there is [sic] quite a few others that would very gladly donate their time to an NBC set-up or CBS program, and I am quite sure that Olin Mathieson [Winchester-Western] or du Pont [Remington Arms] would very gladly donate their money for a program of that type. That is the only hope for the NRA and every gun owner in the United States." °

By April 9—less than a week after the close of the NRA convention—an appeal was on its way to the NRA's 700,000 members asking them to write letters of opposition to their senators, congressmen and even the President and "to insist that public hearings" be held on S. 1592. In the month since his crime message to Congress, President Johnson had received only 50 letters opposing his position. Yet one month after the April 9 NRA mailing he had received, if not

---

° As the NRA convention was in progress, a nostalgic footnote to it was provided by a news item datelined Miami. It announced the death of William J. Sinnott, 78, former bodyguard for President Franklin D. Roosevelt. Sinnott died of pneumonia in a hospital not far from where he had been shot back in February 1933 while trying to thwart the attempted assassination of F.D.R.

a million letters, 12,000 in opposition. Letters descended on both houses of Congress by the tens of thousands, much of it to Senator James O. Eastland of Mississippi, chairman of the Judiciary Committee. Senator Roman L. Hruska of Nebraska reported receiving more than 3,000 letters opposing the bill, compared to only 3 in support of it.

A staff member of the Judiciary Committee's Juvenile Delinquency Subcommittee voiced his perennial optimism and discounted the possibility of hearings. "All eight members of the subcommittee are for the bill," * he said. "With sixteen members on the parent committee we need only nine votes and we'll get those. We should have a report in a week or two and the bill should be up for a vote by the end of June. That will give us July and August to get it through the Senate."

However, less than a week later, Dodd's Juvenile Delinquency Subcommittee announced that public hearings on the bill would begin May 19. *The New York Times* reported: "Most observers here give the Administration bill little chance of passage. They point out that Senator Dodd's milder measure, reported last year and this year to the full Commerce Commitee, has never come to a vote in the full committee."

Attorney General Nicholas Katzenbach, one of four high Administration officials to appear the first day on behalf of the bill, told the subcommittee: "There can be no more vital concern today than the increasing growth, the increasing sweep and the increasing violence of crime."

Declaring that "the ability to get guns through mail order just for the heck of it makes murder easy," he also said that "amateur felons" armed with mail-order weapons, including armor-piercing antitank guns, were partly responsible for a 9 per cent increase in murders and a 27 per cent increase in bank robberies over the year before.

Referring to the Italian-made mail-order Carcano on display in the hearing room, the Attorney General said, "As long as I live, I can never forget that it was a mail-order rifle—sent to a post-office box

* When hearings opened, the subcommittee make-up was changed from the year before. Senator Jacob K. Javits of New York replaced the defeated Kenneth Keating, and Joseph D. Tydings of Maryland replaced Sam J. Ervin, Jr., of North Carolina. The members remaining, in addition to Dodd, were: Philip A. Hart of Michigan; Birch Bayh of Indiana; Quentin N. Burdick of North Dakota; Roman L. Hruska of Nebraska; and Hiram L. Fong of Hawaii.

that had been rented under an assumed name by a man with an established record of defection and mental instability—that killed President Kennedy."

Tearing into the objections raised by the NRA, the Attorney General denounced as "preposterous" the NRA's argument that the legislation could lead to the elimination of all private ownership of guns, and devoted much of his statement to citing other "misleading" objections made by the organization.

For example, he characterized as misleading the NRA objection that the bill would forbid dealers to sell to nonresidents of their state. "The bill does forbid such sales of handguns," said Katzenbach, "but it specifically excepts weapons like rifles and shotguns most commonly used by sportsmen and least commonly used by criminals." Citing another "misrepresentation" in the NRA's April 9 letter, the Attorney General said, "I cannot believe that was an innocent mistake," and called attention to the fact that the NRA had told its members: "If the battle is lost, it will be your loss, and that of all who follow."

"It is impossible for me to understand the NRA's view of what battle is being fought and what the stakes are," Katzenbach said. "In my view, we are all joined in a nationwide battle—a battle against rape and robbery and muggings and murder—and the stakes are public order and safety for every citizen.

"In a country in which half the suicides each year are committed by firearms, many of them assuredly obtained by mail, congressional action is called for now.

"In a country in which 26,000 aggravated assaults were committed last year involving firearms, Congressional action is called for now.

"In a country in which 216 law enforcement officers have been murdered with firearms in the last four years, compared with only 9 by other means, Congressional action is called for now."

Secretary of the Army Stephen Ailes assured the subcommittee that enactment of the proposed legislation would not adversely affect the national security. Nor, he said, would the legislation hinder in any way the Army's civilian marksmanship program. In fact, Ailes said, the Army, worried about the charges that some of the guns sold or lent under the program might be falling into improper hands, was making a study to determine the value of the program in terms of its contributions to the national defense effort.

Pending the outcome of the study, it had also decided it would be best to curtail the sale of U.S. surplus weapons to all NRA members except those participating in the marksmanship program.

The appearance of Senator Robert F. Kennedy before the sub-committee on the following day must have brought back a flood of painful memories. He refused to pose beside the Carcano on display and avoided direct reference to the assassination of his brother. However, he urged immediate enactment of the Dodd bill to "save hundreds of lives in this country and spare thousands of families all across this land the grief and heartbreak that may come from the loss of a husband, a son, a brother or a friend."

"For too long, we have dealt with these deadly weapons as if they were harmless toys," Kennedy said. "Yet their very presence, the ease of their acquisition and the familiarity of their appearance have led to thousands of deaths each year—and to countless other crimes of violence as well. It is past time that we wipe this stain of violence from our land."

Like the witnesses of the day before, Kennedy denounced what he called "a massive publicity campaign" being waged by the National Rifle Association against the bill of which he was a co-sponsor, and said that the campaign was doing the nation "a great disservice."

Testifying that the bill would not unduly curtail the use of fire-arms for legitimate sport shooting or hunting, he charged that the campaign had "distorted the facts of the bill and misled thousands of our citizens." *

"Those responsible for this campaign," he said, "place their own minimal inconvenience above the lives of many thousands of Americans who die each year as the victims of the unrestricted traffic in firearms."

As Kennedy walked slowly with his head bowed out of the hearing room, his wife Ethel, who had been in the audience, ran after him.

The hearings stretched from May through July. One of the final witnesses was California's state finance director, Hale Champion who, together with his wife and 19-month-old daughter, had been kidnapped at gunpoint several weeks before by two fugitives wanted for bank robbery, murder and rape. The Champion family

* For Dodd's questioning of the NRA about the distortions, see notes to this chapter.

was held in custody by the kidnappers for 24 hours before being released at the Nevada border. Recounting the harrowing experience for the subcommittee, Champion said that, while in the custody of the escaped convicts, he had seen them buy two .30-30 Winchester rifles in Nevada hardware stores in a matter of minutes without having to show identification.

At the close of the hearings on July 27, Senator Dodd said that the full Senate Judiciary Committee would report a bill out within a month and that the Senate would approve a strong bill, "hopefully before the adjournment of the current session." However, Dodd's hopes were probably too high in view of a number of developments that had already taken place. On July 1 it was reported that of the eight Juvenile Delinquency Subcommittee members, only two were in favor of the Dodd bill. Four, including New York Senator Jacob Javits, were opposed to it, one was said to have "strong reservations" and one was publicly uncommitted, according to an informal poll of the subcommittee. Because of this, said the New York *Journal-American*, "it is almost impossible now for Mr. Dodd—unless he can do some strong convincing—to get the bill out of the subcommittee intact."

Several weeks later it was reported by the Chicago *Daily News'* Washington bureau that the Administration was "retreating on gun legislation," with the groundwork for an "about-face" laid at a secret two-and-a-half-hour meeting on July 14 in the office of Representative Cecil King of California. King, an NRA director, was then presiding at House Ways and Means Committee hearings on Administration firearms proposals identical to those introduced by Dodd. In attendance at the secret meeting were representatives of the Secretary of the Treasury and the Attorney General, a spokesman for the gun manufacturers, and the NRA's Executive Vice President Franklin Orth.

Dodd said he was neither invited to the meeting nor informed of it, although he did hear rumors of it afterward. "You might say it was clandestine," Dodd declared.

Larry O'Brien, then in charge of White House congressional liaison, said the July 14 meeting was held to see if there wasn't "some way we can get that legislation moving."

Assistant Secretary of the Treasury Joseph Barr, one of the participants, said a report on the "areas of agreement" reached at the meetings was to be turned over to Attorney General Katzenbach, who had authorized the meeting at the suggestion of the manufacturers.

To what extent these reports give an accurate account of what went on at the secret meeting is difficult to say. But on August 20, in the wake of reports that the Administration might be prepared to water down the legislation still tied up in committee, Attorney General Katzenbach said the Administration would not compromise on its firearms measures.

"I would say, as strong as I can say it: I am not going to have a phony gun bill passed by Congress," he said. "I am perfectly happy to make concessions—if it is going to be a forward step toward law enforcement," he added.

Katzenbach also emphasized that President Johnson firmly backed the legislation, in spite of the whispering by opponents that this was not the case.

"There is a very powerful lobby working against the bill, and it is hard to get gun control legislation. We recognized that before we started," said Katzenbach, conceding that it was unlikely that the bill would be passed during the current session.

A month later, on September 28, the Washington *Post* reported that "action in this session seems doubtful," although, it said, "the Senate subcommittee was continuing to hammer out its proposal in hopes of bringing something to the floor as soon as possible."

While Congress delayed, backing for the bill came from the powerful American Bar Association, even though the NRA had lobbied vigorously against it among lawyers. Franklin Orth put in an appearance at the bar association's annual convention in August at Miami Beach, where he denounced the Dodd bill as an "unwarranted intrusion" into personal liberties. However, Senator Joseph Tydings, upholding the other side of the debate at the bar meeting, said that the bill had been subjected to "twisted, misleading" propaganda from gun lobbyists, and denied that it would in any way restrict the legal use of weapons by hunters and sportsmen. The bill, Tydings said, was, in fact, needed by the states to make their own control laws effective.

Originally, the ABA's usually conservative policymaking house of delegates had been so divided that it could make no recommendation on gun law. But President Lewis F. Powell, Jr., rose to identify the bill with "law and order," and said that the vote taken by the ABA would indicate its seriousness about combating crime. He joined other supporters of the bill in proclaiming his love of hunting. "We all have our private arsenals," he said. "I have three shotguns, two rifles and two pistols and I have been trying to hit birds since I was a little boy."

"But in all seriousness," Powell said, "this bill is a moderate and rational approach to an admittedly difficult problem. It will give enforcement officers a strong hand in the war on crime."

The opposition eventually collapsed, and a resolution favoring enactment of S. 1592 was adopted by a vote of 184 to 26.

Later that month, the apparent need for gun controls was brought home by an outbreak of violence in the Watts section of Los Angeles. One of the worst race riots in the nation's history, it left more than 35 dead and nearly 900 injured. A phenomenon of the five-day event was the frantic run on the stock of gun shops. Dealers all over the city stayed open nights to sell their wares. The Dodd subcommittee learned that 4,000 guns were sold in a single day (only 37 of them to Negroes), and that pistol sales increased 250 per cent during the first weekend of the riots. "Throughout California, there were actually lines of people, some a block long, waiting to purchase weapons," said Senator Dodd. The rioters also snatched up thousands of additional weapons by ransacking and looting gun dealers and sporting goods stores and pawn shops. Police, though eventually confiscating some 3,000 guns from rioters, acknowledged that these represented probably less than 10 per cent of the firearms in their possession. "Ironically, a high percentage were rifles and shotguns which the National Rifle Association contends are used for sport, seldom for crime," commented columnist Drew Pearson, who, along with other columnists and newspapers across the country, suggested that the Dodd bill be reconsidered—and even strengthened.

In October, the International Association of Chiefs of Police, meeting in Miami, unanimously adopted a resolution urging support of the Dodd bill.

"The chiefs of police—the men who have had the most direct and intimate experience with the crime problem in this country," editorialized the Washington *Post* on October 8, "have said that existing firearms controls are entirely inadequate. They have said that this carelessness is the 'major factor' in contemporary lawlessness. What more does the country need to hear on this subject? How loudly must the police whistle be blown before Americans wake up?"

The first session of the Eighty-ninth Congress ended on October 23, 1965. Congress was hailed for its prodigious labors and record of achievement, perhaps the most productive in all of U.S. history, implementing about 85 per cent of the Great Society program. Busy as it was, the Congress, at the President's special request, also managed to put through Lady Bird Johnson's Highway Beautification bill and a bill to restrict the illicit traffic in "goof balls" and pep pills.

What about the traffic in guns? At adjournment after ten months, the measures to restrict the traffic in guns were still bottled up in the Senate Judiciary and the House Ways and Means Committee.*

* *Postscript:* In early March 1966, long after the start of the second session of the Eighty-ninth Congress and just one year after President Johnson's crime message, the Administration's firearms control measures were still holstered in committee. Without another message on their behalf by President Johnson, the likelihood of any action on the bills was considered extremely remote in an election year. Meanwhile, the NRA, in a *Rifleman* editorial, said that the bills had "the wrong emphasis," and reminded members and affiliates that Congress would "appreciate the views of the voters." In letters dated February 11, the NRA also offered free marksmanship training to the sons and daughters of members of Congress and their staffs.

12 Forgotten Local Lessons of the Assassination

What transpired in Washington also took place on a smaller, though no less intense, scale in state capitals and municipalities throughout the land. All across the country, the National Rifle Association fared equally well in defeating gun control proposals of all kinds.

In New York State, where nearly 80 bills were introduced in 1964, and the senate majority leader had called for an end to the "intolerable" situation permitting the free sale of shotguns and rifles, the firearms lobby triumphed as early as January. The state's joint legislative committee on firearms and ammunition flatly declined to recommend a bill requiring the registration of all weapons. Not long before, on the eve of the Kennedy assassination, committee members had been feted at a dinner by the New York State Rifle and Pistol Association, an NRA affiliate. The dinner featured a keynote speech by NRA Executive Vice President Franklin Orth. Sixteen guns were distributed as door prizes.

"The unfortunate incident at Dallas on November 22, 1963, created new problems," said the annual report to NYSPRA members a year later. Nonetheless, the report was able to bring "a message of accomplishment—good cheer and hope to the many sportsmen and gun owners in the State of New York and throughout the nation who are vitally interested in preserving the right of citizens of good repute to own and use firearms for lawful purposes." In New York State, the report said, the year was one of "progress and accomplishment in that no harmful anti-gun bills were enacted, although many were proposed."

The futility of relying on state and local legislatures (and another striking example of the power of the NRA) is also demonstrated by what took place in Maryland that year.

In early 1964, Leonard S. Blondes, a personable thirty-four-year-old Silver Spring attorney and state delegate, received phone threats that he would be "bumped off" unless he stopped pressing for a firearms control bill he had just introduced. His wife, his three children, aged four to ten, and his secretary and maid were also the recipients of mysterious calls warning of the dire fate that awaited him. In addition, Blondes and his wife were subject to a stream of abusive mail.

From one who signed himself "True American" came these words:

Why you old bustard. How can you be so unAmerican. Were your parents married? Does your wife do unnatural things. What are you catholics and commies trying to do? Take our guns away, and niggers will break into our houses and rob and rape and kill. Who is behind all these things anyway? Who pays you for this? You might as well give up this unpatriotic way of life as we will outvote you and when you buck up against the NRA, you have something to beat. Get wise to yourself; you cannot beat we gun lovers and lovers of freedom.

What sort of legislation had Blondes proposed? His proposal would simply have required safety instruction for gun buyers and would have limited gun sales to persons whom police could determine were of good character and mental competence and, of course, without criminal records.

The year before, Blondes, as a freshman delegate from Montgomery County to the state legislature, had introduced a similar bill; that one, however, affected only juveniles. It stemmed from his growing awareness of the dangers inherent in Maryland's free and

easy attitude toward firearms. Maryland's law was a model of tolerance. Anyone could buy any sort of gun, if he were eighteen—or
looked eighteen.

Those obviously younger could also buy a gun if they had the
"expressed permission" of a parent or guardian; and, as Blondes
learned, the permission that satisfied many dealers was often a
phone call or forged written note. "In other words," says Blondes,
"no matter how old or how young, you could purchase a gun without regard to physical condition, mental stability or criminal background. I was present in a store when one young man said he was
fifteen, presented a note he could have scratched out himself, and
said he knew firearms. Nor did the dealer have any way of checking
if a minor was even giving his right name; the law did not require
him to check."

To remedy this situation, Blondes proposed a measure early in
1963 which would require those under eighteen to receive not only
parental but also police permission in order to buy a gun. A police
certificate would also have to accompany all juvenile mail-order gun
orders. Police would also license all gun dealers.

The bill served as Blondes' initiation into the ways of the NRA.
Soon after its introduction, a torrent of telephone calls, letters and
telegrams descended on him. One message, terming the bill "a disgrace to the state of Maryland," suggested that Blondes avail himself of NRA membership and "learn a few things that are
worthwhile—because you're not learning a thing at the Statehouse
except to make a fool of yourself." Other more temperate letters
conceded Blondes' thoughts were good and well-intentioned, but
nonetheless advised consultation with NRA officials to correct what
they felt to be the bill's few flaws.

Blondes' brainchild was unceremoniously throttled in committee
by a 32–0 vote; committee members objected that the bill would be
too difficult to enforce and infringed on the right to bear arms.
Blondes then proceeded to meet with the NRA's legislative experts,
and with their advice he worked out what was felt to be a mutually
satisfactory bill. Its provisions were similar to the earlier Blondes bill
but, among other things, now also called for compulsory safety
training for minors under eighteen.

"The compulsory firearms safety training program is a rather
loaded issue," Daniel J. Mountin of the NRA's legislative staff

wrote Blondes while the new bill was being worked up. "A bill like this might be very good, but you must first be positive that the state of Maryland is prepared to conduct a compulsory firearms safety training program." Mountin then suggested that Blondes contact General Milton A. Reckford, the state adjutant general and a former NRA executive vice president, for advice on "the most desired and workable approach to a compulsory firearms safety training program." "After my lengthy discussion with the General," recalls Blondes, "I felt that the NRA was practically a co-sponsor of the new bill."

Blondes, however, was soon disabused of this notion. On the very same day his new bill came to the floor of the House, the NRA dispatched a legislative bulletin to "all NRA members and clubs in Maryland," stating that "the present bill by Mr. Blondes is in no sense an improvement over his previous bill."

A flood of NRA-inspired messages to members of the state's House Judiciary Committee resulted in the speedy suffocation of this proposal too. "It was literally laughed to death in Judiciary," Blondes recalls.

It was the death of President Kennedy that impelled Blondes to try again in early 1964 with his even stronger proposal making an instructional course mandatory for gun owners and prospective buyers of all ages. It also specified a three-day waiting period between purchase and delivery. This would give the police time to check if the would-be gun buyer was a drug addict, had been convicted of a felony or serious misdemeanor or had ever spent time in a hospital or institution for mental illness.

The practicality of the proposal was dramatized by two local tragedies which had just taken place, both already described in an earlier chapter. In one, Elizabeth Takagi, a fifty-three-year-old mentally unstable Maryland housewife, shot and killed her three teenage children and then took her own life with a gun she had bought in a Silver Spring shop (coincidentally, not far from Blondes' office) less than forty-eight hours before. Less than two weeks later, in nearby Fairfax County, Virginia, a housewife, Mrs. Judith Cox, walked into a store and walked out with a revolver, although she had been twice committed to a mental institution. Before the day was out, the woman had killed herself and her four children.

Nonetheless, the NRA, unimpressed, registered its disapproval of the Blondes proposal through a bulletin mailed just three days after its introduction. And again came the rude telephone calls, the vitriolic letters. Only this time there were more!

Many of the letters began with the same clause: "I have just received a bulletin from the National Rifle Association..." Others left no doubt as to their source of inspiration, quoting as they did verbatim passages from the bulletin. Much of the mail was filled with unreasoning hate, reflecting the sickness of the letter writers. Inevitably, Blondes was threatened with the customary reprisals at the ballot box, as in the following message from one who said he had been chosen to write for the rest of the "shootin' gang": "The point of this letter is merely to say that in the next election there are seven votes that you cannot count on for sure and I imagine we can speak for our wives as they pretty much follow along with us."

On the telephone, Blondes was the recipient of even worse threats. One day a deep-voiced caller warned the maid to tell her boss to "give up on the gun bill or else he'll be bumped off." The Blondes' children, too, were warned about the fate that might befall their father.

"What really concerns me is that a person who would make such threatening phone calls is exactly the type that should not be allowed to buy guns without controls and screening," said Blondes.

For a short time there was hope for legislation, particularly when the Blondes bill was referred to the legislative council. Though this marked a big step forward, the proposal, in Blondes' words, "died a glorious death under the pressures of 'the unregistered, unrecognized, nonlobbying entity known as the NRA.'"

After the Maryland legislature failed to act, the Montgomery County Council met to consider a bill giving police in the county seventy-two hours to check on prospective gun purchasers. More than 100 persons showed up at a public hearing, most of them gun collectors and dealers, sportsmen and members of gun clubs. The only one to speak in favor of the bill was Police Superintendent Colonel James S. McAuliffe, in whom the bill invested authority to approve all gun transactions. The bill, in McAuliffe's opinion, would make it more difficult for criminals to get guns and would prevent sales to the temporarily deranged. "The seventy-two-hour waiting period," he added, "will not prove a very great imposition for someone wanting a gun for a legal purpose."

While many of the others declared themselves favorable toward the intent of the bill, they found little else in its favor.

"Guns don't kill people—people kill people," proclaimed the coach of the University of Maryland Rifle Team. A representative of the National Rifle Association said that he was "particularly unhappy" with the authority invested in the police superintendent, calling this "a surrender of sovereignty."

A councilman suggested that the bill be postponed until "a study committee has been appointed and we hear from them," the committee to be made up of members of the National Rifle Association and various pistol and gun clubs. The decision to table the bill, on May 22, was by unanimous vote.

In 1965 the Montgomery County Council, in response to public pressures, finally saw fit to enact an ordinance requiring a five-day waiting period before anyone could purchase a gun. The ordinance also forbade the sale of handguns to anyone under twenty-one and the sale of shotguns or rifles to anyone under eighteen. Maryland's Prince Georges County also managed to adopt an ordinance requiring a five-day waiting period. This, however, applied only to handgun purchasers. Although both ordinances were denounced by the gun lobby, they could not of course be fully effective in the absence of a statewide law. But no such law was enacted in Maryland in 1965 in spite of the efforts of Blondes and other state legislators.*

That year more than 350 firearms bills were introduced in our state legislatures, about twice as many as in 1964. Not one deemed "restrictive" by the NRA was enacted.

A bill in Illinois came closest. Introduced by Representative Abner Mikva of Chicago, the bill would have required the licensing of all handguns in the state, forbidding them, of course, to minors, mental patients, narcotics addicts and ex-convicts. An estimated 100,000 handguns were in the hands of such persons in Chicago alone, noted the city's Police Superintendent Orlando Wilson, in favoring the bill. It was also supported by the state's Democratic leader, Chicago Mayor Richard J. Daley and his Committee on Organized Crime Legislation. It was supported by the Illinois Police Association, the Chicago Crime Commission, and Charles Siragusa, executive director of the Illinois Crime Investigating Commission. Polls also indicated that more than 70 per cent of Illinois voters were in favor of it.

---

* A state law requiring a seven-day waiting period, enacted in 1966, preempted the county laws.

However, the NRA and its perhaps most powerful affiliate, the Illinois State Rifle Association, organized a massive campaign to defeat it just as they had similar legislation in the state since 1934. Three bulletins were dispatched from Washington to Illinois members and gun clubs who crowded the state capitol's largest hearing room in Springfield. Upward of 5,000 letters and telegrams descended on legislators.

Just before the vote on June 21, Representative Adlai E. Stevenson III of Chicago, chairman of a house judiciary subcommittee responsible for amending the bill (it originally covered all types of guns), said it was merely intended to "disarm persons who are morally and physically unequipped to own pistols," and that the bill could be "the most effective anticrime legislation" of the session. An opponent, however, said that the possession of guns by storekeepers would be a "greater deterrent to crime than licensing."

The letter campaign almost boomeranged because of the character of much of the mail. Peoria's Representative John E. Cassidy, formerly a strong opponent of the measure, said he would now vote for it because letters to the bill's sponsor had accused him of "leaning toward the Communist party."

"If that's the type of opposition that exists," said Cassidy, "the bill can't be nearly as bad as the nuts on the far right."

One legislator, however, objected to the implication that all opposition letter writers were "nuts", and described letters he had received from target shooters and a farmer who said he needed a pistol to kill rodents.

The vote was 79 to 75 against the bill.

Its defeat, said the Chicago American the next day, "was an unusually clear lesson on the power of a really well-organized and financed pressure campaign."

Some legislation is of course designed to impose controls not so much on the purchase or possession of guns, but simply on their use.

A year before the Kennedy assassination, the director of Indiana's Department of Conservation, Donald E. Foltz, had complained of his state's lax hunting laws. "I am forced by law to issue hunting licenses to anyone who has the fee, even the feeble-minded or half-blind," he wrote in an article, "Boobs in the Woods," which appeared in *The Saturday Evening Post* of October 15, 1962. The terrible consequences of such leniency on the part of the state, Foltz charged, could be seen in a countryside full of incompetent gunners —and their human victims. "In three out of every four hunting accidents," wrote Foltz, "the gunner is unscathed; the victim is usually a child, a farmer, a passing motorist or a fellow hunter." The national hunting toll was considerable, Foltz pointed out, citing National Safety Council statistics to the effect that 700 people had been killed and 9,000 wounded by hunters in 1961. "That year," said Foltz, "there were three times as many hunting deaths as passenger deaths in commercial airline crashes, train wrecks and bus accidents combined."

"Our states are strict about granting licenses to drivers," he wrote, "because a car can be a lethal weapon; but they will give almost anyone a hunting license. All states require drivers to pass eyesight tests, but no state checks the eyesight of the hunters. All states require motorists to prove their knowledge of safety rules of the road and car handling, but forty-seven states will issue a hunting license to a grown man who doesn't know the difference between a double-barreled shotgun and a Colt .45. And thirty-eight states will turn over hunting licenses to children after asking only one question: 'Do you have the license fee?' "

Foltz promised that he would press for the adoption of three key proposals at the next session of the Indiana legislature: "(1) Anyone who is granted a hunting license for the first time should have to prove that he is capable of hunting safely; (2) before receiving a license, every hunter should pass an eyesight test; and (3) no one under sixteen should be permitted to hunt." To give Hoosier hunters and their possible victims even more protection, Foltz also said he would ask for a number of other laws, including one to make it illegal to hunt while drunk, and another calling for stiffer penalties for accidental shooting by negligent nimrods.

Generally, the penalty for killing or wounding another person while hunting is insignificant. Often no penalty is meted out at all. A classic illustration furnished by Foltz came from Colorado, where seventeen hunters were once killed during a two-week preseason hunt. "Not a single hunter who caused a death was prosecuted, but three men who killed a calf during the same shooting spree were fined $600 each and put on five years' probation."

That hunting laws are intended to protect wildlife rather than human life is borne out by the fate of Conservation Director Foltz's proposals before the 1963 Indiana legislature. Though aimed at protecting human life, not one was enacted. However, the legislature did enact a law to fine hunters found guilty of "carelessly or wantonly" destroying or injuring "any cow, hog, horse, sheep, chicken, turkey, duck."

Some Indiana citizens sought action at the county level to protect human life from the hunters. In Vanderburgh County, an ordinance was proposed to prohibit shooting within 1,000 feet of a residence. If only to make life somewhat safer for farm animals, as well as for rural and suburban citizens, the proposal seemed reasonable enough. "This was something that was almost bound to occur as the county's population grew and residential areas developed outside the city limits," said the Evansville *Press*, the principal county newspaper. "It has long been against the law to discharge firearms inside the city. But the county area outside, rural in nature and thinly populated, has been popular with hunters of all ages. With our population pressing outward, this situation is changing. The mothers' fear that a stray rifle bullet could easily kill or injure a child is a legitimate one."

The proposal grew out of complaints by mothers in Melody Hills, a suburban area containing about 300 homes, 2 miles northwest of Evansville, and was drawn up and presented by F. Wendell Lensing, an attorney representing the Melody Hills Benefit Association. "One mother said that some hunters came around and were shooting maybe 100 feet away from her house," Lensing, a genial ex-judge, told me. "When she told them to stop, they just laughed at her. She didn't at all like the idea that you had to keep your children in the house to keep them from being shot at. Others complained about having shots actually rattle off the side of their houses."

The ordinance was proposed on November 11, 1963—just eleven days before the Kennedy assassination. On November 29 the NRA dispatched a legislative bulletin to its Vanderburgh County members and followers. The bulletin called attention to what it said were at least two flaws in the proposal:

1. It makes no exception for a private range in the basement of one's home or an outdoor or indoor range that is operated in a safe and sane manner and located on privately or publicly owned land.

2. No provisions are made for the discharge of firearms where necessary to protect the life and property of one's self or that of another.

NRA members were asked to make their presence felt through letters to the Metropolitan Plan Commission or by their attendance at a public meeting to be held on December 9. At the hearing, strongly worded arguments came from both sides in a courtroom jammed to twice its capacity; however virtually all of the 200 people in attendance were opposed to what by now had become a controversial ordinance.

A farmer was one of the half dozen or so who appeared to speak for the measure. Against a frequent chorus of catcalls and boos, he said that on at least three recent occasions hunters had fired shots that, after whizzing by him, had struck his farm buildings. "If someone were hit by one of those shots," he said, "the hunters could leave and no one would ever know who fired the shot."

On the other side, a sheriff's deputy told the commission that the ordinance would jeopardize hunting in the entire county. A representative of the Izaak Walton League charged that the ordinance was "unconstitutional," saying it infringed on "the right to bear arms and use them." He told the commission that "you are trying to approach this thing by prohibiting hunting.

"It should be approached by education," he said. "We [hunters] are being indicted by some because of the acts of others." Then he warned, "If you adopt an ordinance here, it will spread to other counties."

The ordinance, maintained still another of its opponents, would prevent a farmer from shooting a fox in his own backyard, even if the fox was in the act of stealing the chickens. Still others quibbled about the 1,000-foot distance set as the boundary for no-man's land. The commission was still mulling over the matter two months later when Lensing, in a desperate attempt to get the proposal through, told the commissioners that he would not object if the distance were reduced from 1,000 to 500 feet, and he would agree to allow people, like the fox-plagued farmer, to use firearms where necessary, even closer than 500 feet, for the protection of life and property. To meet the remaining objections registered by the NRA and others, Lensing said he would also exempt firing ranges in private homes and organized gun clubs, the shooting of meat animals for slaughtering purposes, and he would eliminate all restrictions against hunting in agricultural areas with dwellings, as opposed to residentially zoned areas.

However, his concessions fell on deaf ears. The commissioners voted unanimously against his recommendations. One commissioner said he believed that there were already sufficient laws for the protection of homeowners from hunters' guns.

"Some people," said the disappointed Lensing, "told me that if there was going to be a law passed, it ought to be a state law. Then I suppose if you'd get the state legislature to consider a law, they would say it ought to be a Federal law—every state should have it, not just the state of Indiana. And then, I suppose, if you'd suggest a Federal law, they would be in favor of a state law, and so it starts all over again. What they do is use every excuse possible just to delay and procrastinate."

13 Safety Education Versus Safety Laws

Sometime we shall probably have a hunting license test to determine a man's knowledge of guns before a license is granted. Sometime we may have a law which would take away the hunting license of a drunken gun carrier, but such regulation will help only to the extent that driving tests for automobile licenses, and drunken-driving laws help to eliminate the *worst* risks from the road.

The only *real* answer is education and training. The only real answer lies in the hands of the rifle, pistol and shotgun clubs throughout America. The club that has no time "to bother with tyros" is failing utterly to carry its part of the load to eliminate reckless gun accidents. The club that "can't fool around with a bunch of kids" is doing its bit to bring closer the day when someone will try to correct the situation by means of unworkable antigun laws."

— Editorial, *The American Rifleman*, November 1937

Although the National Rifle Association is mistrustful of most laws, even those aimed at making shooting safer, it has a long-standing and deep-abiding faith in the powers of education. This faith in education is a key element in the standard stratagem of many lobbyists. When a Federal law to eradicate some existent evil threatens, stave it off by calling for state or local laws. When no really valid arguments can be mustered to oppose these, stall still further by suggesting "education" as the only appropriate answer.

Accordingly, the NRA, along with its industry allies, has over the years mounted a massive firearms safety education program which, it says, is one of its two major reasons for existence (the other: marksmanship training). Though the education program is no doubt

233

well-intended, a cynic might see a certain inconsistency between the organization's relish for safety education, and its distaste for safety laws. However, this is not so inconsistent to one familiar with the machinations of the collective NRA mind.

What better way than education to woo the young? "Through firearms safety education and marksmanship qualification shooting . . . the NRA has wide contact with the youth of America," says the NRA. Referring to its corps of more than 86,000 "certified instructors" and "training counselors," the NRA declares: "It is through the unselfish devotion of these dedicated members that much of the work of spreading the influence of the National Rifle Association is accomplished. These volunteer instructors give thousands of hours annually to the introduction of new people to the shooting sport."

For the most part, the instruction is aimed at teenagers. Since 1950, when the NRA Hunter Safety Training Program was instituted, about 2½ million young shooters have completed the four-hour course. Thirteen states * now require youngsters under a prescribed age, usually sixteen, to pass the course before they can be issued their first hunting licenses.

In recent years, three of the states (Connecticut, Rhode Island and New York) have made their laws applicable to all new license applicants regardless of age. Otherwise, no state requires adults to prove knowledge of safe gun handling.

In deference to the fact that more accidents take place at home than on the hunt, the NRA in late 1962 expanded its program by starting a home firearms safety course. During the next two years the course was given in nearly 300 places, ranging from church and civic group meetings to schools and youth organizations. So far, nearly 9,000 persons have completed the course, many of them women. Probably millions of youngsters have also learned the rudiments of gun safety while learning to aim and fire in NRA Junior Rifle Clubs—now more than 4,100 in number—under a program started in 1925.

All this does not include the educational efforts, some independent of the NRA, sponsored by the Sporting Arms and Ammu-

* California, Connecticut, Massachusetts, Minnesota, Montana, New Hampshire, New Jersey, New York, Oregon, Rhode Island, South Dakota, Utah and Washington.

nition Manufacturers' Institute (SAAMI), the National Education Association, the National Safety Council, the Izaak Walton League and countless schools, police departments, community, civic and other groups.

Safety hints and admonitions are summed up succinctly by the firearms industry in a SAAMI leaflet entitled "The Ten Commandments of Safety," which exhorts:

1. TREAT EVERY GUN WITH THE RESPECT DUE A LOADED GUN.
2. WATCH THAT MUZZLE! Carry your gun safely; keep safety on until ready to shoot.
3. UNLOAD GUN WHEN NOT IN USE; take down or have actions open; guns should be carried in cases to shooting area.
4. BE SURE BARREL IS CLEAR OF OBSTRUCTION, and that you have ammunition only of the proper size for the gun you carry.
5. BE SURE OF TARGET BEFORE YOU PULL TRIGGER; know identifying features of game you hunt.
6. NEVER POINT A GUN AT ANYTHING YOU DO NOT WANT TO SHOOT; avoid all horseplay.
7. NEVER CLIMB A TREE OR FENCE OR JUMP A DITCH WITH A LOADED GUN; never pull a gun toward you by the muzzle.
8. NEVER SHOOT A BULLET AT A FLAT, HARD SURFACE OR WATER; at target practice, be sure your backstop is adequate.
9. STORE GUNS AND AMMUNITION SEPARATELY, beyond reach of children.
10. AVOID ALCOHOLIC BEVERAGES before or during shooting.

Firearms firms pack a copy of this gospel with every gun, and the leaflets are also distributed by the tens of thousands to stores, schools, state game departments (who give them out with each hunting license), and to thousands of youth groups, gun clubs, conservation, civic and service organizations and other groups. No less than 50 million copies of the commandments have been printed and delivered into the hands of the public since 1946, according to the National Shooting Sports Foundation.

With all this information and wealth of instruction, one would wonder why there should be any firearms accidents at all. Yet, during the past decade and a half or so, there has in fact been no significant reduction in mortality from firearms accidents. In 1950, the year the NRA Hunter Safety Training Program got underway, the annual death rate from such injuries was 1.4 per 100,000 population. It was 1.3 in 1964, having fluctuated between 1.2 and 1.5 in the intervening years.

How, in the face of common sense, can such fatal accidents continue to happen—an estimated 2,400 in 1964—on the hunt, at home and elsewhere? For over five years I culled clippings of cases which provide strong evidence that, although guns in themselves may be safe, the combination of guns and people very often is not. Here are some of the strangest items in my collection, which are offered in rebuttal to that specious NRA adage: "Guns don't kill people; people kill people!"

One incident, which had as its culprit a car door, involved a Nebraska nimrod who was getting out of his car after a hunting trip. A gust of wind blew the door shut on his coat pocket. In the pocket was a rifle shell. Bang!

No less senseless was the incident involving a Californian who was wielding a rake he had always regarded as trustworthy. He was raking some rubbish into a bonfire when he soon learned that in the rubbish was a shotgun shell. Again, bang! And then there was the Ohioan who, while mowing his lawn, suddenly found himself shot by his lawnmower. It had hit and set off a .22-caliber cartridge lying in the grass.

Although fish stories are often greeted by raised eyebrows, no one could doubt the story of a Texas angler named Bobby Wright who reported that he had been shot by a fish. He had the fish, the gun and the wound to prove it! It seems that a freshly caught catfish, flopping around in the bottom of Bobby's boat, struck the trigger of his rifle and shot him in the arm. In Michigan a man was sitting in the front seat of his car when a friend's dog leaped into the rear on a loaded 12-gauge shotgun lying there. The gun discharged and killed the man. A twelve-year-old Iowa farm boy placed his rifle against the ladder in the barn and started to climb to the loft. His dog jumped on the ladder, struck the rifle trigger with his paw and shot his ascending master.

Finally, there is the story of the pheasant's revenge. The bird, presumed dead, had been hung over the hunter's shotgun stock when it apparently kicked the trigger while in the final throes of a death twitch and peppered the back of the hunter's wife with bird shot.

However, apart from such occasional oddities, how do most of the year's 800 or so fatal hunting accidents—the type most amenable to control through licensing and laws—happen? The most comprehensive and certainly the only widespread and continuing study is that contained in the NRA's annual Uniform Hunter Casualty Report which is compiled from official statistics now received from 40 states (and also 7 Canadian provinces). The report analyzes and breaks down the hunting casualties (fatalities and injuries, all involving firearms) reported into all kinds of comparisons and percentages according to cause, circumstance, shooter and victim. It makes for fascinating, if rather grim, reading.

For example, the 1963 report, covering a ten-year period, tells us that 18 per cent of the casualties are fatal, and that about two-thirds of all casualties are accounted for by shotguns, and most of the rest by rifles.

In only about 3 out of every 10 casualties, we also learn, the shooter shoots himself. In most instances (69 per cent) he shoots somebody else, and not necessarily a fellow hunter. In Claverack, New York, for instance, a four-year-old boy playing in his backyard was hit by a hunter shooting in a wooded area 700 feet away.* A mother hanging clothes in her backyard in a Buffalo, New York, suburb, was killed by another hunter. A bridegroom of one week was driving along a country road when a door leaped across the road in front of his car. Immediately a battalion of hunters materialized and opened fire on the deer; one hunter's bullet penetrated the windshield, killing the driver.

Virtually all hunting casualties, according to the NRA survey, occur in one of many nonsensical ways. More than half of the mishaps (53 per cent) result from the "unintentional discharge" of a gun—that is, the hunter fires the gun unintentionally, usually under circumstances when the gun should not even have been loaded: he stumbles and falls; lets the trigger catch on brush or some other object; is removing the gun from or placing it in a vehicle; is riding in a car with the loaded gun; is crossing a fence, indulging in horseplay, or even clubbing some beast with it.

---

* A shotgun can kill or injure a person up to anywhere from 150 to 300 yards away; the danger range of a rifle, depending on its type and the ammunition used, is from about three-quarters of a mile for a .22 short to as much as 3½ miles for a high-powered job.

The remaining casualties (47 per cent)—classified as victims of "intentional discharge"—are a result of the shooter firing at an animal or bird, or what he thought was some such creature, and hitting a human target. In most instances, the unfortunate victim is hit simply because he is out of sight of the shooter or suddenly moves into his line of fire. But in far too many cases, the victim is actually mistaken for the species of fauna coveted by the hunter. The stories are legion. Indiana's Conservation Department Director Donald Foltz tells of the hunter who thought he saw a squirrel move in a hickory tree. He fired, and out tumbled the body of his fourteen-year-old nephew—dead. Foltz also cites the bizarre case of a West Virginian who "thought he saw a turkey in the brush; he took aim and fired. The 'turkey' was a man. He jumped up, and the shooter fired another round, this time thinking he had a woodchuck in his sight. Fortunately he was still off target, so his victim survived, although peppered from head to foot with buckshot."

During one hunting season, a Michigan father killed his fourteen-year-old son and a Pennsylvania boy hunter of the same age slew his father. Each had mistaken his blood relation for a deer.

To commemorate the countless news items about people who have shot other people under the impression that the latter were deer, rabbits, squirrels or other fauna, composer-humorist Tom Lehrer once wrote a hunting song to herald this trend in trophies. To savor the song's full flavor, one has to hear Lehrer play and sing it, but the opening lyrics go like this:

> I always will remember
> 'Twas a year ago November
> I went out to hunt some deer
> On a morning bright and clear.
> I went and shot the maximum the game laws would allow—
> Two game wardens, seven hunters, and a cow.*

Why do such accidents happen? In an attempt at an explanation, the NRA, in the preliminary remarks to one of its annual casualty reports, says that "substantially all are caused by ignorance, carelessness or both."

Youth, however, is also quite likely an underlying factor of considerable importance. For the 1963 report reveals that teenagers,

* Copyright 1953 by Tom Lehrer.

though comprising (in the fifteen- to nineteen-year-old age group) only 7 per cent of the population, account for almost half (45 per cent) of all hunting accidents. In other words, with from six to seven times more teenagers involved in hunting accidents than the population at large, this age group is seemingly as accident-prone with guns as it is with hot rods. More significantly, the situation with this segment of the population has not been getting any better; it has in fact been getting worse. The proportion of teenage shooters involved in such casualties was 34 per cent in 1950, the year the NRA Hunter Safety Training Program, aimed particularly at young shooters, was started. By 1956, the proportion had risen substantially to 46 per cent, about what it is in the most recent (1963) NRA report.

What good, then, are education and training in curbing carelessness and ignorance, and perhaps other factors? Certainly there can be no question that safety training must have some effect. Nonetheless, in California in 1963, youngsters with training were involved in 5 fatal and 8 nonfatal accidents; untrained juniors were responsible for 5 fatal and 3 nonfatal accidents. Of the total of 64 hunting accidents in South Dakota in 1964, as many as 30 were caused by youngsters, 8 of them age thirteen or younger—one was only eight, another three! Of the 30 youngsters, 21 had passed the course in hunter safety. Of the 157 negligent shooters in Minnesota the same year, another state with a safety program, 102 were teenagers or younger; 7 were under twelve. It is indisputable, based on these and other reports, that youngsters, trained or untrained, are involved in a disproportionately high number of hunting accidents, as well as others involving firearms. Yet, in most states, young people of fourteen, and sometimes only twelve or even younger, can get a license to hunt. In most states, too, both adult and child can hunt without bothering to take a safety course or displaying any proficiency in the handling of their weapons.

Then again, safety is not a halfway affair. It often doesn't do you much good to practice it unless everyone else does. None of the safety programs, even where they have legal force, is aimed at reforming grown men who have gone hunting for years and will continue to go, without learning the rudiments of hunting safety. And so California, even after having a safety training program since 1954, had 27 hunting fatalities in 1964, its highest number in a decade and double the number of casualties recorded in 1962.

One wonders, too, just how much a four-hour safety course can accomplish. To find out, I enrolled in the NRA course given at a New York armory in the company of 16 would-be woodsmen, mostly sweater-attired males in their late teens or early twenties. The instructor was an NRA volunteer. He began by saying that he hoped that each of us, soon after the completion of the course, would get a deer, but that in the process he hoped we would come back alive.

To emphasize this point, he unfolded a tale of a man who, while hunting, had shot and killed his own son. The son, it seemed, had gone behind a bush to urinate and then had proceeded to make his way back to his father by a circuitous route behind the bushes. The father, seeing something move, had fired away. In rapid succession, we then learned of the NRA and its efforts to encourage firearms safety, the history of firearms, the anatomy and operation of the basic types, the proper handling of a weapon in each of its possible positions of use (prone, sitting, kneeling and standing). We were instructed in such things as the trigger squeeze and sight pictures and, of course, introduced to the "Ten Commandments."

Strangely, although the sessions were occasionally punctuated by the sound of guns booming from the armory, and although the NRA Instructor's Guide suggests that "the students handle guns as much as possible," none of us was ever called upon to handle any of the guns used in the demonstration, much less fire one. My feeling, or rather hope, is that this is not the situation in the typical NRA safety course.

At the conclusion of the course, we were put through a written test which called for us to answer such questions as: When should the safety on a gun be on the "off" position? (Only when it's about to be fired.)

If three hunters are advancing abreast down a field and a rabbit runs back through the line of hunters between the middle hunter and the one on his left, which hunter takes the shot? (No hunter should fire.)

Why is it dangerous to have a loaded gun in an automobile? (The motion of the automobile may cause the gun to slide or fall. Dogs or passengers, especially children, may contact the trigger.)

What are the three primary rules of gun safety? (1. Treat every gun as if it were loaded. 2. Always point the muzzle in a safe direction. 3. Be sure of your target.)

Since no licenses are required for the purchase of rifles or shotguns, anyone, no matter what his physical or mental condition, can take the course. If he does not pass the test, he can take it again and again until he is an accredited and licensed safe shooter.

The NRA, in its Instructor's Guide, cautions teachers to be on the alert "to identify at the earliest moment possible those students who have dangerously defective vision which is not corrected by suitable glasses." But just how this is supposed to be done escapes me, at least on the basis of the course I took.

I don't mean to derogate the NRA's safety measures—they are highly commendable as far as they go. My main criticism of the NRA is based on its refusal to allow safety measures to be extended even further. An important point, of course, is that to learn safety rules and to practice them are two different things. Just as most motorists are generally acquainted with rules of the road, most hunters are acquainted with the rules of gun safety, which, after all, are largely only a matter of common sense. Yet allowing those of tender years to have guns, even though the user is trained, is an invitation to disaster.

An analogy would be allowing a child to play with matches simply because he has learned to "Close Cover Before Striking." Children generally are not fitted to discharge the responsibility that goes with being placed in an adult situation or one requiring a certain degree of maturity, such as that calling for the handling of anything potentially dangerous, be they matches, guns or cars.

In criticizing the NRA's shooting program for boys and girls, some only nine years old (and even younger, in some cases), Professor Ross Stagner, chairman of the Psychology Department of Wayne State University in Detroit, questions the reasoning that holds that children should be taught to shoot simply because there are guns in our society. "We have restrictions against nine-year-olds for marriage, driving cars and the armed services, so why would anyone want to teach them to shoot?" he asks. "Instructing children in the use of weapons because they might fire one when they grow older is not very sensible," he added.

"Guns are symbols of power and sometimes used by people who have not achieved a power status," psychologist Stagner also says. "With a weapon in their hands, these people feel they can control events around them. This is especially true of children. They are weak and at times emotionally unstable—far too immature to handle a lethal weapon."

What good do safety rules and training do when most accidents, as the NRA says, are caused by sheer stupidity and ignorance as well as by the thoughtlessness and carelessness, to which too many human beings seem prone?

Some people, it seems, never learn even by experience. There is, for example, the case of the California hunter who one day accidentally shot himself in the right foot. Just returned from the hospital, he demonstrated to friends just how he had done it by pointing a 20-gauge shotgun at the freshly healed foot. He then pulled the trigger, and back he went to the hospital, this time for treatment of a new shotgun wound.

Far too many hunters habitually break all manner of laws, written and unwritten. During one New York season, 12 of 44 persons (all with safety training) involved in hunting accidents were found to be hunting in violation of the law when the accident occurred.

Then, there are other human frailties, physical and psychological, which make hunting dangerous and which all the safety education, training and advice in the world cannot control. One peculiar aspect of hunting as a sport is the dominant role that emotionalism plays in it. In the sheer excitement of the chase, when the heart is pounding and adrenalin is pumping into the system, some hunters are aroused to such a pitch that they will shoot at the slightest movement they see.

"Even after taking a safety course and passing the test," my NRA safety instructor confessed, "a hunter becomes a changed person in the woods. When I used to hunt on public land, no sooner would I start out than I would find bullets popping around me everywhere. One landed in a tree 2 feet from my head. I actually saw hunters aiming at me. A hunter often becomes uncivilized and acts like a maniac as soon as he gets into the woods, just as some people do when they get behind the wheel of a car. If the hunter has not bagged anything in five to ten years, and many don't, he is likely to shoot at anything he sees."

What can also contribute to conjuring up rosy visions of game is alcohol. The NRA says that "no more than about 1 per cent" of the casualties reported to it involve persons "under the influence." But one wonders if this figure isn't somewhat on the conservative side. It is doubtful that tipsy shooters, apart from being difficult to detect, would be reported as such. When Donald Foltz asked one of his officers in Indiana what he would do if he came across a hunter who had been drinking, the answer was, "I'd run like hell!" In an *American Rifleman* editorial, the NRA once sternly warned: "There are too many 'hunting' parties whose primary interest is befuddling their minds as the members hunt for the bottom of the liquor bottle instead of clearing their minds in the matching of wits with the elusive creatures of the wild."

A more likely contributor to those rosy, blurred visions is simply poor eyesight. With 48 in every 100 men shown to have some difficulty with their vision, and with hunters not required to pass an eyesight test anywhere, it is not surprising to hear the story of the man who shot a 6-foot-5-inch companion weighing 240 pounds under the mistaken impression that he was shooting a woodchuck. With most hunting casualties taking place on clear, bright days, in either lightly covered or completely open country, and at relatively short range, there can be little doubt that faulty vision plays at least some part, if not all, in many such accidents.

"Poor eyesight may be involved in as high as 80 per cent of hunting accidents in New York State," said the National Society for the Prevention of Blindness some years ago. Citing figures compiled by the state Department of Conservation, Dr. Franklin M. Foote, the society's executive director, said that of six major causes of hunting accidents in the state that year, "only two—ricocheting and loading or unloading guns—definitely do not involve faulty vision." The other causes, he said, including "in line of fire," "carelessness," "mistaken for game," accounted for 80 per cent of the accidents which injured 118 and killed 12 New York state hunters during the year. "A thorough professional eye examination before the opening of the state deer season," suggested Dr. Foote, "may not only improve marksmanship, but may also save the life of another human being."

Of 74 shooters involved in major Minnesota accidents in 1953, 77 per cent were found to have defective vision. Two-thirds of the negligent gunners had faulty depth perception—which would make it difficult for them to judge whether something—or someone—was within range of their bullets. Astonishingly, most of the hunters with these and other visual defects didn't even suspect their eyesight was faulty, even when their defects were serious.

In the cases studied, all of the hunters who were killed or wounded when mistaken for deer wore red clothing; 60 per cent of the men who shot them were found to be color-blind, compared to from 2 to 5 per cent of the male population at large. (The failing is relatively rare in women.)

What about the emotionally impulsive or unstable type of hunter? A classic examination of this type is in the Minnesota Hunter Casualty Study. It represents probably the most comprehensive analysis of hunting accidents ever made, going far beyond the series of NRA studies in certain respects.

The NRA studies, as we know, deal only with the *physical* circumstances under which accidents take place, cover only part of the total casualties in each area, and are not as a rule based on firsthand information, depending instead on the information sent in by the various reporting localities. The Minnesota study also dealt with physical causes and came up with results not too dissimilar from those in the NRA study. However, the Minnesota study also went further in that it examined the personalities and psychological characteristics of the shooters involved in accidents. To do this involved making exhaustive case studies of 93 of the 130 shooters involved in hunting gun accidents in Minnesota in 1953. (Most of those not studied had, of course, finished themselves off.) Each shooter was given an individual three-hour interview examination by H. Lee Kuluvar, chairman of the Safety Committee of the Minnesota Conservation Federation and outdoor representative of the Jacob Schmidt Brewing Company of St. Paul, which underwrote the study. The examination included the well-known Minnesota Multiphasic Personality Inventory (MMPI) test of 566 questions.

On the basis of the MMPI and other questions exploring the accident and shooter, as well as the latter's gun-and-hunting-safety knowledge, significant differences were found between the shooters who were judged negligent (virtually 95 per cent of them) and the relatively few blameless shooters. Those who could not reasonably be held at fault, often because of the negligence of the victim, were shown to be essentially indistinguishable from the average normal personality. The grossly negligent shooter differed mostly from the norm, according to the study, in being of a type "relatively insensitive to the ordinary inhibitions that help to keep most of us out of trouble." This type of person, the study said, would be less governed by the wishes and precautions of other hunters, would be less affected by what would be punishing situations for others, and so would be less apt to mend his ways or readily learn from experience. On this basis, the study also said, "he would be prone to other accidents."

The study turned up a startling revelation about accident repeaters: On the basis of the number of negligent shooters admitting to previous accidents, it was found that "the shooter who has caused one accident is 100 times as likely to cause another as the average hunter is to have his first accident." The most dangerous age for becoming an accident shooter was fifteen, with fourteen a close second. One fourteen-year-old blithely admitted to 7 accidents in his five years as a hunter!

One of the proposals of the Minnesota Conservation Federation Safety Committee called for a "realistic deterrent penalty on accident shooters—automatic license revocation after an accident, with mandatory report to a game warden. The warden would be empowered to reinstate the license after investigation in minor and non-negligent cases."

"It is felt that the discovery that the most negligent shooters are on the whole recognizable psychologically marks a milestone in hunting accident prevention," said the Minnesota researchers.

Does all this point to an answer to at least one phase of firearms accident prevention? Can the various findings—psychological, physical and others—be used to isolate certain measurable types as probable major offenders in hunting accidents, people who apparently should not be trusted with a gun?

Admittedly it would be difficult to administer a personality test to every hunter, new and old. But to supplement safety training and provide some measure of control, cannot certain minimum requirements be established, to weed out the immature, inexperienced and unstable, as well as those with noncorrectable visual and other mental defects? Can we not disqualify those apt to be most grossly negligent with a gun?

To see how the NRA felt about this, I wrote to the organization. To my question, "Do you feel that an eye test should be made a requirement for a hunting license?" Frank Daniel, NRA secretary, gave only this short and succinct reply: "Actually, it has never been established to what extent visual acuity plays a part in hunting casualties." With regard to allowing the young to hunt, Daniel wrote, "*Most* states have a minimum age for the issuance of a hunting license, or they provide that persons below a certain minimum age may hunt only while in the company of a parent or qualified adult. There would appear to be little or no record of firearms accidents for hunting casualties being committed by youngsters who had received safety training or who were shooting or hunting under adult supervision."

I also wanted to know generally if the NRA felt that applicants for licenses should be screened in any way in an effort to cut down the number of hunters who might turn out to be hazards to others. "We have given a great deal of thought and attention to the various possibilities for screening applicants," said Daniel, venturing the opinion that "it would appear to be most difficult from a practical point of view." To give each applicant even a brief examination such as those given for driver permits, he explained, "would require many, many hours and many personnel which the states at present do not have." Moreover, he saw no purpose to this, he said, stating that the tests given would-be drivers did almost nothing toward weeding out the unsafe drivers. Similarly, it was his feeling that "even a very complex and comprehensive examination would not go far toward determining which hunter will lose his judgment under actual hunting conditions and which will not." Summing up the NRA's stand, Daniel stated: "It has been our very strong feeling that the ultimate solution lies in firearms safety training, and that the best time to give the training is before the youngster starts to hunt."

Although stressing the importance of "training" and making a great to-do about its safety courses, the NRA tries to play down the dangers of hunting which, it would have you believe, are greatly exaggerated.

"Hunting dangerous?" Not at all, according to the NRA's Daniel. "Actually, hunting is not a hazardous sport," he also wrote me, offering some statistics to show how remarkably safe a sport it was. On the basis of the 1,538 casualties, both minor and severe, contained in the 1958 Uniform Hunter Casualty Report, he said, and the number of hunters then estimated in the United States, this worked out to only 1 reported casualty for every 7,800 hunters and for every 113,000 man-days of hunting. (A man-day of hunting is a piece of mythology, meaning one day of hunting by one man.)

These revelations can be seriously questioned, being based admittedly on not necessarily complete reports then from only thirty-three of our states. The National Safety Council some years later estimated the nation's annual hunting casualties at about 9,000, of which about 700 were fatal. The NRA, though continuing with its comparisons and ratios, now shows them only in percentages and, for rather understandable reasons, refuses to give out the figures on which they are based. When I recently wrote to get a count of the casualties currently reported, I was told that the figures were "unavailable."

Nonetheless, the NRA concludes from its calculations that hunting is "a remarkably safe sport," and that the casualties incurred in its pursuit are "statistically not of very great importance." In his letter telling me this, Daniel used the occasion to deplore the fact that hunting accidents "are usually covered much more enthusiastically in the press than such things as industrial accidents and motor vehicle accidents, which are of infinitely greater importance."

The NRA, though disliking to be reminded that drivers are required to have licenses, is particularly fond of comparing motor vehicle accidents and gun accidents and of declaring that cars claim about twenty times as many lives, citing the accidental death figures for each category (in 1964, from motor vehicles, 47,700 or 24.9 per 100,000 people; from firearms, 2,400, or 1.3).

A reliable statistician would weigh the nation's 90 million or so licensed drivers against the perhaps 30 million users of guns. He would also observe that almost everyone rides in cars all year; but only a minority of our population goes hunting, and for a few days each year. He might also want to weigh all the firearms deaths— about 17,000 a year—against all the auto deaths. Proportionately, guns can be said to cause more deaths.

The gun lobby would also like to have the perils of hunting contrasted to the danger of choking on food. "Your chances of getting shot while hunting are quite remote," reads an NRA message to the public. "The national rate for fatal firearms accidents from all causes, per 100,000 persons, is just slightly above the rate of deaths from choking on food."

What the NRA neglects to say is that nearly 4 out of 5 of the some 1,500 choking victims annually are infants or preschoolers, or oldsters over sixty-five. (Moreover, if you choke it's just your own life—not someone else's, as is usually the case in hunting accidents.)

Although gun magazine editors and outdoor editors readily use these statistics, others who use them should know better. Some years ago, *The Saturday Evening Post* ran an editorial on the theme "Gun Laws Shouldn't Be Aimed Wildly at All Sportsmen." It stated: "The rate for fatal firearm accidents was only 1.4 per 100,000 people, scarcely above the 1.2 deaths from suffocating or choking on food." This was an almost verbatim copy of an NRA statement.

Would you also believe that hunting is safer than such sports as golf and baseball, indeed, ranks 16th on a list behind such other perilous pastimes as picnicking, concert attendance and church-going? To "prove" this, the NRA and the National Shooting Sports Foundation often cite a Travelers Insurance Company five-year study of claims paid for "sports and recreation accidents." The study showed, for example, that the company had paid 4,318 claims for football accidents, 824 for accidents incurred by theater-, church- and concert-goers, and only 777 for hurt hunters. Did Travelers intend the number of claims indicated to reflect the relative risk of each activity listed? Not at all, said a company official I telephoned who, indeed, was quite vehement about the use to which the study was being put. "For one thing," he said, "the figures listed represented payment only to people holding *personal* accident policies, not group and other policies, and the sole purpose of the listing was to impress upon the public the fact that accidents do happen in various ways." All that one could conclude from the study, he said, was that more people with personal accident policies happened to go to theaters, churches and concerts than to hunt.

The obvious point, too, is that fatalities, not simply injuries, provide a somewhat more reliable gauge to the dangers of a sport. However, the NRA never sees fit to quote a special Metropolitan Life Insurance Company study of the fatalities suffered by a segment of the company's policyholders as a result of some sport or recreational activity. Of the 315 deaths studied, hunting accounted for 35, ranking only behind swimming, bathing and other water activities (138 deaths), boating (55), and fishing (46). Target shooting accounted for another 3. Far down on the Metropolitan list, in contrast to their high position on the Travelers' list, were baseball (5), basketball (3) and football (2).

Indeed, if the human carnage exacted by hunting were as widely publicized as that of other sports, there would be a loud clamor to have hunting banned in the name of public safety. All the more reason for this would be that the hazards of hunting are unique in that they are by no means confined to its participants, in fact are most likely to number as victims persons other than the negligent hunter; he is often even a nonhunter perhaps as much as a mile or more away from the shooter.

It should be noted that the New York hunter casualty rate is, on the average, far below that estimated for the nation at large. One contributing factor could well be the state's requirement (along with those of Connecticut and Rhode Island) that all first-time hunters, regardless of age, receive safety training. The fact that New York's gun laws are the strictest in the nation could also well contribute to the state's surprisingly low over-all firearms accident death rate. New York's rate of 0.4 deaths per 100,000 population (compared to the national average of 1.2) is the third lowest in the nation, ranking only behind Massachusetts' 0.2 and Connecticut's 0.3. New Jersey's rate is the same as New York's; Rhode Island is only a shade behind with a rate of 0.5. Most of these states, it has already been noted, have at least some semblance of firearms control. On the other hand, the highest firearms accident death rates are found in states with few, if any, controls: Alaska, 4.7; Montana, 3.9; Idaho, 3.9; Utah, 3.5; Mississippi, 3.4; New Mexico, 3.4; Arkansas, 2.7; and Alabama, 2.6.*

In view of all this, what is that source of so many NRA statistics, the National Safety Council, doing to promote firearms safety? Like the American Red Cross, few organizations are so esteemed as the fifty-three-year-old National Safety Council for their service to the public. Chartered by Congress, the NSC, headquartered in a block-long red brick building in Chicago with a staff of 370 employees, is a nonprofit cooperative organization of some 9,000 industrial con-

---

* 1962–63 rates (the latest available), from the June 1965 Statistical Bulletin of the Metropolitan Life Insurance Co.

cerns, insurance and transportation companies, labor unions and other groups from government, education, religion and law.

Among other things, the NSC houses the world's largest library of accident prevention data, churns out hundreds of thousands of posters bearing on every conceivable safety subject, arranges regional and local safety meetings, and helps formulate model safety legislation. Here is the organization which should be the most knowledgeable of all where the prevention of firearms accidents is concerned.

Accordingly, I paid a visit to John P. Fleming, director of the NSC's Public Safety Department, and, as such, responsible for developing programs to keep America safe in its myriad of recreational activities, including shooting. For this Fleming was well equipped both by background and personal inclination. He had acquired a firsthand familiarity with firearms as a former jumpmaster and range officer with the 82nd Airborne Division and as a former instructor at the Illinois State Police Academy; and I learned, too, that he also held membership in the National Rifle Association and its locally affiliated Illinois State Rifle Association. From our conversation, and from scattered writings by Fleming, it soon became apparent that his views on firearms accidents and their prevention coincided with those of the NRA in every important respect. In a guest editorial entitled "Gun Accidents—How Big a Problem?" written for the *Illinois Shooter*, an organ of the state affiliate of the NRA, Fleming left the impression that firearms accidents were not much of a problem at all. At the same time, however, he urged readers to sign up for the NRA's safety courses. For *The World of Guns*, the so-called bible of the pro-gun people, he contributed an article which undertook to explore the whys and wherefores of firearms accidents. Shooting, he wrote, was getting safer all the time. No other cause of accident mortality, he also said, had shown "a corresponding rate reduction." While deploring the more than 2,000 annual deaths from firearm accidents, Fleming pointed to the "more than 20 times as many lives" claimed by motor vehicle accidents. Many of the other "facts" had the familiar ring of NRA propaganda, such as the familiar "choking on food" comparison. As an added fillip, he tossed out statistics to show that "falls" kill about nine times as many people as firearms. He failed to mention that most of the fatal falls are incurred by the aged. Among fifteen- to twenty-four-year-olds, falls account for only about 60 deaths a year, compared with approximately 600 caused by firearms.

Finally, after running through the Ten Commandments of shooting safety (and castigating the carelessness and ignorance of those who violate the commandments), Fleming concluded hopefully: "Education is the answer. The firearms industry and the several national shooting organizations, as well as government agencies, are working at it, but they need the help of every shooter, every gun owner in America. 'Learn yourself; then teach a child.' That slogan, acted upon by every adult, could make firearms accidents obsolete."

Feeling less than satisfied with this panacea and wondering if there wasn't somewhat more the NSC, if not the NRA, could contribute to the prevention of firearms accidents, I later wrote to Fleming and asked the following questions:

Didn't the NSC have some opinion as to the desirability of having all hunters, regardless of age, and including present license owners, pass a safety test, or give some other evidence of their proficiency in the handling of guns? Shouldn't an eye test be made a prerequisite for a hunting license? What about higher minimum age requirements for hunters? Or a requirement that all firearms, including shotguns and rifles, be registered, with the sale of ammunition restricted only to registered gun holders or perhaps only to holders of hunting licenses and members of authorized gun clubs? Shouldn't loaded guns be prohibited within the limits of a city and perhaps within homes? What about laws that would also make it illegal to carry loaded guns in vehicles and to prohibit shooting within 1,000 feet (or some other specified distance) of a residence? How, in general, did the NSC feel about the need for stricter firearms control laws, and what form should these legal controls take?

Fleming said he would bring up these questions at the next meeting of his Recreational Shooting Committee, which, he said, established the guidelines in the firearms area, and so provided the basis on which the NSC staff or management might choose to act. In due course, Fleming wrote to tell me that my letter had been read and "discussed point by point" at a Recreational Shooting Committee meeting, and then reported:

It was the consensus that there would be no significant contribution to accident prevention by suggesting any new regulatory measures or restrictions on gun ownership. On the question of operational procedures and standards for hunters, it was felt that these were subject to continuous study by such organizations as the National Rifle Association and the various state game authorities. . . .

On the matter of recommending any NSC policy with respect to firearms legislation, it was the opinion of the committee that current legislative proposals would have no effect on the prevention of accidents. It was recommended that the council's resources be directed instead to the task of strengthening and supporting the present firearms safety training courses being offered throughout the country.

The chairman of the Recreational Shooting Committee, it should be noted, is Franklin Orth, executive vice president of the National Rifle Association. Orth is also a member of the board of directors of the National Safety Council and a vice chairman of its Public Safety Committee. Another NRA staff member is chairman of the NSC's home safety conference and is also a member of its board of directors. Still another NRA staffer is a member of the Recreational Shooting Committee.

"The tragedy of a hunting accident," says the NRA, "cannot be measured in terms of relative statistical importance. Even one such accident is too many." In its *Hunter Safety Handbook*, the NRA states: "Guns should be unloaded before being put in a car. It is better to case them as well." It seems, therefore, that the NRA would not object to bills that were introduced at about the same time in early 1963 in the Vermont and Montana state legislatures. The bills would make illegal the carrying of a loaded gun in a vehicle; both seemed badly in need of enactment in their respective states. Vermont, the only New England state to have no such law, also has the region's second highest death rate from firearms accidents (1.4), one triple the New England average of 0.5. Montana's rate of 3.9 is the nation's second highest.

Yet the NRA labeled both bills "undesirable" and mustered efforts that resulted in their being killed in committee. "Without defending the act of carrying a loaded firearm in a motor vehicle under circumstances which cause firearm accidents," warned the customary NRA bulletin mailed to these states, "the sportsmen must decide to what extent it is proper to enact an ostensible safety measure to law."

Introduced in the Montana state legislature at about the same time, however, was a bill which would allow children under the age of fourteen years to carry or use firearms under certain circumstances with parental permission. (Montana children over fourteen can freely buy guns without anyone's permission.) This bill was labeled "good" by the NRA, and with its blessing was duly enacted into law.

14 Personal Protection, Crime and Punishment

One is forever being told, "You don't need to protect yourself; that's the job for the police." What kind of talk is this for America? Are we becoming a nation of defeatists, devoid of personal pride and content to rely entirely on our police for protection?

— The National Rifle Association, quoted in the *New Republic*, December 14, 1963

The National Rifle Association and its followers, in opposing firearms control, claim that the Second Amendment to the Constitution gives citizens the right to keep and bear arms for personal protection, national defense and recreation. How valid is this claim? Granting the purpose guns may have served in the days of the Founding Fathers, do privately owned firearms have a place in a twentieth-century civilized society? Does the American of today have a "right" to a gun, either by law or by necessity?

Those who argue against gun control laws say yes. Apart from invoking the Constitution, they use two main lines of argument. For one thing, they contend that stringent regulations make it difficult for citizens to own and use guns to protect themselves against criminals. They also argue that such regulations, in discouraging our citizens from acquiring guns, would deprive the country of a much-needed private arsenal in time of national danger. A related argument holds that regulations requiring all gun owners to register would provide a master list that would facilitate a take-over by a foreign power or domestic revolutionaries. The somewhat less prac-

254

tical benefits of recreation are also cited to justify the use of guns in the various shooting sports.

Assuming that these arguments are offered in good faith and sincerity, let us subject them to scrutiny, considering in turn the main points of debate—personal protection or self-defense, protection in terms of the national defense, and recreation. Closely related is the alleged constitutional "right" to pursue these purposes.

In Brooklyn in August 1965, Thomas Cox, a disabled merchant seaman, armed with a gun and a seemingly limitless supply of ammunition, held off 40 policemen during a two-hour siege of a house that was not a home. Arraigned on charges of felonious assault and Sullivan Law violation, Cox offered a unique defense: self-defense. The house, explained the 6-foot-4-inch 274-pound Cox, had been robbed several times before, although he could give no plausible reason for shooting at what was plainly a coterie of police on an official mission.

The notion that a man's home, however casual, is his castle is rooted in the old common law governing self-protection, and holding sacred chattel, children, house and self. And, in the view of many, the need—indeed, the obligation—for man to be prepared to take militant means to defend his person and property has persisted from the Dark Ages down to this very day. Some, in fact, view the need as more important now than ever before.

The firearms lobby often complains that crime in this country receives an exaggerated amount of press attention, far beyond its actual seriousness. Paradoxically, at other times, it paints a picture perpetuating the myth of the nation today as a twentieth-century Tombstone. From this it follows that every citizen should be a law unto himself, with a gun at the ready available for instant use.

Although the fact is that there are police today where few, if any, were on duty in the old days, the NRA continues to preach the right and need for self-defense. To inspire readers, *The American Rifleman* features a monthly column, "The Armed Citizen," an account of heroic episodes in which citizens use firearms to kill or wound robbers, burglars and other criminals. However, there is never any mention in this or other *Rifleman* columns of the many more citizens who are killed or wounded while in the process of attempting these heroic deeds. Nor is there mention of the many accidental or other deaths due to firearms, or of the high rate of crime by firearms in the United States compared with most other countries.

Column fodder is provided by newspaper clippings solicited from *Rifleman* readers. A typical example:

Los Angeles, California, jewelry store operator Edward Kovacs was alone in his store when three men walked in and demanded his money. When one of the robbers drew his gun, Kovacs pulled out a .25 automatic and fired. One of the bandits fell wounded and the other fled.

Another:

Joe Christian, manager of a grocery store in Owensboro, Kentucky, saw his cashier, Ronnie Payne, being held up. Christian got a .45 automatic and followed the robber out the front door. The man turned and hit Christian and then began to run. After he failed to heed Christian's command to halt, the store manager fired three shots, seriously wounding the robber.

Although such exploits have unquestionably thwarted occasional crimes, it does not require a very discerning person to see their foolhardiness. One critical *Rifleman* reader wrote the magazine's editor a letter which questioned the wisdom of "advertising the poor judgment and often unlawful behavior of these inept toters in 'The Armed Citizen' column." The letter writer suggested that the magazine mention that a "proper and effective means" of protecting property is by insurance. He also mentioned the possibility of an agitated armed citizen hitting an innocent bystander. He concluded with the suggestion that, at the very least, "before a man places a gun in his store, presumably located in a populated area, a minimum test of competence be required," and urged the NRA to press for legislation to this effect. His letter was never published.

The official NRA viewpoint on the righteousness of resisting a criminal effort was voiced this way by its former president, Karl T. Frederick, in a recently issued NRA pamphlet:

How contemptible, how degrading is the advice of those who tell us to submit meekly and without resistance to the depredations of the bandit. . . . Let them follow their counsels of cowardice if they prefer to surrender the privileges and the rights of manhood, but let us resist by every legitimate means the effort to impose upon us their doctrine of nonresistance; let us reject utterly their effort to abolish the right of self-defense.

Such sentiments, which see physical resistance as an expression of self-respecting manhood and view as cowardice what others would call common sense, are rejected by virtually every law enforcement authority of any standing. Indeed, with crimes of violence increasing, it is important that our citizens think soundly on how they can best protect themselves, both to stay alive and to stay within the law.

You may not shoot and kill someone just because he gives you a dirty look, annoys you, or even strikes or threatens to kill you. You have to be in danger of death or serious injury. Even then, on the basis of the present-day modification of the old English so-called "retreat law," you're not supposed to shoot or use some other form of extreme resistance if you can get out of harm's way—that is, safely retreat without increasing your peril.

Should you for some reason be unable to retreat and so avoid a fight, you're still not necessarily in the clear if you kill. Of course, if it's plain that the other person wants to murder or seriously maim you or yours, anything goes. Generally, however, you are legally permitted to use only "reasonable" force—that is, no more than necessary for the purpose—to repel an aggressor. What is reasonable is a matter of court interpretation, and judges may differ in what they consider reasonable. In a Washington, D.C. restaurant several years ago, an attractive girl was approached and patted on the buttocks by an admiring stranger. The girl snatched up a table knife and stabbed the stranger in the stomach—an act the district attorney considered a somewhat more than reasonable use of force under the circumstances. As a result, it was the girl, rather than the man, who was arrested and charged with assault.

Should you disregard any of these rules and kill someone, even in self-defense, you can wind up being booked for homicide, with the burden of proof on you to show that it was legally justifiable or excusable.

Generally speaking, you can't shoot to kill just to defend property, if no threat to life or limb is involved. But you are allowed by law to shoot to prevent a felony, such as robbery, burglary, arson, murder or rape—which would cover someone's making off with some of your property, for example.

For the same reason, somewhat different rules would apply in the defense of your home, store or other place of business. The fact that a surprise visitor has broken into your premises is in itself good evidence of felonious intentions, and, accordingly, you can take whatever means you deem necessary without having to retreat. However, the state laws on this can be rather tricky. In some states it is legal to shoot an intruder in one's house, but not one halfway through the door, or a prowler on the porch or in one's yard.

With all this in mind, there is nothing to prevent you from legally using a gun for self-defense within the specifications set by your local gun laws. Most states permit any law-abiding citizen to buy a pistol or other concealable weapon and carry it with him or keep it at home. All states permit the free, unlicensed purchase and owner-ship of shotguns and rifles. So every citizen nowadays does have access to some sort of gun, and, contrary to the charges of the NRA, even laws requiring the registration of all guns would not interfere with anyone having a firearm to protect himself from armed burglars and other criminals.

Some women, hesitant to carry lethal devices or living in places banning the carrying of conventional concealed weapons, carry such items as pepper shakers, hatpins, tear-gas pens and guns, and other protective devices aimed at repelling attack while not inflicting last-ing injury. Tear-gas dispensers, though frowned on by some law enforcement agencies, are legal in most states.* One popular device of this type, called "Pengun," is a pencil-sized tube about 4 inches long which, according to the accompanying directions, "discharges a blast of a radically new, powerful tear gas that temporarily incapaci-tates man or beast." Priced at $6.95 with two "cartridges" (having a carrying power of 10 feet with a 3-foot spread), the little weapons were reportedly selling at the rate of 1,500 a month in a District of Columbia store-chain.

Also moving into the promising do-it-yourself protection field are pocket-sized aerosol spray dispensers that shoot out a temporarily eye-stinging chemical at an attacker. One such defender is the lipsticked-size "Rebuff," priced at $1.98 and firing up to twenty-five "shots" at a 15-foot distance. "The chemical is powerful and painful

* Among the notable exceptions: California, Illinois, New York and Wisconsin.

enough to send a thug running and screaming for help," one ad promises, adding the humane note: "Leaves no harmful after-effects."

Whether or not you should use a gun or other defensive weapon or irritant, even where the law is on your side, is of course another matter. (Though the law may be on your side, reason often is not.) Most competent police officers think not. Indeed, I could not find a single law enforcement authority or police officer of any stature to justify the value of a gun as a defense weapon. Many, in fact, regard its use as dangerous by a victim of an intruder or hold-up man, and consider the armed citizen who chooses to defend himself and manages to survive as lucky.

When I applied for my pistol permit in New York, the precinct officer in charge said, "Most of the permits we issue go to people like jewelers and liquor store or gas station owners. But they don't do a bit of good. The store owner is the person usually shot, not the criminal. And after the shooting, the criminal winds up with another gun to add to his collection."

In California, I spoke to Sergeant Jess C. Gonzalez, a twenty-year veteran of the Los Angeles Police Department's robbery division. A heavy-set man who certainly looks capable of defending himself, Gonzalez has testified before Congress and played a key role in tracing the telescopic sight used on the Kennedy murder weapon. Gonzalez, who is an NRA member, has this to say:

"Having a gun for protection only gives you a false sense of security. Many people think that if a criminal knows you're armed, he won't bother you. Well, criminals know that most liquor store owners are armed, and yet they are the ones most liable to be held up. [One reason: because they stay open late]. The liquor store owner has all the odds against him. For one thing, the criminal has the drop on him. When someone comes in to commit a crime, the element of surprise is on his side. He is alert, armed, and ready to shoot. All he has to do is pull the trigger and you're dead. In many cases, the store owner doesn't even have the chance to reach for his gun.

"Let me cite two recent cases. One was a liquor store owner who had been lucky enough to kill six or seven holdup men. Well, the next one got him. Another happened in a drugstore. As the holdup man started out of the door with the loot, the druggist ran after him with his gun. The holdup man took one shot and the druggist was dead.

"Too many people get killed to protect a lousy $40 or $50—which is covered by insurance anyway—and leave families of four children. But these people never think of protecting the orphans and the widows. If I owned a store, I wouldn't have a gun in the place."

In the street or home, too, experienced police officers like Gonzalez advise discretion as the better part of valor. "If anyone holds you up," they will tell you, "the best thing to do is to turn over what he wants."

In the home, police officers agree, the armed citizen is also almost always at a disadvantage. "Remember, the intruder is usually wide awake, while you might just have been awakened from your sleep," said one police chief. "If you hear any suspicious noises, the best thing is to call the police. If the intruder is in your room, don't panic. Lie still and call the police the first chance you get. Actually, you seldom have any choice. In most cases, all the intruder wants is your valuables—and these should be insured."

An article in the July 1965 *Better Homes and Gardens* suggested that the armed homeowner could well be more lethal than the average burglar, and cited the comments of another police chief: "If anyone asks me about arming himself against prowlers, I don't encourage it." The officer recalled a case where a homeowner heard a noise, grabbed his gun and, still half asleep, shot a "prowler." The prowler turned out to be his son, returning late from a movie. The boy died instantly. Another widely publicized incident of this sort took place about a decade ago in Oyster Bay, Long Island, when socially prominent Mrs. William Woodward, Jr., shot and killed her financier husband after mistaking him for a prowler.

Innumerable news stories tell of similar incidents involving not only family members but also friends, neighbors, servants and relatives—all on the list of persons killed or seriously wounded because they were mistaken for prowlers and shot at by armed citizens. A young brother and sister at home alone, frightened by the sound of footsteps on the driveway, grabbed a gun and shot a next-door neighbor who, knowing the children were alone, had decided to stop by and check to see that they were all right. In Scarsdale, New York, a seventeen-year-old boy, seeking to pay a call on a doctor's daughter in the early hours of one morning, was mistaken for a burglar and shot by the girl's father. And in Herkimer, New York, a man who had joined the search for a prowler was shot by a woman who mistook him for the hunted man; it was only after she had fired fourteen shots at her helpful friend that she learned who he was.

In her *Life* column of October 23, 1964, Shana Alexander, after noting that the sale of handguns for feminine protection had risen sharply in her pleasant, suburban Southern California community, reported on a colloquy with her friendly neighborhood firearms dealer. The vendor suggested either a .22 automatic, which, he assured Mrs. Alexander, "could run a hemstitch right up anybody's gut," or a .25-caliber revolver, the preferred tool for "slower but more accurate needlework."

After going through his sales spiel, he was finally frank enough to say, "Women with guns are idiots. Fortunately, only one woman in a hundred buys a gun, and only one in a hundred who buys it will ever use it. And only one woman in *that* hundred will ever hit anything with it."

Reflecting the views of every leading law enforcement authority with no known exception, the Washington *Post* has editorialized: "The best defense against armed lawbreakers, we think, is not to arm the law-abiding and thus turn our cities into unrestricted shooting galleries, but to disarm the lawless."

Strangely enough, the NRA is somewhat vague about the *modus operandi* of the law-abiding armed citizen. It does not go so far as to suggest that all of our citizens walk the streets fully armed. And it has gone on record against loaded guns in the home. In its home firearms safety courses, the NRA is firm in its insistence, according to its own rules, that "all guns be stored under lock and key, *unloaded*," and that "all ammunition be stored in a separate place, also under lock and key, preferably out of sight." With these restrictions, one wonders, how would a gun then be readily available for protection?

In one of its more lucid moments, the NRA once made the matter clear. "Simply don't allow a loaded gun in the house," the NRA's director of training activities, Stanley Mate, told the readers of *The New York Times*. "Even for protection. It's far too easy in the dark to shoot down a member of your own family in mistake for a burglar; it happens over and over. And an intruder seeing you armed is much more likely to shoot you."

Do these statements seem to contradict the NRA's other views about the value of a gun for protection? Or, is it of little concern to the gun lobby what our citizens do with guns, just so long as they buy them?

In its pronouncements on the problem of crime, the NRA speaks in other puzzling paradoxes. On one hand, the association professes deep concern over the rising crime rate, but on the other it stoutly resists any effort at legislation that would effectively keep guns out of the hands of actual and potential criminals or other undesirables.

In terms of the kind of firearms legislation that the NRA will support, the association says that it does favor "legislation designed to prohibit the possession of firearms by persons who have been finally convicted of a crime of violence, fugitives from justice, mental incompetents, drug addicts, and persons while adjudicated an habitual drunkard." But the NRA at the same time opposes any laws that will require some check on a customer's background. Thus, in what is the equivalent of locking the barn after the horse is stolen, the NRA will, as was recently the case in New York State, back a bill which makes it unlawful for some persons convicted of a serious crime, or having a history of mental illness, to possess rifles or shotguns. The bill was passed, an achievement the NRA considered an epic step forward in the battle against crime. Such laws, however, do not really prevent the proscribed persons from buying rifles or shotguns and carrying out some mischief before being caught. Former U.S. Bureau of Prisons Director James Bennett, as a result of a survey of his inmates, found that 80 per cent had obtained their guns immediately prior to the crime. No questions were ever asked by the seller as to their identity, although the vast majority of persons arrested are repeaters.* The guiding principle of the NRA is that the only justifiable laws are punitive rather than preventive ones—in other words, those providing stiffer penalties for people who commit crimes with guns.

* In 1963 and 1964, 76 per cent, according to the FBI's *Uniform Crime Reports*.

The NRA ignores the fact that in practically every state statutes on the books do *already* provide additional penalties (usually five years or more, in some states up to life imprisonment or even death) for crimes committed with guns. The Federal Bank Robbery Act also has such a provision. The heavier penalties, however, are seldom a crime deterrent and, in fact, are seldom meted out. Hoping that a heavier penalty would be a deterrent, Kentucky in 1946 amended its law to make the carrying of a concealed weapon a felony rather than a misdemeanor. However, the chief effect of this was to make conviction more difficult. "Possibly in Kentucky, a state composed of people . . . known for their gun-toting propensities," commented the *Kentucky Law Journal*, "it is too much to ask a jury to find a fellow guilty of a crime which will subject him to a minimum of two years in the state penitentiary."

In Minnesota, a 1905 statute applying exclusively to hunting accidents makes a "mistaken for game" killing a criminal offense—first-degree manslaughter, punishable by imprisonment from five to twenty years. However, there hasn't been a conviction under this statute in the sixty-one years since its enactment: county attorneys won't prosecute and juries won't convict, because they regard the penalty as too severe.

Indeed, some people literally get away with murder. A *Newsweek* item headed "Murder Mop-up" reported on some of the cases disposed of in Houston, Texas, during a sixteen-day period in 1952:

Mrs. Margie Zeglen, a thirty-four-year-old strawberry blonde former rodeo queen, had killed her second husband with the same gun she had used to kill her first husband six years ago. She had been no-billed for the first crime. This time she was sentenced to five years.

John H. Crumpton, a fifty-six-year-old house painter, had shot his son-in-law—the second son-in-law he had killed in ten years. Though relatives called for a death sentence, he got five years.

Most of the cases were homicides by firearms [reported *Newsweek*]. The incidence of repeaters—people who had killed before and had received light sentences or acquittals—was high. In seventeen months, there had been only one death penalty in Houston.

But assembly-line justice was no answer to Houston's high murder rate. District Judge Frank Williford blamed it on the fact that the city has no strong law forbidding people to carry firearms. "Every character goes

into a beer tavern with a pistol," he said. "He has five bottles of beer—
is easily insulted. It is immediately necessary for this same Southern
gentleman to defend his honor."

Even where offenders are dealt with to the fullest extent the law
permits, there is considerable doubt that the threat of punishment is
an effective deterrent to crime. The prospect of prison may deter
some persons from some crimes, but it is by no means certain. Does
the death penalty, for example, really deter murder? Apparently it
did not deter the 315 men and women who now * sit in Death Row
in American prisons. Deterrents matter little in the many murders
committed in the heat of passion. Most stem from brawls between
family members, relatives, lovers, friends, acquaintances and neighbors.

On the other hand, it would seem that preventive rather than
punitive measures would have some effect in keeping guns out of
the hands of some miscreants, minors and mental incompetents. The
latter, in particular, would be unmindful of the punishments attached to their misuse of guns. But the NRA says that preventive
measures, such as a registration requirement or some other form of
regulation, would neither stop lawbreakers from obtaining guns nor
reduce crime. In giving voice to this organizational view, NRA
Executive Vice President Franklin Orth tosses off statements like
this: "Nowhere can be found any proof that the permit or license
requirements foisted upon the law-abiding citizen has any apprecia-
ble affect on the relative ease of accessibility of firearms to the
criminal element."

To support this thesis, the NRA goes back 2,000 years and invokes the authoritative words of one Kung-sun Hung, said to be an
imperial chancellor of the Han Dynasty. In a July 1965 *American
Rifleman* editorial bearing the aptly Confucian heading "Wisdom
and Understanding," the NRA, quoting from what is supposedly a
history of the Han Dynasty, has Hung counseling the Emperor to
reject a proposal that he prohibit the public ownership of bows or
crossbows. The argument quoted against the proposal reads: "The
crime of attacking and robbing is subject to death; yet the reason
they have not been stopped is that the great lawbreakers do not

* At the time of writing, late 1965.

care, indeed, to avoid severe punishment. Should the suggested prohibition be enforced, your subject fears that wicked persons will still carry weapons and the officials will not be able to stop them."

Needless to say, the Emperor was won over by these words. The NRA relishes this story so much that it was used, identically worded, as the editorial in an issue six years before (January 1959). Yet it unwittingly reveals another of the many contradictions inherent in the NRA's stream of arguments. If, as the ancient tale plainly says, the "great lawbreakers" of old were not deterred by "severe punishment," specifically death, why should the lawbreakers of today?

Reaching even further into antiquity, the NRA goes back to Genesis and, citing the appropriate chapter and verse, asks with what gun Cain killed Abel. The inference here is that people in a murderous mood will lay their hands on, if not a gun, some other lethal tool. In an effort to support this thesis, the NRA can find only one modern authority. In its pamphlet entitled "The Gun Law Problem," the NRA quotes Dr. Marvin E. Wolfgang, a University of Pennsylvania sociology professor, as stating the following in his work, *Patterns in Criminal Homicide:*

It is the contention of this observer that few homicides due to shooting could be avoided merely if the firearm were not immediately present, and that the offender would select some other weapon to achieve the same destructive goal. Probably only in those cases where a felon kills a police officer, or vice versa, would homicide be avoided in the absence of a firearm.

Apart from seemingly professing a callous unconcern for the 50 or so policemen murdered annually by felons, the statement as quoted didn't ring quite true coming from a man of Professor Wolfgang's stature. He is listed in *American Men of Science,* which shows him to hold memberships in the Academy of Political and Social Science, the International Society of Criminologists and the American Sociological Association, and to be the author of two criminology books other than *Patterns in Criminal Homicide.* Yet no other criminologist or sociologist to whom I showed the statement would agree with it as the NRA quoted it. One said, "Whether a homicide would result if a gun were not immediately available would also depend on the extent of the provocation. If the provocation weren't strong enough or the heat of passion blew over, the aroused person could forget about getting a gun or some other weapon." The words are those of Dr. Walter Bromberg, one of America's leading psychiatric criminologists and for many years on the staff of Bellevue Psychiatric Hospital and director of the Psychiatric Clinic of the Court of General Sessions in New York.

Another leading criminologist, North Carolina State College's Professor Elmer H. Johnson, indicates in his standard text, *Crime, Correction and Society*, that the availability of weapons in a society, apart from bearing some relation to the prevalence of violence, "may spell the difference between aggravated assault and homicide."

Yet the Wolfgang statement, invested with the authority of its author, is quoted endlessly by opponents of gun legislation. At least two witnesses, one a former NRA president, read it at the 1963–64 Senate Commerce Committee hearings on the Dodd bill. Few apparently have ever bothered to read the rest of the Wolfgang work. However, Professor Wolfgang's other statements are of considerable interest, as I learned from a diligent study of *Patterns in Criminal Homicide*. Immediately preceding the one torn out of context by the NRA (from page 83 of the work) is the sentence:

Research would require determination of the number of shootings that would have been stabbings, beatings, or some other method of inflicting death had no gun been available.

Immediately following the statement was the sentence:

There appears to be a cultural preference or selection for particular types of methods of inflicting death and of weapons used to kill.

Then Wolfgang went on to speak of the "*significant* race and sex preferences for weapons employed in criminal homicide" (the preference, for example, by Negroes for "stabbing weapons"), and the relationship existing between the age of the offender and his predilection for certain types of weapons. Pointing to the high use of pistols and revolvers in the younger (under twenty) and older (fifty-nine) age groups, Wolfgang wrote: "It may be that offenders under twenty years of age and those over fifty require (as do women who slay men) some weapon to maintain distance between themselves and their victims, and to offset their limited physical power when involved in an episode of violence."

The Wolfgang book, an expansion of his doctoral dissertation, is based on a study of 588 cases of criminal homicide in Philadelphia during the five-year period of 1948–1952. The NRA, in its literature, also quotes one other fragment from the Wolfgang study:

... It is probably safe to contend that many homicides occur only because there is sufficient motivation or provocation, and that the type of method used to kill is merely an accident of availability; ...

What had this been sandwiched between? What did each intriguing ellipsis represent? I located the statement on page 79 of the Wolfgang work. Immediately preceding it was the sentence:

Although there are many factors which must converge before homicide occurs, there can be little doubt that accessibility of a weapon, cultural traditions of carrying and employing certain types of weapons, and individual perspectives associated with various means of inflicting death are important factors.

Immediately following it were the words:

... that a gun is used because it is in the offender's possession at the time of incitement, but that if it were not present, he would use a knife to stab, or fists to beat his victim to death. On the other hand, the small physical size of the offender relative to that of his potential victim, or the offender's physical repugnance to engaging in direct physical assault by cutting or stabbing his adversary, may mean that in the absence of a firearm no homicide occurs.

How, I wondered, did Professor Wolfgang himself feel about the NRA's use of some fragmentary fruits of his scholarly study? I decided to write him. In his reply, Professor Wolfgang was obviously irate about the NRA's use of his material. Furthermore, he said that he was "in favor of very restrictive legislation on firearms."

"I want nothing to do with them in any way," said Wolfgang in a March 19, 1964, letter to former U.S. Bureau of Prisons Director James V. Bennett. "While it may be true that firearms can be purchased illegally and many of them for relatively small sums of money, I find no reason to offer firearms for sale to the public." In his letter to Bennett, Wolfgang, the only contemporary authority on crime quoted by the NRA, also had this to say:

I think there is no serious question about constitutional rights of individual citizens to protect themselves, for our society and culture have considerably changed from the time of the eighteenth century when our Founding Fathers felt it important that each private citizen be able to stock himself with arms. The elaborate machinery of law enforcement which has grown up in the United States, the facilities for providing protection to our citizenry, are such that there should be no need for an individual to be issued firearms for his own protection.

I am one of those persons who believe that violence and instruments of violence breed violence. Legislation which makes more restrictive the manufacturing, sale and distribution, and licensing of firearms is, I think, desirable in almost any form. If pushed to the wall, I would probably support the Japanese ruling that no one except a police officer should be allowed to possess or carry a pistol.

Moreover, I fail to understand why rifle associations look upon restrictive legislation as threats to their organizations. If some people insist on finding pleasure in practicing marksmanship with weapons, I can conceive of such organizations existing under the most restrictive type of firearms legislation, for it would be possible to require that all weapons used for such recreational purposes be retained on the property of the organization, never to be taken off the property by individual members of the organization, and that all practice be kept within certain spatial limitations. . . . Certainly the extremely permissive legislation that exists in many of our states can only encourage rather than discourage the flow of firearms into wrong hands.

In other declarations, the NRA prefers to quote only what it wishes from the FBI's *Uniform Crime Reports*, just as it does from other material. In its literature, the NRA, quoting from an introductory page in these reports, reprints a list of various environmental factors which, in the FBI's opinion, "affect the amount and type of crime that occurs from place to place." *

---

* Some of the factors: Poverty, population density and composition; climate; standards and efficiency of law enforcement, and attitudes of the people toward law and order.

The NRA then says that in the FBI report, "There is no mention of the impact of firearms controls on crime." Yet those bothering to flip a few pages through the report (page 7 in the report for 1963) will find FBI Director J. Edgar Hoover saying this, which the NRA chooses to ignore:

The use of weapons in murders varies by geographic region, city, suburban, and rural areas. In 1963 firearms accounted for 53 per cent of the murders in American cities, 62 per cent in the suburban area, and 68 per cent in the rural area. By region, a firearm was used in 37 per cent of the killings in the Northeast, 53 per cent in the Western states, 56 per cent in the North Central states, and 64 per cent of the murders in the Southern states. The easy accessibility of firearms and the lethal nature of the gun are clearly apparent in these murder figures. When assaults by type of weapon are examined, a gun proves seven times more deadly than all other weapons combined.

How effective are firearms control laws in hindering or preventing the use of firearms in crime, whether by criminals or "sportsmen"? The NRA claims that such laws are generally ineffective. As the association can muster no evidence whatever to substantiate this thesis, it singles out for vilification the best-known and strictest state gun law, New York's Sullivan Law. NRA Director-Congressman Robert L. F. Sikes of Florida testified at the 1964 Senate Commerce Committee hearings: "New York State has the toughest gun laws in America and probably the highest crime rate." This point, however, Sikes did not choose to document. If pressed, he would have been forced to reveal his own state of Florida to have about a 25 per cent higher crime rate. Florida's homicide rate is also about double that of New York.

However, in an effort to make out some sort of case against New York, the NRA resorts to its "other weapons" gambit, which, as contained in an NRA "fact" sheet entitled "Statistical Study of Firearms in Accidents and Crime," reads like this:

In New York City, in 1963, there were 549 homicides. Knives and other sharp weapons accounted for 225; physical force accounted for 109; pistols and revolvers accounted for 101; rifles and shotguns accounted for 37; all other means accounted for the balance.

These figures [the fact sheet concludes] are revealing in two ways: (1) the entire state of New York has the most restrictive limitations on the sale, possession and carrying of handguns in the United States, yet 101 murders were committed with handguns; and (2) 411 murders were committed by means other than firearms.

The figures, however, are revealing in a way the NRA does not care to publicize. When analyzed, the figures show that in New York City, covered by the admittedly "restrictive" strict Sullivan Law, only 138 * out of 549 murders, or 25 per cent, were committed with guns in 1963. In Philadelphia and in Detroit, where there are also strong local regulations, the percentages of homicide by guns were 36 per cent and 40 per cent, respectively. In Los Angeles and Chicago, two other cities with gun laws, the murders accounted for by guns were, respectively, 43.5 per cent and 46.4 per cent. On the other hand, in the city of Dallas, where there are no gun controls whatever, 72 per cent of all homicides were effected with a firearm. In the United States as a whole that year, a gun was used in 56 per cent of all homicides.† Unquestionably, there seems to be some relationship between the percentage of murders committed with guns and the strictness of firearms controls in a given geographical area.

How do these controls, however, possibly affect over-all homicide rates? In 1963, New York City's homicide rate was 7.0 per 100,000 population. In Philadelphia and Detroit, the rates were 6.4 and 7.7, respectively. Los Angeles and Chicago, also with gun controls, though in states with no controls, had rates of 7.5 and 10.4. But the city of Dallas, with no controls and in a state with no controls, had a homicide rate of 15.1, perhaps the highest of any major city in the nation.

Referring to an often overlooked value of New York's Sullivan Law, former New York City Police Commissioner Michael J. Murphy points approvingly to "the simple fact that we are able to make arrests for the illegal possession of pistols and revolvers before the possessor has had the opportunity to commit a crime of violence. On this score we have had a substantial degree of success. We have

* With pistols and revolvers, 101, plus 37 with shotguns and rifles.
† In just our cities, 53 per cent.

been able to prevent many crimes of violence by such arrests. Many of those convicted for illegal possession of pistols and revolvers were planning on robberies, assaults and even homicides.

"I would like to underscore as strongly as possible this latter vital point of crime prevention," Murphy told an American Bar association panel on criminal law on August 12, 1964. "One of the most important theories in criminal law—one of the most important functions of law enforcement—is the prevention of crime wherever possible. In many areas the law makes certain conduct illegal and criminal before the actual violent act has occurred. The whole theory of prosecuting for conspiracies and for attempts reflects the community desire to afford protection whenever possible by stopping a course of criminal conduct before it has erupted. We should not have to wait idly by until robberies have been perpetrated or citizens murdered before the forces of law and order are brought into play."

All told, the New York City Police Department property clerk reported the receipt of 5,461 pistols and revolvers in 1963. "A sampling made by his office," said Murphy, "indicates that of this total, 2,741 or 50.2 per cent of these weapons were received as evidence in the commission of a crime. This would, of course, include arrests where the crime charged was the possession of the pistol or revolver. It would also include arrests for other crimes wherein the use or possession of the weapon was an element of the crime."

No proponent of firearms legislation contends that tightening up gun laws will completely abolish homicide, or keep guns completely away from someone who wants a weapon badly enough. No law, for that matter, is completely effective, but all the evidence, both from this country and abroad, indicates that licensing or registration requirements will reduce homicide, and cut other crimes as well as accidental tragedies and suicide, by making it more difficult for unscrupulous and irresponsible people to get guns. Even some who have at times been mentally unstable are upset by the ease with which they can obtain a gun. A case in point was the following startling story, reprinted just as it appeared in Bill Gold's daily column in the Washington *Post* of July 13, 1965.

The other night I had quite a conversation with a woman of obviously superior intelligence. Very early in our chat I formed the impression that she is probably considered a valuable employee by the firm she works for—the kind of person that can be depended on to get the job done with skill and dispatch. Her manner was one of calm self-assurance.

So I was a bit surprised to hear her say: "I've been terribly upset about a news story that I read in the paper this morning."

"Which story?" I asked.

"The one about the two men who were released from prison a few days ago, and within a week they had bought pistols and a shotgun and had killed a policeman, robbed a bank and kidnaped a woman and child," she said. "What bothers me is that ex-convicts find it so easy to arm themselves."

"Yes," I agreed, "but of course that's an old, old story. Even if we some day get strict Federal gun control laws, we'll still have to contend with black market guns being passed from one criminal to another."

"True," she said, "but at least it won't be quite as easy to buy a gun. For example, I shouldn't be permitted to have one, and I know it. But there's nothing to stop me from buying one."

I didn't quite know what she was getting at, but she spared me the trouble of trying to word the question that was on my mind.

"I'm a graduate of Chestnut Lodge," she said. "You know what that is, don't you?"

"Yes," I said, "it's a sanitarium out in Rockville."

"You don't have to beat around the bush," she said. "It's a mental institution. I was off my rocker."

"I see," I said.

"What's more," she went on, "I had strong suicidal tendencies."

I didn't interrupt, and after a few moments she continued. "One day," she said, "I walked out of there with some sort of half-baked idea in my head, and I went to apply for a driver's license.

"But as soon as I listed Chestnut Lodge as my address, they stopped me. They said I'd have to get a letter from my doctor saying that it was all right for me to drive. Well, of course I couldn't get any such letter, so I left. My next stop was at the [deleted] store, where I bought a pistol to kill myself with. Again I gave the Chestnut Lodge address, but the salesman couldn't have cared less. In five minutes I had my pistol."

"Luckily you didn't use it," I said.

"By the grace of God I didn't use it," she said.

"How long ago was that?" I asked.

"Oh, don't worry," she said, "I'm all right now. I got rid of the gun and I'll never touch one again—I hope."

She was silent for a moment. Then she said: "But what worries me is that it's so easy for me, or even an ex-convict, to just walk in and buy a gun. You might want to tell my story in your column some day to illustrate how incongruous our laws are. The state won't permit me to drive an auto unless my doctor gives assurance that I won't be a public menace; but the state doesn't give a hoot about a mental patient buying a gun. That's the story you ought to tell some day."

15 "A Nation of Riflemen"

> Fighting in the next major war will not be confined to the battle-field alone. It is inevitable that our homeland will be attacked. ... More than ever, the individual soldier and the individual citizen will be forced to rely on the weapon with which he is armed, and on his ability to use it effectively, if he is to survive.
> —*The American Rifleman*, May 1957.

An armed citizenry, it is argued, is needed not only for self-defense but, more altruistically and importantly, for the defense of the Republic itself. Ever since our earliest history, the ever-ready Minute-man has been enshrined as our champion of liberty. Today this symbol survives in the articles of faith linking firearms and freedom, and the fanciful notion of "a Nation of Riflemen." This notion has long held that each of our able-bodied men should be ready in America's hour of need to reach for a metaphoric musket and do battle against a hostile horde—redskins, Redcoats or Reds.

This Minuteman mystique completely ignores the fact that a good part of the world has changed between the American and Russian Revolutions, and that in this age of nuclear weapons, tactics suited for use against the Redcoats might be quite ineffective against the Reds.

Certainly the assertion by the National Rifle Association that the Russians, armed with atomic devices, hesitate at attacking us because of the fear that "30 million Americans own and know how to use firearms" smacks of sheer fantasy. No less preposterous is the idea of an armed citizenry fighting a house-to-house, ditch-to-ditch defense against a fancied "Communist takeover" of the United States. To compound the inconsistency, the modern Minutemen and other extremists of the firearms fringe say that, firearms or no firearms, we will surely be subjugated by the Communists anyway, and even venture some date, such as 1973, for this unhappy occurrence.

With similar inconsistency, gun control laws are seen as a facet of a gigantic and all-embracing Communist conspiracy, reaching from the highest to the lowest in the land, and stretching from the Supreme Court, Senate and even the Chief Executive all the way to Moscow and Peking. Why, in the face of this, the Communists condone the shipment of Russian rifles and revolvers here for purchase by American civilians is a rather puzzling maneuver in this imagined "conspiracy."

It is argued that gun control laws would somehow "disarm" the populace by discouraging or making difficult the acquisition of private firearms. This, the reasoning goes, would deprive the nation of a private arsenal, to say nothing of a well-trained shooting citizenry, that might be needed to repel the Red hordes.

Pointed to as a horrible example of what this could mean is a poor, prostrate Britain, facing Nazi invasion during those dark hours after Dunkirk, the country virtually defenseless, with a citizenry armed with little more than brooms, beer bottles and pikes. This was all a consequence, says the NRA, of England's 1921 national firearms act, which, in the words of the NRA, "so curtailed small arms practice that a whole generation was prevented from knowing anything about the fundamentals of firearms," and also reduced the civilian market for arms and ammunition to "almost zero." If it were not for such armament as rifles and revolvers shipped to Britain by the sportsmen of America, it is suggested, the course of events in Europe might have been entirely different.

Paradoxically, the gun lovers assert that gun control laws wouldn't disarm our nation. The NRA says that, if need be, "honest, loyal Americans" would obligingly, if reluctantly, register their weapons, though criminals wouldn't. But, the NRA warns in its classic argument against gun registration, our honest, patriotic citizens could later be disarmed if our registration lists were seized by subversive agents or by an enemy occupying force. The handy lists, it is claimed, would lead to the seizure of all private arms.

To indicate that this is not at all a far-fetched possibility, *The*

American Rifleman, in an April 1948 editorial entitled "Pattern in Red," said that an FBI fingerprint check of 401,211 Federal government employees had shown 8.5 per cent to have "criminal records." "State and municipal government employees would probably check out with a similar average record," said the editorial, adding, "people with a criminal tendency are quite likely to become useful tools for foreign agents or subversive groups."

The mind boggles at the obvious implausibilities in this profusion of arguments. Registration laws, we are told—often in the same breath—would both disarm and yet not disarm the nation. Assuming the latter, we are also asked to believe that it is the nation's sporting guns and other small arms that would deter a Soviet ICBM from landing in our midst. If the widespread possession of small arms is meaningful in national defense, how, one wonders, could a significant number of insurrectionists and invaders ever manage to storm our city halls, pick up those neat lists of registered personal weapons and eventually gain the upper hand by grabbing the guns that all loyal citizens are presumably dedicated to die with? If, on the other hand, small arms are not a meaningful factor against even the incursions of insurrectionists or a sparse alien police, what good would small arms do against a tyrannical government backed by military force?

One answer is provided by the abortive Hungarian revolt of 1956. Though the nation's shooting clubs had been dissolved eight years earlier, the valiant Freedom Fighters were armed. True, ammunition was in somewhat short supply. But all the small arms and ammunition in the United States would probably have been of little avail against those Russian tanks, artillery, bazookas and flame throwers. Yet an NRA pamphlet asks:

"Need any more forceful example be given of the place of firearms in the social structure than the heroic struggle of the Hungarian Freedom Fighter and in the merciless crushing of this revolt by the Red Army?" One is hard put, however, to find a more fitting example of the futility of small arms in the hands of a civilian mob.

In resorting to such sophistry, the NRA is as casual with history as it is with statistics. It makes much of the alleged Nazi use of firearms registration lists to disarm and conquer Europe. However, if such a tactic were employed, it must be accounted one of the best-kept secrets of the war, for I could find no reference to it whatever in the histories of that era. I have spoken to correspondents with an intimate knowledge of German affairs, and they too disabused me of the notion that this was an element in the Nazi invasion tactics or, as is also said, in Hitler's rise to power. Said Sigrid Schultz, a journalist in Germany since 1919: "Hitler used lists to take over Germany? Why, that's perfectly silly, absolutely ridiculous. He didn't need the guns of the people. He had virtually all the people. He had the Storm Troopers and he had the Army. His forces were literally armed to the teeth. If Hitler had any list of guns, he didn't need them."

Another veteran correspondent, Norbert Muhlen, with a half dozen books on Germany to his credit, tells me of a German friend of his: "He was a vehement anti-Nazi, but they never took away his gun. In fact, he even became a hunting inspector."

I also wrote to the American Embassy in each of the countries who so supposedly succumbed to the Nazis. From Denmark came this typical reply: "The Germans did not disarm Danish civilians and so facilitate the German invasion and occupation of Denmark." From Finland: "The Library of War Sciences has not heard of any such activity."

I also write with firsthand personal knowledge of invasion and military occupation techniques from the relatively unusual experience of having served with our own Army during the occupations of *both* Germany and Japan. In Germany we did use lists. These were not of guns, but rather of Nazi party members who were picked up by our Counter Intelligence Corps agents through lists drawn from the records in the office of each *Landkreis*. In Japan, shortly after the war, I recall making the rounds of some villages near Tokyo with a Military Police team charged with the mission of confiscating guns, swords and other weapons. In each village the team leader looked up the local elder (or the man with the longest beard) and told him to tell his townsmen to turn in whatever weapons they had. The collection was made in a matter of minutes. If we had wanted to go to the time-consuming trouble of doing this with Japan's firearms registration lists, we probably wouldn't have been able to read those available anyway.

The fact of the matter is that dictators or other authorities don't depend on lists to grab guns or anything else they may want. They order house-to-house searches, broadcast or issue proclamations, and warn recalcitrants of severe penalties if orders are not complied with.

In Germany, U.S. Military Government procedures specified the posting of notices and other measures "to advise the civilian population" to surrender an array of "such articles as firearms including shotguns, ammunition, explosives, radio transmitting, and similar supplies." * The German armed forces, in *their* occupation procedures, also resorted to proclamations. A German proclamation dated May 10, 1940, to the Occupied Territory of Belgium, and typical of those used elsewhere in occupied Europe, read: "The surrender of weapons and other implements of war has been ordered by special proclamation," and ordered guns to be surrendered to the mayor.†

How the Nazis themselves typically operated can also be seen not through the tactics envisaged in the NRA imagination, but more concretely through Operation Sea Lion, the code name given to the Nazi over-all plans for the invasion and occupation of Britain. These plans were worked out in considerable detail in the instructions headed "Orders Concerning the Organization and Functioning of Military Government in England." They were signed by Field Marshal Walther von Brauschitsch, Commander-in-Chief of the German Army, on September 9, 1940. The orders, among other things, specified "armed insurgents of either sex will be dealt with with the utmost severity," and provided that anybody failing to turn in his firearms or radio sets within twenty-four hours would be subject to immediate execution.‡

What firearms did Hitler have in mind if, as the NRA says, Britain then had only "a negligible amount" of gun owners? It is pure NRA myth that Britain's firearms laws had so stripped the citizenry of small arms that it took the generosity of American sportsmen to prevent Britannia from going under. This was accom-

---

* From *Public Safety Manual of Procedures, Military Government of Germany, Supreme Headquarters, Allied Expeditionary Forces, September 1944.*
† From *Key Laws, Decrees and Regulations Issued by the Axis in Occupied Europe, Board of Economic Warfare, Blockade and Supply Branch, Reoccupation Division, December 1942, Belgium Administration.*
‡ *The Rise and Fall of the Third Reich,* by William L. Shirer, page 782; *Operation Sea Lion,* by Peter Fleming, pages 263–4.

plished, we are told, by our sportsmen sending the British sporting rifles, shotguns and sidearms in huge number—variously estimated at 200,000, or 500,000 or even more. Actually, the number of such arms a so-called American Committee for the Defense of British Homes managed to muster and ship abroad, was only 7,000.

It is true that Britain needed every bit of weaponry it could get, but the country was far from disarmed, at least as far as civilian firearms were concerned. Then as today, any acknowledged hunter or member of a shooting club could buy a gun, though admittedly with somewhat less abandon than is possible here.

"The legend that at the time of Dunkirk the Home Guard was extensively armed with pikes is, like many other legends of the period, not in accordance with the facts," writes Peter Fleming, distinguished as both a soldier and a journalist, in his book *Operation Sea Lion.* "I can say most firmly that the laws in England did not strip the nation of sporting firearms and ammunition," says Drew Middleton, for many years the highly respected chief of *The New York Times* London Bureau. Middleton recalls that "in 1940 when the Home Guard was first raised against invasion, the men were armed primarily with sporting weapons, rifles, shotguns, etc." No less an authority than Winston Churchill confirms this, writing in *Their Finest Hour* (page 55): "All over the country, in every town and village, bands of determined men came together armed with shotguns, sporting rifles, clubs and spears. From this a vast organization was to spring. But the need of Regulars was also vital."

Contrary to another popular misbelief, the members of the Home Guard, which, within a few months, was to have a strength of more than a million, were not bereft of any knowledge of the fundamentals of firearms. In fact, the majority, Fleming tells us, were old soldiers or sailors "whose combined experience covered a vast diversity of campaigning."

The chief problem faced by the British was a lack of *military* arms and ammunition. Almost all available to the Army had been sent overseas and much had also been lost, men as well as matériel, in the weeks preceding Dunkirk. This shortage cannot be correctly attributed, as the NRA would have us believe, to Britain's firearms laws' drying up the nation's arms industry, for the British situation was by no means unique. Indeed, America was militarily and industrially weak too, at the time. "In May 1940, America had a small regular army of 75,000 men, a one-ocean navy and an air force with a total strength of less than 25,000 men," writes Fleming. "When the spectacular German successes in Europe brought home to her the urgent need for expansion, her industry was not producing armaments in any important quantities."

Some indication of this is seen in the fact that the first half a million rifles shipped from America (from government arsenals, not from the racks of sportsmen) were of World War I vintage, containing the coating of grease in which they had been embalmed more than twenty years before.

One great value of the British Home Guard was that it assumed certain duties that the Regulars of the Home Forces would otherwise have had to. But it is questionable as to whether even the Regulars would have been able to stave off the Nazi invasion, which, for reasons still unknown, was never launched. In any event, what saved England were not guns from America, but rather its Royal Air Force pilots—the famous "few" hailed by Churchill in his historic tribute to the heroes of the Battle of Britain.

Even if any lists of firearms owners would be useful to an enemy of the United States, undoubtedly the single largest and most useful such master list would be that of the more than 1 million names and addresses conveniently maintained on Remington Rand tabulating cards in the membership division at NRA headquarters. (New York City's list of 17,000 registered handgun owners is minuscule compared to this.) Vastly larger collectively are the lists of about 19 million hunting licenses on file with the conservation (or fish and game) departments in the capital cities of our fifty states.

But old myths live on and on. And so we have the Honorable Robert L. F. Sikes, Representative from Florida, telling Congress quite seriously: "Great Britain, after Dunkirk, had only a few thousand small arms available to the entire country, and was requesting the people to contribute swords and crossbows for defense. This was the dilemma they faced, because they did not have an armed civilian population to fall back on. Britain has tight gun laws." *

Another military expert is fish-and-game man Thomas L. Kimball of the National Wildlife Federation. Kimball, in filing his brief for the citizen-soldier, told the same Senate committee:

* 1964 Senate Commerce Committee hearings, January 23, 1964.

U.S. Armed Forces deployed an entire armored division from the United States to West Germany in three days. Is it so unconceivable that our enemies could perform the same feat? In my humble opinion the day will never come when war becomes so sophisticated that the occupation of land will become unnecessary. The role of the foot soldier and armed citizen fighting from hedgerow to hedgerow and from house to house can never be discarded as a significant military force if this nation is determined enough to protect its basic freedom.

What, though, happened to the poor German foot soldier and armed citizen when the United States and its allies swept across Germany? Texas Senator Ralph Yarborough, who is an NRA member, told his Senate Commerce Committee colleagues who had listened to Sikes and Kimball:

I was on the staff of an infantry division and I saw the invasion of Germany. Hitler called on every German to die in his home, at his post, and the first time a sniper fired in a town at an Allied soldier they learned. These men were trying to be nice to the civilians, but the snipers fired. After that, the towns were simply sawed down. And pretty soon there was a total surrender.

As we advanced in Germany, not only towns surrendered but every house. They put bed sheets out the windows; rolled bolts of cloth out; the whole sheet was a waving series of white flags, from the length of a bolt of cloth to a pillowcase. Each house would put a white surrender pillowcase in every single window of a house to keep it from being fired at. They realized this idea of civilians sniping at soldiers is obsolete, that it is not feasible, simply because firepower is so great in modern armies.

You just look at military tactics. This [armed citizen idea] just won't work in a civilized country. The only place where this kind of thing might work is with a people that are impoverished, as in the swamps of South Vietnam, who have nothing to defend.

It doesn't work in a civilized country, with modern technology and modern cities. You are not going to have a defense force out there that is going to defeat an invading army, unless you do it with trained military forces, with tremendous firepower and superior weapons. . . . If we thought this was the best way to defend the United States, to disband the Army and let every man have a scope-sight rifle, that would be so much cheaper, there wouldn't be any point in spending $50 billion a year to defend this country with intercontinental ballistic missiles and Polaris submarines armed with nuclear warheads and the many other expensive devices and satellites in the sky for spying on the other powers, and the tremendously expensive technological equipment required in modern warfare. Only an industrialized nation can really sustain prolonged modern warfare. And that is by highly trained, highly skilled forces of highly motivated men.

*   *   *

What argument do the anti-gun reformers have to offset the uncomfortable fact that Switzerland (which requires practically every able-bodied male to keep a gun in his home) has always had the lowest crime rate in Europe *not* excluding England?

—Editorial, *The American Rifleman*, November 1948

The NRA and other gun groups share an unbounded admiration for that land of cuckoo clocks, chocolate, secret bank accounts and scenery—Switzerland, which *Guns* magazine once admiringly described as "not just a nation of riflemen, but *the* nation of riflemen."

The basis for this praise stems from that small country's unique system of national defense, which provides for compulsory military training for all able-bodied men, with each citizen militiaman keeping his weapon at home between tours of training duty.

Does Switzerland really have "the lowest crime rate of any nation," * as the NRA and its friends often declare? Since no evidence is ever offered to document this claim, I decided to do some checking by visiting my local Swiss Consulate. Evidently, the NRA and its friends are privy to information which ordinary mortals do not have, for I was told that the Swiss government, much as it would like to, could furnish no data to document the contention that it was the least crime-ridden country on earth.

Turning next to the United Nations, I could find no comparative over-all crime statistics there either. The reason soon became obvious: each nation keeps its crime records differently. However, over-all homicide statistics were available. Comparing those for the 17 European countries listed, I found 8 countries to have homicide rates lower than Switzerland's 1.0 per 100,000 population. The countries included England (0.7), Belgium (0.6), Denmark (0.5), Iceland (0.0), Ireland (0.4), the Netherlands (0.3), Norway (0.4) and Sweden (0.16). Equaling Switzerland's homicide rate were two countries—Austria and Portugal. Only 6 countries had higher homicide rates: Finland (2.7), France (1.6), West Germany (1.2),

* *American Rifleman* editorial, August 1948.

Greece (1.5), Hungary (1.9) and Italy (1.1). That of the United States was 4.9 in the same year.* I could not compare rates on homicides due to firearms, because Switzerland is the only country that does not furnish this information. Nor does it release any figures on firearms suicides.

What about suicides from all causes? Switzerland's rate of 18.8 was exceeded by only four countries: Austria (22.4), Denmark (19.0), Finland (22.1) and Hungary (24.9). Twelve other countries had lower suicide rates. The United States' rate was 11.0.

Information from Switzerland was, however, available on accidental deaths due to firearms. Switzerland's rate of 0.46 was higher than that of every other country except France (0.56). The Netherlands had the lowest rate (0.1). Among the lowest were those of England (0.17), West Germany (0.17) and Belgium (.22). The United States' rate for the same year was 1.1.

As can be seen, the Swiss rates in each category, except for suicide, are much lower than those for the United States as a whole. Interestingly, however, I did find New York State's firearms accident death rate of 0.4 † to be about the same as that of Switzerland. Seeking to learn to what extent the Swiss system might account for all this, I spoke to officials at the Swiss Consulate.

Yes, I was told, the country has no standing army, and, in fact, at certain times of the year there is not a single man under arms in all of Switzerland. The constitution expressly forbids the country to maintain standing troops. The Army's only full-time professional soldiers are contained in a small cadre of about 500 commissioned and noncommissioned officers and some instructors. Otherwise the army is made up of most of the country's adult male citizens, who, when not going about their regular business, are organized into nine divisions forming four army corps, together with some special troops.

Military service is obligatory for all able-bodied males between the ages of twenty and sixty; those exempted for physical disability or other reasons must pay a special tax. The initial basic training period of four months is followed by regular short training periods.

In a sense, the Swiss militia system is not unlike that of our own National Guard and reserve units. One peculiarity of the Swiss sys-

* 1962 figures, latest available for all countries mentioned.
† 1962–1963 average figure.

tem is that, continuing an ancient tradition, every Swiss citizen soldier, when not undergoing training, keeps his weapon at home along with twenty-four rounds of ammunition, his uniform, haversack, helmet and other military paraphernalia. From this point on, I learned a number of astonishing things that the NRA either doesn't know or wouldn't care to have known.

I asked one of the Consulate officials how his government kept track of all those guns.

"Why, they're *registered,* of course," he answered. I asked him to explain how. "The serial number of each weapon, whether a pistol or machine gun, is recorded by several authorities together with the name of the person to whom it is given," he said, showing me his *Dienstbüchlein,* or military service book, in which was inscribed the serial number of the gun he had been issued (a carbine) and also the number of rounds of ammunition (twenty-four) he had been issued for it. "The soldier also has no right to use his weapon or his ammunition without authorization," he also said. "Each round of ammunition issued must be accounted for."

I also learned that in order to buy any other sort of gun in Switzerland (shotguns are excepted in some cantons), you have to get a permit from the police in the canton, or state, where you live. Permits are not issued to those under eighteen, or to drunks or to those found to have criminal records, backgrounds of mental illness or emotional instability. No mail-order sales are allowed. You have to show your face to a dealer, who, contrary to custom here, must be licensed. The dealer verifies your permit and keeps the record of the date of sale, your identity and the serial number of the gun you're getting. This information is forwarded to the canton authorities. In other words, this gun is registered too.

I'm not quite so sure that the gun lobby would really care for the Swiss system as it is actually maintained.

Although Swiss fighting men have been justly famous, to what extent they could defend Switzerland in light of the changing methods of modern warfare is a moot question. In purely military terms, there is probably little doubt that a few well-placed bombs could blast Switzerland and its army to bits. In our nuclear age, particularly, a citizen militia is as outmoded as the antimacassar. In fact, this has probably long been the case. Even a present-day patriotic Swiss is prone to forget that the French under Napoleon had no trouble at all invading his land as far back as 1798, conquering it in but a few months and occupying it for fifteen years. Nor does the gun lobby in this country care to recall this bit of history.

During the eighteenth century, too, the idea that an army composed largely of part-time civilian soldiers was a military force to reckon with was a dangerous illusion that almost cost us the Revolution. Nonetheless, a considerable body of legend has developed to the contrary. Indeed, had we depended on our Minutemen and colonial militia alone we would still be living under the Union Jack. The shortcomings of our colonial militia stemmed from something more than the fact, as Daniel Boorstin says,* that it was even "a most unmilitary outfit by European standards."

"A large proportion of the recruits," Charles and Mary Beard note,† "were brave men who fought courageously, but they were accustomed to serve for short terms, were undisciplined, not inured to long and grueling campaigns. At the beginning few among them had ever seen a real battle." A majority were Emerson's "embattled farmers" who preferred to stay close to their homes and families and attend to their personal needs.

For the most part they were not only unmilitary, but also undependable and unreliable. The normal term of enlistment was for one year and, as the Beards write, "hundreds of militiamen insisted on quitting as soon as their terms of service were over, no matter how grave the danger to the American cause and despite the pleas of their officers."

"The young men's favorite contribution to the war was to turn out for a short campaign with the militia, then go home to plant the corn, get in the hay or harvest the wheat, according to the season," writes Samuel Eliot Morison.‡ "Typical of the attitude of the average American is the story of Reuben Stebbins of Williamstown, Massachusetts. He had not seen fittin' to turn out until he actually heard the firing at Bennington. He then saddled his horse, called for his musket and remarked as he rode off, 'We'll see whose goin' t' own this farm!' "

Many citizen soldiers went home even before their terms were up,

* *The Americans: The Colonial Experience,* p. 355.
† *A Basic History of the United States.*
‡ *The Oxford History of the American People.*

and there were desertions by the droves; in fact they assumed epidemic proportions. Several weeks before the Battle of Bennington in 1777, as many as 400 militiamen (of the 1,600 present and fit) disappeared or, in present-day Army parlance, "went over the hill." At the siege of Newport, less than a year later, some 5,000 militiamen deserted within a few days, so weakening General John Sullivan's forces (originally, about 10,000 men) that he had to give up his plan of attack.

Not uncommonly, large numbers fled in panic at the sound of gunfire or the sight of blood. After one miltiaman was hit at the Battle of White Plains, "the whole regiment broke and fled immediately and were not rallied without much difficulty," says a journal of the encounter. At the Head of Elk, during the Philadelphia campaign, a view of the British and Hessians disembarking was enough to cause four companies of militia to flee "without firing a shot."

The inadequacies of the militia system, particularly in times of crisis, almost drove General George Washington out of his mind. "The subject... is not a fit one to be publicly known or discussed," he once bitterly wrote a nephew. "I am wearied to death all day... at the conduct of the militia, whose behavior and want of discipline has done great injury to the other troops, who never had officers, except in a few instances, worth the bread they eat."

Time and again, Washington complained to the Continental Congress about the conduct of the armed citizenry and pleaded for an army of regulars authorized to enlist for three years or for the duration. According to Christopher Ward's *The War of the Revolution*, Washington also urged the Congress to put no dependence in "a militia or other troops than those enlisted and embodied" for longer periods than were then in vogue and declared his conviction that "our liberties" might be lost 'if their defense is left to any but a permanent standing army; I mean, one to exist during the war."

It wasn't until Washington's pleas were heeded and he finally had a large enough body of well-trained and well-disciplined regulars— the so-called Continental Line—that there was really any hope for victory at all. Even then, the militia had to be carefully deployed and watched so that they would be of some use or, at least, wouldn't cause any trouble by retreating. One way was by putting them in the first line, as did General Daniel Morgan at Cowpens. He asked his militia men there for just two rounds of fire before they quit the battle: "Two rounds, my boys, and then you may fall back!" With the militia almost as much a hindrance as a help, the final victory over Cornwallis at Yorktown could most likely not have been achieved without the aid of the French.

"America," George Washington also warned, "has been almost amused out of her Liberties" by the proponents of the militia. "I solemnly declare I never was witness to a single instance, that can countenance an opinion of Militia or raw Troops being fit for the real business of fighting. I have found them useful as light Parties to skirmish in the wood, but incapable of making or sustaining a serious attack . . . The late Battle of Camden is a melancholy comment upon this doctrine. The Militia fled at the first fire, and left the Continental Troops surrounded on every side, and overpowered by numbers to combat for safety instead of victory."

"However pacific the general policy of a nation may be," Washington later wrote, "it ought never to be without an adequate stock of military knowledge for emergencies. . . . The art of war is at once comprehensive and complicated; it demands much previous study." To this end he urged the creation of a military school which was later to materialize as the United States Military Academy at West Point.

However, the militia system continued to linger on. "The periodic local muster, its participants often overdressed in gaudy outfits to compensate for their lack of militaristic temper, sometimes with no equipment at all, was in its latter days primarily a social occasion," writes Marshall B. Davidson in his *Life in America*. "Few nations have felt so free to play at the arts of soldiering and to work at the arts of peace."

It was purportedly to help some segments of our citizenry to improve their marksmanship, so as to be better prepared for military emergencies and possibly even the threat of war, that the National Rifle Association came into being in 1871. Later, as we have also already learned, the Federal government, acting with the NRA in 1903, set up the so-called National Board for the Promotion of Rifle Practice, now an arm of the Defense Department. It is hard to estimate just how much of the taxpayers' money the NBPRP has spent on behalf of the national security and of the National Rifle Association during the sixty-odd years of its existence. When the question was put to him by the Senate Juvenile Delinquency Subcommittee on May 19, 1965, Army Secretary Stephen Ailes was unable to give a ready answer. However, the figure could probably run well in excess of $100 million. During the five-year period ending in 1964, the National Board program cost taxpayers at least $12 million, largely for the ammunition and other expendables used in target shooting.

Is the purpose of this largesse simply to promote shooting as a sport? Or do the expenditures really do any good in terms of what they are ostensibly expected to accomplish—the promotion of our national defense? Is it, as Army Secretary Ailes has wondered, "creating a reservoir of personnel trained in a basic military skill on which the Armed Forces may draw in time of need and . . . providing us with a fair number of new recruits who have had some previous experience with the rifle"?

"If these training programs are not helping us," Army Secretary Ailes told the Senate Juvenile Delinquency Subcommittee during its 1965 hearings, "then there is little justification for them."

Surprisingly, no one ever bothered to find out the answers to these questions until the spring of 1965, when the Army hired the prestigious management engineering firm of Arthur D. Little, Inc., of Cambridge, Massachusetts. Little's board chairman is General James M. Gavin, former Army Research and Development chief. Its task was to conduct a study to determine the benefits actually accruing to the military from the activities of the NBPRP. One interesting area of the study, which was to be completed in November 1965, is a comparison of the marksmanship proficiency of soldiers who have had pre-service marksmanship experience with those who have not. All these years we have been paying for it, without knowing if it was worthwhile.*

A question pertinent to the study is the relative importance of the

* Nor did we know as recently as mid-March 1966. An Arthur D. Little official had told me that the "final edition" of the report of the study, which reputedly cost $100,000, was to be delivered to the Secretary of the Army by December 31, 1965. However, if the findings are favorable to the marksmanship training program, the Army is apparently in no great rush to convey these tidings to the public. In early February I wrote to the Army and inquired about the study. The Army informed me on February 17 that the study was still "under review," and hoped that "some release of information would be forthcoming" during the next few days. A month later I had not yet received it. Meanwhile, *The New York Times* reported (February 13), presumably on the basis of informa-

rifle-bearing soldier in the present and future military way of things. There are many persons, of course, who think of him as somewhat of an anachronism in this nuclear age. But let us for the sake of argument concede the foot soldier to continue to have a role of some importance, even if more limited than before. Yet, whatever the results of the Arthur D. Little study, one cannot help wondering how many participants in the National Board–NRA Marksmanship Program would ever qualify for active military duty—for example, female shooters. Many others, of both sexes, would be disqualified because of age, or for other reasons.* A study for the year 1962, showed that of the 1.1 million men who reached age twenty-six that year, only about 58 per cent—or 640,000—had seen service. The remaining 42 per cent were either rejected as mentally or physically unfit (27 per cent), or were disqualified or deferred for academic, occupational or marital reasons.

Should they and others unlikely ever to wear a military uniform be allowed to indulge in free government-sponsored target shooting, on the grounds that they might be helpful in the event of a foreign invasion? Asked about how the people at the Pentagon felt about such use of the citizenry in the light of present-day concepts of warfare, Army Secretary Ailes in 1965 told the Senate Juvenile Delinquency Subcommittee:

I have not seen any contingency war plan where the citizenry was included. As you know, we have a National Guard and the Reserves in the states that we go to great pains to train. That program costs us over one billion dollars a year. This is something that is very important, but those are combat troops and support troops which would be called in wartime. But I am not familiar, myself, with any plan in high levels of government to call out the armed citizenry as at Bunker Hill.

If not, then one can wonder with the Washington *Post* whether the National Board program does not represent quite a lot of

---

tion leaked to it, that the study had recommended "tighter measures of control" on the Army's marksmanship training program and that participating NRA club officers be fingerprinted. (One State Attorney General had earlier acknowledged to me his difficulties in checking the names sent him in connection with the Little study because of the absence of fingerprints.) The Army refused to comment on the *Times* story.

* Even NRA members have been frank enough to tell me that they regard the program as a waste of taxpayer money because, as one pointed out, "many of the people who participate are too old to ever go back into the Army."

largesse at the public expense. In an editorial dated March 29, 1965, the *Post*, after conceding that "shooting is good, clean fun," quite reasonably asked:

Why does not the Defense Department exhibit equal generosity to hiking clubs (very good training for the Infantry), to polo teams (excellent for the Cavalry), to sailing and yachting groups (fine experience for the Navy, you know) or to the improvement of baseball, football, tennis, skiing, golf, hockey or swimming (all body-building sports calculated to produce hale and healthy young men for the Armed Services)? Can it be that the National Rifle Association got the drop on Congress?

What with all the government-subsidized "marksmanship training," one would think us to be a nation of Deadeye Dicks. Moreover, one would think Americans to be shooters without peer anywhere, because of the numerous other indigenous advantages in our favor: our tradition and heritage of arms; a culture in which children are virtually weaned on weapons, real or facsimile; an arms industry, not only the largest anywhere, but turning out the world's best guns, scopes and ammunition; the free-and-easy accessibility of guns to virtually anyone, and a high-powered propaganda campaign to encourage their use; many places to hunt and shoot; and more leisure time and money to do it with than other countries have.

Yet, with all this, Americans are really no great shakes as shooters, or at least not as good as they should be. The teams comprising the cream of our shooters do pretty well in most international competition. But in the matches that really count, those of the Olympic Games, we're traditionally better at running than shooting. Time and again, the firearms-registered Russians, Rumanians, Hungarians, Germans, Finns, Italians, Austrians and others outshoot us with just about everything that shoots—small rifles, big rifles, shotguns and pistols. This result cannot be explained away, as in the case of other Olympic sports, on the ground that the foreign shooting teams are government-subsidized and better trained. Our shooting teams are also government-subsidized; in fact they are the only teams of U. S. Olympic competitors which are. And it cannot be said that our shooters lack opportunity to practice, or enough ammunition to do it with.

A singular and recent exception to our usual performance in the

Olympics, one that may perhaps presage a renaissance of the rifle-man, took place at the 1964 Games in Tokyo, where, in the six shooting events, U.S. marksmen won 2 gold medals, 2 silver medals and 3 bronze medals, or 7 of the total of 18 possible marksmanship awards. This superlative feat, however, exactly matched that achieved by the Russians in Rome in the previous Games, in 1960. Then the United States won only 1 gold and 1 silver medal, and in the 1956 Olympics, only a silver medal.

Our 1964 victory in the free or high-power rifle match, one of the six Olympic shooting events, was our first since 1924. Our other 1964 gold medal came in the three-position small-bore (.22-caliber) rifle match, an event we had never won before. We have not managed to win the small-bore rifle prone match since 1948, nor the clay pigeon or trap event since 1920. Our pistol shooting has also been relatively mediocre: we have not won the free pistol event since 1952; and our 1960 gold medal in the automatic rapid-fire was our first in this event since 1924.

Though our best shooters have come from the military,* which has occasionally produced outstanding marksmen, the average American soldier, whether in the Olympics, peace or war, has been found wanting in weaponry. His shooting conduct, to say nothing of his battlefield behavior, was criticized during the Revolution. It was also, as we have seen, a subject of dismay during the Civil War, and again during the Spanish-American War. The criticism continues even today, via occasional carping in the gun magazines.

"What has happened to American marksmanship?" asked a Canadian critic of ours in a February 1964 *Shooting Times* article entitled "You Yanks Are S-L-I-P-P-I-N-G!" "World War II showed the Allies up badly," charged the Canadian. "We simply weren't ready. Of the thousands of volunteers, only a small portion could shoot well enough for the fighting battalions. A mathematician figured that it took over 12,000 rounds of small arms ammo to down one enemy soldier."

Lest one think this a biased opinion, some years ago a group of Army researchers, a Department of the Army pamphlet reveals, came up with this startling conclusion: "Revolutionary War soldiers did a better job with their muskets than soldiers of World War II

* In the 1964 Olympics, all our team members were service-connected or on active duty.

and Korea were able to do with their superb rifles." And there is also Colonel Charles Askins of our own Army asking in the May 1962 *Guns:* "Why Are Army Riflemen Bum Shots?"

Why? The fact that our soldiers are poorly motivated may be one answer. The lack of ambition on the part of most to be crack shots may be another. The world of difference between firing on a peaceful—if noisy—range, and under combat conditions may be still another. Our marksmanship training program, both military and civilian, may be at fault.

Most likely, bull's-eye marksmanship training for every able-bodied male no longer makes any sense in training for war. Even in World War II, if a front-line company had some sniping to do, the commander called on one of his best shots to do it. Actually, a relatively small proportion—only 1 out of every 4—of the roughly 14 million American men in uniform during World War II ever fired a shot in combat. Those who did scored an astonishingly low percentage of "hits" compared to the total number of rounds fired. Very few were the ones who even got off carefully aimed shots. It was a war primarily of planes, bombs, tanks, trucks, artillery, mortars and machine guns—and these were what ultimately made the difference between victory and defeat. Bull's-eye shooting was relatively unimportant.

After the war, a board of Army infantry experts assembled to mull over our marksmanship mediocrity. There was general agreement that our rifle trainees receive more realistic training by, among other things, firing at "surprise" man-shaped targets, and this procedure is now part of our military marksmanship program. The board was also emphatic in its condemnation of the bull's-eye target.

Still the worship of the venerable bull continues as the present-day standard for competitive match shooting in our civilian marksmanship training program. In this program many men participate who will never be called to the colors or, if called, probably will never fire a shot in combat.

Sociologists say that there is always the tendency for organizations, particularly those of a nonprofit character, to turn away, if only partially, from their original, ostensible goals. It would be less than natural if the NRA, like other organizations, were not concerned with its self-perpetuation and growth, an aim manifest in its

"A Nation of Riflemen" 293

current campaign to "shoot for a million." To this end, the entice-
ment of a shooting program made possible with free or cut-rate
government arms and ammunition is a powerful recruiting inducement. The patriotic phrase exhorting Americans to exercise "The
Right to Bear Arms" is also as enviable a rallying call as any organization could want, although to the NRA it is evidently of little
consequence who chooses to answer the call.

16 *What* Right to Bear Arms?

The problem of the misuse of firearms in the United States is growing at an alarming rate.... It has made a mockery of Federal and state laws.... Yet the blind, almost mindless, efforts of a segment of the gun enthusiasts, with their shabby, time-worn slogans, were successful in defeating my efforts. The number-one slogan, piously repeated by these people, is the *last half* of the Second Amendment which states "the right of the people to keep and bear Arms, shall not be infringed." They leave out the first half which stipulates that the right is contingent upon the maintenance of a militia. It is apparent to me that in considering the intent of the Amendment, we must, of necessity, consider it in its entire context, rather than to consider only one clause as so many seem to do in their public pronouncements.

—Senator Thomas Dodd, from an address before the Ford Hall Forum in Boston, March 8, 1965

"Do we, as law-abiding citizens of the United States, possess an inalienable right to bear arms comparable to our right of assembly, our freedom of speech, and our freedom of worship?" rhetorically asked the National Rifle Association in one of the many editorials it devotes to its favorite constitutional subject. As usual, it gave itself the expected answer: "Undoubtedly there is an inalienable right to own and to use private weapons for lawful purposes. This right is not cast in doubt by state laws controlling certain actions under their police power."

This judgment, often delivered with a stirring reference to the Bill of Rights, is based on a fundamentalist, out-of-context reading of the Second Amendment, which the firearms faction seldom bothers to quote in full, though it consists of but a single sentence. *Guns* magazine, which of late likes to speak of the "constitutional right to own

294

and *enjoy* arms," once devoted an entire 3,000-word article to the Second Amendment without ever quoting its full text.

The Second Amendment to the Constitution, also sometimes referred to as Article II of the Bill of Rights, says:

A well regulated Militia, being necessary to the security of a free State, the right of the people to keep and bear Arms, shall not be infringed.

"We prefer to believe that the simple, straight-forward language means exactly what it says," editorialized the NRA in the July 1955 *American Rifleman*. But what does it mean? The NRA, though its beliefs are clear enough, querulously declares: "There has been so much conflicting 'expert' opinion, so many interpretations of constitutional law, that it is hardly surprising that widespread confusion exists in the minds of sincerely interested persons."

If widespread confusion exists, it is one that the NRA itself has compounded, for the only body of "conflicting 'expert' opinion" is its own.

Its leading legal authority is a Tacoma, Washington, Superior Court Judge, Bartlett Rummel, who is a recent Past President of the NRA. Rummel's nearly 100 scholarly papers on firearms legalities and related matters,* published during a recent six-year period have appeared largely, if not exclusively, in the pages of *The American Rifleman*. None, as far as I have been able to determine, have seen print in any legal periodicals.

"It has been asserted that the Second Amendment refers only to the militia as an organization," Judge Rummel said in 1964 on the *CBS Reports* television program devoted to the firearms problem. "In other words, it doesn't give the individual the right to have and bear arms, and we dispute that because we believe there isn't a basis for that either in history or in any great number of court decisions." Referring to a celebrated case involving firearms, *U.S. v. Miller* (307 U.S. 174), Rummel said that the United States Supreme Court in ruling on the case in 1939 held "that we have to interpret these things in the light of history, and what the laws were at the time the Second Amendment was adopted; and if we go back into that situa-

* "To Have and Bear Arms," "On the Right of Self-Defense," "New Court Cases on Self-Defense," "Federal Protection of Migratory Birds," and so on.

tion, we find that people individually were entitled to have their arms, and this matter of the militia just as an organization is something that we dispute, and believe is not a correct interpretation of the law."

To this another program participant, the distinguished Harvard Law School Professor Arthur E. Sutherland, retorted: "The Supreme Court of the United States held in the Miller case that as the arms in question were of the type which had no conceivable relation to the conduct of the organized militia of the states, nothing prevented the Congress from forbidding their use by the defendant Miller."

In *U.S. v. Miller*, the United States Supreme Court upheld the constitutionality of the National Firearms Act by ruling against one Jack Miller and one Frank Layton, who had been convicted of violating the act by transporting an unregistered sawed-off shotgun from Oklahoma to Arkansas. The act, the Court held, did not violate the Second Amendment. The Court stated that there was nothing to show that a sawed-off shotgun "at this time has some reasonable relationship to the prevention, preservation, or efficiency of a well-regulated militia." Therefore it could not say that the Second Amendment guaranteed "the right to keep and bear such an instrument," because the weapon was not part "of the ordinary military equipment or that its use could contribute to the common defense."

The Court further declared that the obvious purpose of the Second Amendment was to render effective the provisions in the Constitution that provide for "calling forth the Militia to execute the Laws of the Union, suppress insurrections and repel invasions," * and said that the Second Amendment "must be interpreted and applied with that end in view."

In its decision, the Court recognized that at the time the Constitution was drafted, the militia was considered to be a "body of citizens enrolled for military discipline" and that "ordinarily when called for service these men were expected to appear bearing arms supplied by themselves and of the kind in common use at the time." However, the Court also took note that as of 1934, most, if not all, of the states had adopted provisions regulating the right to keep and bear arms and concluded that none of these laws affected the right of the Federal government to adopt the National Firearms Act.

Many other court decisions and virtually every leading legal

* Article I, Section 8, Clause 15.

scholar and constitutional expert in the land agree that the intent, wording and meaning of the Second Amendment, in its full context, refer only to the people's *collective* right to bear arms as members of a well-regulated and authorized militia. It is not an individual right, they also agree, in the same sense as others the Bill of Rights specifies, such as trial by jury and freedom of speech and religion.

Moreover, no serious student of the law seriously believes that it precludes the reasonable regulation of firearms. This is already evidenced in the many unchallenged laws now on the books requiring licenses and permits, or prohibiting the carrying of hidden weapons.

Even the NRA knows this. An official brochure reads: "The courts have repeatedly held that many laws regulating the purchase, carrying or use of concealable firearms are constitutional." And, though it manages to leave the impression that its favorite whipping dog, New York's Sullivan Law, is unconstitutional, it also admits, at the same time, that "the notorious New York 'Sullivan Law,' which requires a police permit to own a handgun for any reason, even in one's home, has consistently been held to be constitutional."

In the Georgetown University library reposes an interesting typewritten document dated June 1959 and entitled "The Right to Bear Arms." The dissertation is the master's thesis of Jack J. Basil, Jr., of the NRA's legislative staff. On page 66 Mr. Basil writes:

Certain principles may be deduced from the history of the construction, interpretation and administration of the right to bear arms: (1) The Second Amendment operates as a limitation against the National Government only; (2) The States, under their broad political powers, may regulate the possession and use of firearms in furtherance of the health, safety and general welfare of the people; (3) The prevalent assumption appears to be that the possession and use of firearms by an individual is conditional on the legislative and administrative mandate of the States; (4) The keeping and bearing of arms is a collective and not an individual right.

The United States Supreme Court has ruled on at least five occasions on the meaning of the constitutional right to bear arms. In the case of *U.S. v. Cruikshank* (92 U.S. 542), decided in 1876, the issue was whether a group of white citizens had conspired, in violation of the Enforcement Act of 1870, to deprive two Negroes of certain constitutional rights, including the right to keep and bear arms.

"The right to bear arms is not granted by the Constitution," said the Court in holding the indictment to be defective. "Neither is it in any manner dependent upon that instrument [the Constitution] for its existence."

The Second Amendment, the Court also held, meant nothing more than that the right "shall not be infringed by Congress. This is one of the amendments that has no other effect than to restrict the powers of the national government." People, the Court said, should look to the states for protection against any violation or infringement of the right. The Court suggested, too, as *U.S. v. Miller* was to later, that the purpose of the Amendment was to ensure only the continuation of a well-regulated militia.

The Court reiterated this principle and carried it a step further a decade later in the 1886 case of *Presser v. Illinois* (116 U.S. 264). In this case, one Herman Presser had been convicted of violating an Illinois law by marching a group of about 400 armed men in the streets of Chicago. The group, called the *Lehr und Wehr Verein*, was what we would think of today as a cross between the Nazis and the Minutemen. Found guilty in Cook County Criminal Court for parading and drilling a "body of men with arms" not authorized by the governor, Presser took his case to the Illinois Supreme Court, where the original judgment was affirmed, and then to the Supreme Court of the United States. His brief was based on the right to keep and bear arms. In upholding the Illinois law, the Supreme Court said that a state could regulate the possession and use of weapons. For a state to be wrong in prohibiting its citizens from keeping and bearing arms, the Court added, it must be shown that this would "deprive the United States of their rightful resource for maintaining the public security, and disable the people from performing their duty to the general government."

This principle was made still more explicit in the later Supreme Court decisions of *Miller v. Texas* (153 U.S. 535, 1894) and *Robertson v. Baldwin* (165 U.S. 275, 1897). In the latter case, the Court ruled that the right specified in the Second Amendment was not a fundamental or absolute right when it observed:

The freedom of speech and of the press (Article I) does not permit the publication of libel, blasphemous and indecent articles, or other publications injurious to the public morals or private reputation; the right of the people to keep and bear arms (Article II) is not infringed by laws prohibiting the carrying of concealed weapons . . .

U.S. *v. Miller* remains the most recent and the leading U.S. Supreme Court interpretation of the Second Amendment. For in it the Court for the first time in 150 years had the opportunity to pass squarely upon the nature of the right to keep and bear arms.

From all these decisions rendered by the highest court in our land, it is difficult to challenge the two conclusions that emerge regarding the interpretation of the Second Amendment. One is that while it places a restriction on the Federal government, it does not on the states. Second, the right to carry arms is not individual, but rather, collective, and applicable even in this sense to only the sort of arms which a "well-regulated militia" would carry. Decisions in the lower Federal courts have reiterated these principles and gone even further.

The NRA's legal authority, Judge Bartlett Rummel, stoutly contends that the so-called right to keep and bear arms *is* a basic right. To this end the Tacoma Superior Court Judge cites as his *sole* authority another judge, Sir William Blackstone (1723–1780). The eminent English jurist terminated an unsuccessful legal practice to turn to teaching, and later encompassed his endless stream of learned lectures in a four-volume work called *Commentaries on the Laws of England,* which, though the most monumental and best-known history of the doctrines of English law, has long lost the favor it once had in the United States. Rummel quotes bits of Blackstone to show "that the right to have and bear arms was considered a basic right under the old English common law."

However, going through a list of law journal articles commended to constitutional scholars in an NRA bibliography headed "Notes and Sources on the Right to Keep and Bear Arms," one finds the following: "The right to bear arms, whether collectively or individually, was not a right guaranteed by common law," says John Brabner-Smith, holder of a doctorate in jurisprudence from Northwestern University, in *Law and Contemporary Problems* (I, 1934). "The right to keep and bear arms was not a common-law right," says Willimina Montague in *Southern California Law Review* (XIII, 1939). And in the *Harvard Law Review* (XXVIII, 1915) Lucilius A. Emery states, "The guarantee does not appear to have been of a common law right, like that of trial by jury." As evidence, all three constitutional scholars (and countless others) cite the English Statute of Northampton which, as already mentioned, declared as long ago as 1328 that no man should "go nor ride armed by night or by day in fairs, markets, nor in the presence of the justices or other ministers, nor in no part elsewhere."

An armed citizenry was by no means an American invention, says historian Daniel Boorstin, who calls it a prime example of American "regression." "It was a revival of the medieval Assize of Arms (1181), from which the English had developed a *militia* consisting of every able-bodied freeman, each required to provide himself with arms, to train periodically under a local officer, and to be ready on sudden call."

At the time of the restoration of the monarchy in the person of Charles II in 1660, no other armed force was recognized as lawful. The survival of the English militia system and its persistence on these shores grew out of a series of experiences that had several years before seen a citizen army under Oliver Cromwell defeat Charles I, sending him into exile in France.

During his exile in France, Charles II had been much taken with the idea of a professional standing army independent of the people —an institution that apparently contributed to the splendor of France and enabled Louis XIV to maintain his autocratic ways. Accordingly, upon his return to England and his ascension to the throne in 1660, Charles II started the nucleus of such a force, armed, equipped and paid for out of the royal revenues, in order to guard both his palace and person. This was a sensible enough precaution in view of the long-ranging struggle between the Crown and Parliament.

When Charles II succumbed to an apoplectic stroke in 1685, his brother and successor, James II, long vastly unpopular with the masses and especially hated by the Whigs, built the nucleus of household troops into a regular army fit for general military service. This force, though not large, was put to good use in the suppression of a rebellion by the Duke of Monmouth, a Protestant claimant to the throne.

The fact that James II was a convert to Rome was to have grave consequences down to this very day. Flushed with the victory over

Monmouth and now at the height of power, he continued the emergency practice of commissioning Catholics as officers and installing them in key posts. There was also an infusion of Irish recruits, also Catholic, into the ranks. Holding that the militia, who had augmented his regular forces against Monmouth, was useless, James II said that a strong, standing army was necessary for the preservation of peace in the realm and the security of the government. Accordingly, he strengthened the royal forces. They were soon to grow to 30,000 in number. In disenfranchising the militia he accomplished the disarmament of the Protestant populace, and to add insult to injury, quartered his Catholic troops in the homes of what was becoming an increasingly rebellious people.

In the ensuing Great Rebellion of 1688, James II fled to France. Parliament, with the assent of the Protestants William and Mary, and in protest against the grievances committed by their predecessor, passed a Bill of Rights. One of its provisions declared "that the raising or keeping of a standing army within the kingdom in time of peace unless it be with the consent of Parliament is against the law." The next clause said "that the subjects which are Protestants may have arms for their defense suitable to their condition, and as allowed by law."

The Bill of Rights confirmed an earlier declaration proclaimed by Parliament immediately after the flight of James. In this declaration his acts were referred to as an "endeavor to subvert and extirpate the laws and liberties of this kingdom" and as "contrary to law." Lucilius Emery comments: "It is quite evident from the foregoing that in the seventeenth century in England the assertion of the right of Protestant subjects to have arms was to preserve 'the laws and liberties of the Kingdom' and not at all to enable a subject to violate them."

Willimina Montague, referring to the 1840 Tennessee case *Aymette v. State*, which touched on the trials of the English under James (and sustained the validity of a regulation prohibiting the carrying of concealed weapons), has also commented: "The evil caused by disarming the people was that the King could compel them to submit to the most arbitrary measures, whereas, if they had been armed, they could have resisted. Their grievances were of public character; no private defense was contemplated."

And so the uniquely English militia system persisted and, along with the old English regulations governing the possession of arms and ammunition, was exported to America and established in the colonies. Short of funds and beset with enemies from all sides, the colonies required all able-bodied males of military age to provide themselves with specified arms and ammunition for the common defense. In the province of Massachusetts, in 1632, any unmarried man who was not properly armed could be hired out as a servant. The colonies maintained no standing armies whatever; the only regular troops were those from England, and they were under the direct command of royal, rather than colonial, officers. Needless to say, their presence was generally distasteful to the people of the colonies.

Contributing to this, of course, particularly after the time of James II, was that traditional English fear of a standing army. This is manifest in the Declaration of Independence, which lists as a grievance against the King: "He has kept among us, in times of peace, Standing Armies without the consent of the legislatures. He has affected to render the Military independent of and superior to the civil power."

Though the Founding Fathers here had George III in mind, there were those atavistic memories of James II; our forebears therefore still envisaged the possibility of a defenseless citizenry at the mercy of an armed force when they drafted the Second Amendment.

This amendment, as well as the rest of the first ten amendments comprising the Bill of Rights of our Constitution, was based on the earlier English Bill of Rights, in inspiration and meaning. In this sense, the new Bill of Rights was therefore not really a radical departure from any already accepted principles of government. Our Supreme Court was later to state in the case of *Robertson v. Baldwin* (1897) that the retention of the principles established by the original Bill of Rights had implicit recognized exceptions. These included the power of the state to regulate the promiscuous carrying of deadly weapons:

The law is perfectly well settled that the first ten amendments to the Constitution, commonly know as the Bill of Rights, were not intended to lay down any novel principles of government, but simply to embody certain guaranties and immunities which we had inherited from our English ancestors, and which had from time immemorial been subject to certain well-recognized exceptions arising from the necessities of the case. In incorporating these principles into the fundamental law there was no intention of disregarding the exceptions, which continued to be recognized as if they had been formally expressed.

The Second Amendment did not win acceptance without considerable controversy. "The people who enacted the Bill of Rights were very much afraid of a central tyranny," says Harvard Law School Professor Arthur Sutherland. "We had gotten rid of one King George. We didn't want another George to be a tyrant. Fantastic, from the present point of view, but it had a great influence with the people who ratified the new Constitution, proposed in 1787. And one of the things they were very much afraid of, and this emerges in the ratifying debates, was that the traditional source of state independence, the militia, the armed citizenry called to Lexington, or to Concord, that this would be eliminated, and we would be in the power of a central tyrant in the national capital. This is pretty silly in the light of our present point of view, but this was a real fear." *

As originally proposed by James Madison in the first session of the First Congress, the amendment read:

The right of the people to keep and bear arms shall not be infringed; a well-armed and well regulated militia being the best security of a free country; but no person religiously scrupulous of bearing arms shall be compelled to render military service in person.†

This proposal, along with a number of others, was referred to a Select Committee of Eleven from which the following emerged:

A well regulated militia, composed of the body of the people, being the best security of a free state, the right of the people to keep and bear arms shall not be infringed; but no person religiously scrupulous shall be compelled to bear arms.

This draft apparently provoked some debate in the House, though this centered largely on the religious provision; the proposals were obviously aimed in part at protecting the individual conscientious objector. Of interest, incidentally, is that in each he is referred to in

* *CBS Reports,* Murder and the Right to Bear Arms, June 10, 1964.
† *Annals of Congress,* Volume 1, p. 451, June 8, 1789.

individual terms, that is, "person"; on the other hand, in referring to the right to bear arms, both proposals use the collective term "peo-ple."

Shorn of its religious clause and sharpened somewhat, the Second Amendment, as finally adopted in 1789 and ratified two years later, is now known in full or in part through these words:

A well regulated Militia, being necessary to the security of a free State, the right of the people to keep and bear Arms, shall not be infringed.

The majority of our state constitutions (35) have similar provisions variously worded.* In Massachusetts and Kansas, for example, the language is: "The people have a right to keep and bear arms for the common defense. And as, in time of peace, armies are danger-ous to liberty, they ought not to be maintained without consent of the legislature, and the military shall always be held in exact subor-dination of the civil authority, and be governed by it." Some states use the same language as that in the Second Amendment, and in some it is condensed simply to: "The right of the people to keep and bear arms shall not be infringed." In no state is the right given directly to the individual citizen without some restriction.

Let us take a close look at the semantics of the Second Amend-ment:

"A well-regulated Militia, being necessary to the security of a free State ..."

"The purpose of the Second Amendment is set forth in this phrase," says John Brabner-Smith. "The right of the people to bear arms is protected by the Constitution because a well-regulated militia is necessary for the security of the state. The entire provision must be read in the light of this expression, and no regulation or restriction of firearms or weapons is in conflict with this amendment unless it substantially impedes the maintenance of a militia suffi-ciently well-equipped to assure the safety of the state."

What is a "well-regulated militia"? In 1903, Congress passed a law

---

* The fifteen states with no provisions: California, Delaware, Illinois, Iowa, Maryland, Minnesota, Nebraska, Nevada, New Hampshire, New Jersey, New York, North Dakota, Virginia, West Virginia and Wisconsin.

providing that the "regularly enlisted, organized, and uniformed active militia in the several states" should constitute the "organized militia" and be known as the National Guard, or some such other name as the state might give. (The organized Naval Militia was created by a 1914 act of Congress.) The act also provided that all other able-bodied men between the ages of eighteen and forty-five should be known as the "reserve militia." However, the act specified that Federal equipment could be distributed only to the *organized* militia; and that a state could procure additional arms from the War Department only if its organized militia met certain specified training requirements. Our remaining eligible manpower was to form the "unorganized militia." This, however, was to have no official status until its members were actually called into the National Guard under state or Federal law. This distinction between the organized militia and the unorganized reserves is also followed in state laws.

"... the right of the people ..."

As used in the Constitution, if not in an everyday sense, the term "right of the people" is used to refer a collective right, and "people" connotes our citizens in a collective sense. A familiar example from the Preamble is the phrase, "We the people of the United States ..." Where the Constitution refers to individuals or individual rights, three different terms (but never "people") are invariably used: "person" (and "persons"); "citizen" (and "citizens"); and "subject" (and "subjects").

Interestingly, the collective and individual terms are both used in the Fourth Amendment: "The right of *the people* to be secure in their *persons*, houses, papers, and effects, against unreasonable searches and seizures, shall not be violated, and no Warrants shall issue, but upon probable cause, supported by Oath or affirmation, and particularly describing the place to be searched, and the *persons* or things to be seized."

Awareness of this distinction (as used not only in the Federal Constitution but also in state constitutions) is also evident from many court decisions. A leading case is that of *City of Salina v. Blaksley,* where the Supreme Court of Kansas in 1905 stated that "the word 'people' means only the collective body, and that individual rights are not protected by the constitutional clause." In this case, the court also unequivocally held that no body of citizens other than the organized state militia or other military organizations provided for by law may be said to have a constitutional right to bear arms.

"... to bear arms ..."

"Arms" is traditionally a military term, as is also the phrase "to bear arms," in contrast to such a phrase as "to carry weapons." One simply does not think of a single individual or members of other than a military group as "bearing arms." Indeed, to speak of a hunter "bearing arms" to stalk a deer in the woods, or even a policeman "bearing arms" to stalk a criminal smacks of the ridiculous. Unless you are a member of an organized military group, the only arms you can properly be said to have are those dangling from your shoulders. This point was made plain in the 1874 Georgia case of *Hill v. State* where the court said:

The very words, "bear arms," had then and now have, a technical meaning. The "arms bearing" part of a people, were its men fit for service on the field of battle. That country was "armed" that had an army ready for fight. The call "to arms" was a call to put on the habiliments of *battle,* and I greatly doubt if in any good author of those days, a use of the word arms when applied to a people, can be found, which includes pocket-pistols, dirks, swords-canes, toothpicks, Bowie-knives, and a host of other relics of past barbarism, or inventions of modern savagery of like character. In what manner the right to keep and bear these pests of society, can encourage or secure the existence of a militia, and especially of a well regulated militia, I am not able to divine.

"... shall not be infringed."

In *Hill v. State,* the court also concluded that "the right to keep and bear arms is not infringed if the exercise of it be by law prohibited at places and times when a proper respect for the majesty of the law, a sense of decency and propriety, or the danger of a breach of the peace forbid it." "Only persons of military capacity to bear arms in military organizations are within the spirit of the guarantee," wrote Emery in the *Harvard Law Review* back in 1915, long before the passage of the National and Federal Firearms Acts. "Women, young boys, the blind, tramps, persons *non compos mentis,* or dissolute in habits, may be prohibited from carrying weapons.

Military arms may not be carried in all places even by persons competent to serve in the militia. They may be excluded from courts of justice, polling places, schoolhouses, churches, religious and political meetings, legislative halls and the like [and even] in street parades and other public demonstrations."

Other legal scholars like D. J. McKenna in a commentary on "The Right to Keep and Bear Arms" for a 1928 issue of the *Marquette Law Review,* concede *at the most* that "the Second Amendment only forbids Congress so to disarm citizens as to prevent them from functioning as state militiamen." From such statements, as well as the countless court decisions, it follows that any Act of Congress which does not in fact prevent an *eligible* citizen from functioning as a state militiaman is not proscribed by the Second Amendment. This is in line with the uncontested view that the Second Amendment merely affirms the right of the states to organize and maintain militia. McKenna went so far as to suggest that future courts might even say "that the states may have their well-regulated militia even though individuals possess no weapons of their own, provided the states supply the necessary armament upon mobilization," something they already do.

With all this in mind, it is clear that Congress, under the great central clauses of the Constitution, can impose or permit the imposition of firearms control through its commerce and taxing powers and through the residual police power of the states. Their validity has withstood the constitutional tests of time, courts and scholarly opinion.*

Nonetheless, the members of the firearms lobby, individually and collectively, continue to prate about the "absolutes" in our Bill of Rights. "They must be cherished and protected from those who would impair them," reads a *Rifleman* editorial of April 1960. Reiterating its cherished belief that "the price of liberty is eternal vigilance," the NRA frequently invokes the words of Justice Louis D. Brandeis: "Experience should teach us to be most on guard to protect liberty when the government's purposes are beneficent. Men born to freedom are naturally alert to repel invasion of their liberties by evil-minded rulers. The greatest dangers to liberty lurk in insidious encroachments by men of zeal, well-meaning, but without understanding."

* See pages 174, 179.

The unknowing reader, noting these words in a *Rifleman* editorial or article on the right to bear arms, would naturally be inclined to accept them as a favorable commentary by this eminent jurist on the NRA's interpretation of the Second Amendment. For the NRA never chooses to mention in what context the late Justice Brandeis uttered these words. They are a fragment of his dissenting opinion in the 1928 U.S. Supreme Court case of *Olmstead v. U.S.*, in which the Court upheld the Federal government's use of wire-tapping evidence to apprehend some violators of the Prohibition Law. In this opinion, Brandeis was commenting not on the Second Amendment, but rather on the Fourth (unreasonable search and seizure) and Fifth (self-incrimination through the use of the captured conversations). Nor does the NRA care to mention that Kentucky-born Brandeis, though an active outdoorsman, loathed firearms.

The gun lobby also mutters warnings about tampering with the Constitution and calls for support upon the Founding Fathers, notably that fierce lover of freedom, Thomas Jefferson, to whom are attributed the words, "No free man shall be debarred the use of arms." In this attitude, the gun lobby is of similar mind to those who hold that any changing of the Constitution is a violation of our sacred inheritance. No one, of course, has suggested anything about tampering with the Constitution. Indeed, no change whatever is needed, even in the Second Amendment, to validate additional firearms legislation. But if any were, one would suspect that such NRA "friends" as Jefferson and the rest of the Founding Fathers invoked, to say nothing of Brandeis, would be all for it. The name Brandeis is enshrined as one of our great jurists because of his oft-stated view that laws had to be related to the needs of society and, accordingly, had to change with the times.

As for the framers of the Constitution, they too were well aware that a man cannot wear the same coat he wore as a boy (as Jefferson put it), and that changes in the mode of life of the nation would create a need for amendments to the Constitution. There was no more staunch proponent of this view than Jefferson. And as Max Lerner has commented, America in Jefferson's time "did not have the kinds of mental illnesses that have become widespread today, perhaps even among those who so fiercely want the freedom of guns."

17 Guns, Recreation and Conservation

Conservation and sportsmanship are personal things—growing from the conscience, from the soul. That is why hunting is cherished by Americans as a legacy to be shared by sportsmen today, but to be conserved for generations yet unborn. . . . So why not take a boy or girl on your next trip!
—From an editorial in *The American Rifleman*, November 1964

Most authorities on youth agree on the value of proper shooting training in developing both personal and shooting responsibility. Recreational and physical education leaders consider marksmanship superior and rewarding exercise; they value its contributions to good physical and mental growth. . . . With this skill comes a lifetime ability to be proud of—the respect of chums, the standing of a man among men.
—Pamphlet, Sporting Arms and Ammunition Manufacturers' Institute

If guns in the hands of our citizenry serve no practical patriotic or protective purpose, what valid reason remains for people to possess them? Their only other ostensible use is largely for recreation—to some extent for target shooting, but for the most part for hunting. This in turn touches on what is often ambiguously called conservation.

We have already touched on the alleged social, psychic and civic values of target shooting. No serious objection can be registered to the continuance of this pastime, as long as its practice and the instruments necessary to its pursuit are confined, as Dr. Marvin E. Wolfgang has previously suggested, to "certain spatial limitations."

The values of hunting, on the other hand, must be more carefully examined because of the annual toll of perhaps 800 lives exacted in its pursuit. It is evidenced almost every day during the hunting season by such recurrent headlines as: "Hunter Accidentally Kills Pal; Thought He Was Porcupine."

Hunting is also properly a matter of public concern because the intended targets, our wildlife resources, are usually government property. Most game animals are owned by the states; and migratory birds, because they cross state lines, belong to Uncle Sam before they are bagged.

The practitioners of probably no other sport are as notoriously bad-mannered as hunters. Their too-common misdeeds include traipsing without permission on the property of others, performing such acts of vandalism as breaking down fences, peppering away at NO HUNTING signs, littering the woods with whiskey bottles, indiscriminately gunning down proscribed species of bird or beast, or firing their weapons too close to homes.

In view of all this, open to serious challenge is the whole host of wholesome values usually attributed to hunting, generally by those having some economic interest in it. We should remember that this is an industry worth upward of $1.5 billion annually. A blunt statement of its money value was given by a game warden, or conservation officer, to use the more modern term, who, wrote Joseph Wood Krutch in *The Great Chain of Life*, "protested hotly against the exhibition in a state park of a young deer which children were allowed to pet because, so he said, making pets of wild animals creates a prejudice against hunting. And to leave no doubt concerning the ultimate reason for his attitude, he is said to have added, 'After all, guns and ammunition are big business.'" This business, we should also remember, goes to paying the conservation officer's salary.

Then there is The American Humane Education Society, which charges the gun and ammo makers with exploiting the emotions of the average citizen:

Their ads suggest that most of our famous statesmen and pioneers were outdoorsmen, not strictly soldiers or scholars, but typical rugged, fighting settlers who won freedom for America. However, they play down the fact that the use of firearms was a necessity in those pioneering days for obtaining necessary food, driving off marauders and for self-protection. Instead, they glorify the hunt and exalt the kill in phrases such as ... "Thrill to the crack of a rifle, whether in search of game or for the mere excitement induced by the sport itself." ... The advertisers attempt to influence the average man in envisaging himself as a "man with a musket" and thus become a living example of the so-called American legend. The subtle desire seems to be to add hundreds of thousands of youngsters and adults to the list of gun enthusiasts, *not to enjoy the outdoors as such, but to use it merely as a backdrop for hunting.*

The primary purpose of our forebears in hunting was, of course, to get meat for food, as well as to use the hides for clothing and other needs. Among our primitive progenitors elsewhere throughout the world, hunting also originated as a necessity. No one seriously questions the value—indeed, the need—of hunting for this purpose except vegetarians, and anthropomorphic animal lovers. But with the food-foraging era long past, one may fairly wonder what value is now served in "rehearsing this aspect of the history of our race," to use a phrase of Roland C. Clement, staff biologist for the National Audubon Society.

Today's hunters, however, have developed a number of interesting rationales for hunting. They are aired over and over in conversation and burst forth in endless repetition from the editorial and advertising pages of the gun magazines. They include physical exercise, furtherance of the father-and-son relationship, and communion with one's companions and with nature. But these, according to the defenders of hunting, are merely subsidiary to certain more practical benefits.

Following the good old American tradition of bringing home food for the family is still said to be one, though hunting is no longer really necessary or even practical for this purpose. This pursuit may cause venison, for example, to cost the hunter something like a hundred dollars a pound. Actually, not more than half of all hunters, according to surveys, claim meat as their motive. Of these, probably only a negligible number bother or even care to eat what they shoot. In fact, many have trouble giving the meat away.

Some antivivisectionists and vegetarians regard killing game for sheer sport as something savage and barbaric. During the hunting season their letters pour into the newspapers, castigating hunters as sadistic, bloodthirsty creatures, and uttering reminders to the effect that humans are the only members of the animal kingdom who kill for fun. One correspondent referred to the episodes described in a series of hunting articles in the Detroit *News* as "good reminders of the innate brutality in some men," and sneered at the "brave Americans, well-armed with guns, who gain pleasure in the killing of wild animals. . . ." Author Cleveland Amory, a staunch antivivisectionist, once waggishly formed a "Hunt the Hunters Hunt Club." One rule specified: "After you've bagged your hunter, don't drape him over your automobile or mount him when you get home; merely the cap or jacket will suffice."

It should be said that those opposed to hunting, whether for food or fun, are not necessarily fuddy-duddies or desiccated souls who hate everybody who walks between them and the sun. Many, indeed, are gun enthusiasts, often former hunters, who now get their enjoyment from popping away at inanimate targets because they can no longer enjoy shooting at living things.

However, hunters vehemently reject the proposition that they are bloodthirsty creatures bent on nothing but killing. In fact, they declare themselves, as did the Detroit *News* outdoors writer, "the best friends of the wildlife of the world." Under some circumstances, hunters have even been known to describe themselves as "humanitarians."

Hunters, this argument goes, are performing an act of mercy, and actually doing a beast or bird a service by doing him in before he is killed by a fellow bird or beast, or by the hardships of nature. "A hunter's well-placed bullet is a far more swift and merciful death for a deer than that brought by a bear," says a February 1963 *American Rifleman* article entitled "The Humane Side of Hunting." It explains further: "Black and grizzly bears leave proof of their kill, a partially consumed carcass that tells how cruel nature can be." Speaking of the deer's special nemesis, the cougar, the article goes on to say: "Young cougars, just learning to hunt for themselves, make many mistakes which leave slashed and bleeding deer in the woods." One might add that so does many a novice nimrod.

Dwelling further on the cruelties of nature, the article points to the plight of the deer who do not survive a winter in the woods, or who are so weakened by starvation "that they fall prey to minor predators or to disease." Though the deer may not see it quite the same way, obviously shooting is preferable to starvation. This leads to a related and often-used argument that hunting is *necessary* in order to prune—"harvest" is the usual euphemism—certain kinds of animals which would otherwise become overnumerous to the detriment of trees, crops and, eventually, even themselves, because of the inability of their natural habitat to support their swollen population. This leads to a decline not only in the quantity but also in the quality of the species, as Bert Popowski points out in an exhortatory article, "We *Must* Kill More Deer!," published in the May 1964 *Shooting Times.*

In this argument, the hunter is cast as a conservationist. It is pointed out that the money he spends on license fees, special Federal taxes and contributions is used to preserve and increase game.

"Next time an anti-hunter knocks the shooting fraternity as a blood-lust bunch of animal murderers, set 'em straight as to who's *really* responsible for the game we have available," reads a blurb in the August 1964 *Guns & Ammo* introducing an article called "Hunters *Are* Conservationists" by Dr. Joe Linduska.

"One thing that makes me sore," begins Linduska, "is the recurrent suggestion that hunters and conservationists are different people. Nothing could be further from the truth. The fact of the matter is that the great mass of hunters are dedicated conservationists, even if a bit prejudiced at times in favor of their pet game species." Linduska then goes on to declare that "with hunters making the difference, a number of game species are reaching new peaks of prosperity."

Though *Guns & Ammo* does not identify him as such, its conservation proponent, Dr. Joe Linduska, is ordinarily occupied as a public relations director of Remington Arms, which since 1816 has had more than a casual interest in the sale of sporting weapons and ammunition. In the Remington files there is a letter, dated October 5, 1873, from an early customer, no less than General George Armstrong Custer, attesting to his satisfaction with a company product for which he had paid $91.50, and had used, he said, to bag forty-one antelope, four buffalo, four elk, eight deer, two wolves and "geese, prairie chickens and other feathered game in large numbers." The letter, omitting the list of game bagged, is reprinted in Remington's sales literature.

The du Pont-controlled Remington, it should also be remembered, is a prime financial support of the Wildlife Management Institute, as well as other leading conservation voices in Washington which have close ties with the Sporting Arms and Ammunition Manufacturers' Institute. Furthermore, as we may also remember, special Federal taxes on the sale of sporting arms and ammunition now provide more than $20 million annually for the development of wildlife resources. Among other things, the funds help pay the salaries and other expenses of the nation's conservation and wildlife (or fish and game) departments.

This program derives its authority from the Federal Aid in Wildlife Restoration Act (the Pittman-Robertson Act), passed in 1937 with the strong support of Remington, du Pont, and Winchester-Western. The program is administered by the Bureau of Sport Fisheries and Wildlife of the Department of the Interior. Some years ago, the Interior Department ruled that Eskimos in Alaska might not hunt ducks out of season, even though the meat is used there to feed hungry children. The killing of the ducks up North, it was noted, would reduce the numbers later available for the sojourn in the South on flyways frequented by sportsmen.

With all this in mind, one may reasonably wonder whether the purpose of conservation is to preserve wildlife, or to provide game for hunters to shoot at for the ultimate benefit of the arms industry. Or is it possible that one goal is not inconsistent with the other?

The answers, to a large extent, will depend on what one takes conservation to mean. Conservation, Joseph Wood Krutch once said, is like virtue in that "it has no declared opponents, but like virtue again it is defined in so many ways that it needs no enemies." To most laymen, the term has the connotation of preservation and protection, and as it applied to wildlife this purpose was clearly specified in the 1916 Act of Congress which created the National Park Service. A frequently quoted passage of the Act states that its purpose is "to conserve the scenery and the natural historic objects and the wildlife therein and to provide for the enjoyment of the same in such manner and by such means as will leave them unimpaired for the enjoyment of future generations."

In a sense the parks were established as refuges, with their animal population protected against hunting, and this philosophy of protection is still followed today; generally, no public hunting is allowed in our national parks. This protective philosophy stemmed from the excesses of our hunters in the 1800s when America witnessed what was undoubtedly the greatest mass slaughter of wildlife in world history. At one time, anywhere from 75 million to 125 million buffalo (bison), according to various estimates, ranged our plains. As late as 1868, a train of the Kansas-Pacific Railroad was described as traveling "one hundred and twenty miles through a continuous herd of buffalo packed so densely that the earth was black and the train was compelled to stop several times."

But by 1872 the plains were aswarm with buffalo hunters, many taking only the hides and tongues, and leaving the meat to rot. During the next three years nearly 3.7 million buffalo (5 million, according to some estimates) were slaughtered. In his first eighteen months at his specialty, Buffalo Bill Cody accounted for 4,280. By the late 1870s only 500 remained in all of America, and by 1900 the species was regarded as doomed. Fortunately, the survivors were saved, and today there are some 8,000 under careful protection.

In less than 150 years, almost forty species of birds and mammals have disappeared entirely from America, about half of them since 1900. One, the heath hen, saw her last here as recently as 1932. Even more incredible than the virtual disappearance of the buffalo was the fate of the passenger pigeon. A century ago no bird was more common, and it accounted for an estimated 40 per cent of this country's bird population. A single flock was estimated by John James Audubon as containing more than a billion birds. Yet, like the buffalo, they too were coveted by market hunters. Apart from the birds' providing good eating, the feathers were also in great demand for ticking. There were also sport shooters, trappers and nest raiders. During the 1870s a hard-working hunter could net 15,000 birds in a single day. Within fifty years every last one was gone. The last wild passenger pigeon was shot in 1900. Of three then still captive in the Cincinnati Zoo, the last, a female named Martha, died in 1914 at the age of twenty-nine. Her body was shipped to the Smithsonian Institution in Washington where she now perches under glass, as *Time Magazine* has noted, "a plumed reproof to man's destructiveness."

Meanwhile, as the conservation movement began to gain momentum, particularly under the leadership of Theodore Roosevelt, a problem of another sort arose, one that was to give rise to quite a different concept of conservation. The problem is typified by a case cited frequently by conservationists as a classic example of game mismanagement, one that took place in the Kaibab country of northern Arizona. In 1906 President Roosevelt made the 735,000-

acre region a national game preserve in order to protect its magnificent herd of 4,000 well-nourished mule deer. Deer shooting was ended in the preserve. To build up the herd, government hunters also began a systematic campaign to wipe out the predators. Within the next twenty-five years nearly all of the deer's natural enemies—mountain lions (cougars), wolves, coyotes and bobcats—were eradicated. By 1924 the deer population had increased to an estimated 100,000, far beyond the capacity of the environment to support it. As the supply of vegetation was eaten up by the deer, starvation and disease took their toll. Deer died by thousands and, according to a history of the national parks, "those who lived ate every leaf and twig till the whole country looked as though a swarm of locusts had swept through it, leaving the range torn, gray, stripped and dying." By 1930 the Kaibab's deer population had plummeted to around 30,000. By 1940 even this number had been cut in half, and many of the deer were sickly.

Before this disaster, the deer, the Navajo (who killed only the deer he needed for food, clothing and trading), the mountain lion and other creatures of the Kaibab lived in peaceful, if primitive, coexistence. But this and other examples of what Peter Farb has called "injudicious tampering" with the environment led to a philosophy of conservation—more properly, wildlife management—born from the need of controlling a game population within the limitations of the carrying capacity of its environment. This concept, chiefly concerned with the production of wildlife for recreational hunting, sees our wildlife as a sort of self-replenishing resource, to be built up to produce a surplus that can be "harvested" just like timber, corn or other crops. "Game management and care sees to the sowing," says a Remington Arms history. What contributed to the deer overpopulation problem, both in the Kaibab and elsewhere, is the fact that man wiped out virtually all of his natural wild enemies. Today there are no significant numbers of mountain lions, wolves and other deer predators in this country, at least in close proximity to large deer populations in public hunting areas. The deer's most serious predator today—except for man himself—is the dog.*

The reintroduction and encouragement of natural predators, fea-

* To be entirely fair a big factor underlying the deer problem in many places has been the inroad of civilization itself. Logging and the clearing of forests at first creates an ideal habitat for deer, which thrive on twigs, shrubs, saplings and leaves from low trees. Under these conditions, deer multiply. The in-

sible for some species and in and around such areas as national parks, can no longer be relied on entirely for controlling such ungulate (hoofed mammal) species as deer, moose and elk. Moreover, wolves and mountain lions cannot readily be introduced into areas near large communities where they would pose hazards to humans.

All of which seems to leave shooting as perhaps the simplest and most practical means of control in the case of such animals as deer. Whether hunting for this purpose should be entrusted to the armed citizenry is, however, another matter.

If deer or other species are too numerous and the so-called conservationists are really concerned about the health of the herd, it would be more efficient and humane to leave the "thinning out" to competent, professional hunters, who are expert marksmen, as is the practice in our national parks.

One would, of course, expect the humane society people to suggest this and to challenge the rationale of hunters that animals must be killed to prevent overpopulation and consequent suffering. "We believe this is merely specious justification," says Oliver Evans, president of the Humane Society of the United States, who also ventures the belief that "99 per cent of the hunters are in the field for the joy of the kill and not because of altruistic concern for the health of the herd. Perhaps there are situations where excessive numbers must be reduced but, in my opinion, this should be carried out by professional hunters whose shots will kill and not wound, rather than by the large army of unqualified amateurs who go into the field every year."

However, even the nation's leading ecologists, zoologists and game management authorities, hunters themselves, regard as specious the conservation claim advanced to justify the need for public hunting. I contacted the University of California's A. Starker Leopold, son of Aldo Leopold, father of wildlife management in this country, who back in the 1920s had pioneered the philosophy that wildlife populations could be "harvested." The younger Leopold wrote me:

The real basis for a defense of hunting, in my opinion, is not as a biological tool but as a recreational outlet. Many thousands of people, in-

creased number, however, soon outgrow their food supply as they overbrowse the range. (The low, young trees, for example, begin to grow out of reach.) This, plus the absence of predators, compounds the overpopulation problem.

cluding myself, hunt because they enjoy it. It offers a form of mental and physical exercise not duplicated by any other form of sport with which I am acquainted.

Harold E. Anthony of the American Museum of Natural History, one of America's most honored zoologists, also a hunter, has written:

The wise sportsman does not defend himself by reminding us that certain animal populations, such as the deer in our West, must be periodically pruned, else the extermination of natural predators like cougars will bring an increase in deer population beyond the carrying capacity of the range. For otherwise, unmanageable deer populations could be controlled by utilitarian state commissions; sportsmen shouldn't beg the issue by claiming that they are best serving the interests of deer by shooting them. Sportsmen shoot because they want to shoot, because they believe it is a good sport that enriches life—not for the deer, but for man.

Interestingly, one hears the conservationist argument for the need of hunting to "harvest" the surplus only in connection with such game species as deer and doves, but never in connection with the hunting of predators which, ironically, would provide a natural and more efficient means of controlling that much-worried-about surplus.

Among the predators that have largely been killed off by man are the panther in Florida and the gray, or timber, wolf in Michigan. One can also point to the polar bear, now also threatened with extinction because of the manner in which he is now hunted in Alaska by well-heeled Americans. The technique employed is a modern version of the methods formerly used by buffalo hunters to gun down their victims a century ago. Two small planes are used, one plane to corner the bear on an ice floe and chase him around until he drops from exhaustion, the other to land a hunter to finish off the bear. *The New York Times* reported that some 300 bears were killed like this in the winter of 1964–65. The sole object is a trophy; the carcass is left to rot. Both Russia and Canada forbid the hunting of polar bears for sport; only Alaska and Norway encourage it as a tourist promotion.

Our national symbol, the bald eagle, though protected by Federal law, has also been on the downgrade for years. A recent National Audubon Society study showed that of 118 eagles reported dead in a two-year period, 91 had apparently been shot. A Washington *Post* article on the impending extinction of Potomac eagles mentioned that those shot by hunters had been mistaken for crows.

A recent report to the Audubon Society tallied 200 Swainson's hawks found dead at the foot of 200 telephone poles along a short stretch of Kansas highway. The birds, which habitually perch on telephone poles, had been slaughtered by hunters using .22-caliber rifles and cruising in cars.

In the past twenty years the population of the California condor, the nation's largest soaring land bird, with a wingspread of nearly 10 feet, has declined to only 38, according to a recent census. Again, a primary cause is shooting by sportsmen who don't know what a condor is—or don't care.

And there is the classic case of the whooping crane, teetering on the edge of oblivion since around 1910. By December 1965, just 44 birds had survived hunters and the draining of prairie sloughs (needed for corn and wheat); the whoopers now winter in a special 47,000-acre wildlife refuge on the Gulf Coast of Texas.

The rare Kaibab squirrel, often termed Arizona's "whooping crane," furnishes a recent example of the frequent conflicts that arise between gun-oriented game commissions and those genuinely concerned with the preservation of wildlife. The Kaibab squirrel (once described by Theodore Roosevelt as "the handsomest squirrel I have ever seen") is not only very rare, but is also unique in that it is found in only one place in the world: a 30-by-70-mile strip adjacent to the Grand Canyon. Never abundant in number, this distinctive squirrel (it has an all black body and a white plume-like tail) has for many years been in a precarious position facing extinction. It is listed by the United States Fish and Wildlife Service as an endangered species, and is classified by the International Union for Conservation of Nature and Natural Resources as a rare mammal. For sixty years it was under rigid protection; to be caught with one meant a fine of $500.

Yet in 1964 the Arizona Fish and Game Department sanctioned an open nine-day season on the squirrel, with twenty-seven squirrels allowed per hunter, and no limit on the number of hunters. The season, announced despite the opposition and advice of field members of the Grand Canyon National Park and Kaibab National Forest, as well as two Arizona Fish and Game Department members, provoked a storm of protests from naturalists, scientists and conservationists.

Carl Buchheister, president of the National Audubon Society, said:

> The incident is illustrative of a peculiar myopia that afflicts many game departments whose administrators and technicians have been trained in the game management philosophy that any shootable species, no matter how limited in range or numbers, is "going to waste" unless hunters are permitted to "harvest the annual crop."
>
> Unable to recognize a public interest broader than that represented by licensed hunters, who do in fact support their program, these departments argue that sportsmen "have a right" to harvest the crop.

The Audubon Society, though not opposed to hunting per se, does not always agree with state wildlife agencies and other so-called conservation groups. Much of the program advanced by these groups is conservation in the good old-fashioned sense of the term. In its bi-weekly packet of news releases and bulletins, the gun industry-subsidized Wildlife Management Institute, for example, is clearly on the side of the angels in its approbation of the efforts taken to save the whooping crane and the also endangered Attwater's prairie chicken, of which 1,335, at last count, remained in coastal Texas. (After all, to wipe out the few remaining would hardly use up any ammunition.) The conservation groups and gun enthusiasts also make much of their noble efforts to fight water pollution and drainage programs and to oppose the U.S. Army Engineers' "destructive" river-basin and other projects. But why such efforts?

When the U.S. Army Corps of Engineers talked of plans to clear a brushy strip in order to ease the flow of flood waters near Phoenix, Arizona, the Wildlife Management Institute saw this not only as a "serious setback" to doves but, more important, to dove hunters. "The Arizona Game and Fish Department says that more than 834,-000 doves use this brushy strip," read an WMI bulletin of February 12, 1965. "Hunting is excellent, and shooters spend approximately $1 for various kinds of sporting goods and services for every dove they bag." Consequently, the bulletin went on to say, the financial loss to the affected communities, if the Corps' plan were to go into effect, would amount to $317,000 annually "based solely on hunter expenditures," this not counting the incalculable loss of "recreational opportunity."

"Directors of the state wildlife agencies are the chief spokesmen for hunters and other shooters in their states," also says the WMI in one of its frequent bulletins opposing firearms bills: "They have a responsibility to foster and to expand the recreational interests of hunters and shooters."

The only other practical justification for hunting is the argument that it is needed to get rid of animals and birds who are threats to crops, poultry and livestock. Again, we are once more dealing with predators in the sense that every creature is a predator, but in this justification they are now also commonly referred to as pests, vermin or—in the vernacular of shooting circles—"varmints."

The subject, inherently complex from a purely biological or ecological point of view, "is further complicated beyond all reason by inherited prejudice, vested interest, and genuine economics," says Purdue University's famed wildlife management expert Durward L. Allen. In 1964 A. Starker Leopold, heading a blue-ribbon group appointed to advise Interior Secretary Stuart Udall, issued a report stating that "far more animals are being killed than would be required for effective protection of livestock, agricultural crops, wildland resources and human health."

For instance, coyotes, it has long been known, though they do pose some problem in ranching country, are not the great threat to livestock they are popularly believed to be. They bother cattle only rarely, and it is only individual coyotes that threaten sheep. Postmortem studies of coyotes conducted by James Anderson of the Oregon Museum of Science and Industry showed that those examined had not killed sheep or lambs.

"It is a fallacy to believe that every bobcat or coyote is lurking in the shadows, waiting to prey on domestic stock," says Montana State Senator Arnold Rieder, chairman of his State Committee on Stockgrowing and Grazing. "The predator's natural prey happens to be rodents and other wild species. When a particular coyote or bobcat is killing lambs and chickens, he, by all means, should be exterminated. Then the trouble will stop, and predation will resume its normal course in the wild where it is vitally needed."

Other studies confirm that *individuals* in a species differ in how they act, just as humans do, and that therefore all coyotes, like all hunters, cannot be condemned by the actions of just one or a few. Besides, their beneficial effects have to be weighed against their possibly harmful effects.

As a Missouri Conservation Commission report points out: "For example, we might study the food intake of a number of coyotes and find that of their total foods, they killed about $500 worth of poultry and livestock. But most of the rest of the food was mice and rats, which, if predators hadn't eaten them, would have ruined $700 worth of crops. The answer seems clear: We have a $200 profit in those coyotes on their animal food alone, to say nothing of the many other nonpredator values most creatures have."

One of the most controversial predators and so-called pests is the fox, about whom there are many strong opinions. With few chickens raised on open ranges today, he may be a problem in certain areas. But is he really the pest he is believed to be?

Again we have to go into the dynamics of the complex predator-prey relationship. Normally, the fox diet consists of mice, rabbits, chipmunks, insects, fruits and berries, grouse, pheasant, small birds and, but only occasionally, chickens. In his case too, the damage done by the fox has to be assessed in terms of his other values to the farmer. As explained by Maurice M. Alexander of the New York State University College of Forestry in the *New York State Conservationist* of Febuary–March 1959:

The fox might be killing the farmer's chickens and so the fox is greatly reduced in numbers in the wild community. But foxes at the same time were doing much to control the small mammals. With the evil chicken-eating foxes gone, the mice increase, do damage to the farmer's trees, grains and stored feeds until the hawks and owls (pretty good predators in their own right) take advantage of this new supply of rodents as food. Then the population of hawks and owls increase and, in addition to feeding on the mice, they take a few of the farmer's chickens. It might be asked if the farmer gained in killing the foxes.

Alexander also reminds us:

It should be kept in mind, too, that fox predation on chickens may be the action of an individual or family. This is true in most cases and so does not warrant the removal of all foxes. The guilty party can be caught and further control may not be necessary. This could be stated for many of our predators because only a few overcome an acquired fear of man and visit his immediate areas.

In any event, the farmer may be justified in shooting an occasional fox. But this is a far cry from the wanton shooting of all foxes—and, for that matter, woodchucks, squirrels, coyotes, crows, hawks and owls—under the guise of "varmint hunting."

Contributing to the predisposition of people to do this are prejudices built up from childhood. The fantasies fostered by fairy tales, old wives' tales, and the stories of nature writers which have personalized the predator have endowed him with the worst human characteristics. Thus we are conditioned by legends of the cruel coyote, the sly fox, the ruffian red squirrel, the big bad bear, the wicked wolf—all of whom, we are warned, are out to get us.

And, indeed, old legends die hard, fortunately for the sporting arms and ammunition industry, which sees the promotion of varmint shooting as a tremendous source of sales. One recent Colt ad showed a scared squirrel staring at a sign reading, "Varmints Take Notice: This land is protected . . . make yourself scarce, varmints." A quite logical suggestion. A deer hunter can go through a whole season without firing off a single shot, except perhaps at another hunter. Varmint hunting, on the other hand, uses up a lot of ammunition. Seemingly, it is of little importance that the "sport" kills creatures that have a place in the scheme of things, are beneficial and are attractive and interesting to look at.

Writing of the indiscriminate shooting of hawks and owls and other predatory birds, Durward Allen says:

Probably there is no category of wildlife so generally appreciated by people who enjoy the out-of-doors as birds of prey. A growing awareness of the high esthetic value of these birds is behind an increasing trend toward total protection in progressive states—a trend well supported by responsible sportsmen's federations. The attempt in certain states to protect some predatory birds while others are left unprotected is meaningless and completely ineffective. The average gunner does not know one from another. . . .

All this, I realize, does not consider the animal's or bird's side of the question. However, some men will continue to feel the irresistible, periodic urge to kill something, or watch something or someone get killed. Killing for fun and sport has been with us since ancient times, and every culture has had its own particular way of enjoying it. Perhaps civilization can be said to have advanced in that our entertainment of this sort has evolved from watching lions disembowel an old woman in an amphitheater to concentrating our violence in shooting down members of the animal kingdom. As members of a so-called higher order, some members of the human race may, I suppose, take this prerogative to satisfy what they consider deep-felt needs.

I do not propose to dwell on the moral aspects of this, since I am concerned here largely with the ostensible practical values of hunting. But hunters do themselves a disservice when they say that killing a caribou is no more wrong than killing a cockroach: the extension of this line of reasoning would also justify the killing of human beings—say, the "surplus" of starving, teeming Indians— supposedly to strengthen the human species. Nor is it any less specious to suggest, as does Vance Bourjaily in a *Saturday Evening Post* article entitled "Hunting is Humane," that there is not much of a moral difference between "the unnatural rearing and drab, bloody slaughter of meat and fowl commercially, and the system of game management which raises crops of wild birds and animals to be harvested by men who find challenge, and excitement, health and pleasure, in trying it."

No matter how one tries to avoid it, all these are rationales for the guilt in a game that involves killing.

Hunting solely for food is perhaps the least of the advantages that "accrue to the nation's well-being," concedes a history of Remington Arms. It also states: "More important, by far, are the benefits to the nation's health and virility; the easing of the terrible tensions of modern living; the wonderful companionship of men, and women, too; the joyous friendship of father and son bound together by enjoyment of an ageless sport." The same benefits, of course, could be attributed to such activities as bowling and baseball, or mountain hiking or skiing.

Is it, then, as is also claimed, the glory of the great outdoors, and not the love of killing, that sends the huntsman forth? If this is so, asks Alan Devoe, one of America's great nature writers, "why in the holy name of sanity does he burden himself with that long, heavy, unnecessary object that has a butt at one end and is likely, if he isn't careful, to go *bang?* It's just the fun of exercising the *skill* of shooting, is it? Dr. Roy Abbott, a biologist, has remarked that no living bird or beast calls forth this skill more prettily than does a beer can tossed in the air."

Or, one may also ask, why does not the outdoors lover do his shooting with a camera—something, incidentally, calling for far more skill than a gun.

Many sportsmen do in fact give up hunting with guns in favor of hunting with cameras, not necessarily for moral reasons, but because of the belief that a good photograph may be a more satisfying trophy than the dead animal. Many other sportsmen also give up hunting for a great variety of reasons. Some find they can no longer stand the pace. Getting up at three in the morning and tramping the chilly woods, or waiting in a damp duck blind, is something that palls after a while. Others give it up because of an unfortunate experience—being fired at, for example, or accidentally firing at someone themselves, or seeing a dreadful accident.

Others finally heed the warnings of their families to stay out of the woods. With all the careless shooters a forest conceals, it can be a really dangerous place during the hunting season. Then there are those who give it up for deeply personal reasons, who decide gradually or suddenly that interfering with the lives of their fellow creatures is a game hardly worth the candle. Dr. Karl Menninger wrote me that part of his motivation in giving up hunting came from watching "a few animals die after heroic efforts to escape my long-distance bludgeoning. I decided the fun I was having making animals gasp and quiver wasn't worth the suffering it was costing them."

To former *New York Herald Tribune* rod-and-gun columnist Edmund Gilligan the decision came as he shot down an antelope at close range. The account of his experience, published in *The Saturday Evening Post* of December 1, 1962, is one of the most eloquent and moving personal statements ever offered by one who gave up hunting.

Even a dedicated hunter like Vance Bourjaily confesses that the only reasoned defense of hunting, like that of drinking whiskey or going to the theater, is the pleasure it provides—in the case of hunting, finding and killing a creature. Of similar mind is Harold

Anthony, though he uses the term "general sense of well-being" as something perhaps far transcending the term "pleasure." Not that the sportsmen may at the moment of truth give any thought to killing per se. He may be depersonalized. Like a soldier in combat, the hunter may, as Anthony says, merely consider killing as a "routine action to reach the goal of capture or hitting the target."

Yet Remington Arms and other of the rationalists are fond of quoting the words of outdoorsman Theodore Roosevelt, a patron saint of the hunting fraternity:

> In hunting, the finding and killing of game is after all but part of the whole. The free, self-reliant, adventurous life, with its rugged and stalwart democracy; the wild surroundings; the grand beauty of the scenery; the chance to study the ways of woodland creatures . . . all these unite to give the career of the wilderness hunter its peculiar charm. The chase is among the best of all national pastimes; it cultivates the vigorous manliness for the lack of which in a nation, as in an individual, the possession of no other qualities can possibly atone.

The words recall the characterization of T.R. by a close friend: "You must always remember," said the friend, "that the President is about six."

T.R.'s ringing words also bring to mind the question posed by Alan Devoe: "Is the sport of hunting, as such, a man-worthy thing or isn't it?" And his answer: "*Manly?* It doesn't take a man to kill something. Any animal can do that. What it takes a *man* to do—and he is the only creature on all the earth that can do it—is to feel pity and show mercy, to feel gratitude for aliveness and give the thanks of restraint, to be so very strong in his manhood that he can be gentle."

18   17,000 Lives a Year— Can They Be Saved?

All that is necessary for the triumph of evil is for good men to do nothing.

      Edmund Burke

What is the solution to the gun problem? Is there any way of preventing firearms accidents; of protecting the average citizen against armed assault or murder, possibly even from a member of his own family, of preventing the frequent firearms suicides? Unfortunately, in a nation that has grown up with guns and where children are virtually weaned on weapons, there are no easy answers.

One possible solution presents itself immediately: Ban all weapons for civilian use. Indeed, this is a solution suggested by the only authority the National Rifle Association chooses to mention in its literature—Dr. Marvin E. Wolfgang of the University of Pennsylvania's Center of Criminological Research.

Under these hypothetical circumstances, there would eventually be no firearms problem. Some people would undoubtedly continue to bludgeon, stab and throttle others to death, but firearms fatalities and accidents would recede to the vanishing point as all guns were rounded up.

However, to require all sportsmen and hunters to give up their shotguns and rifles is unrealistic. On the other hand, the need for any private citizen to own a revolver or pistol can be more seriously questioned. These weapons are rarely used for hunting—in fact many states already forbid their use for this purpose—and probably no more than 50,000 or 60,000 Americans use them for serious target shooting.

The only other ostensible use for handguns is for self-defense. In the home a shotgun or rifle can also be used for this purpose. And, as any police officer will tell you, if anyone should break into your house or hold you up, the safest thing to do is to avoid showing resistance. Some believe that if all hand weapons were prohibited, so that lawless elements found it impossible to get them, their need for protective purposes would diminish, too. Others would have this ban extend even to the police. Although such a plan may seem utopian, it has long been the practice in England, where, with pistols and revolvers virtually outlawed since 1922 and the police unarmed, there are very few homicides compared to the number in this country.

Our carefully trained police officers are responsible for their quota of killings too—often involving innocent bystanders, their fellow officers and members of their own families. During a recent ten-day period, a Brooklyn patrolman accidentally shot and killed his best friend—another patrolman who was trying to help him break up a sidewalk brawl. And two off-duty policemen in civilian clothes, each suspicious of the other for having a gun, exchanged eleven shots in a Manhattan bar. Another policeman, casually playing with his gun in the kitchen of his home, accidentally killed his pregnant wife. And a fifteen-year-old girl shot her policeman father with one of his service revolvers after he had supposedly beaten her.

Short of outlawing all firearms, what can be done to at least reduce their danger to all of us?

The gun lobby is forever full of suggestions. It argues that since guns don't commit crimes, laws should not be aimed at guns, but only at the unlawful shooter. It suavely suggests punitive laws, ignoring the fact that such laws are already in existence. Moreover, it does not say how one can undo or prevent the damage done by a person who gets a gun and puts it to some nefarious use, unmindful of punishment.

The gun lobby is a staunch advocate of local, rather than national, laws, without saying how any law can be fully effective in one jurisdiction when there is none in a neighboring jurisdiction.

It professes faith in a uniform state law, knowing full well that a strong law won't be acceptable to the states, as the past four decades have demonstrated, and that a weak law is meaningless. It knows that the most recent efforts to draft a uniform state law have already been declared a failure.

The truth, of course, is that the gun lobby wants no laws at all or, if any, a so-called "pro-gun" law relaxing the few controls we now have.

The gun lobby believes in harsher punishments for the misuse of firearms and for crimes committed while carrying them; but it does not agree to laws that would provide any feasible means of keeping firearms out of the hands of persons likely to misuse them or commit crimes with them.

It professes to favor safety rules, commandments or principles, but obstructs any efforts to enact these into law.

It manifests a concern as to the type of citizens who should and should not have guns, yet the NRA, for example, does nothing to prevent literally anyone from availing himself of membership in the organization, and so making himself eligible to receive *free* or bargain-priced government guns and ammunition.

The gun lobby refuses to recognize the correlation between strict firearms controls and the low incidence of firearms deaths where controls are in effect, both in the United States and abroad. It protests that controls are an inconvenience. It cloaks its objections in the "patriotic" raiments of protection, both of the national security and constitutional rights. But it masks its real objections, which stem from monetary motives, as well as from vague, misguided fears.

In its objections, the gun lobby could very well be short-sighted and doing itself a disservice. As New York City Mayor John V. Lindsay, while still a congressman, told the Senate Commerce Committee:

Responsible sportsmen and gun owners find their sport or hobby degraded by the greedy practices of irresponsible gun sellers and the murderous practices of irresponsible gun buyers. I cannot see how it helps bona-fide gun lovers and even the dealers and manufacturers to have a national sport become a national scandal.

Against the gun lobby is the opinion of experts with no commercial ax to grind. This opinion is almost unanimous that the status quo cannot be maintained, and that stricter controls of some sort are necessary.

"We already have controls on tobacco, alcohol, narcotics, poisons and, of course, any food or drug that might be dangerous for human use," says former Federal Bureau of Prisons Director James V. Bennett, who has stated that the traffic in handguns, at least, must be similarly supervised, preferably by Federal laws. "I recognize that Federal legislation alone will not provide the necessary measure of control," he says, "but it would help and it might stimulate more effective local efforts which are now so largely excercises in futility."

"Handguns suitable for concealment are basically the weapons of the assassin, not of the militia," U.S. Court of Appeals Judge George Edwards of Detroit told a 1964 American Bar Association panel on the gun problem. "Acquaintance with this problem as a judge, as a former police commissioner of the city of Detroit, as a former infantry officer, and at least an occasional hunter," declared Judge Edwards, "convinced me that these three steps should be taken to lessen our criminal carnage."

1. The manufacture and sale and possession of handguns suitable for concealed weapons should be prohibited by state and Federal law, except where sale and possession is the subject of a permit provided by state law. Such laws should provide for court review of denial.

2. The purchase and possession of rifles or shotguns should in my judgment be a matter of right for any law-abiding citizen. Such weapons should, however, be registered under state law and sold only on proper identification. The purchase and/or possession of a rifle or shotgun by a person with a felony record should be made illegal, unless he possesses a permit for the weapon issued on a showing of a subsequent record of good citizenship of some length.

3. Interstate mail order sale or delivery of firearms of any kind should be banned by Federal law.

Most serious students of the gun problem would also go beyond the mail-order restrictions proposed by Senator Dodd, and are of the firm opinion that all guns, like cars, should be registered. Moreover, they feel that guns should be sold only to persons at least eighteen or twenty-one years old with permits or licenses. Another wise precaution suggested is that the families of permit applicants, of whatever age, be checked and placed on notice that a member of the household—husband, wife, sister, brother, or child—is about to buy a gun.

Such a permit system would prevent the impulsive purchase of weapons, make it more difficult for criminals and mental incompetents to buy them, and would enable law enforcement officers to keep track of who was armed with what in case of a shooting. All guns now without any form of identification on them would have to be stamped with serial numbers and other identifying information, a practice already followed by many manufacturers. Gun purchasers would have to show identification and sign their names before being allowed to pick up their guns after the specified waiting period. In most states now, the dealer need take only whatever name and address the purchaser gives him, but not his signature.

Ammunition, it then follows, would be sold only to holders of firearms licenses or permits, which would be required of present as well as prospective gun owners. Each of their guns would also be registered.

"If a person has nothing bad in mind," a Treasury Department official told me, "there is no reason in the world why he should object to there being a record of the fact that he has a gun." Or as U.S. Attorney General Homer Cummings put it three decades ago, "No honest man can object to registration. Show me the man who doesn't want his gun registered, and I will show you a man who shouldn't have a gun."

If gun buyers are licensed, it also follows that gun dealers should be, too. Only twenty-three states and the District of Columbia license handgun dealers. Much more care should be taken in the issuance of licenses. The Federal licenses required of interstate dealers are given out indiscriminately to anyone who can pay the $1 cost. The proposal for more rigid screening does not seem unreasonable in view of the fact that dealers in products such as liquor and drugs are usually licensed, to say nothing of astrologers, house movers, parking lot attendants and private detectives.

Because of the large number of people killed in gun accidents (now about 2,400 a year), in spite of the NRA's preachments and safety training efforts, it might be well to require safety training before issuing licenses to all gun owners, not merely those below a certain age or first-time shooters. If safety instruction is deemed necessary for some, it stands to reason that all should have it.

For safety's sake, many authorities like former New York City Police Captain Frederick J. Ludwig, now a practicing attorney, are of the opinion that it should be made a crime for anyone to have a *loaded* weapon in the home, on the street, or anywhere else except where it is intended for use. "Unless you're in the woods," Ludwig says, "there is no need for you to keep your gun loaded unless you're planning to kill another human being."

Going even further is the suggestion frequently made that no guns, whether loaded or unloaded, be allowed in the home at all, but rather be kept in central storage places, a possibility that Walter C. Reckless, Ohio State University criminologist, suggests in his standard work, *The Crime Problem.* "Why keep a weapon around the house or anywhere indoors if you use it only for hunting or target practice?" asks Ludwig. He mentioned as possible storage places the local police station, government armories and arsenals, from which ammunition could also be made available. "The weapons could be stored for possibly a small fee and drawn out whenever needed," says Ludwig. Having them in a central storage place would also minimize the possibility of their being stolen. Psychologist Anatol Rapoport, in a behavior study on accident research, also suggests the advantage of renting weapons at their place of use to eliminate the need for having to store them in the home.

Where does all this leave the gun collector? There is no reason why he shouldn't be permitted to keep his souvenir and trophy weapons at home as long as they are registered and permanently deactivated.

Experts believe that the archaic distinction in most of our own laws between the carrying of concealed and unconcealed weapons should be eliminated. "This a hang-over from the frontier days," says Ludwig. "You can do just as much harm, if not more, with a weapon out in the open and ready for use as with one tucked away in your pocket with the safety catch on."

In addition to all these preventive measures, penalties—but meaningful ones—should face the person misusing guns, whether intentionally or unintentionally. Overzealous hunters mistaking other hunters for wildlife, or shooters directly responsible for other types of accidents should be subject to more than a mere slap on the wrist. They should face the loss of their gun and shooting privileges, perhaps permanently.

James V. Bennett sees as "the ultimate" in firearms legislation a Federal statute imposing an excise tax on those who own, purchase or possess firearms. "This law would make it possible to feed this information into a data-processing machine, and within an hour or so the police could trace any gun that they found had been used in the commission of a crime." Very likely such a procedure would also prevent the commission of many crimes.

Should the private ownership of all, or at least some, firearms be completely prohibited? Could this be done without infringing on the Constitution? To answer this question, I went to Cambridge, Massachusetts, to see one of the nation's ranking authorities on constitutional law—Harvard Law School Professor Arthur E. Sutherland. After finishing Harvard Law School in 1925, Sutherland was selected to serve in the highly coveted post of law clerk to U.S. Supreme Court Justice Oliver Wendell Holmes, himself a distinguished authority on Constitutional law. Later, Sutherland was a practicing lawyer for fifteen years, served as Commissioner on Uniform State Laws of New York, and has been a professor of law for the past twenty years. Since 1955, he has held the distinguished Bussey Professor Chair of Law at Harvard.

"In our kind of civilization, I can't tolerate any kind of weapon," Sutherland told me. "The romantic attachment for guns doesn't go with our urban way of living. In our present crowded society, there is simply no place for guns.

"Law enforcement? In Boston not long ago, there was a shooting fray between cops and robbers. None of them got hurt. But a girl who was walking along the street got killed. Hunting? Hunters say they shoot to keep down the deer population. If there are too many deer let the game wardens worry about them, instead of our self-appointed ecological missionaries. The average hunter doesn't really care about conservation. The guy goes to a store, buys a red hat and red coat and feels the stir of the great outdoors and the Old West. This, he thinks, makes him feel like a man."

Does this sound like a disgruntled ivory-towered dreamer, a do-gooder with no knowledge of firearms? In addition to his legal and teaching duties, Sutherland has served in our National Guard long enough to rise in the ranks from basic private to major. On a wall of his book-lined office is a photograph showing Sutherland in uniform at Anzio with General Mark Clark whom he served as aide-de-camp. During World War II he served four years with the Fifth Army, the First Infantry Division and the Office of the Undersecretary of War, being discharged with the rank of colonel, the Legion of Merit with cluster, the French Cross of War (awarded to him twice) and other foreign decorations. All in all, he has more than a casual familiarity with firearms.

As a young lawyer, Sutherland handled a case involving a two-year-old girl, who once was as normal and happy as any two-year-old can be. "Her brother was pulling her on a sled," he recalls, "when she suddenly started to cry. Her laughing squeals of joy suddenly turned into cries of anguish. The brother brought her home, and there he saw blood coming out of her head. An X-ray revealed a bullet in her brain, the result, as it turned out, of two teenage target shooters whose bullets had missed their mark.

"I held the X-rays up in court and managed to get some judgment against the store which had sold the guns to the boys. It was small solace for the child, whose brain was never the same. Fortunately or unfortunately, she lived on to become an imbecile. Nothing could be done to the boys.

"In our present crowded society the availability of concealed weapons in particular is an anachronism. It's a bad thing. I feel the handgun has no place in America today. If I were a dictator I would eliminate handguns from the American way of life."

But would he have to be a dictator to do this? "I don't see how a handgun you can buy in a hardware store has much to do with the maintenance of a state militia, and I've spent enough time in the New York National Guard to know this," said Sutherland. "I will even go so far as to eliminate the 1911 Colt from use by the military. I've cleaned the gun, carried it all over the war but never had any occasion to fire it. I've never known anybody to fire it in combat. The only time I ever knew it to be fired was behind the lines when someone fired off one in anger. An Army colonel got the seat of his pants shot off."

What about pistol practice making one a better shot with the rifle? "I don't see this at all," said Sutherland, "and I've shot expert with the handgun and rifle. I don't see instruction in one making you a better shot with the other. The techniques are completely different. The handgun in our society, civilian or military, is simply a nuisance."

Congress, Sutherland is firmly convinced, has all the power it needs to require the registration or otherwise regulate the possession of all firearms, shotguns and rifles as well as handguns, and even prohibit the private possession of them.

"The rationale," he said, "is this. Entrusted to Congress by the Constitution are roughly two broad things: one is the power to regulate our foreign affairs in peace and war; the other is to regulate the national economy. This is largely spelled out in Article I, Section 8, Clause 3, which gives Congress the power"—he opened a copy of the Constitution to get the exact wording—"to 'regulate commerce with foreign nations, and among the several states, and with the Indian tribes.'

"Now, this commerce clause has an elastic concept. It gives Congress sweeping powers to regulate just about anything that even remotely affects interstate commerce, even things not directly involving commerce as long as they somehow affect the national economy. For everything we do can be said to have some bearing on interstate commerce, whether we realize it or not. For this reason, the Supreme Court has even upheld Federal controls over wheat grown and consumed on the same farm, ruling that the combined output of many even small farmers affects the total flow of interstate commerce. Supreme Court decisions have upheld the constitutionality of Federal legislation regulating child labor, the extractive industries, narcotics, gambling, labor relations, and most recently in the field of civil rights, public accommodation—all passed under the commerce power.

"Now, if we can regulate all these things, the Federal regulation and registration of firearms seems to me fairly easy, and there is little doubt in my mind that control of the whole traffic in arms and ammunition is well within the commerce power. Guns usually move in interstate commerce or are made from some parts that cross state lines.

"Taking the taxing power of Congress, there would seem to be nothing more illogical about imposing a Federal tax on guns than in imposing one on slot machines which are made and sold locally. And, of course, the National and Federal Firearms Acts have already been upheld by the Supreme Court as valid exercises of the taxing and commerce powers."

"Let us now take the Second Amendment," Sutherland continued. "Does it forbid the regulation of firearms? To say that the Second Amendment forbids the Federal government from stopping any Tom, Dick and Harry from buying a shotgun or rifle or handgun in a hardware store is not at all convincing to me. Now let us look at Article I, Section 8, Clause 16, which gives Congress the power 'to provide for organizing, arming, and disciplining the militia.' The Second Amendment doesn't repeal this. Now, if Congress, exercising this power, were to say, 'We will prescribe that the militia use only certain weapons of a specified type, and no longer use this or that weapon,' and furthermore say that all the prescribed arms be kept locked up in an armory, and that except for these arms, no other arms could otherwise be manufactured, sold or carried—well, that would be the end of that.

"Now, let's take a typical case that might then come up before the Supreme Court. Joe Doakes is charged with selling a buyer some sort of weapon. The buyer's defense is: 'Well, look, Judge, it says right here in the Second Amendment that I have the right to bear arms.' The judge can then turn right around and say, 'This isn't the kind of weapon the militia is supposed to use. I'm sorry, you have no defense.' Actually, as we know, the Court has already ruled this way in the case of certain types of weapons. There is no reason why it wouldn't do the same in the case of any other weapon not prescribed for official use."

How would Sutherland go about drafting a Federal firearms statute? "I wouldn't use just one constitutional peg. I would use the taxing, commerce and all the other possible powers. The statute would start off something like this: "Whereas the United States is getting crowded, and most of its people live in cities, and whereas the frontier is gone and so we no longer need to ride horses or shoot Injuns, now therefore do we establish this statute to promote the general welfare and public safety, using any and all of the constitutional powers of the Congress . . .'"

"Then," he continued, "the statute would list the taxes and commerce regulations, specify the arms to be used by the militia, and so on. To be realistic, though, I would first aim the statute at handguns and require them all to be registered. Of course, lots wouldn't be, but we would confiscate all those that turned up illegally and so take them gradually out of circulation.

"I know some people say that there's no point to trying to control guns, because you can be killed by something else, but this is like saying that people shouldn't be immunized for polio because they might get smallpox."

There can be no question that banning privately owned firearms from our lives would bring firearms deaths to a virtual end in this country. It is conceded that certain fringes of our population would somehow manage to keep them because of the limits there are to law enforcement. It is also conceded that fatalities will also continue to occur through the use of knives, sticks, rocks, baseball bats and other lethal instruments frequently mentioned by the gun lobby.

The idea of banning all firearms seems farfetched in a society where violence is often equated with virtue, where Ku Kluxers, madmen and Minutemen can freely buy guns with no questions asked. Yet these are among the ones who wrap themselves in the American flag, and with the shrill cry of the superpatriot, represent the dominant voice in the halls of Congress and in our state legislatures. And it seems likely that they will have their way for a time in continuing to thwart any effort at meaningful firearms control.

This is by no means a unique situation. The fate of many other legislative proposals in other fields has often been sealed, if only temporarily, by a well-organized, ardent minority able to generate a noisy clamor in the press and a flood of mail to legislators out of all proportion to its size.

One relatively recent happening that could help bring about an eventual change is the historic U.S. Supreme Court "one man, one vote" reapportionment decision of June 15, 1964. This ruling is aimed at eliminating the inequities which have given sparsely populated districts equal representation with the more populous urban ones. One likely result of the ruling will be a continued dilution of the power of rural interests, generally opposed to firearms control, which have usually dominated most legislatures, and a corresponding strengthening in state affairs of urban voices, which have generally favored stricter firearms control.

A serious barrier to any change, however, during the foreseeable future, is legislative lethargy. Even more important is public apathy.

The vast majority of our citizens, including those who own and use guns, have repeatedly expressed themselves as being in favor of firearms control. But, whereas the gun lobby is organized and vocal, those favoring controls are unorganized and silent and, as memories of the Kennedy assassination or less-heralded local tragedies fade, increasingly apathetic.

"You can't run into anyone who really doesn't want some form of gun legislation," says New York Supreme Court Justice John E. Cone, head of the National Committee for the Control of Weapons, a well-meaning but fundless organization with perhaps 200 members. "But they're not willing to express themselves any more. They all say let the next fellow do it."

Yet concerned citizens can press the issue by making themselves heard, by writing to their senators and congressmen and to their state and local legislators, by persuading their friends and neighbors to do the same, and by enlisting the aid of their civic organizations. The government can and will act, even in spite of the partisan considerations of individual legislators, when it knows that the public is aroused in sufficient numbers. Such an aroused public opinion has ultimately been the decisive force behind many of our social and legislative advances, most recently the enactment of Medicare. A similarly aroused public under the leadership of such well-organized groups as the League of Women Voters can, in the end, command far more political power than the firearms lobby.

In failing to do anything much about the indiscriminate sale of firearms, virtually all of us must bear some measure of responsibility for that terrible deed in Dallas, as well as for the 50 lives that firearms claim every day in this country.

"What paralysis of feeling, what hideous complacency, what failure of will and understanding allow this kind of human sacrifice to be continued without an effort to prevent it?" asked an editorial in the Washington *Post* on October 22, 1965. "All of us—Congress and country alike—have sat apathetic and bemused by the perverted nonsense of the gun lobby about the right to keep and bear arms. There has now been too much of this human slaughter. Let us stop it."

Certainly, not even the most stringent proposed restriction would deprive any mature, law-abiding, physically and mentally fit and gun-competent citizen of any constitutional right, real or imaginary.

Even with handguns banned, any bona-fide hunter or target shooter would still be able to buy or rent any gun he needs. Evidently, one would be able to shoot just as well with a registered as with an unregistered gun. A special dispensation could no doubt even be worked out for bona-fide gun collectors, and perhaps even for pistol targeteers who shoot on carefully supervised ranges and leave their guns there, except when on a journey to a match. The purchase of ammunition would be no problem whatever to anyone with a gun permit or license, or one holding membership in an approved gun club.

The laws specifying these controls would, of course, involve some small sacrifice of personal convenience, as do all laws involving the public good. But what would this sacrifice amount to, compared to the far greater sacrifice we are already making—the annual sacrifice of nearly 17,000 human lives, and of many times that number of maimed bodies?

How many of these lives would be saved? Admittedly, no gun control laws—nor, for that matter, any laws—can bring an end to crime. And even the most stringent laws will not prevent some people from getting guns illegally. But at least it can be made far more difficult for them to secure civilized society's most deadly portable weapon.

There will also be a quota of ordinarily law-abiding and seemingly normal people in legal possession of guns who, in a moment of despondency or a fit of passion, use a gun to take a human life, possibly their own.

No doubt hunters will continue to blow out one another's brains in the woods, as they always have. This is the price occasionally paid in a sport which, in spite of the protestations of the NRA, *is* somewhat less safe than taking a bath. However, with their sporting weapons not allowed in the home, hunters would confine their carnage almost entirely within their own ranks.

On the other hand, it is also reasonable to assume that the restrictions suggested would reduce the number of guns in the hands of actual or potential criminals, the known mentally ill and disturbed, the unscrupulous, the irresponsible and the immature. There would therefore be fewer sudden suicides, impulsive murders and senseless accidents for which such people are responsible.

The comparatively few firearms deaths in England and Japan

and, even with much less stringent restrictions, in our own New York State give every indication that this would be so. Obviously, the more rigid the screening procedure the better.

To those who rise in protest, one could well ask: Why should those of our civilians who wish to use guns be subject to any less screening than our citizens accepted for military duty and members of the police? To those who suggest that police discretion may at times be abused in the issuance of licenses, it may be said that this is so in every use of power. It can be easily resolved, as Judge George Edwards has suggested, through the use of the courts or special appeal boards. There is little evidence, on the basis of the firearms laws now in effect, that there has been such an abuse of police power anywhere.

How many lives would be saved? With the restrictions suggested, *very few of the tragedies described in this book might have taken place.*

Let us not say that 17,000 lives a year would be saved. Would controls be worthwhile if they would save 10,000 lives a year? This is about the annual number that firearms carry to a suicide death. It is true that some people would have succeeded in ending their lives by other means. But who can say how many might have lived if a gun were not so readily available at a crucial time?

Would the "inconvenience" of controls justify the saving of 5,000 lives a year—a number equal to those murdered annually by firearms? Many homicides are not premeditated, but are the product of a sudden fit of irritation, or a deranged mind, plus the convenient availability of a gun.

Would saving 1,000 lives a year be a good bargain? Banning guns from the home would surely save this number of lives—the number lost in those home accidents where a usually "unloaded" gun somehow manages to go off. Of this number of victims, 500 are children. Should society trade the privilege of allowing guns in the home for the guarantee of saving this many young lives every year?

Would controls of any kind be worthwhile to save 100 lives? Or even just one life, that of another President?

Or perhaps even your own?

Appendices

APPENDIX I

Digest of Federal Firearms Laws

A. *The National Firearms Act of 1934*, as amended, imposes a tax on the making or transfer of certain kinds of firearms, those commonly thought of as "gangster weapons," and requires that they be registered with the Treasury Department. The Act is administered by the Alcohol and Tobacco Tax Division, Internal Revenue Service, United States Treasury Department. It covers machine guns, submachine guns and all other fully automatic weapons, all short-barrel (or cut-down or sawed-off) shotguns and rifles, and also such things as mufflers and silencers. The Act does not apply to pistols and revolvers, ordinary sporting or target-type rifles and shotguns, flintlock and percussion weapons of all types, and ammunition.

The principal provisions of the Act are as follows:

1. The transfer or making of any of the following firearms requires the payment of a $200 tax:
    a. All fully automatic firearms, all rifles with barrels less than 16 inches in length and all shotguns with barrels less than 18 inches in length;
    b. All firearms made from a rifle or shotgun and having an *overall* length of less than 26 inches;
    c. All pistols with shoulder stocks and having barrels less than 16 inches in length;
    d. All firearms with combination rifle and shotgun barrels less than 12 inches in length;
    e. All mufflers and silencers.

2. The transfer of any of the following firearms (defined as "any other weapon" under the law) requires the payment of only a $5 tax:

a. All shot pistols or revolvers;

b. All firearms with combination rifle and shotgun barrels *at least* 12 but less than 18 inches in length;

c. All weapons or devices (except conventional pistols or revolvers) capable of firing a shot if such weapons or devices can be concealed on the person. (Examples: all Handy Guns, tip-ups, burglar guns, cane guns, pen guns, etc.)

3. Although the transfer tax on any firearms under the "any other weapon" category is only $5, the tax for *making* such a firearm is $200.

4. Both the transferor and the transferee are jointly and severally liable for the tax imposed on the transfer of firearms where such firearms are transferred without payment of the tax.

5. Manufacturers and importers of, and dealers and pawnbrokers in, firearms coming within the National Firearms Act must pay the full occupational tax in order to engage in business for a year or part of a year. There is no proration of this tax.

6. Manufacturers or importers of firearms under subparagraph 1, above, must pay an occupational tax of $500 a year; dealers (other than pawnbrokers) in firearms under subparagraph 1, above, $200 a year; pawnbrokers, $300 a year; manufacturers of, and dealers in, firearms under subparagraph 2, above, $25 and $10 a year, respectively.

7. No weapon defined as a "firearm" under the National Firearms Act may be imported or brought into the United States or any territory under its control or jurisdiction unless the purpose is shown to be lawful, and such firearm is unique or of a type which cannot be obtained within the United States or such territory.

8. Firearms incapable of being fired with fixed ammunition (i.e., a fixed metallic cartridge or a fixed shotgun shell) do not come within the tax and registration provisions of the National Firearms Act.

B. *The Federal Firearms Act of 1938,* as amended, also administered by the Alcohol and Tobacco Tax Division of the Internal Revenue Service, regulates the interstate and foreign commerce in *all* types of firearms, parts of firearms, and pistol or revolver ammunition by requiring the licensing of manufacturers and importers of, and dealers in, firearms or ammunition, or components thereof. (The term "ammunition" does not include shotgun shells, metallic ammunition suitable for use only in rifles or any .22-caliber rimfire ammunition.)

Two key provisions of the Act are the following:

Section 902 (c). It shall be unlawful for any licensed manufacturer or dealer to transport or ship any firearms in interstate or foreign commerce to any person other than a licensed manufacturer or dealer in any state the laws of which require that a license be obtained for the purchase of such firearms, unless such license is exhibited to such manufacturer or dealer by the prospective purchaser. [*Comment:* If a person has a Federal dealer's license, it would not be unlawful for anyone to ship him a handgun, even if the person lives in one of the states requiring a special permit or license for the purchase of handguns. Nor would the person receiving the handgun be violating Federal law. However, he would of course be violating state or local law.]

Section 902 (d). It shall be unlawful for any person to ship, transport or cause to be shipped or transported in interstate or foreign commerce any firearm or ammunition to any person *knowing or having reasonable cause to believe* that such person is under indictment or has been convicted in any court of the United States, the several states, territories, possessions or the District of Columbia of a crime punishable by imprisonment for a term exceeding one year or is a fugitive from justice. [*Comment:* As the words emphasized suggest, the shipper is acting illegally only if it can be proved that he *knowingly* made delivery—or is himself a convicted felon, a fugitive from justice, or under indictment.]

Among other things, the Act also provides:

1. No person may knowingly ship, transport or receive stolen firearms or ammunition, or firearms from which the serial number has been removed, obliterated or altered.

2. Every licensed manufacturer, importer and dealer must maintain complete records of the production, disposition and receipt, at wholesale or retail, of all firearms.

3. The term "manufacturer" means any person engaged in the manufacture or importation of firearms or ammunition or cartridge cases, primers, bullets or propellent powder for the purpose of sale or distribution.

4. The term "dealer" means any person not a manufacturer or dealer actually engaged in the business of selling firearms or ammunition or cartridge cases, primers, bullets or propellent powder, or any person engaged in the business of firearms repair or of manufacturing or fitting special barrels, stocks, trigger mechanisms or breech mechanisms to firearms. Included in the term "dealer" are wholesalers, retailers and pawnbrokers.

5. A gunsmith can be either a manufacturer or dealer, depending upon the scope of his gunsmithing activities.

6. Application for a license is made to the Director of the Internal Revenue District in which the applicant resides. The fee for a manufacturer's or importer's license must be renewed annually.

C. *Postal Laws and Regulations.* Concealable firearms, such as pistols or revolvers, may not be shipped through the mails, except to the following classes of persons in connection with their official duties: (1) active and reserve officers of the Armed Forces and the state militia; (2) enforcement officers and employees of enforcement agencies; (3) watchmen of government property; (4) Postal Service employees; (5) licensed firearms manufacturers and dealers. *Mailable* are unloaded rifles and shotguns, and antique or unserviceable pistols and revolvers sent as curios or museum pieces.

D. *Regulations Governing the International Traffic in Arms.* These regulations, administered by the Office of Munitions Control, Department of State, provide that: (1) manufacturers, exporters and importers of firearms and ammunition or components thereof (except shotguns and .22-caliber rimfire rifles or ammunition for these guns) must register with the State Department at an annual fee of $75; (2) such persons must obtain an export or import license (no charge) for each shipment; (3) a person may enter or leave the United States without a license, with a maximum of three firearms and 1,000 rounds of ammunition when these articles are part of his baggage and intended for his personal use, not for resale; (4) firearms manufactured prior to 1898 may be exported or imported without a license.

E. *The Tariff Act of 1930,* as amended, provides that firearms not designed to fire or incapable of firing a fixed metallic cartridge or fixed shotgun shell are exempted from import duty.

F. *The Internal Revenue Code of 1954* imposes a Federal tax on sales by manufacturers, producers or importers of firearms and ammunition. Taxable at 10 per cent are pistols and revolvers; taxable at 11 per cent are other firearms and shells and cartridges.

G. *The Federal Aviation Act of 1958,* as amended, provides that no person may without special authorization (as prescribed in regulations by the Federal Aviation Agency) carry a deadly or dangerous weapon aboard a commercial air carrier. Unloaded firearms are permissible if in baggage not accessible to the passenger while he is aboard the aircraft.

H. *National Parks and Monuments.* Hunting, or the use or display of firearms, is not permitted in the areas administered by the National Park Service,

Department of the Interior. Firearms may be taken into such areas only if the guns are sealed by a ranger, or are broken down and not readily accessible.

[*Source:* Condensed from the various Federal laws and regulations and from material prepared by the NRA Legislative Service. However, the comments given are the author's.]

APPENDIX II

Digest of State Firearms Laws

All 50 states and the District of Columbia have some statutory provisions relating to the control of firearms. While rifles and shotguns are included in the statutory provisions of many states, the provisions are largely aimed at prohibiting the sale of these firearms to certain persons (such as minors, aliens or convicted felons) or relate to their discharge in certain areas or to their use in hunting. However, no state requires a permit or license for the purchase, possession and carrying of rifles and shotguns.

Therefore, shown in the following table are only the major provisions directed at concealable firearms, such as pistols and revolvers, or the firearms commonly called handguns. As can be seen, the statutes controlling handguns vary widely. Supplementing and strengthening the frequently ineffectual state laws, there may also be local ordinances (county, city, town or village); a few are mentioned in the notes to the table. To learn of any such ordinances in your area, contact your county or municipal clerk or local police officials.

STATE	A Is license or permit required to purchase handgun?[1]	B Is waiting period required between purchase and delivery of handgun?	C Are handgun sales reported to police?[9]	D Is license required to sell handguns at retail?[13]	E Minimum age requirement to buy or receive handgun?[14]	F Is permit or license required to own handgun (keep at home or place of business)?[16]	G Is permit or license required to carry handgun openly on person?[18]	H Is permit or license required to carry handgun concealed on person?[18]
Alabama	No	48 hours	Yes	Yes	18	No	No	Yes[a]
Alaska	No	No	No	No	18[15]	No	No	Carrying prohibited
	N…	No	No	No	18[15]	No	No	Carrying

State	Time required for granting of permit						
California	No[2]	72 hours	Yes	Yes	18[15]	No	No	Yes[28]
Colorado	No	No	No	No	No	No	No	Yes
Connecticut	No[2]	Delivery next day	Yes	Yes	18	No	Yes	Yes
Delaware	No	No	Yes	Yes	"Minor"	No	No	Yes
District of Columbia	No	48 hours	Yes	Yes	21	No	Yes[3]	Yes[8]
Florida	No[2]	No	No	No	16	No	Yes	Yes
Georgia	No[2]	No	In certain municipalities	Yes	18	No	Yes	Carrying prohibited
Hawaii	Yes		Yes	Yes	20	No	Yes[3]	Yes[3]
Idaho	No	No	No	No	16	No	No	Yes
Illinois	No[2]	No	No[11]	No	18	No	No	Carrying prohibited
Indiana	No	48 hours	No[11]	Yes	21	No	Yes[3]	Yes[3]
Iowa	No	No	Yes	Yes	21	No	No	Yes
Kansas	No	No	No	No	"Minor"	No	No	Carrying prohibited

[1-29] Footnotes for Appendix II begin on page 351.

APPENDIX II (cont.)

STATE	A — Is license or permit required to purchase handgun? [1]	B — Is waiting period required between purchase and delivery of handgun?	C — Are handgun sales reported to police? [9]	D — Is license required to sell handguns at retail? [13]	E — Minimum age requirement to buy or receive handgun? [14]	F — Is permit or license required to own handgun (keep at home or place of business)? [18]	G — Is permit or license required to carry handgun openly on person? [18]	H — Is permit or license required to carry handgun concealed on person? [18]
Kentucky	No	No	In certain municipalities	No	"Minor"	No	No	Carrying prohibited
Louisiana	No [2]	No	No	Yes	21	No	No	Carrying prohibited
Maine	No	No	No [11]	No	16	No	No	Yes
Maryland	No [2]	7 days	Yes	Yes	21	No	No	Carrying prohibited
Massachusetts	Yes	Time required for granting of permit	Yes	Yes	21 [15]	No	Yes	Yes
Michigan	Yes [8]	Time required for granting of permit	Yes	Yes	21	No [19]	No	Yes [8]
Minnesota	No [2]	No	No	No	18 [16]	No	No [20]	No [20]

State		for granting of permit	(To circuit clerks)						prohibited
Montana	No	No	No	No	14	No	No	No	Yes
Nebraska	No[2]	No	No	No	18	No	No	No	Carrying prohibited
Nevada	No	No	No	No	18	No	No	No	Yes
New Hampshire	No	No	No[10]	Yes	"Minor"	No	No	No	No[35]
New Jersey	Yes	Time required for granting of permit[8]	Yes	Yes	18	No	No	No	Yes[25]
New Mexico	No	No	No	No	No	No	No	No	No[27]
New York	Yes	Time required for granting of permit	Yes	Yes	16	No	Yes[16]	Yes	Yes
North Carolina	Yes	Time required for granting of permit	No[11]	Yes	21	No	No	No	Carrying prohibited
North Dakota	No	No	Yes	In certain counties	17	No	No	Yes	Yes
Ohio	No[2]	No	No	No	17	No	No	No	Carrying prohibited

1-29 Footnotes for Appendix II begin on page 351.

APPENDIX II (cont.)

STATE	A Is license or permit required to purchase handgun?[1]	B Is waiting period required between purchase and delivery of handgun?	C Are handgun sales reported to police?[9]	D Is license required to sell handguns at retail?[13]	E Minimum age requirement to buy or receive handgun?[14]	F Is permit or license required to own handgun (keep at home or place of business)?[13]	G Is permit or license required to carry handgun openly on person?[13]	H Is permit or license required to carry handgun concealed on person?[13]
Oklahoma	No[2]	No	No	No	"Minor"	No	Carrying prohibited	Carrying prohibited
Oregon	No	No	Yes	In certain counties	14	No	No	Yes[23]
Pennsylvania	No[3,4]	48 hours	Yes	Yes	18	No[4]	No	Yes[23]
Rhode Island	No[5]	72 hours	Yes	Yes	15	No	Yes	Yes[23]
South Carolina	Handgun sales prohibited[6]	See Col. A	See Col. A	Handgun sales prohibited	See Col. A	No[6]	Carrying prohibited	Carrying prohibited
South Dakota	No	48 hours	No	Yes	18	No	No	Yes[5]
Tennessee	No	15 days	Yes	Yes	"Minor"	No	No[21]	No[21]
Texas	No	No	No[12]	Yes	"Minor"	No	Carrying prohibited[23]	Carrying prohibited[22]

Virginia	No[2,7]	No	In certain counties[7]	In certain counties[7]	18	No	No	Yes
Washington	No	48 hours	Yes	Yes	21	No	No	Yes[20]
West Virginia	No	No	Yes	Yes	21	No	Yes	Yes[22]
Wisconsin	No[2]	No	No	No	"Minor"	No	No	Carrying prohibited
Wyoming	No	No	No[11]	No	21	No	No	Yes

[1] Where purchase permits are required, they generally cover only purchases in the state. Consequently, they do not prevent residents from making purchases outside the state, either in person or by mail order. Out-of-state mail-order firms may also legally ship to Federal firearms dealer license holders, although the latter may be violating local laws. Obviously, purchase permit requirements also do not generally prevent someone from buying a gun and giving it to someone else (see Col. F).

[2] For city or cities requiring purchase permits in this state, check the following list: Arlington (Va.), Baltimore, Birmingham, Canton, Chicago, Columbus (Ga.), Columbus (O.), Fresno, Hartford, Jacksonville, Kansas City (Kan.), Memphis, Milwaukee, Miami, Montgomery, Nashville, New Haven, New Orleans, Norfolk, Oklahoma City, Omaha, Peoria, Philadelphia, Raleigh, Richmond, Rockford, Sacramento, Salt Lake City, Savannah, Springfield, St. Paul, Tulsa, Wichita Falls, Youngstown. However, other cities in the state may also have purchase permit requirements.

[3] Exempt from requirement are "regularly enrolled members of organizations authorized to purchase or receive firearms from the United States or the state"—notably, members of the National Rifle Association.

(*Footnotes continued on next page*)

4 Philadelphia's recently enacted (1965) statute is the strictest municipal law in the nation; it requires a police permit for the purchase or possession of *all* firearms.

5 For in-state sales, Rhode Island requires a waiting period of seventy-two hours after an application for purchase. For out-of-state purchases, police must certify the applicant as free from any "disqualification" (fugitive from justice, narcotic addict, habitual drunkard, mental illness). In a sense, this may be considered a form of permit, although the applicant is not screened as rigorously as in other states.

6 The law is a bit ambiguous. Although it forbids any person, firm or corporation to "manufacture, sell, offer for sale, lease, rent, barter, exchange or transport for sale into this state any pistol" less than 20 inches long and 3 pounds in weight, it goes on to say that it does not apply "to the carrying or keeping of pistols by persons while on their own premises." The law also specifies that no person may give any firearm to a child under twelve years of age. The interesting question arises: Where do the state's over-twelve-year-olds get the firearms they keep on their premises? Many, of course, come in from out of state.

7 Virginia requires a permit to purchase or sell handguns in counties having a population density of more than 1,000 a square mile. Covered by this requirement are Arlington county and Alexandria.

8 In New Jersey, the permit is granted or denied within seven days; in other states requiring permits, the time is generally longer.

9 Requirement for reports generally apply only to dealers within the state.

14 Note that even states requiring a permit to buy a handgun do not require a permit to own one. The sole exception is New York, which requires a permit to both purchase and possess a handgun.

15 However, a Michigan statute requires all those who come into possession of a handgun to present it to a police chief or county sheriff for safety inspection and certification.

16 For the reason for the legal distinction between carrying handguns openly (in full view) and concealed, see page 151. Even where permits are required or carrying is generally prohibited, exceptions are often provided for certain contingencies and categories of persons—for example, sportsmen, deputy sheriffs and "travelers." Some of these are indicated in the notes. The carrying of a handgun in a vehicle is often considered the same as carrying it on the person if it is within easy reach of the driver. The same permit requirements or prohibitions therefore generally apply. However, some states requiring a license to carry on the person do not require a license to carry in a vehicle. Other states may require a license only if the gun is loaded.

19 Arkansas prohibits only carrying "as a weapon" (that is, to fight with).

20 State law prohibits only carrying "with intent to assault."

21 Tennessee prohibits only carrying "with the intent to go armed" (that is, to fight with).

22 However, exempt from the prohibition are persons "traveling."

23 Exempt from requirement are members of organizations in note 3; also members of target-shooting clubs while at or going to and from established target ranges; also licensed hunters or fishermen while engaged in, or going to or re-

[11] However, require that sales records must be available to the police.

[12] Report must be made to the Texas Department of Public Safety.

[13] Dealers buying or selling across state lines must have a Federal firearms dealer's license. See Appendix I.

[14] The minimum age frequently differs from that for rifles and shotguns. Where "minor" is listed, the discretion is generally left to the dealer. This is also usually the case where a certain minimum age is specified—few dealers bother to ask for birth certificates. Note that in some states, age requirements are not specified at all.

[15] Younger with consent of parent or guardian.

[26] Exempt from requirement are licensed hunters going to or returning from hunting, and members of government civilian rifle clubs (enrolled with the Office of Department of Civilian Marksmanship and the NRA) while at, going to or returning from, target practice.

[27] May be carried only unloaded. Carrying of loaded handguns concealed is prohibited.

[28] Exempt from requirement are those in note 23. However, hunters and fishermen must register their handguns with the county treasurer.

[29] Exempt from requirement are those in note 23, plus members of gun collector clubs going to and from "their collector's shows and exhibits."

The usual term of the permits and licenses issued in one year, although the Georgia license (for carrying a handgun concealed) is for three years. License fees vary from 50 cents (Ga., Mass., Ore., S.D.) to $10 (Hawaii) and even twenty dollars (W.Va., N.Y.). Customarily, full age, good character and absence of a criminal record are required. The latter is variously defined, ranging from conviction of a felony, through conviction of a crime of violence, to conviction of any crime. However, only six states (Calif., Mass., Mich., N.J., N.Y., R.I.) make the taking of fingerprints compulsory. The majority of the states require that the license be carried with the firearm and be produced on demand by a law enforcement officer. Two states (Del., W.Va.) require the applicant to publish notice that he is applying for a license to carry firearms. Five states that license the carrying of firearms require the posting of security, amounting to $100 (Fla., Ga.), $300 (R.I.), $2,000 (certain licenses in Mississippi) or $3,500 (W.Va.). The bond in W.Va. is forfeited to any person injured by the accidental, negligent, improper or unlawful use of the firearm.

Many states also restrict or prohibit the possession of firearms by aliens, narcotics addicts, adjudged drunks, mental incompetents, Indians (Colorado), prostitutes (D.C.), and others of supposedly immoral character. However, as pointed out on page 13, these restrictions and prohibitions work somewhat better in theory than in practice.

Source: National Rifle Association, Senate Subcommittee on Juvenile Delinquency, *Sports Afield 1965 Gun Annual,* and individual state statutes.

APPENDIX III

Deaths Due to Firearms in the United States

Death Registration Area, 1900–64 *
Total Number and Rate per 100,000 Population

YEAR*	HOMICIDE		SUICIDE		ACCIDENT		TOTA
	Number	Rate	Number	Rate	Number	Rate	Number
1900	—	—	835	—	1,139	—	1,974
1901	—	—	913	—	1,082	—	1,995
1902	—	—	953	—	1,196	—	2,149
1903	—	—	1,052	—	1,151	—	2,203
1904	—	—	1,185	—	1,294	—	2,479
1905	—	—	1,435	—	823	—	2,258
1906	—	—	1,714	—	1,074	—	2,788
1907	—	—	2,027	—	897	—	2,924
1908	—	—	2,468	—	986	—	3,454
1909	—	—	2,395	—	944	—	3,339
1910	1,852	—	2,561	—	1,161	—	5,574
1911	2,347	—	2,859	—	1,327	—	6,533
1912	2,449	—	2,796	—	1,369	—	6,614
1913	2,821	4.5	2,930	4.6	1,572	2.5	7,323
1914	3,077	4.7	3,286	5.0	1,579	2.4	7,942
1915	2,885	4.3	3,608	5.4	1,501	2.2	7,994
1916	3,241	4.5	3,386	4.7	1,613	2.3	8,240
1917	3,793	5.1	3,269	4.4	1,730	2.3	8,792
1918	3,727	4.6	3,350	4.1	2,013	2.5	9,090
1919	4,567	5.4	3,302	3.9	2,350	2.8	10,219
1920	4,477	5.1	3,169	3.6	2,262	2.6	9,848
1921	5,509	6.2	4,122	4.6	2,346	2.6	11,977
1922	5,714	6.1	3,912	4.2	2,514	2.7	12,140
1923	5,648	5.8	3,900	4.0	2,578	2.7	12,126
1924	6,028	6.1	4,280	4.3	2,571	2.6	12,879
1925	6,216	6.0	4,333	4.2	2,570	2.5	13,119
1926	6,377	6.1	4,616	4.4	2,593	2.5	13,586
1927	6,310	5.8	4,989	4.6	2,741	2.5	14,040
1928	6,857	6.0	5,437	4.7	2,839	2.5	15,133
1929	6,540	5.6	5,660	4.9	3,015	2.6	15,215
1930	7,190	6.1	6,833	5.8	3,120	2.6	17,143
1931	7,532	6.3	7,543	6.3	3,041	2.5	18,116
1932	7,458	6.2	8,075	6.7	2,928	2.4	18,461
1933	7,863	6.3	7,798	6.2	3,026	2.4	18,687
1934	7,702	6.1	7,296	5.8	3,023	2.4	18,021
1935	6,506	5.1	6,830	5.4	2,854	2.2	16,190
1936	6,016	4.7	6,771	5.3	2,882	2.2	15,669
1937	5,701	4.4	7,073	5.5	2,696	2.0	15,403

YEAR*	HOMICIDE		SUICIDE		ACCIDENT		TOTAL	
	Number	Rate	Number	Rate	Number	Rate	Number	Rate
1938	5,055	3.9	7,357	5.6	2,629	2.1	15,108	11.6
1939	4,799	3.7	6,944	5.3	2,582	2.0	14,325	11.0
1940	4,655	3.5	7,073	5.4	2,390	1.8	14,118	10.7
1941	4,525	3.4	6,385	4.8	2,414	1.8	13,324	10.0
1942	4,204	3.1	6,117	4.6	2,741	2.0	13,062	9.7
1943	3,444	2.6	5,076	3.8	2,318	1.7	10,838	8.1
1944	3,449	2.6	4,808	3.6	2,412	1.8	10,669	8.0
1945	4,029	3.1	5,321	4.0	2,454	1.9	11,804	9.0
1946	4,966	3.5	6,276	4.5	2,816	2.0	14,058	10.0
1947	4,922	3.4	6,691	4.7	2,386	1.7	13,999	9.8
1948	4,894	3.3	6,660	4.6	2,270	1.6	13,824	9.5
1949	4,235	2.9	7,215	4.9	2,326	1.6	13,776	9.4
1950	4,179	2.8	7,377	4.9	2,174	1.4	13,730	9.1
1951	3,898	2.5	6,873	4.5	2,247	1.5	13,018	8.5
1952	4,244	2.7	7,013	4.5	2,210	1.4	13,467	8.6
1953	4,013	2.5	7,293	4.6	2,277	1.4	13,583	8.5
1954	4,115	2.6	7,539	4.7	2,281	1.4	13,935	8.7
1955	3,807	2.3	7,763	4.7	2,120	1.3	25,283	8.3
1956	4,039	2.4	7,817	4.7	2,202	1.3	14,058	8.4
1957	4,010	2.4	7,841	4.6	2,369	1.4	14,220	8.4
1958	4,230	2.4	8,871	5.1	2,172	1.3	15,273	8.8
1959	4,457	2.5	8,788	5.0	2,258	1.3	15,503	8.8
1960	4,627	2.6	9,017	5.0	2,334	1.3	12,978	8.9
1961	4,753	2.6	9,037	4.9	2,204	1.2	15,994	8.7
1962	4,954	2.7	9,487	5.1	2,092	1.1	16,533	8.9
1963	5,126	2.7	9,595	5.1	2,263	1.2	16,984	9.0
1964	5,090 †	2.6 †	—	—	2,400 ‡	1.3 ‡	—	—
TOTALS	265,122		339,195		139,741		744,058	

here were more firearms deaths during this period than the table indicates. This is because
e death registration area did not represent the whole United States until 1933. In 1900, the
ear the annual collection of mortality statistics began, the death registration area consisted
only 10 of our then 45 states plus the District of Columbia and a comparatively small
umber of cities located in nonregistration states. By 1913, the registration area had increased
the point where its population was estimated at 63,200,000, or only about two-thirds of
e total population of the United States. No population estimates for the registration areas
e available for the years prior to 1913; for this reason, death rates cannot be shown for
ose years. The rates for the years 1913–32 are based on the population estimates of Dr.
rederick Hoffman, a prominent actuarial expert for the Prudential Life Insurance Company
ho died in 1946). The rates for the years since are based on Bureau of the Census pop-
ation reports. The number of deaths for the years since 1900 are from the Division of
ital Statistics of the Department of Health, Education and Welfare.

ata not available   † From FBI *Uniform Crime Reports* for 1964

reliminary estimate by National Safety Council

APPENDIX IV

Deaths Due to Firearms in 16 Countries of the World

Total Number and Rate per 100,000 Population

COUNTRY (Year is the latest for which figures are available)	HOMICIDE Number	Rate	SUICIDE Number	Rate	ACCIDENT Number	Rate
United States, 1963	5,126 †	2.7 †	9,595	5.1	2,263 †	1.2 †
Australia, 1963	61	.56	336	3.1	87	.80
Belgium, 1963	24	.26	64	.69	10	.11
Canada, 1963	99	.52	556	2.9	150	.8
Denmark, 1962	6	.13	59	1.3	15	.32
England and Wales, 1963	24	.05	161	.34	77	.16
France, 1962	584 *	1.3 *	777 *	1.7 *	265	.56
German Federal Rep., 1962	68	.12	438	.80	93	.17
Ireland, 1963	—	—	7	.25	15	.53
Italy, 1962	351 *	.70 *	362 *	.73 *	181	.36
Japan, 1962	37	.04	93	.10	90	.09
Netherlands, 1963	3	.03	11	.09	4	.03
New Zealand (excl. Maoris), 1962	4	.17	39	1.7	6	.26
Scotland, 1963	3	.06	20	.38	13	.25
Sweden, 1963	8	.11	163	2.1	27	.36
Switzerland, 1962	—	—	—	—	26	.46

† For 1964 figures see Appendix III.

* 1961 figures, latest available

— Data not available. For comparison of Swiss over-all homicide and suicide rates with other countries, see page 282.

Source: Reports and previously unpublished data from the World Health Organization, Geneva.

APPENDIX V

Statement of Policy *of the National Rifle Association*

A. The National Rifle Association believes that firearms legislation is of insufficient value in the prevention of crime to justify the inevitable restrictions which such legislation places upon law-abiding citizens. In those cases where legislative bodies, nevertheless, determine that some firearms control legislation is necessary, the position of the NRA is as follows:

1. The NRA is opposed to control measures which levy discriminatory or punitive taxes or fees on the purchase, ownership or use of rifles, shotguns, pistols and revolvers.

2. The NRA is opposed to proposals to license the possession or purchase of a rifle, shotgun, pistol or revolver. The inevitable result of such licensing regulation is to vest the arbitrary power to say who may and who may not own a gun in the hands of an appointed or elected official. It is the illegal use and not the ownership of a firearm which should be the subject of legislative control.

3. The NRA is opposed to the theory that a target shooter, hunter or collector, in order to transport a handgun for lawful purposes, should be required to meet the conditions for a permit to carry a weapon concealed on his person.

4. The NRA is opposed to the registration on any level of government of the ownership of rifles, shotguns, pistols or revolvers for any purpose whatever. Regardless of professed intent, there can be only one outcome of registration, and that is to make possible the seizure of such weapons by political authorities, or by persons seeking to overthrow the government by force. Registration will not keep guns out of the hands of undesirable persons, and few people seriously claim that it will.

5. The NRA is opposed to legislation which denies, or interferes with, individual rights of our citizens or is designed purely for the convenience of law enforcement officers or for the purpose of circumventing due process of law in order to obtain convictions more easily. The desire to see our laws adequately enforced is not justification for any law which can make a prudent, law-abiding citizen an unwitting violator, or which denies the right of self-defense.

B. The National Rifle Association of America does not advocate, propose or suggest any restrictive gun legislation at any level of government. When, nevertheless, firearms legislation is enacted, it should never exceed any of the following four provisions:

1. Legislation designed to prohibit the possession of firearms by persons who have been finally convicted of a crime of violence, fugitives from

justice, mental incompetents, drug addicts and persons while adjudicated an habitual drunkard.

2. Legislation providing severe additional penalties for the use of a dangerous weapon in the commission of a crime.

3. Legislation making the sale of firearms to juveniles subject to parental consent and the use of firearms in public by juveniles subject to adequate supervision.

4. Legislation regulating the carrying of concealed handguns should be reasonable and the requirements for such carrying should be clearly set forth in the law. The conditions having been met, the issuance of a "license to carry" should be mandatory and should license the act of carrying, not the handgun itself.

Bibliography

Many of the books in the Bibliography are referred to in the text; others I read simply for background information. All are listed here for the benefit of those who may wish to pursue any aspect of this subject further. In preparing *The Right to Bear Arms*, I also pored over many specialized works such as the reports of the annual North American Wildlife and Natural Resource Conferences and the various publications of the National Rifle Association. I also consulted such standard reference sources as the *Statistical Abstract of the United States*, the *World Almanac*, the *Information Please Almanac* and William L. Langer's *Encyclopedia of World History*, to say nothing of countless court decisions, Federal and state statutes, reports and hearings of congressional committees.

ALLEN, DURWARD L. *Our Wildlife Legacy*. Funk & Wagnalls Company, New York, 1962.

AMBER, JOHN T. *Gun Digest*. Follett Publishing Company, Chicago, 1965.

ARDREY, ROBERT. *African Genesis:* A Personal Investigation into the Animal Origins and Nature of Man. Atheneum Publishers, New York, 1961.

BEARD, CHARLES and MARY. *A Basic History of the United States*. Garden City Publishing Company, Inc., New York, 1944.

BLOCH, HERBERT A., and GILBERT GEIS. *Man, Crime and Society:* The Forms of Criminal Behavior. Random House, Inc., New York, 1962.

BOORSTIN, DANIEL J. *The Americans: The Colonial Experience*. Random House, Inc., New York, 1964.

BOYLE, ROBERT H. *Sport: Mirror of American Life*. Little, Brown and Company, Boston, 1963.

359

BROMBERG, WALTER. *Crime and the Mind: A Psychiatric Analysis of Crime and Punishment.* The Macmillan Company, New York, 1965.

————. *The Mold of Murder: A Psychiatric Study of Homicide.* Grune & Stratton, Inc., New York, 1961.

CARPENTER, JOHN. *Extremism U.S.A.* Associated Professional Services, Phoenix, Arizonia, 1964.

CARY, LUCIAN. *The New Lucian Cary on Guns.* Arco Publishing Company, New York, 1960.

CHAPEL, CHARLES EDWARD. *The Complete Book of Gun Collecting.* Coward-McCann, Inc., New York, 1960.

CHURCHILL, WINSTON S. *A History of the English Speaking Peoples: The New World.* Dodd, Mead & Company, Inc., New York, 1956.

————. *The Second World War: Their Finest Hour.* Houghton Mifflin Company, Boston, 1949.

CODDING, GEORGE ARTHUR, JR. *The Federal Government of Switzerland.* Houghton Mifflin Company, Boston, 1961.

DAVIDSON, MARSHALL B. *Life in America.* Houghton Mifflin Company, Boston, 1951.

DE LARUE, JACQUES. *The Gestapo: A History of Horror.* Dell Publishing Company, Inc., New York, 1965.

DUBLIN, LOUIS I. *Suicide: A Sociological and Statistical Study.* The Ronald Press Company, New York, 1963.

ELLIS, EDWARD R., and GEORGE N. ALLEN. *Traitor Within: Our Suicide Problem.* Doubleday & Company, Inc., Garden City, New York, 1961.

FARB, PETER, editor. *The Forest.* Life Nature Library, Time, Inc., New York, 1961.

FLEMING, PETER. *Operation Sea Lion.* Simon and Schuster, Inc., New York, 1957.

GESELL, ARNOLD, and FRANCES ILG. *Infant and Child in the Culture of Today.* Harper & Brothers, New York, 1943.

GREEN, ARNOLD W. *Recreation, Leisure and Politics.* McGraw-Hill Book Company, 1964.

GREY, HUGH, and ROSS MC CLUSKY. *The Field & Stream Treasury.* Henry Holt and Company, Inc., New York, 1955.

GUTTMACHER, MANFRED S. *The Mind of the Murderer.* Farrar, Straus & Co., 1960.

HADDON, WILLIAM, JR., EDWARD A. SUCHMAN, and DAVID KLEIN. *Accident Research: Methods and Approaches.* Harper & Row, Publishers, Incorporated, New York, 1964.

HAMILTON, ALEXANDER, JOHN JAY, and JAMES MADISON. *The Federalist.* Modern Library, Inc., New York, 1937.

HATCH, ALDEN. *Remington Arms in American History.* Rinehart & Company, Inc., New York, 1956.

HENRY, ANDREW F., and JAMES F. SHORT, JR. *Suicide and Homicide.* The Macmillan Company, New York, 1964.

HOWARD, ROBERT WEST, editor. *This Is the West.* New American Library of World Literature, Inc., New York, 1957.

HOWE, WALTER J., editor. *National Rifle Association Firearms and Ammunition Fact Book.* National Rifle Association, Washington, D.C., 1964.

JANSON, DONALD, and BERNARD EISMANN. *The Far Right.* McGraw-Hill Book Company, New York, 1963.

KENDEIGH, S. CHARLES. *Animal Ecology.* Prentice-Hall, Inc., Englewood Cliffs, New Jersey, 1961.

KESTING, TED. *The Outdoor Encyclopedia.* A. S. Barnes & Co., New York, 1957.

KRUTCH, JOSEPH WOOD. *The Great Chain of Life.* Houghton Mifflin Company, Boston, 1956.

KOLLER, LARRY. *Handguns.* Maco Magazine Corporation, New York, 1957.

————. *The Fireside Book of Guns.* Simon and Schuster, Inc., New York, 1959.

KUENZLI, FREDERICK A. *Right and Duty or Citizen and Soldier: Switzerland Prepared and at Peace.* National Defense Institute, New York, 1916.

KVARACEUS, WILLIAM C. *The Community and the Delinquent.* World Book Co., Tarrytown-on-Hudson, New York, 1954.

MANN, E. B., editor. *The World of Guns.* Publishers' Development Corporation, Skokie, Illinois, 1964.

MENNINGER, KARL. *The Vital Balance: The Life Process in Mental Health and Illness.* The Viking Press, Inc., New York, 1963.

MIKES, GEORGE. *The Hungarian Revolution.* Andre Deutsch, London, 1957.

MORISON, SAMUEL ELIOT. *The Oxford History of the American People.* Oxford University Press, Fair Lawn, New Jersey, 1965.

PALMER, STUART. *A Study of Murder.* Thomas Y. Crowell Company, New York, 1960.

PETERSON, HAROLD L., editor. *Encyclopaedia of Firearms.* E. P. Dutton & Co., Inc., New York, 1964.

————. *The Treasury of the Gun.* Golden Press, New York, 1962.

RAINE, WILLIAM MACLEOD. *Famous Sheriffs and Outlaws.* Garden City Publishing Company, Inc., New York, 1929.

RANDOLPH, JOHN W. *The World of "Woods, Field and Stream."* Henry Holt and Company, Inc., New York, 1962.

RECKLESS, WALTER C. *The Crime Problem.* Appleton-Century-Crofts, Inc., New York, 1961.

RICKETTS, HOWARD. *Firearms: Pleasures and Treasures.* G. P. Putnam's Sons, New York, 1962.

RITTER, GERHARD. *German Resistance.* Frederick A. Praeger, Inc., New York, 1958.

ROBINSON, BEN C. *Woodland, Field and Waterfowl Hunting.* David McKay Company, Inc., New York, 1946.

ROOSEVELT, THEODORE. *Hunting and Exploring Adventures of Theodore Roosevelt.* The Dial Press, Inc., New York, 1955.

RUSSELL, CARL PARCHER. *Guns on the Early Frontiers.* University of California Press, Berkeley, California, 1957.

RUTLAND, ROBERT ALLEN. *The Birth of the Bill of Rights, 1776–1791.* Collier Books, a division of Crowell-Collier Publishing Co., New York, 1962.

SCHLESINGER, ARTHUR M., JR. *The Coming of the New Deal.* Houghton Mifflin Company, Boston, 1959.

SHIRER, WILLIAM L. *The Rise and Fall of the Third Reich.* Simon and Schuster, Inc., New York, 1960.

SHNEIDMAN, EDWIN S., and NORMAN L. FARBEROW, editors. *Clues to Suicide.* McGraw-Hill Book Company, New York, 1957.

TAYLOR, WALTER P., editor. *The Deer of North America: Their History and Management.* The Stackpole Company, Harrisburg, Pa., 1956.

TREFETHEN, JAMES B. *Crusade for Wildlife: Highlights in Conservation Progress.* The Stackpole Company, Harrisburg, Pa., 1961.

————. *Wildlife Management and Conservation.* D. C. Heath and Company, Boston, 1964.

WARD, CHRISTOPHER. *The War of the Revolution.* The MacMillan Company, New York, 1952.

WARREN COMMISSION, THE. *Report of the Warren Commission on the Assassination of President Kennedy.* McGraw-Hill Book Company, New York, 1964.

————. *The Witnesses.* McGraw-Hill Book Company, New York, 1965.

WERNER, M. R. *Tammany Hall.* Doubleday, Doran & Company, Inc., New York, 1928.

WILLIAMSON, HAROLD F. *Winchester: The Gun That Won the West.* Combat Forces Press, Washington, D.C., 1952.

WINANT, LEWIS. *Firearms Curiosa.* Bonanza Books, New York, 1955.

WOLFGANG, MARVIN E. *Patterns in Criminal Homicide.* University of Pennsylvania Press, Philadelphia, 1959.

ZILBORG, GREGORY. *The Psychology of the Criminal Act and Punishment.* Harcourt, Brace and Company, Inc., New York, 1964.

Among periodicals, the *Congressional Record* was a prime and invaluable source of information. Others, of course, were the various gun and outdoor magazines. I read through a good portion of the files of many of these, notably *The American Rifleman, Guns* and *Guns & Ammo,* in order to select the articles referred to at various points in the text. As the text also indicates, the accounts of firearms homicides, accidents and suicides came, for the most part, from newspapers across the country. For its detailed coverage of these as well as of the firearms efforts before Congress, I am indebted particularly to the Washington *Post,* which is truly one of the best and most public-spirited newspapers in the United States.

Acknowledgments, Notes and Sources

I can recall the exact day this book probably had its genesis—December 2, 1958. On the front page of most New York newspapers that day was the story of a fourteen-year-old boy who suddenly got up from his stamp collection, took a .22-caliber rifle from his closet, and killed his mother, his sister and himself in their Great Neck, Long Island, home. While leafing through the same newspapers, I noticed another item, datelined Mauston, Wisconsin, which told of a seventeen-year-old girl who shot her parents to death with a pistol. On still another page was an account of a Bridgeport, Connecticut, housewife who shot her husband four times (the shooting was later described as "accidental"), supposedly as a prelude to an attempt on her own life.

At first, I thought it rather unusual for so many shootings to be reported in a single day. But as I perused the newspapers in the days that followed, I soon saw that such incidents were fairly commonplace, indeed so commonplace that I, like most people, had been inured to the frequency with which they were reported. It was difficult to pick up a newspaper without finding an account of at least two or three fatal shootings; and these, I soon learned from government statistics, represented only a fraction of the average of nearly forty—homicides suicides, and accidents—then taking place every day in this country. By comparison, I also learned, there were relatively few firearms fatalities in most other countries of the world.

When I mentioned these findings to Herbert R. Mayes, then editor of *McCall's* magazine, he assigned me to write what turned out to be the first comprehensive article ever published by a major mass-circulation magazine on

America's gun problem. The article (it ran about 10,000 words) appeared in the July 1959 issue of *McCall's* under the title, "This Very Day a Gun May Kill You." Since the article was in a sense the progenitor of this book, I am deeply indebted to Mr. Mayes, one of the great editors of our time, for his encouraging my work on the article.

In the article I concentrated largely on pointing out the laxity of our firearms laws, and touched only secondarily on those chiefly responsible for this situation—the members of the gun lobby. However, I continued to study their activities over the years, particularly after another memorable date—November 22, 1963. In an article that was published in the December 1964 *Harper's*, I gave a detailed account of just how the lobby managed to kill all of the eighteen-odd firearms control bills introduced in Congress immediately after the murder of President Kennedy. In preparing this article I was aided by a grant from the Society of Magazine Writers, to which I am therefore also indebted for indirectly making this book possible. A word of appreciation is also due John Fischer, Russell Lynes and Marion K. Sanders of *Harper's* for their assigning and allowing me a free hand in the preparation of the article that was to blossom into this book.

Otherwise, all of the persons, organizations and companies mentioned in the book have had some role, directly or indirectly, in its creation. Among those who gave generously of their time, knowledge, and advice were: James V. Bennett, former director of the U.S. Bureau of Prisons; Frederick J. Ludwig, attorney and a former New York City police captain and legal consultant to the New York State Joint Legislative Committee on Firearms and Ammunition; Rudolph Kales, the U.S. Treasury Department's veteran regional firearms coordinator for the North Atlantic states; and Carl L. Perian, Eugene Gleason and Elizabeth Knipe of the Senate Subcommittee to Investigate Juvenile Delinquency.

Lest anyone read anything of special significance into the above selection of names, I should say that among those also solicitous about keeping me well informed were: Charles Dickey of the National Shooting Sports Foundation; Frank C. Daniel, Jr., and Louis Lucas of the National Rifle Association; and officials and executives of other shooting sport and industry groups, as well as of individual manufacturers and publications.

All of the mortality and crime statistics that may appear uncredited came from official records of the Department of Health, Education and Welfare, the Federal Bureau of Investigation, and (in the case of the international comparisons) the World Health Organization. For some special material prepared for or furnished me (and appearing in print for the first time in this book), I am especially grateful to Dr. Anders S. Lunde, acting chief of the Mortality Statistics Branch, Division of Vital Statistics of HEW; Jerome J. Daunt, chief of the FBI's Uniform Crime Reporting Section; and Ed. G. Ruff, statistician-supervisor of WHO in Geneva.

I also called on literally scores of specialists in the many areas with which this book necessarily has had to deal—criminology and conservation, military affairs and constitutional law, sociology and psychiatry, to mention only a few. Many of these people are cited, along with their contributions, in the text.

Others would prefer to remain anonymous for reasons that should be obvious. To all, however, plus those whose comments were useful for background information, I am equally indebted.

My wife, Shirley, unflinchingly helped me maintain my "morgue" of now some 10,000 clippings of such items as "Boy, 1½, Shot Accidentally by Babysitter," and "Ex-Mind Patient Slays Four Sons, Husband and Self." And finally, I owe a special word of thanks to my friend Alden Todd, for dissuading me from using more of these items in the book; his editorial acumen was otherwise of immeasurable help in preventing the book from being longer than it already is.

Needless to say, none of those named or others mentioned in the book are responsible for any errors that may have somehow crept into it. Nor should they be held to account for any opinions not directly attributed to them. Everything else in the book represents the shots as I have seen fit to call them.

To make for easier reading, I have tried to avoid cluttering the main body of the book with too many footnotes and citations. Accordingly, for the benefit of those interested in such matters, what now follows is a chapter-by-chapter breakdown of additional notes, sources, acknowledgments and personal comment.

CHAPTER 1 (*pages 1–6*)

The Steinmetz quotation on the page opposite the opening of the chapter is from his book, *The Romance of Duelling*, published by Chapman and Hall of London in 1868.

Government records show a total of 736,568 gun deaths—homicides, suicides and accidents—from 1900 through 1963. (The year-by-year figures are itemized in Appendix III.) Adding the 17,000 more estimated for 1964 and another 17,000 for 1965 would bring the total well over 750,000.

The battlefield deaths totaled 529,460 through the year 1965, according to figures from the Department of Defense. By major conflict, the casualties are as follows: Revolutionary War, 4,435; War of 1812, 2,260; Mexican War, 1,773; Civil War, 140,414; Spanish-American War, 385; World War I, 53,402; World War II, 291,557; Korean War, 33,629; Vietnam, 1,605.

The incidents described throughout the chapter were culled from some 60 newspapers all over the country published on November 22, 1963, and the days immediately following.

Our assassinated Presidents, in addition to Kennedy, were Lincoln (1865), Garfield (1881) and McKinley (1901). Shot, but escaping assassination, was ex-President Theodore Roosevelt in 1912 while again campaigning for the Presidency. Shot at but unhurt were President-elect Franklin D. Roosevelt in 1932, and Harry S. Truman in 1950. For details of the F.D.R. assassination attempt, see page 167.

CHAPTER 2 (*pages 7–29*)

Kennedy's statement on behalf of his bill appears in the *Congressional Record* of April 28, 1958, page 7442. The House debate on the companion Morano measure is in the *Congressional Record* of May 14, 1958, pages 8729–8734. The NRA's opposition to the measures represented one of the few instances in which the Association's views have not coincided with those of the firearms manufacturers.

The estimate of the number of foreign weapons imported from 1959 through 1963 is by the Senate Juvenile Delinquency Subcommittee.

The shotgun is also used in the clay target sports of trap and skeet shooting as well as in hunting. A shotgun's size, or "gauge," is a measure of its bore diameter expressed as the number of round lead balls of that diameter required to weigh a pound. For example, a 12-gauge gun has a diameter which will accommodate a ball of such a size that twelve of them together weigh a pound. Most shotguns today come in one of six popular sizes: 10 (largest), 12, 16, 20, 28 and .410. The latter, the one exception to the gauge method of determining shotgun size, refers to a gun whose barrel diameter measures .410 inches. Shotguns may also be loaded with a solid rifle slug for big game. Rifles are generally used for conventional target shooting as well as hunting, and handguns, largely for target shooting, in police work and for protection. These guns accommodate many sizes of cartridge, of which the bullet or projectile is one component. The projectile size or caliber is determined in this country and in England by the diameter of the interior of the gun barrel expressed in inches. Thus, a .30-caliber bullet is three-tenths of an inch in diameter. Continental European ammunition and guns are based on the diameter in millimeters. The revolver, because it is somewhat more dependable and trouble-free than a pistol, is now the preferred handgun of all our police agencies. The pistol, though it is apt to jam now and then, does however offer certain advantages over the revolver: rapidity of fire, quickness of loading, large ammo capacity (some accommodate ten-shot clips). A pistol, because of its flatness, is also a bit easier to carry and conceal inside a breast pocket or shoulder holster. For these and various other reasons, it is the general favorite among Europeans and James Bond types.

The statements by James V. Bennett and Sergeant K. T. Carpenter were made during the firearms hearings of the Senate Juvenile Delinquency Subcommittee in 1963. The hearings filled a 348-page volume of small type.

The incident of the two-year-old girl buying a machine gun is described in an article, "Murder Weapons for Sale," by Ashley Halsey, Jr., published in *The Saturday Evening Post*, February 8, 1958.

AP reporter Gavzer's experience was reported in the Chicago *Tribune*, February 14, 1965; Rugaber's appeared in the Detroit *Free Press*, March 14, 1965.

The conversation with the clerk about the "Nigger Getter" was reported in *Life*, August 27, 1965; that with Val Forgett, Jr., appeared in the New York *Journal American*, November 27, 1963.

CHAPTER 3 (*pages 30–40*)

The U.S. crime figures are from the Federal Bureau of Investigation's *Uniform Crime Reports*. The FBI's figures have been challenged by some sociologists and criminologists. The feeling of some is that the figures are too low because not all crimes are reported. On the other hand, there are those who feel that the figures are too high, for one thing, because arrests rather than convictions are reported, for another, because of the statistical techniques used and the failure to consider such factors as racial violence and weather. However, the fact remains that the FBI figures represent the only national statistics we have.

The foreign homicide figures are from the United Nations' World Health Organization.

J. Edgar Hoover's comment about killing on impulse is from the FBI *Law Enforcement Bulletin,* June 1963.

The account of the Senate Juvenile Delinquency Subcommittee hearing in New York City is based on reports in *The New York Times,* September 24, 1959, and in *Time,* October 5, 1959. The findings by the police in other metropolitan areas are summed up in detail in a subcommittee report of August 7, 1964.

The incidents described by Bennett comprised part of his testimony before the Senate Juvenile Delinquency Subcommittee on March 7, 1963.

The statement of the Joliet inmate to a CBS reporter was made on the network's *CBS Reports: Murder and the Right to Bear Arms* telecast, June 10, 1964.

J. Edgar Hoover's statement about firearms being seven times more deadly than all other weapons combined is from the FBI's 1963 *Uniform Crime Reports,* page 7.

A postscript to the Liuzzo slaying: Collie Leroy Wilkins, a twenty-two-year-old Klansman, after being tried three times on charges relating to the murder, was finally found guilty of conspiring to violate the constitutional rights of civil rights workers. The conviction calls for a possible ten-year prison term. In January 1965, Wilkins was also sentenced to a year and a day in prison for violation of probation in connection with an earlier conviction for having a sawed-off shotgun. This was the result of an arrest (a year before the Liuzzo slaying) to which Wilkins pleaded guilty and was let off with a suspended sentence and two years' probation.

CHAPTER 4 (*pages 41–67*)

Newspapers were the source of virtually all the shooting incidents described in this chapter as well as in other chapters.

The nineteenth-century art critic who killed a woman friend because she had thick legs was Thomas Griffiths Wainewright. The incident is described by Murray Teigh Bloom in an article, "Hows and Whys of the Perfect Murder," published in *Playboy,* May 1965.

Another excellent and more recent work by Bromberg is his *Crime and the Mind,* listed in the Bibliography.

Dr. Hartog's comments on suicide and guns was made on the CBS-TV program, *Murder and the Right to Bear Arms,* telecast on June 10, 1964.

The Dublin estimate of the number of suicides is from his definitive book, *Suicide;* that of Farberow and Shneidman are from their *Clues to Suicide.* Both are listed in the Bibliography.

The incident of the nine-year-old who killed himself because his horse,

Cindy, had been sold is from a report on "Teenage Suicide" by Jhan and June Robbins in *Good Housekeeping*, October 1964.

The quotation by Lourie is from a symposium on suicide reported in the December 1965 *Medicine at Work*, a publication of the Pharmaceutical Manufacturers Association.

The article in *Today's Health*, entitled "A Psychiatrist Examines Suicide," by Dr. Paul Friedman, appeared in the publication's December 1963 issue.

The Yolles quotation is also from *Medicine at Work*, mentioned above.

Senator Thomas Dodd estimates the number of gun victims at more than 200,000 annually. Making up this estimate are the 17,000 homicide, suicide and fatal firearms accident casualties, the 26,000 or so victims of aggravated assaults and another 40,000 victims of armed robberies, plus 120,000 persons, many of them innocent bystanders, he estimates are maimed or wounded by firearms every year.

I am indebted to F. Roy Keaton of the American Medical Association for furnishing the medical papers which served as background and reference material for the section on wounds.

CHAPTER 5 (*pages 68–92*)

The opening quotation is from *Sports Illustrated*, December 11, 1961. This article and one in the December 15, 1961, issue of *Life* furnished the basis for much of the material on fast draw in this chapter.

The 19,058,809 purchasers of hunting licenses, tags, permits and stamps in 1963 may represent some duplications in the case, for example, of persons hunting in more than one state. Some states also require special permits or tags to hunt such animals as elk, deer or turkey.

The explanation of the joy of trap shooting came from a participant on the CBS-TV show, *Murder and the Right to Bear Arms*, as did also the quote from the instructor at the California fast-draw school.

For my account of the activities of the North-South Skirmish Association, I drew on an article in the Washington *Post*, April 4, 1965.

The quotation by Samuel Grafton is from his article, "Climate of Crime," in *McCall's*, March 1965.

Although there is a dearth of material on the psyche of the shooter, some inquiries have been made into his socio-economic-cultural makeup. A 1961 survey by Ohio State University's Dr. Tony Peterle of 6,800 of the state's hunting license buyers showed the average hunter to be thirty-five years old, with 77 per cent married, 81 per cent in the under-$7,000-a-year income bracket (grouse shooters were found to have the highest income, woodchuck and raccoon hunters the lowest), and 6 per cent college graduates. Among other things, music was also found to be the favorite non-hunting entertainment, with nine times as many preferring rock and roll as opera.

Jeff Cooper is quoted in *Guns and Ammo*, September 1964, Lucian Cary in his book on guns (see Bibliography), and Oscar Godbout in *Esquire*, February, 1965.

The finding that more than half of all hunters couldn't be satisfied with a hunt if they didn't kill is from the Peterle survey mentioned above. Results of the survey appeared in the Transactions of the Twenty-Sixth North American Wildlife and Natural Resources Conference (held in 1961), published by the Wildlife Management Institute. The Minnesota study referred to is described in Chapter 13, page 244.

Dr. Lois Barclay's comments appeared in an article, "Children and Toys," in the December 17, 1963, *Look*. Those by Dr. Benjamin Spock were in his *Redbook* column of November 1964. The comments by Dr. Michael Rothenburg and *The New York Times* quotation about Oswald as a boy appeared in the December 21, 1963, *New Republic*.

CHAPTER 6 (*pages 93–127*)

The policy statement of the International Association of Chiefs of Police was read by the organization's executive secretary, Leroy E. Wike, before a hearing of the Internal Revenue Commission on August 27, 1957.

The indictment of Minutemen leader Robert B. DePugh was reported in *The New York Times* of August 17, 1965. For a detailed, recent account of the character and activities of the various extreme right-wing groups, see the book by Janson and Eismann, listed in the Bibliography. A report of William B. Edwards' work as a recruiter for the Minutemen was given in the San Francisco *Examiner* of February 12, 1965.

Rounding out the $1.5 billion estimated annually is upward of $150 million spent a year for hunting license fees and for dues and contributions to wildlife and conservation organizations.

The April 24, 1935, dinner meeting at the Waldorf-Astoria is described on page 269 of Trefethen's *Crusade for Wildlife*, listed in the Bibliography.

CHAPTER 7 (*pages 128–148*)

Much of the material in this chapter was based on an exhaustive (and exhausting) study of the file of *The American Rifleman*, NRA literature, and the organization's annual reports. About the most detailed account of the organization's history in print appeared in its 1947 report.

The Proxmire and Kennedy comments on the Lobbying Act are from an article, "Washington's Money Birds," by Larry L. King in *Harper's*, August 1965. The NRA's tax exemptions were discussed in an article in the Washington *Post*, January 10, 1965.

As mentioned earlier, the Kennedy and Morano measures marked one of the rare occasions that has seen the gun lobby divided. Favoring the measures for quite obvious reasons was the Sporting Arms and Ammunition Manufacturers Institute. Opposing them were importers, mail-order houses and other dealers selling the guns the measures sought to ban, and the NRA. The latter's explanation for favoring the Sikes proposal instead, according to NRA Secretary Frank Daniel, was: "We did not feel that it was just or proper to curtail the importation of all military arms and ammunition." The House debate on the Morano measure included this interesting statement by Sikes:

"Just a few minutes ago I talked by telephone to the executive director of the National Rifle Association and here is what he told me: Yes, he had seen Mr. Morano's language. It is better than the original language of the bill. A hand with one finger is better than a hand with no fingers, but not much better. The members of the NRA do not want the original language or the substitute language" (*Congressional Record*, May 14, 1958.)

CHAPTER 8 (*pages 149–165*)

Lucian Cary's statement is from page 137 of his book on guns, listed in the Bibliography.

No one knows who invented the gun or just when and where it first appeared on the world scene. However, Saracen records describe the use of the earliest-known guns—stone-throwing cannon—in the 1247 defense of Seville. The oldest surviving illustration of a gun is found in a royal instruction book, *De Officiis Regium* (On the Duties of Kings), prepared in 1326 for the edification of the prince who was to become England's Edward III. The first guns, like almost everything else, have also been attributed by some to the Chinese.

Frederick J. Ludwig has pointed out to me the interesting fact that our early state laws were precisely the opposite of English common law: our statutes prohibited (and most still do today) concealed rather than openly carried weapons. I am indebted to Ludwig and also to Lieutenant John H. Berryman of the New York City Police Department for furnishing background information on our early state laws.

The commentary on the Kentucky law is by Karl T. Frederick, from an address before the 1951 NRA annual convention. His statement to a newspaper interviewer appeared in the Chicago *Tribune*, November 1, 1951. Other statements attributed to Frederick are from his NRA pamphlet, *Pistol Regulation: Its Principles and History.*

Tim Sullivan's statement on the Senate floor was quoted in the New York *Herald Tribune*, July 19, 1964.

The New York State Investigation Commission findings are included in a 68-page report, "Concerning Pistol Licensing Laws and Procedures in New York State," published in November 1964.

The National Conference is the offshoot of a special committee set up by the American Bar Association in 1889 to draft and promote uniform state laws. The commissioners—practicing attorneys, law school teachers and judges—are appointed by the governor of each state. Each state has from three to seven commissioners.

The McLaughlin letter came to my attention in Lieutenant John M. Berryman's master's thesis, "The Controversy Surrounding Firearms Legislation," written in 1962 in fulfillment of the requirements for his degree from the City College of the City University of New York.

Professor Sam B. Warner's comments are in the *Journal of Criminal Law and Criminology*, November–December 1938, and also from his report to the Firearms Committee of the Interstate Commission on Crime in 1937.

CHAPTER 9 (*pages 166–187*)

The comment of the mail-order dealer who decided to discontinue selling handguns was quoted in an address by U.S. Attorney General Homer Cummings before the annual convention of the International Association of Chiefs of Police on October 5, 1937.

A detailed account of the assassination attempt on Roosevelt is given in Arthur M. Schlesinger, Jr.'s *The Crisis of the Old Order*.

J. Weston Allen's remarks were from a paper read before the Attorney General's Conference on Crime in Washington, D.C., on December 12, 1934.

Cummings' comments on the need for a Federal law is from his address cited above. So are the figures on the number of weapons registered after the passage of the National Firearms Act.

The testimony on the various bills discussed is from reports and newspaper accounts of the hearings.

The account of the 1957 Internal Revenue Service hearing and the events leading up to it are based on a transcript of the hearing, the recollections of persons present, articles in *The American Rifleman* and NRA legislative bulletins.

CHAPTER 10 (*pages 188–210*)

The testimony, statements and exhibits of the Senate Commerce Committee and Juvenile Delinquency Subcommittee hearings covered in this chapter fill three reports totaling 880 printed pages. To prepare this chapter, I also read many newspaper and other accounts of the hearings as well as the pertinent references to them in *The American Rifleman*, and was fortunate enough to be able to attend several of the sessions. I also interviewed many of the persons mentioned in the chapter.

CHAPTER 11 (*pages 211–221*)

Of interest to the statistical-minded may be the fact that the testimony, statements and so on that occupied the attention of the Senate Juvenile Delinquency Subcommittee and House Ways and Means Committee in 1965 filled three reports of small print totaling 1,570 pages. Space limitations have precluded me from reprinting more of the fascinating material found in these reports. However, a pertinent footnote to this chapter may be Senator Dodd's questioning of NRA executive vice president Franklin Orth about the association's April 9 letter which, Orth said, had been composed by an NRA committee made up of "two presiding Superior Court Judges and four prominent practicing attorneys."

In view of this, Dodd expressed astonishment at the errors in the letter which, he said, had "caused a great deal of confusion" and done considerable harm as reflected by the mail received by Congress. After citing some of the errors already referred to in the chapter, Dodd read a sentence from the letter that said: "Anyone engaged in the manufacture of ammunition will be required to have a $1,000 manufacturer's license." Orth conceded that the figure should have been $500.

Further on in the letter, Dodd quoted this paragraph: "If you transported your rifle or shotgun to another state for a lawful purpose such as hunting, you would have to comply with such burdensome restrictions and red tape as might be required under the regulations."

"Now this is patently untrue," said Dodd. Orth, while not disputing the senator's view, lamely attempted to explain that the learned judges and lawyers on the NRA committee might somehow have gotten this impression from reading the bill.

Going through the letter from beginning to end, Dodd found an error in virtually every paragraph, and suggested that the NRA should correct its "mistakes" and set matters straight with a new mailing. NRA president Harlon B. Carter, sitting at Orth's side, said Dodd's request would be given consideration. "We feel a keen sense of responsibility," Carter said.

The new mailing requested was never sent. Instead, Orth addressed an open letter to NRA members in the December 1965 issue of *The American Rifleman*. The letter began: "First, I would convey my compliments to you individually for your response to my April letter. Probably no issue before the first session of the 89th Congress drew the volume of mail that poured in to the nation's lawmakers in opposition to S. 1592. Letters by the thousands were received by virtually all members of the Senate and House of Representatives. That these letters were effective in preventing the passage of S. 1592 is beyond question. Each of you who played his part is entitled to be proud of his participation in the democratic process."

Also playing a part in the "democratic process" was the National Shooting Sports Foundation, which had also put out a letter echoing many of the points in the NRA letter. During the hearings Dodd confronted the NSSF's Charley Dickey with his organization's letter, said that it was "replete with false statements," and asked: "What are you trying to do? Are you actually trying to tell the truth about this bill or are you trying to confuse the sportsmen of this country?"

"As you know," said Dickey, "there has been a great amount of confusion about the various versions of your bills among sportsmen in the last three or four years."

"Yes, and I think you have helped create it," said Dodd.

Thomas J. Siatos, editor of *Guns & Ammo*, offered a rather unique explanation for his refusal to appear voluntarily. (He had to be subpoenaed.) "We felt that our case had been pretty well presented by the National Rifle Association and the National Shooting Sports Foundation," said Siatos in his opening remarks. "We felt it would be redundant to appear."

Nevertheless, Dodd read into the record an article entitled "The *Real* Facts behind S. 1592" from the magazine's July 1965 issue, and said that of the 28 paragraphs in the article referring to the bill, 27 were "not anywhere near the truth."

"All I can say is this is what we call editorializing," Siatos ventured.

"Some people call it lying," snapped Dodd.

. CHAPTER 12 (*pages 222–232*)

The sniping at state and local bills continued unabated into 1966. In New Jersey, for example, the National Rifle Association urged its thousands of members to defeat a bill that would require persons wishing to buy rifles or shotguns to have a special identification card provided them by the police. The bill was written by State Attorney General Arthur J. Sills, who told a hearing on the bill that studies showed that more and more people were using these guns to commit violent crimes. Sills, speaking against a chorus of angry mutterings and scattered boos, denounced objectors to his bill as "people who just don't want any legislation," adding, "They would prefer to roam the streets to make a jungle out of the United States." He also mentioned that he had received 335 critical letters after testifying in Washington for the Federal gun bills introduced there the year before. Of these letters, he disclosed, about 25 had come from persons found to have records of arrest.

CHAPTER 13 (*pages 233–253*)

Most of the freak shooting accidents described are from the files of the National Safety Council.

Since we have statistics on just about everything else, it may seem odd that there are no precise figures on fatalities due to hunting accidents. However, the figure is now estimated at from 600 to 800 annually by the National Safety Council, and is probably somewhat higher.

The danger range given of shotguns and rifles is from the National Safety Council's Firearms Data Sheet, which also says that the range for pistols and revolvers "varies from about one-half mile for one loaded with a .22 long rifle [cartridge] to about a mile with a heavier weapon."

The stories by Donald Foltz are from his article, "Boobs in the Woods," published in *The Saturday Evening Post*, October 15, 1962.

I am grateful to Tom Lehrer for permission to reprint the lyrics of his hunting song.

The figures for the accidents among young hunters are from the conservation departments of the states mentioned.

The comments of Ross Stagner first appeared in the Detroit *Press*, July 18, 1965.

The study of defective vision among hunters was also part of the Minnesota Hunter Casualty Study.

The estimate of the percentage of color-blind males is from a booklet of the American Optometric Association. Other estimates run as high as 10 per cent. Applying even the 2 per cent estimate to the approximately 19 million people who now apply for hunting licenses, tags and permits (and assuming all were men) would mean that 380,000 hunters would be unable to recognize a bright red cap or jacket if they saw it!

Actually, giving eye tests to hunting license applicants would not present any unsurmountable difficulties. The California and Montana Optometric Associations offer free eye tests to hunter safety students, although eye tests are not required by law. In New York, eye tests (for drivers) are available free at the Department of Motor Vehicles when a driver's license comes up for renewal.

The accident statistics uncredited are from the National Safety Council's annual statistical reference book, *Accident Facts* (1965 edition), and from the U.S. Department of Health, Education and Welfare.

CHAPTER 14 (*pages 254–273*)

The statement by Karl T. Frederick is from the NRA pamphlet, *Pistol Regulation: Its Principles and History*, reissued in 1964.

Our sole exception to the "retreat law" is in Texas where an attacked person can stand and fight it out under any circumstances. Not surprisingly, Texas also has one of the nation's highest homicide rates.

The comment from the *Kentucky Law Journal* is from a paper, "Criminal Law—The Law as to Concealed Deadly Weapons," by Gardner L. Turner, in the Summer 1955 issue.

The item from *Newsweek* was in its December 5, 1952, issue.

The city homicide figures are from data, some previously unpublished, provided by the Federal Bureau of Investigation.

Bill Gold's column is reprinted by permission of the Washington *Post*.

CHAPTER 15 (*pages 274–293*)

In the section on foreign homicides, suicides, etc., I used the statistics for 1962 because these were the latest available for all the foreign countries mentioned. However, 1963 figures are available for some of the countries, as indicated in Appendix IV.

The unattributed quotes about the Revolution and by George Washington are, for the most part, from Boorstin, Ward, and Davidson—all listed in the Bibliography. For background information I am also grateful to my friend Thomas J. Fleming, author of many fine books on the Revolution.

Representative Henry B. Gonzalez of Texas is among those estimating the cost of the Arthur D. Little study at $100,000. In the *Congressional Record* of January 26, 1966, he also described his difficulties in getting information about the results of the study.

The draft study for the year 1962 was reported in *The New York Times*, May 16, 1965.

The Department of the Army pamphlet commenting on the relative ineptitude of our modern shooters is No. 355-14, entitled "Trainfire Troop Topics."

CHAPTER 16 (*pages 294–308*)

The NRA quotation opening the chapter appeared in *The American Rifleman*, July 1955.

The astonishing editorial feat performed by *Guns* was in its July 1964 issue;

the article was "Right to Keep and Bear Arms—Is the '2nd' Obsolete?" by Charles T. Erion. The only portion of the Second Amendment quoted was "to keep and bear arms."

Judge Rummel's commentary on Blackstone (actually, on a book called *Jones' Blackstone*) was before the Senate Commerce Committee on January 23, 1964.

The quotation by Boorstin is from his *The Americans: The Colonial Experience*, listed in the Bibliography.

It is interesting to speculate whether there ever would have been a Second Amendment if not for the Catholics and James II.

According to a memorandum, "Federal Firearms Control and the Second Amendment," prepared by the General Counsel of the Treasury Department in May 1965: "There in no indication in the Annals [of Congress] as to how the final language of the Second Amendment was decided upon. While the religious-scruple clause was omitted, the final version does retain the use of the collective term 'the people,' and debates which are reported support the view that the Second Amendment was designed to protect and preserve the state militias. No mention was made of any individual 'right' to possess, carry or use arms and there is no indication of any concern with this."

For the section defining the militia, I have also relied on the memorandum cited above.

In analyzing the judicial construction, or semantics, of the Second Amendment, I have retrod some of the ground first plowed by John Brabner-Smith in *Law and Contemporary Problems* (I, 1934).

McKenna is quoted from the *Marquette Law Review*, XII (1928), pp. 138–49.

For information as to the source of the Brandeis quote and about Brandeis himself, I am grateful to the late Justice's daughter, Mrs. Susan Brandeis Gilbert, and to her husband, Mr. Jacob M. Gilbert. Another authoritative source of information was Alden Todd, author of *Justice on Trial*, an outstanding book on Brandeis.

CHAPTER 17 (*pages 309–326*)

The charge by The American Human Education Society appeared in the magazine *Our Dumb Animals* (February 1964), published jointly by the AHES and the Massachusetts Society for the Prevention of Cruelty to Animals.

A Federal Fish and Wildlife survey some years ago showed that hunters bring in only 250 million pounds of dressed meat annually. On a per capita basis, this represents an extremely small fraction of the 170 pounds of meat the average American eats every year.

The ruling against the Eskimos (141 were arrested) was in accordance with treaties between the United States, Canada and Mexico for the protection of migratory birds. The treaties stipulate the period between March 10 and September 1 as the closed season on migratory game birds. At the time the treaties were drafted no recognition was given to the customs and needs of the Eskimos and Indians as far as waterfowl are concerned.

The story of the slaughter of our wildlife has been widely told. Among the many sources I consulted were Allen's *Our Wildlife Legacy*, the *Field and Stream Treasury*, and publications of the U.S. Department of the Interior.

The Kaibab deer problem is described in detail in Trefethen's *Crusade for Wildlife*, Farb's *The Forest*, and Allen's *Our Wildlife Legacy*.

The Remington Arms history referred to is the one by Alden Hatch.

Another method of controlling deer—trapping and transplanting—is generally impractical in terms of large deer populations, for one thing because of cost.

Harold Anthony's comments appeared in *The Saturday Review*, August 17, 1957.

The Kaibab squirrel controversy was reported in *Defenders of Wildlife News*, August-September-October 1964.

The full 1964 report of the blue-ribbon group headed by Leopold, one of America's most distinguished zoologists and wildlife management authorities, appears in the Transactions of the Twenty-ninth North American Wildlife and and Natural Resources Conference, pp. 27–49.

The comments by Allen are from his *Our Wildlife Legacy* and from a paper, "Predators and Public Policy," he delivered before the annual meeting of the National Audubon Society in 1962. In the paper Allen also said: "Depredations by coyotes on cattle do occur occasionally, but these appear to be minor problems that mainly call for the control of individual animals."

The Rieder Statement appeared in a Defenders of Wildlife News Bulletin dated April 1964.

The report of the Missouri Conservation Commission, one of the nation's most progressive and enlightened, was issued in 1955. The report was entitled "Predator Control—Why and How."

As of 1964, only 19 states gave blanket legal protection to owls and hawks, though providing in carefully spelled-out provisions for the elimination of individual birds causing damage; 26 states protected only some species; and the remaining states protected none of their birds of prey.

Bourjaily's comments appeared in *The Saturday Evening Post*, February 15, 1964; Devoe's were in *Our Dumb Animals*, April 1951, reprinted from an article originally published in the *New American Mercury*.

Theodore Roosevelt is quoted in Hatch's *Remington Arms;* the characterization of him by a friend is from Boyle's *Sport: Mirror of American Life.*

CHAPTER 18 (*pages 327–340*)

The remarks by John Lindsay were made during his appearance before the Senate Commerce Committee on January 30, 1964.

Judge George Edwards of the U.S. Court of Appeals, Sixth Circuit, made his recommendations at the annual meeting of the American Bar Association in New York on August 12, 1964.

The Rapoport study is from *Behavioral Approaches to Accident Research*, Association for the Aid of Crippled Children, New York, 1961, pp. 164–178. It is also reprinted in *Accident Research*, listed in the Bibliography under

Haddon. In his study, Rapoport whimsically poses the following interesting hypothesis:

> What some pre-industrial cultures achieve by the ritual of blood sacrifice, including human, we may be "achieving" by our yearly slaughter of innocents. We would shrink from the idea of drawing lots to decide which 100,000 men, women, and children were to be killed each year. [The figure represents the fatalities from all types of accidents in this country every year.] But in effect, we are essentially doing just that, and our explanations of what actually occurs—*i.e.*, the notion of "accident," where the events are attributed to the will of chance (just as in other cultures blood sacrifices are rationalized as pleasing to the gods)—could well be mere rationalizations.

Somewhat related was the following thought in a Washington *Post* editorial of October 10, 1965:

> To regard a shooting as an "accident" is more comforting to the community conscience than to regard it as a "homicide." But in simple truth no shooting can be considered genuinely accidental—not even the kind of shooting one reads about so frequently of a wife by a husband who mistook her for a prowler or the unfortunate shooting of a husband by a wife annoyed by some supposed misconduct on his part. In the true sense of the term, these are not "accidents" because they have a readily discernible causation. And no community which permits the indiscriminate proliferation of firearms can escape a responsibility for the tragedies they cause.

Index